THE HISTORY OF LEXICOGRAPHY

AMSTERDAM STUDIES IN THE THEORY AND
HISTORY OF LINGUISTIC SCIENCE

General Editor
E. F. KONRAD KOERNER
(University of Ottawa)

Series III - STUDIES IN THE HISTORY OF THE LANGUAGE SCIENCES

Advisory Editorial Board

Volume 40

R.R.K. Hartmann (ed.)

The History of Lexicography

THE HISTORY OF LEXICOGRAPHY

PAPERS FROM
THE DICTIONARY RESEARCH CENTRE SEMINAR
AT EXETER, MARCH 1986

Edited by

R.R.K. HARTMANN
University of Exeter

JOHN BENJAMINS PUBLISHING COMPANY
AMSTERDAM/PHILADELPHIA

1986

340437

c

Library of Congress Cataloging in Publication Data

Dictionary Research Centre Seminar (1986: Exeter, Devon)
  The history of lexicography.

(Amsterdam studies in the theory and history of linguistic science. Series III, Studies in the history of language sciences, ISSN 0304-0720; v. 40)
Bibliography: p.
1. Lexicography -- History -- Congresses. I. Hartmann, R.R.K. II. University Exeter. Dictionary Research Centre. III. Title. IV. Series.
P327.D544   1986   413'.028'09   86-20577
ISBN 90-272-4523-1 (alk. paper)

CONTENTS

PREFACE

Most dictionaries have forerunners, and all have imitators; an understanding of the historical foundations of dictionary-making is therefore one of the preconditions of further progress in academic lexicography.

The two dozen or so papers which were presented at the 1986 Exeter Seminar surveyed most of the lexicographical traditions in the world, some tracing them right back to their beginnings. The programme was divided into eight sessions (see Appendix B), with the following concentrations of topics:

(1) Three classical traditions (represented by papers on bilingual Chinese lexicography by Chien & Creamer, on intercultural problems in the bilingual dictionary since ancient Sumer by Snell-Hornby, and on the entry structure of the conventional monolingual Arabic dictionary by Haywood);

(2) the early history of European lexicography (papers by Filipović on Croatian and other Central European dictionaries since the 15th century, by Kibbee on Renaissance, chiefly French, lexicography, and by Steiner on three centuries of Spanish-English dictionaries);

(3) the beginnings of English lexicography (Dolezal on viewing the evolution of the English dictionary as varations on a text, Osselton on a recently discovered pre-Cawdrey dictionary manuscript, and Stein on 16th-century English-vernacular dictionaries);

(4) further aspects of English lexicography (papers by Hüllen on Wilkins thesaurus, by McArthur on the origins and value of the thematic mode, by Bronstein on pronunciation in the English dictionary, and by Read on the emergence of an American dictionary tradition);

(5) the Background of diverse national developments (Haugen on 17th-century Scandinavian lexicographers, Magay on Országh and dictionary-making in Hungary, and Piotrowski on monolingual Polish lexicography);

(6) specific features of national developments (El-Badry on English-Arabic dictionaries, Gouws on Afrikaans lexicography, and Hatherall on the German Duden spelling dictionary);

(7) pioneers of three genres (papers by Bray on the influence of Richelet on dictionaries of the 17th and 18th centuries, by Merkin on the forerunners of historical lexicography, and by Wolfart on early field-work for dictionaries of indigenous languages in Canada), and, finally;

(8) recent trends in the English dictionary (Ilson on tracing multiple editions, Allen on the history of one Oxford dictionary, and Cassidy on the role of computers in a regional dictionary).

Many cross-currents were uncovered, for instance the relative priority of the monolingual or the bilingual dictionary, the role of commercial and ideological constraints, or the functions of the compiler and the user. An opportunity also arose for discussing resource centres for research into the history of lexicography, and a survey of dictionary collections and training establishments was initiated (which will be reported on elsewhere). It might have been possible in this volume to arrange the papers in chronological or topical sequence as above, but for practical reference purposes it was decided to present them in alphabetical order of authors. In spite of the editor's insistence on uniformity of presentation, the individual character of the various contributions has been retained to reflect the diverse approaches taken. References to dictionaries and other literature are given in each paper, and Appendix A lists all dictionaries cited in alphabetical order of titles, with full bibliographical details.

Thanks are due to all contributing authors (Cassidy's and Wolfart's papers will be published elsewhere); to Exeter University conference and catering staff (especially Jackie Cressey) for providing a pleasant atmosphere; to Professor R. L. Collinson for advice at the main stages of planning; to my secretary Veryll Nuttall for administration; to David Chien, Trevor Learmouth, Stuart Macwilliam, Paul Auchterlonie and Nawal El-Badry for checking references; to Rufus Gouws for selfless help during and after the Seminar; to Avril Smith and my son Stefan for assistance with word-processing. This is also the appropriate place for acknowledging the generous financial sponsorship of the British Council, the Fulbright Commission, the British Academy, and the British Association for Applied Linguistics, which allowed several scholars from abroad to participate. Finally, to Konrad Koerner and the John Benjamins Publishing Company goes full credit for accepting the volume for publication in their series.

Exeter, May 1986

Reinhard Hartmann

A CONCISE HISTORY OF THE COD

Robert E. Allen

In 1985 I began work with three colleagues on the eighth edition of
the COD. Our primary objective, in addition to revising the text, is to
bring the book into the computer age by turning it into an electronic
database. COD's own vocabulary will reflect this by taking account of
the language of the computing world, and the book will therefore continue to be a product of its age. The start of a new revision is a good
time to look back on the work of predecessors, and as I did so - with
the help of OUP's archive material - another theme emerged: plus ça
change, computers notwithstanding, as familiar problems (some still
unresolved) emerged from the editorial correspondence of the 'twenties
and 'thirties. What follows then is a brief survey concentrating on certain aspects of continuity and change where lessons may be learned. (1)

The CONCISE OXFORD DICTIONARY was the first English dictionary published by the Clarendon Press apart from the partially issued OED. The
decision to publish a 'short dictionary' (as it was called) was a commercial one. A number of rivals were already published, most notably
CHAMBERS' 20TH CENTURY DICTIONARY, which had appeared in 1901. All of
these had drawn on the material made available by the publication of
the first fascicles of the OED, and it would have been foolish for the
Clarendon Press, which owned and had direct access to the material, not
to do the same as a means of recovering some of its investment in the
OED. Nonetheless the decision remained unimplemented for several years,
mainly because suitable editors could not be found. Then as now the
professional lexicographer waiting for work was a rare thing. In 1906
the Delegates of the Press decided on two brothers living on Guernsey,
Henry and Francis Fowler (hereafter HWF and FGF), who had recently completed work on a prescriptive manual of grammar, The King's English.
Before that they had undertaken a translation of the Greek writer
Lucian, the work that first brought them into contact with the Clarendon
Press. Charles Cannan, then Secretary to the Delegates of the Press,
was influenced in this decision mainly by the Fowlers' proven powers of
scholarship and by their record of keeping to schedule and delivering
manuscripts on time. In this respect they again fulfilled their promise; they forecast a period of five years' work and the book was indeed
published five years later in 1911. (2)

The distinctive features of the COD then as now will be familiar.
A style of presentation that depended on drastic abbreviation and the
use of telegraphese enabled more information per square inch to be presented than had been achieved by any rival. The Fowlers used the word
telegraphese in their preface, but evidently overlooked the fact that
they had not put it in the dictionary; later the oversight was noticed
and put right in the first set of addenda published in the impression of
1914. Much store was put by the use of multiple illustrative examples,

whereby in the treatment of functional words such as by and the the
space devoted to exemplification was at least as great as if not greater
than that for definition. Nesting of compounds and derivatives and even
main words is another characteristic that has survived to this day but
is now under review, and the same is true of the embedding of grammatical information in the definitions, a practice acquired from the OED but
carried much further in the interests of compression.

The Fowlers explained their debt to the OED in their preface,
describing its articles "rather as quarries to be drawn upon than as
structures to be reproduced in little". In fact the structural resemblances are very great and the historical treatment of the OED has left
a very definite mark on the layout of entries in the smaller work right
up to the current edition, where archaic and historical senses continue
to receive a prominence due rather to their OED source than to convenience or logical sequence. In one important respect the COD was of
course very different from the OED: it was supported by invented
examples and not by quotations from real sources; this would have required attribution for which there was no space. Invented examples
afford a dictionary compiler the best opportunity of a creative fling,
and the Fowlers´ examples are in many ways exceptionally distinctive,
ranging from the frequently gruesome (minus: returned minus an arm;
wind up: shot his wife and child and wound up by stabbing himself) to
the male-oriented or as some would say now sexist (good: give her a good
beating; better: no better than she should be (repeated under no!));
spectacle: a drunken woman is a deplorable spectacle) and the plain
idiosyncratic or at least throught-provoking (stick: was referred to as
´Winnie´ and the nickname stuck). The Fowlers were occasionally taken
to task over their examples. Under subject the example the Indians are
our subjects was seized on by an Indian nationalist whom HWF assumed
for some reason to be Gandhi. Fowler´s defence was that the sentence
illustrated idiom and not truth, and was no more an insult to Indians
than all men are liars would be to humanity.

Other distinctive characteristics of the Fowlerian approach include a thoroughly analytical view of etymology (in this they were much
encouraged by C.T. Onions) which can be confusing in so small a scale,
and an exceptionally generous coverage of non-naturalized words and
phrases of a kind that must be put down to editorial predisposition.
Many of these were not in the OED (brutum fulmen = empty threat; lues
Boswelliana = ´Boswellian plague´, i.e. the tendency of a biographer to
magnify the importance of his subject; ventre à terre = ´stomach to the
ground´, i.e. at full speed; and many others from all parts of the alphabet). Many from the end of the alphabet were not entered in the OED
although its editors presumably kept an eye on the then available COD,
and they had to wait for inclusion in the SUPPLEMENT of our own day.

A still more remarkable editorial quirk occurs in the addenda of
1914, where a long list of the names of noteworthy streets and build-
ings, most of them in London, are found among the new items. A few
examples will give the flavour: Bond Street (´resort of fashionable
loungers´); Buckingham Palace (´London residence of the King´); South
Kensington (´(used for) the museums of S.K. or their atmosphere of culture & art & instruction in these connexions´). As some of the
formulations show, the lexical point resides in the allusive uses of the

names, and some of the entries, notably <u>Westminster</u> and <u>Whitehall</u>,
rightly survive in the current edition of the COD; but many of the
names, such as <u>Bond Street</u>, <u>Buckingham Palace</u>, and <u>Trafalgar Square</u>, are
not adequately supported by the extension in sense that would justify
their inclusion on normal Fowlerian principles. Evidently the editors
were called upon to account for these new articles; the reply, dated 20
September 1914, is (unusually) from FGF and it recognizes the weakness
of some of the cases:

> <u>Albert Hall</u> and <u>Buckingham Palace</u>, we contend,
> are so far connotative that an uninformed reader,
> meeting with <u>Albert Hall manifestos</u> or <u>an</u>
> <u>intimation from Buckingham Palace</u> will not rest
> content with his knowledge or ignorance of their
> whereabouts; he will want to know how the A.H. is
> used, and who lives at B.P... <u>Albert Memorial</u>
> is an extreme and perhaps indefensible case.

Some but not all of these items were incorporated in the text of the
second edition; many survived to the sixth edition where they were obvious candidates for removal to make way for newer and more straightforward vocabulary items.

When the Fowlers began work on the COD Murray's dictionary had
reached the letter M, and by 1911, when the COD was in the press, it had
advanced to the end of R, with major articles such as Bradley's celebrated entry for set still to come. The deficiency in S-Z must have
appeared irreparable, as when a historian turns to a period for which
suddenly no dependable narrative source is extant. We have little evidence of how the Fowlers filled the gap. On 20 June 1909 HWF admitted
in a letter addressed probably to R.W. Chapman, then Assistant Secretary
to the Delegates:

> Now that we have got beyond the OED, we go rather
> slower, produce rather shorter articles, & have
> always the consciousness, with the words that really
> matter, that a third or so of the senses are likely
> to be escaping us.

In their preface the editors describe their method for this part of the
alphabet as one of collecting quotations "given in the best modern
dictionaries" and other external sources or "from our own heads".

It would be an interesting exercise to make a systematic comparison of various parts of the COD with their OED counterparts and with
other sources. My impression from a more superficial survey is that
HWF's worst fears were not realized. Most revealing in this context
are the written worksheets prepared for the sixth edition of the COD;
references in these to the OED as a corrective to the existing COD
treatment are considerably more numerous in the relevant range S-Z than
in the earlier parts of the alphabet. But they are mainly concerned
with small obscure entries and senses, and reveal a higher than average
occurrence of dubious items (such as <u>tabefaction</u> = emaciation; <u>tain</u> =
tin-foil, and so on) that were either not included in the eventual OED
or included with little supporting evidence. Annotations for major

articles such as take and turn are no higher than for other parts of
the alphabet. The fear that "a third or so of the senses are likely to
be escaping us" is surely not substantiated. On the other hand the
sudden loss of the OED support evidently put the Fowlers somewhat adrift
in the matter of selecting vocabulary and assessing primary source
material.

As soon as a dictionary is finished the work of criticizing and revising it begins. The sources of comments were (then as now) observations of fellow lexicographers and correspondence from the general
public (the great public or G.P. as Henry Fowler called them); only
rarely does a dictionary benefit in its subsequent editions from views
expressed in a published review. Generally speaking the Fowlers (and
here I refer mainly to Henry, whose letters predominate in the files)
were hostile to the newspaper critics but highly receptive to criticisms
from scholars and members of the public. It was not the practice of the
day for editors to correspond directly with the individuals concerned;
the procedure was that Chapman (who succeeded Charles Cannan as Secretary to the Delegates in 1919) would forward any letters to Guernsey (or
after 1925 to Somerset) with his own opinion on the matter and sometimes
a recommendation as to reply. He was always a model of courtesy and
discretion in a way that many very great scholars are, and since Henry
Fowler was not without his scholarly sensitivities it was probably as
well that there was a go-between to pass on the more forthright and often
waspish comments of Craigie and more especially of Onions. An exchange
of letters from the autumn of 1920 illustrates the point. Henry Fowler
was working on the ´abridging of the abridgement´ (his description of
the projected POCKET OXFORD DICTIONARY) and reacted to criticism of his
policy of nesting many compound words such as aircraft and earthquake
in italic type under their first elements. On 22 September 1920 he
wrote to Onions via Chapman:

> I have been beating my brains, vainly, to discover
> why you class railroad among ´exciting words´.

Onions responded a few days later:

> Railroad is an exciting word for me because I don´t
> use it. So is airship, which I have had to learn
> and have had occasion to tell others, is a flying
> machine ´lighter than air´. But azimuthal leaves
> me cold.

Azimuthal leaves me rather cold too. And I agree in general with
Onions. The Fowlerian view of compounds as second-class words only
rarely needing explanation strikes me as their most serious misconcep-
tion, and has in my judgement adversely affected their dictionaries to
this day. One of our main concerns on the new COD (as it was with the
new POD) is to restore the compound word to its rightful place in the
vocabulary.

Francis Fowler died in 1917 and after that HWF worked alone, for a
time with shadowy support from his other brother, A.J. Fowler. Living
in Guernsey, and later in Somerset, he lacked a collection of data about
the language of the kind that was available to Oxford editors then and

(especially) later. As far as we know he never visited Oxford during
these years. This deficiency was just as serious as the non-availability
of OED's S-Z, and effectively ruled out a major revision of the COD for
many years. Preparation of the first OED Supplement in the 1920s provided the COD with material for a large set of addenda published at the
end of the third edition in 1934, but the main body of the original text
remained largely unaffected. The addenda of 1911 comprised three items:
Borzoi (the dog), duple (in mathematics and music), and hangar (the
shed). The addenda of 1914 comprised about 1100 items which included
the proper names already mentioned, and a substantial addition to the
entry for as that must be regarded as another example of Fowlerian inspired idiosyncrasy (and anticipated their POD approach in some ways):
it dealt with the comparative type as...as... found in (as) bald as a
coot, (as) good as gold, and so on, and proceeded to give no fewer than
76 examples including the following oddities: fat as a porpoise, merry
as a grig, plentiful as blackberries, weak as a cat. It also heralded
the first COD appearance of man in the street, of bally (stung by a b.
wasp was the example) and (passing over barmy on the crumpet which had
nothing to do with a liking for women) collywobbles (rumbling in the
intestines), pekinese (another dog), and thermos flask (then with a small
t). A large proportion of the space was given over to allusive and
proverbial phrases such as Caesar's wife must be above suspicion,
beggars must not be choosers, and not worth powder and shot. It is perhaps a little unfair to judge a list of addenda from 1914 in these terms,
but the impression given is one of a distinct paucity of source-material.
The point is of more than historical interest in that it can contribute
to the widespread but false notion that the language was not developing
as rapidly in the first half of this century as it is in the second
half.

The first problem with proprietary terms in COD arose in 1928 with
the term Vaseline. Up to this time all such terms were entered in the
normal way with a small initial and often with no indication of special
status. Fowler added a note on status in the etymology of the second
edition but the lower-case initial remained. This policy was not systematically reviewed until the revision of the 1970s. Fowler took a
pragmatic view of the problem in a letter of 28 September:

> I should say, let us cut out the word & have no
> more fuss about it.

Until the 1933 Supplement material became available the only ident-
ifiable source of new vocabulary was the suggestions of correspondents.
These were passed on by Chapman to Fowler along with other correspondence, again often with a comment. In difficult cases a consultant,
such as Bradley, co-editor of the OED, was brought into the picture. In
1920 someone suggested the inclusion of bumf, and Chapman considered it,
on Fowler's behalf, for POD. He asked Bradley, who replied (14 October
1920):

> Bumf and the word of which it is a shortening
> are in Farmer's Slang & its Analogues, and
> the full form is in the big dictionary... I never
> heard the word myself; no doubt if I had served
> in the army through the war I should have been

familiar with it, and possibly then I might have
taken a more favourable view of its title to
recognition.

Henry Fowler was no prude, he had served in the army, and the word was
allowed into the POD.

Other items thrown up by the random process of suggestion were jig-
saw puzzle and ectoplasm. On 27 August 1924 Kenneth Sisam, later to be
Chapman's successor, wrote to Fowler:

I think ectoplasm deserves consideration –
though possibly you excluded the word doubting
the existence of the thing.

The word had been included in the COD but not in the POD.

In February 1929 Julian Huxley, then Professor of Zoology at King's
College London, sent in a list of suggestions for the COD. He had
already corresponded with Bradley about the OED. Among his suggestions
were Achilles' tendon (it was in fact given under t but a cross-
reference was now added), endocrine, and Mendelian; also ecology, which
he failed to notice under the oe- spelling then common. "Two biological
terms in common use now are chromosome & gene which I think should be
entered", he continued. Gene had already been added to the second
edition; like many scholarly users of dictionaries Huxley was using an
old edition. Chromosome was duly inserted in the addenda of 1934.
Another problem mentioned by Huxley has an even more familiar ring: "can
you not..insert under data "often incorrectly used as singular"?" This
(with the omission of 'incorrectly') had to wait for the sixth edition of
1976 and (for the more prescriptive ruling) for the seventh of 1982.

The main strengths and weaknesses of the COD were aired and considered in an interesting connection; a plan to produce a larger quarto
dictionary of current English, an 'unconcise' as the London publisher
Humphrey Milford called it, the OXFORD DICTIONARY OF MODERN ENGLISH as
it was called on letterheads. Work on the dictionary continued for some
years but it was never finished. The main revisions of policy were to
be a more comprehensive treatment of scientific and technical words and
a more systematic approach to pronunciation. One of the editors who was
to work on this dictionary was Col. H.G. Le Mesurier, who had corresponded with Henry Fowler and had read the manuscript of A DICTIONARY OF
MODERN ENGLISH USAGE (published in 1926) while serving in the army in
India. He proved to be good at defining technical words; as Sisam wrote
to Chapman, "Le Mesurier understands things which were always rather a
mystery to the OED staff". Fowler too had high expectations, as he said
in a letter to Sisam (19 March 1931):

I have..great hopes of Le Mesurier, who approaches
the job in a very coming-on spirit.

As regards pronunciation, in the 1911 edition of the COD this was
given only for especially difficult words, a policy that was severely
criticized by the Oxford lexicographers and abandoned both in the
smaller POD and in the plan for the quarto dictionary; in a letter to

Sisam written in January 1930 Fowler noted among the policy points
"pronounce throughout". The position of the stress mark also was the
subject of heated exchanges between Guernsey and Oxford, with Onions
firmly asserting his view (again not directly) that they should be
placed after the syllable and not inside it (so <u>diaph´anous</u> not
<u>dia´phanous</u>), this being allegedly what the general public could best
understand. On 11 April 1919 Fowler wrote to Chapman:

> I feel bullied. You and Mr. Onions, or Amen Corner
> behind you, have an uncanny insight into the likes
> & dislikes of the G.P. that give you a manifestly
> unfair pull over me in the argument. My own belief
> is that not one in a thousand of the G.P. cares
> twopence where his dictionary puts its accents... I
> have still hopes that you will let the accents stay
> where they are, for England.

In the event no major revision of the practice was undertaken for the
second edition. A syllabic system of the kind recommended by Onions was
adopted in the first edition of the POD in 1927 and in the fourth
edition of the COD in 1951; in the sixth edition of each it was modified
and the stress mark put back to where the Fowlers had wanted it.

This subject was raised in connection with a projected American
version of the COD, for which a number of policy changes were envisaged.
It came to nothing, as did later revivals of the idea. An American
edition of the POD was published in 1927 but soon went out of print and
was not revived. In more recent times Australian, New Zealand, and
South African versions of the POD have been published or are in preparation; the first adaptation of the COD will be an Australian version
to be published in 1986.

Other matters that Fowler considered for the quarto dictionary and
the second edition of the COD included the revision of S-Z ´with OED´,
the introduction ´sparingly´ of diagrams, a fuller coverage of archaic
words found in literature (especially the Bible, Shakespeare, and
Milton), and the addition of Americanisms. This last was an area that
Fowler was fully willing to contemplate but felt ignorant about, as occasional allusions in his correspondence show. This and the expansion
of the technical vocabulary were as far as we can tell the two areas
felt to be most relevant to a revised COD; the others were obviously for
the larger work only. As it turned out neither of these nor any significant revision of the standing matter was implemented in these years,
and the edtion of 1929 carried little that was new apart from incorporation of the addenda of 1914 and some literal corrections. An important reason is that Fowler was encouraged to concentrate on the projected quarto dictionary. Another is that until a fairly late stage it
was evidently assumed that the revision would not involve resetting but
must be on a space-for-space basis with addenda. Certainly Fowler received no encouragement to revise drastically, although a letter of 2
Feb. 1926 shows that he was ready to ´recast´ the entire text ´if able´.
It seems that both parties recognized the need to revise the text, but
were daunted by the size of the task and the practical problems that
stood in the way.

What is really remarkable in the history of the COD is that it survived and sold in thousands of copies for some 65 years and three more
editions without undergoing a major revision. Le Mesurier took charge
of the dictionary when Henry Fowler died in 1933, and operated from his
home in Exmouth. He was concerned only with addenda and minor corrections of the kind thrown up by the chance of correspondence from
interested readers, apart from the material provided by the work done
for the 1933 Supplement. Le Mesurier assembled this material as a set
of addenda to the third edition published in 1934; there were about 2400
items in 61 pages. It was the largest addition, or indeed change of any
kind, that the COD received before the revision of the '70s.

In went activate, artefact, gamma rays, isotope, poppycock,
reflation, and third degree. Most of the items not from the Supplement
were from Le Mesurier's own experience, especially a large number of
Indian and Anglo-Indian words such as chillumchee (a large copper
basin), chupatty (a small bread cake, a familiar term now), gharry (a
kind of carriage), and panchayat (an Indian village council). In one or
two cases he improved on the Supplement definition, as with ekka which
the Supplement defined as a cart drawn by a horse but Le Mesurier knew
could also be drawn by a bullock. Other items such as accountancy,
devil's advocate, and counter espionage were found in other sources, or
were already in the OED and had been overlooked or only lately come to
prominence.

Le Mesurier had little chance to do any more than 'top up' the COD
vocabulary. For some years he produced word lists of scientific vocabulary drawn from the periodical Nature for use on the quarto dictionary,
but these were not added systematically to the COD at this stage. Had
he been a younger man, and had he been given the chance to revise the
COD on a more rigorous basis the results might have been interesting.

The caretaker years continued with the COD in the hands of Edward
McIntosh, a Scottish schoolmaster who knew Le Mesurier and moved to
Exmouth when he was invited to collaborate on the third edition. He became sole editor in 1939 after Le Mesurier's death. He was a retiring
man judging by his extant correspondence, and he acted under close in-
structions from Oxford, issued by Sisam and later by the Academic Publisher, Dan Davin; these were the true custodians of the dictionary
while McIntosh performed the drudgery. His main concern was with
addenda of one kind or another. The expanded 1944 collection is of
special interest in its coverage of words that had come into prominence
during the war years, words such as anschluss, armoured column, bomb
load, and gestapo, and forces' slang such as ack-ack, decko, and prang.
Other interesting items were allergy (a word coined in 1911 but not in
general use until the 1930s), Belisha beacon, bifocal, and hoover (small
initial again).

McIntosh prepared two editions of the COD: the fourth of 1951 and
the fifth of 1964. There was still no attempt to recast the book as
Fowler himself had contemplated, or to revise the spellings or remove
the by now considerable amount of redundant vocabulary, and both
editions were therefore in effect the old version with routine corrections made and addenda incorporated. There were however two innovations
in the fourth edition which greatly affected the general appearance of

the text: the introduction of the swung dash to stand for the headword
when it recurred within an entry (up to then its initial letter had been
used, though only in examples), and the adoption of the syllabic pronunciation system used in the POD, still with the stress mark after and not
inside the stressed syllable. It was evidently McIntosh's idea to use
the swung dash in the COD; the same device had been proposed for the
quarto dictionary (where it appears in one of the extant specimen pages)
and had been used in the LITTLE OXFORD DICTIONARY published in 1930.
It was to be retained for defined items but not for examples in the
sixth and seventh editions. I confess to a strong aversion to it and
shall not use it in the eighth edition; this is partly a matter of taste
and fashion and no doubt a future editor will one day hit on the idea
again in the hope of saving space. Such is the cycle of progress in
dictionaries as in many things.

     A third innovation was made in the fifth edition; a repeated hyphen
at the beginning of the next line to distinguish a permanent hyphen
falling at the end of a line from an accidental word-break. This is the
sort of device that is useful and comforting to editors but goes
unnoticed by most users.

     McIntosh died in 1970. With the appointment of his successor (and
my predecessor) the following year the decision was at last made to revise the dictionary completely on an entry-by-entry basis, as was only
possible with an Oxford-based in-house editor now that so much needed to
be done. The name of J.B. Sykes will be familiar as probably will be
his background. A former astrophysicist, Harwell researcher, and technical translator, he brought a new kind of thinking to the COD from
which the book profited immeasurably: the scientific mind that admits
data to be sound only if verifiable and quantifiable and regards consistency of approach to all elements of information as fundamental. We all
aspire to these principles but find them difficult to achieve. "I think
I have the kind of mind that likes the precision and deduction of the
scientific method, rather than the imprecise and subjective approach
that you find in the arts " he is quoted as saying in an interview published in New Scientist of 4 Sept. 1980, to which readers are referred
for further information. I am not sure that I recognize the distinction
without further qualification (a historian, for example, is precise and
deductive and usually objective), but the qualities were well suited to
the task of dismantling the structure of the COD, then refurbishing it
and reassembling it to produce something new without losing the character
 and best features of the original.(3)

     The main objectives of the revision can be deduced from all that
has been said: removal of items no longer current; revision of basic
questions of policy that had not been reconsidered since the dictionary's beginnings in the Edwardian age; a systematic selection of new
vocabulary based on firmer principles made possibly by the availability
of evidence for the new SUPPLEMENT TO THE OXFORD ENGLISH DICTIONARY
extension of coverage to include the language of other parts of the
English-speaking world, especially North America; the elimination of
inconsistencies and duplications (or combinations of the two) that were
found to be quite numerous; and most important, a line-by-line survey of
the entire text regardless of whether or not particular parts had been
picked out for criticism at any point. The text was typed out on to

some 50,000 6" x 4" slips of paper which were revised by hand to form
the printer's copy in the traditional manner. Summaries of the existing
entries were written out on A4 sheets and subjected to systematic
annotation on the basis of copious primary evidence available in the OUP
Dictionary Department's files as well as other sources, including notably
the OED, as we have seen.

This thorough revision brought the COD into the modern age; its
over-strong literary bias was corrected and the vocabulary of the
sciences was given its due. It recognized English as a world-wide
language and for the first time catered adequately for the American
influence. Its redesigned page, with semibold type cutting a path
through the italic jungle, made it easier to use. In the seventh
edition a small measure of prescriptivism was introduced with the symbols D (= disputed used) and R (= racially offensive use) alerting the
user to the existence of controversial points. I support this, if it is
what readers want, as long as the tone is strictly impartial; I should
not like to see the COD crossing the frontier into the territory of
prescriptive grammars and usage books.

Where then do we go from here with the COD? A great deal has
happened in the lexicographical world since the preparation of the
sixth and seventh editions; fashions have changed and research has been
carried out into what users expect from their dictionaries; rival dictionaries have found new approaches to the presentation of information
and have compelled us to rethink our own. The COD remains a difficult
dictionary to use in the sense that detailed information, because it is
so concisely expressed or more especially because it is implied, is
often overlooked or, worse, misunderstood. Therefore the information
needs to be restructured; in particular, we must rewrite the definitions
in more flowing English and disengage the deeply embedded syntactical
information. We must introduce the International Phonetic Alphabet.
Further de-nesting of subsumed headwords, reordering of senses, allo-
cation of phrases to special sections of articles, and some simplifi-
cation of the over-elaborate etymologies, are all essential. These
revisions have all been thought out in terms of the COD as a printed
book and we have already introduced some of them in the POD. It is
fortunate, but largely fortuitous, that they result in a text that
is well suited to organization as a structured database, because all
the indications are that the COD must move in this direction if it is to
retain its place in a highly competitive market. To achieve this we
have started to keyboard the revised text using software specially con-
figured to accommodate it. I shall have more to say about this on
other occasions as our experience accumulates. Meanwhile the fundamental issue for the editors of the COD now remains largely what it
always has been: how to refurbish it for the present day without
losing the book's essential character. Let us see if we succeed.

Notes

(1) I am most grateful to Dr R.W. Burchfield, and to my COD colleague Dr D.J. Thompson, for reading a draft of this paper and
making many important suggestions. I must also thank Mrs. J.
McMorris and Miss E.M. Knowles for help with the archive material.

(2) On the Fowlers, see Burchfield (1979).

(3) Dr Sykes has described how he went about the revision of the COD
in an article entitled "From A to Zen" (1979).

References

Cited dictionaries (see Appendix):

CHAMBERS TWENTIETH CENTURY DICTIONARY (Davidson/Kirkpatrick)
(THE) CONCISE OXFORD DICTIONARY (Fowler/Sykes)
(A) DICTIONARY OF MODERN ENGLISH USAGE (Fowler)
(THE) LITTLE OXFORD DICTIONARY (Ostler/Swannell)
(THE) OXFORD ENGLISH DICTIONARY (Murray et al.)
(THE) POCKET OXFORD DICTIONARY ... (Fowler/Allen)
(A) SUPPLEMENT TO THE OXFORD ENGLISH DICTIONARY (Burchfield)

Other literature:

Burchfield, Robert W. (1979) "The Fowlers: Their Achievements in
    Lexicography and Grammar". The English Association Presidential
    Address. June 1979
Fowler, Henry W. and Francis G. (1906) The King's English. Oxford:
    Clarendon P.
Sykes, John B. (1979) "From A to Zen" The Rising Generation (Tokyo:
    Kenkyusha) 125,5: 204-207
Sykes, John B. (1980) "The New Scientist Interview: John Bradbury
    Sykes" New Scientist 87, 1217: 718-720

RICHELET'S 'DICTIONNAIRE FRANÇOIS' (1680) AS A SOURCE OF 'LA PORTE DES SIENCES' (1682) AND LE ROUX'S 'DICTIONAIRE COMIQUE' (1718)

Laurent Bray

The DICTIONNAIRE FRANÇOIS (1680) and the lexicographic scene in 17th and 18th century Europe

The DICTIONNAIRE FRANÇOIS by César-Pierre Richelet (1626-1698) is the first fully monolingual French dictionary of definitions. It was published in 1680 - quite a late date in comparison with dictionaries of other Romance languages such as Spanish and Italian.
The Spaniard Fernando del Rosal compiled his ORIGEN Y ETYMOLOGIA DE TODOS LOS VOCABLOS ORIGINALES DE LA LENGUA CASTELLANA as early as 1601 (the manuscript, which is owned by the National Library in Madrid, had not been published; cf. MacDonald 1977:13) and one year later, in 1602, the Italian, Giacomo Pergamini's MEMORIALE DELLA LINGUA appeared, the very first dictionary of definitions dealing with a modern language to be published in Europe. In 1611 Sebastian de Covarrubias y Orozco published his TESORO DE LA LENGUA CASTELLANA O ESPAÑOLA and shortly thereafter, in 1612, the VOCABOLARIO DEGLI ACCADEMICI DELLA CRUSCA appeared.
As we know, entirely monolingual dictionaries of definitions made their appearance in Northern Europe in the course of the 18th century: in England, after the work done by J.K. (NEW ENGLISH DICTIONARY, 1702) and Bailey (UNIVERSAL ETYMOLOGICAL ENGLISH DICTIONARY, 1721; MORE COMPLEAT UNIVERSAL ETYMOLOGICAL ENGLISH DICTIONARY, 1730), the first English dictionary truly comparable to that of Richelet was not published until 1755 when Johnson's DICTIONARY OF THE ENGLISH LANGUAGE appeared.
The Germans were to see their first dictionary of definitions published in five volumes between 1774 and 1786, namely Adelung's VERSUCH EINES VOLLSTÄNDIGEN GRAMMATISCH-KRITISCHEN WÖRTERBUCHES. In the Netherlands, Peter Weiland's NEDERDUITSCH TAALKUNDIG WOORDENBOEK begun in 1799 (vol. 1) was completed in its 11th volume in 1811.
Let us note here that the advent of the first monolingual dictionaries usually corresponds to a period of growing awareness of national or regional identity: the publishing of Richelet's dictionary in 1680 - and later on of those of Furetière (DICTIONAIRE UNIVERSEL, 1690) and the Académie française (1694) - coincides with the apogee of Louis XIV's reign.

The DICTIONNAIRE FRANÇOIS: too liberal to be the dictionary of the 'honnête homme'

The DICTIONNAIRE FRANÇOIS of 1680 signed by Richelet was in fact compiled by a group of scholars: the translators Maucroix and Cassandre,

the barrister Patru and the Jesuits Rapin and Bouhours all participated
in the work. These learned men rejected the lexicographical principles
maintained by the members of the Académie française. Among the practices that Richelet and his collaborators disagreed with was the exclusion of literary quotations from the Academy's dictionary, then in preparation. They also criticized the Academy's slowness and challenged
the lexicographical competence of the Académiciens. Richelet's dictionary can be seen as the fruit of a rebellion against the principles advocated by the Academy. It is known how the dictionary of 1680 was made.
Richelet's collaborators were charged with the task of collecting potential headwords for the dictionary and of recording the literary quotations in which the lexical units appeared. As for Richelet, he reserved
for himself the most thankless task: that of writing the definitions,
which, interestingly enough, recall those of Johnson (1755). Like Johnson, Richelet used his dictionary to criticise his contemporaries and
society in general (cf. Pitou 1949).
But Richelet's dictionary was fated to oblivion - and this for two
reasons. Firstly, it had the misfortune of being eclipsed by two other
dictionaries: that of the Académie (1694), which had succeeded in secu-
ring favour more by its prestige than by its qualities (this dictionary
is not user-friendly because it is ordered by root words; in addition
it only records a relatively small cross-section of the lexicon).
A more formidable competitor of Richelet's dictionary was that of Furetière (DICTIONAIRE UNIVERSEL, 1690) which is characterised by an extensive macrostructure and an impressive encyclopedic component. This dictionary succeeded in completely overshadowing Richelet's work, which,
because it had been completed in only 16 months, could not hope to offer
the same completeness.
Later on, the prominent French lexicologist of the beginning of this
century, Ferdinand Brunot, too hastily stamped a label on Richelet's
dictionary: for Brunot, the dictionary of 1680 is puristic and this
rapid judgement has been adopted - without being verified - by several
generations of language historians (cf. Bray 1985).
Overshadowed by Furetière and by Brunot's judgement, Richelet was
doomed to oblivion.
And yet, Richelet's dictionary is worthy of being restudied. An analysis of the macro- and microstructure of 1680 shows that this work has,
in fact, some very modern characteristics. Richelet provided his user
with a wealth of usage notes on the French vocabulary of the 17th century. This includes information on the situation in which words or
meanings are used, the subject area, the level of usage and the region
they are typical of. He also gives spelling variants and the pronunciation of hard words, and - for the very first time in France - he systematically defines all the words in his dictionary.
Richelet's dictionary has wrongly been labelled the dictionary of the
'honnête homme'. In actual fact, besides stylistically unmarked vocabulary, Richelet incorporates a wide range of marked lexical units
which clash with the French puristic ideal of the 17th century. 'Bien-
séance', 'pureté' and 'honnêteté' in language - none of these traits
are scrupulously respected by Richelet. His dictionary includes vulgar

words, 'dirty' words ('mots sales'), provincial words, words of the
common folk, neologisms and archaic words, all of which the disciples
of Vaugelas condemned. Richelet also records "mots des arts et des
sciences", that is, the vocabulary of specialized languages, which the
'honnête homme' shunned, regarding all that concerns 'science' as sus-
picious and pedantic.
It is the inclusion of popular and technical words and, above all, the
abundant usage notes which make Richelet's DICTIONNAIRE FRANÇOIS desirable to provincials and foreigners seeking to gain a precise image of
the actual use of the French language.

The DICTIONNAIRE FRANÇOIS: a dictionary rich in information which provided a useful starting point to many lexicographers

The DICTIONNAIRE FRANÇOIS was an enormous commercial success: no fewer
than 60 editions were published between 1680 and 1811!
The extensive circulation of the work, its qualities and the diverse
vocabulary which it records explain why it was exploited - openly or
not - by numerous lexicographers of the 17th and 18th centuries.
Richelet is the main source of a number of polyglot dictionaries, for
example the EUROPÄISCHER SPRACH-SCHATZ (Leipzig: J.F. Braun, 1711), a
trilingual German-Italian-French dictionary by Johann Rädlein; he uses
Richelet's dictionary because - as he tells us - it is the best French
dictionary of its time. Another example is the anonymous GRAND ET NOU-
VEAU DICTIONNAIRE FRANÇOIS ET FLAMAND; compiled by a certain L.V.I.V.
I.F., it was published in Brussels by J. de Grieck in 1707. But the
most interesting mention of Richelet was made by one of the most productive European lexicographers and, indeed, one of the most capable
and well-informed metalexicographers of 17th and 18th century Europe,
Matthias Kramer. In 1712, in the preface to his DICTIONARIUM ... FRANT-
ZÖSISCH-TEUTSCH (Nürnberg: Endter) Kramer claims that Richelet's work
is the only French monolingual dictionary of its time which presents
an authentic and critical image of the French language.
Of course, the authors of bilingual dictionaries were not the only ones
to profit from Richelet's work. Frenchmen equally benefitted from Richelet in their work on monolingual specialized dictionaries. But as
opposed to the non-French lexicographers I have just mentionned, Richelet's compatriots lacked the scruples to indicate their source. In the
course of research today one stumbles across many dictionaries which
- although they are presented as original works - are in reality mere
plagiarisms, more or less obvious, of Richelet's DICTIONNAIRE FRANÇOIS.

A comparison of Richelet with Thomas Corneille's DICTIONNAIRE DES ARTS
ET DES SCIENCES (Paris: Coignard, 1694) shows, for instance, that, in
the articles the two dictionaries have in common, Corneille has copied
almost word for word close to 80% of the lexicographical information
given by Richelet already in 1680. This discovery is surprising, to
say the least, when one considers that Corneille belonged to the Académie française which had so severely condemned Richelet's work!

The DICTIONNAIRE FRANÇOIS, the source of LA PORTE DES SIENCES (1682)

I would now like to discuss two dictionaries which are more talked of
than known. The first is a dictionary of hard words published in 1682,
the second a dictionary of slang published in 1718: both of these dictionaries - although their aims are radically different - have Richelet
as a common source. The fact that two authors working 40 years apart
from one another chose to draw their inspiration from one and the same
dictionary to produce two such dissimilar books clearly shows the diversity of information offered in Richelet's dictionary. We see that it
is quite unfounded to seriuosly accuse Richelet of uncompromising pu-
rism as has been done in the past.

In 1682 the Parisians Charles Coignard and Daniel de La Ville published
a small 226 page in-octavo entitled LA PORTE DES SIENCES [sic] OU RE-
CEUIL [sic] DES TERMES ET DES MOTS LES PLUS DIFICILES A ENTENDRE ...
AVEC UN DICTIONNAIRE DE PLUSIEURS AUTRES MOTS & TERMES AUßSI OBSCURS.
The author, whose name is concealed behind the initials D.C.S.D.S.S.,
sets down his aims in the introduction to his book (Av Lectevr, ãiij
r⁰ - [ãv]r⁰): it is written firstly "en faveur des dames pour augmen-
ter leur perfection" that is for the profit of ladies so that they may
increase their perfection; secondly "pour rendre ceux qui n'ont que peu
ou point d'estude capables d'entendre les termes & les mots de la langue Françoise les plus obscurs & les plus difficiles", to render those
who have but little or no education capable of understanding the most
obscure and difficult terms and words of the French language; and
thirdly, "pour servir à l'instruction des Estrangers". That is, to serve for the instruction of foreigners. The author expressly states that
he has excluded vulgar words from his dictionary.
The work of D.C.S.D.S.S. is divided in two parts: the first (1-87), entitled LA PORTE DES SIENCES (the title seems to be modelled on Comenius'
JANUA LINGUARUM RESERATA, 1631) is a thesaurus of hard words. It is divided into 23 headings, 23 'matières', in which are listed (without
any apparent order) and defined the difficult terms of grammar, ethics,
physics, geography, etc. The heading 'Rêthorique', for example, presents and defines 132 obscure rhetorical figures for those "qui n'ont
que peu ou point d'estude": pradiastole , metalepse , antonomasie ,
epenos , schevasme , hipozeuxe ... to name just a few.
The first part of D.C.S.D.S.S.'s work, the actual PORTE DES SIENCES, is
original: it has practically nothing in common with Richelet's dictionary. The second part (1-124), however, entitled the DICTIONNAIRE DES
MOTS OBSCURS, LEUR EXPLICATION A COTE, & COMME ILS S'ORTHOGRAPHENT [sic],
is an abridged but blatant copy of the DICTIONNAIRE FRANÇOIS. The author
of the DICTIONNAIRE DES MOTS OBSCURS simply selected the entries in Richelet's dictionary which he considered difficult and placed them in
alphabetical order. The definitions are those of Richelet. A comparison
of two articles shows how much D.C.S.D.S.S. owes to Richelet:

Richelet 1680:

PALESTRE, s.f. C'étoit le lieu où
   les luiteurs [sic] s'exerçoient
   Voiez Vitruve.[Ici, dans la pa-

D.C.S.D.S.S. 1682:

Palestre. Lieu oû s'exerçoient
les Luiteurs [sic].

lestre unie, les lutteurs font
tous leur êforts. *S.Amand, Rome
ridicule.*]

HAUBANT, *s.m. Terme de mer.* Ce sont
de gros cordages amarrez aux barres de hune & à des caps de mouton. [A la reserve du beaupré chaque mast a ses haubans.]

Haubans. Gros cordages, amarrs
[*sic*] aux barres des hunes & des
caps de mouton, chaque mas a ses
hunes [*sic*].

D.C.S.D.S.S. leaves out Richelet's grammatical information, the examples
and the quotations, retaining an often abbreviated form of his definition.
A comparison of the letter **H** in the two dictionaries (D.C.S.D.S.S.
has only 45 entries) shows that entries peculiar to D.C.S.D.S.S. are
very rare (one in 45: Hipotequaires) and that the definition is almost a word for word copy of Richelet. Only three definitions in **H**
differ from those in Richelet (Hipotequé , Homogene , Horoscope).
D.C.S.D.S.S.'s definitions are rudimentary and just as obscure as the
hard words they are meant to explain. For example:

Richelet 1680:

HOMOGENE, *adj. Terme de Philosophie,*
qui veut dire *semblable.* [Matiere
homogene.]

D.C.S.D.S.S. 1682:

Homogene. Semblable nom à toutes les parties du tout.

HOROSCOPE. Ce mot est *masculin & fé-
minin,* mais le plus souvent *masculin.* L'horoscope consiste à cher-
cher le moment de la naissance
d'une personne & à *voir* sous quel-
le planette est née cette personne
pour lui prédire le bonheur & le
malheur qui lui arrivera avec la
durée de sa vie. [Horoscope bien
dressé. *Vau. Rem.*]

Horoscope. Pour connoître les
evenemens de la vie.

The author of the DICTIONNAIRE DES MOTS OBSCURS is apparently an inca-
pable lexicographer, but nonetheless a lexicographer who is most familiar with Richelet's dictionary. And this is not a mere coincidence.

Although LA PORTE DES SIENCES is known (Quemada 1967 includes it in his
bibliography and Collison 1982:86 makes mention of it in his History
of Foreign-Language Dictionaries), its author has not yet been identified. And yet a short poem presenting the work and signed by D. Georges Conrad Schuter de Leipzig contains an important clue as to the identity of D.C.S.D.S.S., abbreviated to M.D.C. in the short title. It reveals his pseudonym, 'Damon':

Ieune Autheur qui pretens monter sur le Parnasse
Et qui chez Apollon tiens la derniere place,
Vien[s] consulter Damon, sur cent termes divers
des Sciences sans peine il t'ouvrira la porte ...

Now, Damon is not unknown in French literature. He is a mediochre, unsuccessful author often mocked by his contemporaries and whom Boileau
mentions in his first Satire:

> Damon ce grand Auteur, dont la Muse fertile
> Amusa si long-temps et la Cour et la Ville ...

Not only does Boileau make fun of Damon, he also reveals his true identity in a letter to Brossette (edited by Laverdet 1858, 524): Damon,
alias D.C.S.D.S.S., alias M.D.C., is none other than François Cassandre,
M.D.C., Monsieur De Cassandre, who - as I have mentioned earlier - was
one of Richelet's collaborators in work on the dictionary. In a letter
to Maucroix of April 4th 1677, Patru says that Cassandre had been charged with collecting words "qui sont de peu d'usage", that is, the hard
words, the 'mots obscurs'. Cassandre seems to have waited, once he had
delivered his word list to Richelet, for the latter to define the material before discretely including it in his own DICTIONNAIRE DES MOTS
OBSCURS. This hypothesis gains credibility considering the fact that
these two men despised each other.

The DICTIONNAIRE FRANÇOIS, the source of the DICTIONAIRE COMIQUE by Le Roux (1718)

Richelet was not a purist. For him, the language of the common folk
was not without a certain charm: he was a great amateur of linguistic
'libertinage'. As a matter of fact, he even announced, in a note appended to a collection of letters edited by him in 1689, the completion
of his manuscript for a DICTIONNAIRE BURLESQUE: "... le Dictionnaire
burlesque que je ferai peut-être bien-tôt imprimer ...". This dictionary was never published: some authors (Lenglet-Dufresnoye 1737, Goujet 1740) claim that it was Richelet himself who destroyed the manuscript on the advice of his confessor; others (e.g. Billet de Fasnières
1714) maintain that it was stolen: "... on ne sçait ce qu'est devenu
cet ouvrage ... qu'on luy a volé à sa mort". Whether it was destroyed
or stolen, Richelet's DICTIONNAIRE BURLESQUE seems to have well and
truly disappeared. I say "seems to have disappeared" because in fact,
in 1718, twenty years after Richelet's death and four years after Billet de Fasnières' claim that Richelet's manuscript had been stolen, a
book was published in Amsterdam, an interesting collection which,
strangely enough, resumes Richelet's idea from 30 years earlier: namely, to explain "toutes les manières de parler burlesques, comiques,
libres ... qui peuvent se rencontrer dans les meilleurs auteurs".
Could this be a coincidence?
I think not. Philibert Joseph Le Roux's DICTIONAIRE COMIQUE, the book
in question here, is indeed a rather curious work. Giraud justifiably
declared in 1983 that "le livre et son auteur restent assez mystérieux".
Le Roux, of whom we know practically nothing, did not bother writing
an introduction to his book: in 1718 the DICTIONAIRE COMIQUE did not
as yet have a preface. The dictionary is preceded only by a "Catalogue
des auteurs" which, by the way, includes Richelet. It also includes -
and this is quite unexpected in a 'dictionnaire comique' - works of
Jurisprudence (by Patru), Physics (by Rohault), Ethics and Religion
(by Pascal, Nicole, Bossuet) and even translations of Classical lite-

rature (by d'Ablancourt). Giraud, who described the DICTIONAIRE COMIQUE
in 1983, expressed surprise at the inclusion of these books but could
not find an explanation for it. Interestingly enough, all of these authors can be found in the DICTIONNAIRE FRANÇOIS of 1680; we could take
Giraud's line of thinking one step further, and suspect Le Roux of having copied Richelet - this Giraud could not have done, since he had
not compared Richelet with Le Roux. But what he did note was a similarity in the character of the two authors: both have a satirical penchant,
and both criticize their contemporaries. To illustrate his point, Giraud cites the article **insipide** in Le Roux's dictionary. Here we read:

> INSIPIDE ... Les traductions de l'imaginaire Amelot sont
>   insipides en comparaison de celles de l'excellent d'Ablancourt...

But Giraud was not able to explain why Le Roux should attack Amelot and
defend d'Ablancourt. If Giraud failed to understand the motivation behind this statement, it is because its author was not Le Roux but Richelet (DICTIONAIRE FRANÇOIS 1693, s.v. **insipide**). Richelet was, in fact,
a close friend of the translator d'Ablancourt and Amelot de la Hous-
saye's bitter enemy. We see that Le Roux and Richelet have a number of
points in common. A comparison of Le Roux's dictionary of 1718 with the
1693 edition of Richelet's DICTIONAIRE FRANÇOIS (printed in Geneva for
David Ritter by Vincent Miège; a revised and enlarged version of the
1680 edition) shows that the two have more than just a few "points in
common": Le Roux literally pillaged Richelet:

Richelet 1693:

Il n'en a pas fait une panse d'A,
Façon de parler proverbiale, qui
veut dire, il n'y a point travaillé,
il n'en a rien fait, il n'a pas tou-
ché à l'ouvrage dont il est question.

...

Renvoyer quelqu'un à l'a b, c, façon de parler proverbiale, pour dire
traiter quelqu'un d'ignorant.

†AB HOC & AB HAC. Mots latins qui
sont devenus Frãçois & qui signi-
fient sans ordre & sans raison, à
tort & à travers. (Discourir *ab hoc
& ab hac,* parler *ab hoc & ab hac.*)
Ici git Monsieur de Clezac
Qui baisoit *ab hoc & ab hac.*
Ménage, poësies.

Le Roux 1718:

A, PANSE D'A, *il n'en a pas fait
une panse d'a,* façon de parler
proverbiale, pour dire qu'un homme n'a rien fait de l'ouvrage dont
il s'agit, qu'il n'y a point tou-
ché.

...

Renvoyer quelqu'un à l'*A.B.C.* pour
dire, le traiter d'ignorant.

Ab hoc & ab hac. Il ne fait ce
qu'il dit, il en parle, ou il en
discourt *ab hoc & ab hac;* pour si-
gnifier, confusément, sans ordre
ou sans raison.
Ici gît Mr. Clezac
Qui baisoit ab hoc & ab hac.

Le Roux differs from Richelet 1693 only in a few new articles. We may ask,
where do these new articles come from? Were they written by Le Roux himself, or are they taken from the manuscript of the DICTIONNAIRE BURLES-
QUE? In other words: is the DICTIONAIRE COMIQUE of 1718 the same DICTION-
NAIRE BURLESQUE which Richelet announced in 1689? I would not deny it -

but a definitive answer can only be given, if one day, in some dark and
dusty corner of a library, the famous manuscript is found.
Wether Richelet is the author of the dictionary of 1718 or not, one
thing is certain, it was a tremendous success: it was reprinted at least
seven times between 1718 and 1808, and, ironically enough, was in turn
the object of plagiarism: the NOUVEAU DICTIONNAIRE PROVERBIAL, SATIRIQUE
ET BURLESQUE (Paris: Dauvin, 1826; 2nd ed.: 1829) by Antoine Caillot is
an almost word for word copy of Le Roux.
And so with Le Roux's and Caillot's plagiarisms Richelet's lexicographic work was exploited right up to the first half of the 19th century.

To conclude, and because we are here in Great Britain, let me recall
that it was the success which Le Roux's dictionary enjoyed in France
which persuaded Francis Grose of the need for a similar dictionary of
the English Language. In his preface to the DICTIONARY OF THE VULGAR
TONGUE (1785) Grose writes:

> "The great approbation with which so polite a nation as France has
> received the Satirical and Burlesque Dictionary of Monsieur Le Roux,
> testified by the several editions it has gone through, will, it is
> hoped, apologize for an attempt to compile an English Dictionary on
> a similar plan; our language is at least as copious as the French,
> and as capable of the witty equivoque ..."

By the intermediary of Le Roux we can say that, with Grose's dictionary
a part of Richelet's spirit crossed the Channel in 1785; which only goes
to show that tunnels aren't the only means of getting across.

References

Cited dictionaries (see Appendix):

(A) CLASSICAL DICTIONARY OF THE VULGAR TONGUE (Grose)
DICTIONAIRE COMIQUE ... (Le Roux)
DICTIONAIRE UNIVERSEL ... (Furetière)
DICTIONARIUM ... FRANTZOSISCH-TEUTSCH (Kramer)
(A) DICTIONARY OF THE ENGLISH LANGUAGE (Johnson)
DICTIONNAIRE BURLESQUE (Richelet)
(LE) DICTIONNAIRE DE L'ACADEMIE FRANÇAISE
DICTIONNAIRE DES ARTS ET DES SCIENCES (Corneille)
DICTIONNAIRE DES MOTS OBSCURS see PORTE DES SIENCES
DICTIONNAIRE FRANÇOIS ... (Richelet)
EUROPÄISCHER SPRACHSCHATZ (Rädlein)
GRAND ET NOUVEAU DICTIONNAIRE FRANÇOIS ET FLAMAND ('L.V.I.V.I.F.')
JANUA LINGUARUM RESERATA ... (Comenius)
MEMORIALE DELLA LINGUA ... (Pergamini)
(A) MORE COMPLEAT UNIVERSAL ETYMOLOGICAL ENGLISH DICTIONARY (Bailey)
NEDERDUITSCH TAALKUNDIG WOORDENBOEK (Weiland)
(A) NEW ENGLISH DICTIONARY ... ('J.K.')
NOUVEAU DICTIONNAIRE PROVERBIAL ... (Caillot)
ORIGEN Y ETYMOLOGIA ... DE LA LENGUA CASTELLANA (Rosal)
(LA) PORTE DES SIENCES ... ('D.C.S.D.S.S.'/Cassandre)
TESORO DE LA LENGUA CASTELLANA, O ESPAÑOLA (Covarrubias)
(AN) UNIVERSAL ETYMOLOGICAL ENGLISH DICTIONARY (Bailey)

VERSUCH EINES VOLLSTÄNDIGEN ... WÖRTERBUCHES ... (Adelung)
VOCABOLARIO DEGLI ACCADEMICI DELLA CRUSCA

Other literature:

Billet de Fasnières, M. (1714) Bibliothèque des Homonymes françois.
    Paris: Bibliothèque Nationale ms.fr.15273, fol.199-200
Boileau, Nicolas (1701/1966) Oeuvres diverses. Reprint ed. by Fran-
    çoise Escal (Pléiade). Paris: NRF Gallimard
Bray, Laurent (1985) "Notes sur la réception du Dictionnaire fran-
    çois (1680) de Pierre Richelet" Lexicographica 1: 243-251
Bray, Laurent (forthcoming) César-Pierre Richelet (1626-1698):
    biographie et oevre lexicographique (Lexicographica. Series
    Maior). Tübingen: M. Niemeyer
Brunot, Ferdinand (1909-13/1966) Histoire de la langue française des
    origines à nos jours (vol. III, IV/1). Reprint ed. Gérald An-
    toine. Paris: Colin
Collison, Robert L. (1982) A History of Foreign-Language Dic-
    tionaries (The Language Library). London: A. Deutsch
Giraud, Yves (1983) "Le 'Dictionnaire comique' de Le Roux (1718)"
    Cahiers de l'Association Internationale des Etudes Françaises
    35: 69-86
Goujet, Abbé (1740) Bibliothèque françoise, ou Histoire de la
    littérature françoise. The Hague: J. Neaulme
Laverdet, Auguste N. (1858) Correspondence entre Boileau-Despréaux
    et Brossette, avocat au Parlement de Lyon, publiée sur les manu-
    scrits originaux. Paris: J. Téchener
Lenglet-Dufresnoye, Nicolas (1737) Histoire de la Conquête de la
    Floride; Avertissement. Amsterdam: J.F. Bernard
MacDonald, Gerald J. (1977/82) "Lexicography in Spain before the
    18th century: progress, personalities, and milestones" in Papers
    of the Dictionary Society of North America ed. by Donald Hobar.
    Terre Haute IN: Indiana State University/DSNA 9-15
Pitou, Spire (1949) "Richelet, forerunner of Samuel Johnson, and De
    Lormes" Modern Language Notes 64: 474-476
Quemada, Bernard (1967) Les dictionnaires du français moderne,
    1539-1863. Etude sur leur histoire, leurs types et leurs
    méthodes (Etudes lexicologiques 1). Paris: M. Didier

Richelet as a source of LA PORTE DES SIENCES (1682) and Le Roux's
DICTIONAIRE COMIQUE (1718) :

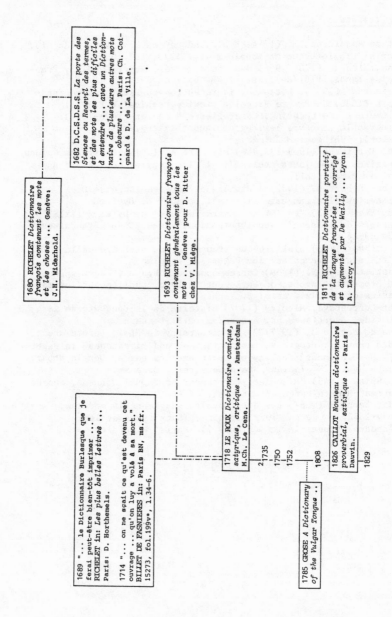

THE HISTORY OF PRONUNCIATION IN ENGLISH-LANGUAGE DICTIONARIES

Arthur J. Bronstein

The indication of pronunciation in English language dictionaries, as we know it today, developed slowly and in very distinct stages, from the 17th century to the present day.

Neither the grammarians nor the orthoepists of the 16th century made any real efforts to define pronunciation standards and although the 17th century was aware of such concepts, attempts to identify and prescribe or note 'correct' or other forms of pronunciation were not lasting. Thus, the very early English language dictionaries, from Robert Cawdrey's A TABLE ALPHABETICALL in 1604 through John Kersey's DICTIONARIUM ANGLO-BRITANNICUM in 1708, neither mentioned nor entered pronounced forms of words.

It was not until 1727, when Supplement II of Nathan Bailey's UNIVERSAL ETYMOLOGICAL ENGLISH DICTIONARY appeared, that the first feature of pronunciation (the indication of an accent on the dominant syllables of words) became an entry in English language dictionaries. That indication came in a dictionary-conscious age, for the middle and late 18th century has been called one that "not only absorbed the innumerable dictionaries of Bailey and Johnson and various other more modest works, but abounded in technical dictionaries and even went to the length of affixing a glossary to any work where language was at all unusual" (Starnes and Noyes 1946, p.126). Thomas Dyche established pronunciation as a requisite feature of English language dictionaries by the manner in which he stressed such on the title page of his A NEW GENERAL ENGLISH DICTIONARY, co-edited with William Pardon in 1735. He extensively developed the treatment of pronunciation in that dictionary's introductory matter.

We know that the 'age of reason' was reflected in the attitudes of the language molders of the period--an antipathy for irregularity and a strong sense of what has been called 'gentlemanly culture'. That century reflected the dictionary editors' departure from the linguistic 'ease' of the previous Elizabethan age, with its freedom of morphological and syntactic forms, as well as the freedom in coining words for an exploding lexicon. Thus the 18th century's devotion to 'correctness' and linguistic regulation, if not support for approaches leading to 'purifying' the language, demonstrated itself, no less, in its indication of pronounced forms of the lexicon. The editors' intents were prescriptive, reflecting the expectations of their readers. The members of a class suddenly risen to power in this century had developed a consciousness that fostered a single social (rather than geographic or regional) standard pronunciation form. Common or regional variants were 'cleansed' from the expected forms.

Samuel Johnson, the most widely quoted and respected lexicographer of the 18th century and the one who "invested the calling with lasting dignity" (Starnes and Noyes, p.196), adopted Bailey's accentuation system in toto in A DICTIONARY OF THE ENGLISH LANGUAGE (1755). He attempted to indicate such features as regional differences, the pronunciation of sounds in languages other than English as they should be pronounced by cultured Englishmen, and voiced/voiceless contrasts. If Johnson did develop a system that was rudimentary and ineffective, (cf. Congleton 1979), he did demonstrate a preliminary understanding of the function pronunciation might play in lexicography.

Like those before Johnson and those lexicographers to follow him in that century, the influence of linguistic rules or conservatism or language control was pervasive. By the end of the century, in 1791, John Walker's highly influential CRITICAL PRONOUNCING DICTIONARY AND EXPOSITOR OF THE ENGLISH LANGUAGE appeared and it was now obvious that pronunciation entries in any English language dictionary were important and expected parts of such works. It became the arbiter for most dictionary readers of the time, meeting the demand for regularity, logic, order, and rules in language use. That influence was not to end with the century.

Almost at the same time as Walker's entry on the scene of 18th century lexicography, another lexicographer, Thomas Sheridan, published his COMPLETE DICTIONARY OF THE ENGLISH LANGUAGE in 1789. Sheridan picked up the linguistic idea within the unsuccessful revolt proposed by John Locke in his Essay Concerning Human Understanding in 1751--the idea that language constantly reflected growth or change. Sheridan was the first major lexicographer to note variations from 'established, correct forms', based on his understandings of certain actual pronunciation usages of educated speakers. His conclusions were based on no extensive surveys--but they were more representative of that period's actual pronunciations by educated speakers. Despite this, Walker's work was considered more authoritative and Sheridan's pronunciation-indications succumbed, in later lexicons, to the dictates of Walker. Both these eminent 18th-century lexicographers had developed detailed respelling systems for the entry of pronunciations "invading territory where Johnson had feared to tread" (McDavid 1980:305). Their dictionaries included not only accent marks placed over the stressed syllables of words, but the use of diacritic systems for representing vowel qualities and consonant forms. Their systems were followed by all 19th-century lexicographers even into the present century. With their dictionaries, pronounced forms had become a feature of all English language dictionaries.

The descriptive revolt, begun in a very small way by Sheridan, continued with Noah Webster and others of the following century who considered 'pronunciation usage' a fact of lexicography. Two men, Noah Webster and Joseph Worcester, dominated 19th-century lexicography. The former's works were more extensively circulated, while Worcester's dictionaries were assumed to possess what Lounsbury (1904) called "a tone of loftier linguistic or rarer orthographical virtue" (pp.54-55). Webster's development as the leading lexicographic authority in the United States began with his COMPENDIOUS DICTIONARY OF THE ENGLISH

LANGUAGE in 1806, followed by his two-volume AN AMERICAN DICTIONARY OF
THE ENGLISH LANGUAGE in 1828. His concept of pronunciation standards was
the first strong attempt to recognize current usage as a factor in pronunciation-indications; despite his later conservatism in listing certain
common variant pronunciations of the time, his attitude towards the
indication of usage was an important influence in the direction following
lexicographers had to take. Joseph Worcester, his powerful dictionary
opponent, published his COMPREHENSIVE PRONOUNCING AND EXPLANATORY DIC-
TIONARY OF THE ENGLISH LANGUAGE in 1830, his UNIVERSAL AND CRITICAL
DICTIONARY OF THE ENGLISH LANGUAGE in 1846, followed by his DICTIONARY OF
THE ENGLISH LANGUAGE in 1860. Worcester's dictionaries adhered strongly
to British patterns of orthography and pronunciations--reflecting a belief that British pronunciations were 'better', 'more accurate', 'more
harmonious and agreeable'--an antithetical notion to Noah Webster's attitude that dictionary entries of 'American pronunciations' in use would
better reflect educated usage in the United States.

During the early 19th century the first pronouncing dictionaries in
the United States appeared--R.S. Coxe's A NEW CRITICAL PRONOUNCING
DICTIONARY OF THE ENGLISH LANGUAGE (1813) and B. Allison's THE AMERICAN
STANDARD OF ORTHOGRAPHY AND PRONUNCIATION AND IMPROVED DICTIONARY OF THE
ENGLISH LANGUAGE (1815). Both were based on the works of British orthoe-
pists and neither showed any real recognition of American English pronun-
ciation forms. Later in the century, D. Smalley's THE AMERICAN PHONETIC
DICTIONARY OF THE ENGLISH LANGUAGE (1855) and W. Bolles' A PHONOGRAPHIC
PRONOUNCING DICTIONARY OF THE ENGLISH LANGUAGE (1846) appeared; neither
was in widespread use.

The twentieth century saw the real development of English pronouncing
dictionaries. A considerable improvement in the notational system for
pronunciation came with the establishment of the International Phonetic
Association in the late 19th century and the development of its IPA
alphabet. One of the first dictionaries to use that alphabet was A
PHONETIC DICTIONARY OF THE ENGLISH LANGUAGE, co-edited by H. Michaelis
and Daniel Jones (1913). It listed English words in phonetic transcription first. This pronunciation-first format proved impractical; it was
abandoned in favor of listing words in their orthographic forms first,
followed by a phonetic transcription--the system adopted by Daniel Jones
in his ENGLISH PRONOUNCING DICTIONARY (EPD).

Jones was the leading British phonetician of this century. A brief
review of his training, publications, and accomplishments, written by
A.C. Gimson, appears in the BIOGRAPHICAL DICTIONARY OF THE PHONETIC
SCIENCES (Bronstein et al.1977,pp.108-109). With his phonetics teacher,
Paul Passy, he was chiefly responsible for the development and growth of
the International Phonetic Association for which he edited, in 1949, the
Principles of the International Phonetic Association. Prior to his EPD,
Jones had published a number of phonetic readers and pronunciation
manuals which, along with his The Pronunciation of English (1909, extensively revised 1917), helped establish his reputation as the pre-eminent
phonetician of his time. The EPD was completely revised in 1937, again in
1956, 1963 and 1967, and finally, extensively revised and reedited by

A.C. Gimson in its 14th edition, 1977. Jones' EPD was the first dictionary to use a fully developed phonetic system to represent the vowel,
diphthong, and consonant forms of the language, the indication of three
degrees of syllabic stress, syllabified consonants, syllable divisions,
symbols for certain non-English sounds, and diacritics to represent
consonant retroflexion, voicelessness, and nasalization. Jones' dictionary represented a particular type of English pronunciation, which he
called 'Public School Pronunciation', a term he later abandoned for
'Received Pronunciation' (RP) in 1926. RP was regarded "as a kind of
standard, having its base in the educated pronunciation of London and the
Home Counties. Its use was not restricted to this region, however, being
characteristic by the 19th century of upper class speech throughout the
country. Thus, though its base was a regional one, its occurrence was
socially determined" (Gimson-Jones 1977, p.x). The current edition of
Jones' dictionary is a record of the pronunciation of approximately
60,000 entries, all in IPA script. In addition to being the most complete record of RP pronunciations for a 60 year period (from 1917-1977),
there are occasional comments about variants for specific words (e.g.
greasy as [grisι] and [grizι]); shifts of stress when contrastive forms
exist: cròwn prínce vs. crówn prìnce; regional variants (mægǝ'zi:n
normally, but['mæg--] as the usual form in the North of England, uncommon
in the South); local, when different from RP, pronunciations, as Polzeath
as [pɒl'zeθ (- zi:θ)], but with the note: "the local pronunciation is
[pɒl'zɛ:θ]"; occasional stylistic forms like 'obsolete' or 'old
fashioned', such as Pontefract [pᴅntιfrækt] with the note "An old local
pronunciation ['pʌmfrιt] is now obsolete. The pronunciation survives in
pomfret cake [pʌmfrιtkeik,'pᴅm--]"). Jones' dictionary remains the reference source for RP speakers, British speakers of dialects other than
RP, and speakers of other languages who wanted to consult an authoritative record of RP pronunciation.

    Two other British phonetic dictionaries have been published, both
written to assist speakers of other languages to learn 'standard'
British-English pronunciations. Both include American pronunciation-
variants. The first was A DICTIONARY OF ENGLISH PRONUNCIATION WITH
AMERICAN VARIANTS (Palmer at al. 1926). Palmer's dictionary was written
to train Japanese students in English. His book was an attempt to replace S. Ichikawa's AN ENGLISH PRONOUNCING DICTIONARY FOR JAPANESE STU-
DENTS (Tokyo 1923) with a more thorough and complete source. Its use was
mainly in Japan and it was never revised nor reissued. The second is a
smaller pronouncing dictionary (approximately 24,000 words) which appeared in 1972, authored by J. Windsor Lewis. THE CONCISE PRONOUNCING
DICTIONARY OF BRITISH AND AMERICAN ENGLISH (CPDBAE), begun in 1964, was
"planned solely for the benefit of users of English as a foreign or
second language" (Preface, p.vi). Like the EPD, the CPDBAE indicates all
pronounced entries in IPA, rather than in the diacritic respelling system
commonly found in American dictionaries, stressed forms are marked, and
variant pronunciations appear.

    Thomas Pyles, in reviewing the Lewis volume in American Speech, noted
that "CPDBAE is an altogether reliable treatment of the most up-to-date
type of British pronunciation.... It is considerably less satisfactory

for American pronunciation." The CPDBAE overlooks recent scholarship
about American English regional and social variants. Lewis "excludes all
American pronunciations with any specific association with ... regions of
the USA giving only those which are most general in the USA and Canada.
This kind of pronunciation is often referred to, with a looseness
convenient to our purposes, as 'General American' pronunciation (GA)"
(Preface, p.xiv).   American phoneticians no longer use the term GA, a
blanket term encompassing pronunciations and other language forms that
are neither Eastern nor Southern. Since the early publication of the
Linguistic Atlas project (the first was H. Kurath's Word Geography of the
Eastern United States in 1949) numerous terms other than 'General
American' are found in the literature. The indication of pronunciation in
the North American continent presents the lexicographer with a difficult
task since no single prestigious standard dialect exists throughout the
country. Despite the large number of local and regional forms, the
differences among most educated speakers are relatively minor, and communicative interferences are not a factor of concern. No one dialect in
the US and Canada is considered more 'desirable' or more prestigious than
another. The differences between them do not easily permit a single
label to cover all of them.

The only major pronouncing dictionary of this century to appear in the
United States was the J.S. Kenyon and T.A. Knott PRONOUNCING DICTIONARY
OF AMERICAN ENGLISH (PDAE 1944). It is "a phonetic pronouncing dictionary of the speech of the United States that might serve, both in the U.S.
and elsewhere, the purposes served for Southern British English by Professor Daniel Jones' ENGLISH PRONOUNCING DICTIONARY" (Preface, p.v).
PDAE was published after six years of data-compiling, authored, as the
book jacket states, by "two of America's best-known dictionary-making
authorities", associated as consulting and general editor, respectively,
of Merriam-Webster's famous unabridged Second Edition of WEBSTER'S NEW
INTERNATIONAL DICTIONARY, 1934.

John Kenyon was the preeminent phonetics scholar in the United States.
His American Pronunciation, first issued in 1924, was reprinted and
revised through 10 editions (the 10th appeared in 1950). It was the
first thorough description of American pronunciation, based on the available scholarship of the time. His "Guide to Pronunciation", in the front
matter of the Merriam-Webster's NEW INTERNATIONAL DICTIONARY, 2nd edition, unabridged, 1934, was the most detailed description of pronunciation to appear in any dictionary up to that time.

The authors of the PDAE noted that their purpose was "to record without prejudice or preference several different types of speech used by
large bodies of educated and cultivated Americans in widely separated
areas and with markedly different backgrounds of tradition and culture"
(Preface, p.v). Kenyon and Knott's volume differed in some obvious ways
from their model, Jones' EPD. Their purpose was to record only colloquial English pronunciation "of the everyday unconscious speech of cultivated people" rather than the "formal platform speech" recorded in
WEBSTER's Second Edition. The PDAE does indicate some modified pronunciations resulting from the influence of surrounding words as well as

phonetic variants resulting from shifts in "rhythm, tempo, intonation,
sense stress, etc" (p. vi).

The PDAE made a strong attempt to include the results of the early
investigations of the Linguistic Atlas project, which placed large
amounts of unpublished materials at the editors' disposal. Ninety scholars throughout the US and Canada provided phonetic transcriptions of
their own speech, sixteen other linguists detailed their impressions of
the phonetic forms in other languages for place and proper names, and
eleven phoneticians and linguists provided collected materials on the
speech of their areas and recordings of sample readings and/or conversa-
tions. It remains, 40+ years since its publication, the most useful
compilation of the pronunciation of 'standard colloquial English' in the
United States and Canada.

Three other 'pronouncing dictionaries' should be mentioned. One is
WORLD WORDS edited by the late Professor W. Cabell Greet of Barnard
College and Columbia University and managing editor of American Speech
from 1933-52 (cf. Bronstein et al. 1977, pp.72-73). First issued as WAR
WORDS in 1944 and then revised and enlarged, WORLD WORDS contained the
"recommended pronunciations" for approximately 12,000 names and words.
This volume was the source for broadcasters at CBS (one of the two larger
broadcasting networks in the U.S. at the time) who couldn't easily locate
pronunciations for so many new proper and place names suddenly appearing
in the news. Greet followed a diacritic-respelling system (rather than
the IPA system) for all entries.

Greet consulted more than a hundred consular agents, foreign language
professors and foreign correspondents for assistance. A glance through
the volume reminds the reader that CBS announcers of the 1940's could
learn the spelled and the 'expected' pronunciation forms of 'old-
fashioned' aeroplane for which both the spelling and pronunciation were
replaced by airplane -- to Aegina in both its English [ɪˈdʒɑɪnə] and its
Greek [ˈɑɪjinɑ] forms.

The other major American network of the time had retained James F.
Bender, formerly chairman of the Department of Speech in Queens College
in New York City, to compile an NBC HANDBOOK OF PRONUNCIATION which
appeared in 1943. Bender used both diacritic respelling and the IPA to
record the pronunciations of more than 20,000 entries (e.g. abandon: uh
BAN duhn, əbændən). The NBC HANDBOOK included geographical and biographical names, as well as words 'commonly mispronounced' (e.g. economics,
either). Its third edition was a revision by Thomas L. Crowell, Jr. in
1964, and it has since been revised and updated in a 4th edition by
Eugene Ehrlich and Raymond Hand, Jr.

The revised NBC HANDBOOK makes no real attempt to discuss foreign
language vowels or consonants, and as such doesn't help the announcer too
much with the 'handling' of foreign place and proper names. Variants do
not appear in this volume: advertisement, abdomen, Caribbean, economics,
kilometer, Kishinev, Los Angeles, Missouri, and oratory are entered with
a single pronunciation. This decision is defended with "...the present

editors supply a single pronunciation for each entry rather than a be-
wildering variety of acceptable pronunciations. This reflects the belief
rather than justification for a particular pronunciation"! (p. 8).

Both of these volumes were attempts to emulate Broadcast English, a
collection of seven pamphlets written by Professor A. Lloyd James of
University College, London for, and published by, the BBC (they appeared
between 1932 and 1939) and the Handbook for Announcers, issued by the
Canadian Broadcasting Corporation in 1942 as a reference guide to the
large number of names suddenly appearing in the World War communiqués.

The third is the BBC PRONOUNCING DICTIONARY OF BRITISH NAMES (Oxford,
1983), G.E. Pointon, editor. This dictionary was first issued in 1971 by
the BBC's Pronunciation Unit. All entries are respelled in the IPA and a
'modified conventional spelling' system (e.g. "Berkyngechirche, A.-S.
(Anglo-Saxon) name for Barking-by-the-Tower, London, 'bɑrkɪŋtʃɜrtʃ,
baarkingtchurtch", "Bernhard, C.n. (Christian name) bɜrnərd, bernard",
"Du Vivier, f.n. (foreign name) ˌduˈvɪvɪeɪ, doovivvi-ay"). This volume
contains approximately 20,000 entries, predominantly British place and
proper names. Five non-English vowels, called 'Exotic Vowels' are
listed, "more or less as in French", and only two non-English consonants
appear: /x/ as in Scottish loch and /ɬ/ as in Welsh llan.

The major English language dictionaries published on both sides of the
Atlantic have been strongly influenced by the pronouncing dictionaries
that exist in both countries. Thus, a check of some British general dictionaries (e.g. THE SHORTER OXFORD ENGLISH DICTIONARY (1973), CHAMBERS
20TH CENTURY DICTIONARY (1983), LONGMAN DICTIONARY OF CONTEMPORARY ENG-
LISH (1978), and COLLINS DICTIONARY OF THE ENGLISH LANGUAGE (1979))
indicates that the front matter contains not only carefully identified
pronunciation keys, including a few symbols for foreign-language sounds,
but separate sections or essays on British pronunciation. Two of these
dictionaries (COLLINS and LONGMAN) use IPA symbols for pronunciation
respelling, while the CHAMBERS uses a diacritic respelling system and the
OXFORD a variation of the IPA. And one (LONGMAN) includes American
pronunciation variants as well as a brief comment on pronunciation differences between British and American English forms.

The major American and Canadian English general dictionaries include
similar guides. THE AMERICAN HERITAGE DICTIONARY (1969) and the RANDOM
HOUSE DICTIONARY OF THE ENGLISH LANGUAGE (1973) include separately
authored essays on pronunciation, usage, and dialects; WEBSTER'S NINTH
NEW COLLEGIATE DICTIONARY (1983), the most recent abridgement based on
WEBSTER'S THIRD NEW INTERNATIONAL DICTIONARY (1961), includes a six-page
essay on pronunciation and a section on spelling and sound
correspondences; THE WORLD BOOK DICTIONARY (1979) discusses certain
phonological rules, and has small sections on American English dialects
and usage; and WEBSTER'S NEW WORLD DICTIONARY (1976) contains a section
on pronunciation, usage, and levels. THE DICTIONARY OF CANADIAN ENGLISH:
THE SENIOR DICTIONARY (1967,1973), based on the THORNDIKE-BARNHART HIGH
SCHOOL DICTIONARY (1965) contains a four-page introductory essay by
Walter S. Avis, one page of which discusses Canadian pronunciation (as

distinct from American or British) with numerous references to specific
'widely-heard' educated Canadian forms not commonly recorded in other
dictionaries, e.g. khaki as (kär'kē), armada as (är mad'ə), longitude as
(long'gə tüd), Trafalgar as (trə fol'gər). A major revision of the above
dictionary appeared in 1983 as the GAGE CANADIAN DICTIONARY. Both contain additional introductory guidelines that treat syllabification,
stress indications,variant pronunciations and advice on the pronunciation
of foreign words. Special attention should be called to EVERYMAN'S
FRENCH-ENGLISH AND ENGLISH-FRENCH DICTIONARY, WITH SPECIAL REFERENCE TO
CANADA (1962), edited by Jean-Paul Vinay and others. That dictionary
contained Canadian English and French respellings (phonetic transcriptions in IPA) as well as a special introductory section on "Ontario
English" with both western and eastern (Canadian) variants. Sheridan's
and Walker's influence, stressing pronunciation as a key feature of a
general dictionary, is obvious. And the influence of phonetic scholarship that made the phonetic-pronouncing dictionaries of the 20th century
possible pervades all the British and American English general
dictionaries.

The first of five volumes of the long awaited DICTIONARY OF AMERICAN
REGIONAL ENGLISH edited by F.G. Cassidy (The Belknap Press, Cambridge,
Mass, 1985) is now on our shelves. DARE, scheduled for completion in the
early 1990's, is neither a general nor a pronouncing dictionary of American English (AE), but it does contain very useful information about AE
pronunciation(s). J.W. Hartman authored an extensive, elucidating essay
on pronunciation in the front matter, including a review of major AE
regional variants. DARE does not include pronunciations for words with
little or no pronunciation variation (e.g. slap), nor for entries with
expected variations (e.g. words with postvocalic /r/), nor for entries
for which the DARE data base does not contain the pronounced forms (e.g.
caballero). The reader will not find pronounced forms for words like
batter, chime, chocolate, cot; nor does DARE enter such words as abdomen,
adult, angina, clangor, coupon, all of which have common alternative
pronunciations in standard AE, but for which no common variant regional
pronunciations exist. But for words like avenue, average, about, bron-
chial, Carolina, carry, and others, the reader will find pronunciation
entries that include vowel, diphthong, and consonant variants, stress
shifts, and regional variants, plus discussions that identify such items
as spelling pronunciations, rare pronunciations, those used by older
speakers, or those with little formal education, as pertinent.

DARE is the first AE dictionary to contain considerable information
on pronunciation variants (other than the PDAE, of course). It does,
and will, provide other lexicographers with needed and useful information
about regional pronunciations of many AE words.

If Great Britain can boast of a reasonably current record of British
(RP) pronunciation usage, as it appears in the Jones-Gimson dictionaries,
the US and Canada are not as fortunate. The PDAE remains the only
significantly comprehensive pronunciation lexicon for American English,
despite the fact that linguistic/phonetic research over the past 40 years
has rendered it considerably out of date. The numerous publications

associated with the vast Linguistic Atlas project (such as those by
Kurath, McDavid, Allen, Shopen, Williams, Wolfram, Pederson among others)
plus the identification of socially-defined pronunciation variants since
the 1960's (cf.,e.g.,such studies by Labov, Bailey, Shuy, Stewart among
many others), and the recent data from DARE were not available to the
PDAE, which reflected the 'classical' phonetic approaches developed by
the structural linguists of the 1930's and 1940's, later known as 'taxonomic' or 'autonomous phonemics'. That theoretical approach was followed
by versions of phonological analysis as first detailed by Jakobson, Fant,
and Halle (1952) and later by Halle (1964), and Chomsky and Halle (1968).
This 'systematic phonemics' approach uses distinctive feature theory to
establish oppositions that occur between and within the segments of a
language. Herein a set of phonological rules is applied to account for
the alternations. The structuralist needed to point to the phonemic
contrast between the final nasals of Sim, sin, and sing to establish
meaningful differences. The generative phonologist recognized that feature analysis, based not only on place and manner of articulation and
production, but also on acoustic-perceptual features provided him with
essential information. Thus the circumstance that pin and pen are always
heard as [pɪn] in a Southern dialect of American English (while pit and
pet always vary) was explainable by a phonological rule (the feature of +
nasality). Similarly the medial consonant in slighting and sliding,
heard as the same voiced flapped sound, in the speech of many if not
most American English speakers, was not easily explained by taxonomic
phonetics. The presence of the longer nucleus in slide, but not in
slight, doesn't explain what happens to the participles, for vowel length
is not a contrastive feature in English (cf. Wolfram and Johnson 1982,
pp. 102-124). The inventory of features is, to a large extent, the
result of acoustic-phonetic research plus research on the physiology and
perception of speech so dependent on recent development of sophisticated instrumentation, little of which was available to earlier
structural linguists.

A substantial lexicographical gap needs to be filled by an updated
pronouncing dictionary of American and Canadian English. The 40 years of
phonetic and linguistic research since the appearance of PDAE provide
much source material. Such a volume is needed on all our shelves.

References

Cited dictionaries (see Appendix):

(THE) AMERICAN DICTIONARY OF THE ENGLISH LANGUAGE (Webster)
(THE) AMERICAN HERITAGE DICTIONARY (Morris/Berube)
(THE) AMERICAN PHONETIC DICTIONARY OF THE ENGLISH LANGUAGE (Smalley)
(THE) AMERICAN STANDARD OF ORTHOGRAPHY AND PRONUNCIATION AND IM-
     PROVED DICTIONARY OF THE ENGLISH LANGUAGE (Allison)
BBC PRONOUNCING DICTIONARY OF BRITISH NAMES ... (Pointon)
BIOGRAPHICAL DICTIONARY OF THE PHONETIC SCIENCES (Bronstein et al.)
CHAMBERS TWENTIETH CENTURY DICTIONARY (Davidson/Kirkpatrick)
COLLINS DICTIONARY OF THE ENGLISH LANGUAGE (Hanks et al.)
COMPENDIOUS DICTIONARY OF THE ENGLISH LANGUAGE (Webster)
(A) COMPLETE DICTIONARY OF THE ENGLISH LANGUAGE ... (Sheridan)

COMPREHENSIVE PRONOUNCING AND EXPLANATORY DICTIONARY OF THE ENGLISH
    LANGUAGE ... (Worcester)
(THE) CONCISE PRONOUNCING DICTIONARY OF BRITISH AND AMERICAN ENGLISH
    (Windsor Lewis)
CRITICAL PRONOUNCING DICTIONARY AND EXPOSITOR OF THE ENGLISH
    LANGUAGE (Walker)
DICTIONARIUM ANGLO-BRITANNICUM ... (Kersey)
DICTIONARY OF AMERICAN REGIONAL ENGLISH (Cassidy)
(A) DICTIONARY OF ENGLISH PRONUNCIATION WITH AMERICAN VARIANTS
    (Palmer et al.)
(A) DICTIONARY OF THE ENGLISH LANGUAGE (Johnson)
(THE) DICTIONARY OF CANADIAN ENGLISH ... (Barnhart/Avis et al.)
ENGLISH PRONOUNCING DICTIONARY see EVERYMAN'S ENGLISH PRONOUNCING
    DICTIONARY
(AN) ENGLISH PRONOUNCING DICTIONARY FOR JAPANESE STUDENTS (Ichikawa)
EVERYMAN'S ENGLISH PRONOUNCING DICTIONARY (Jones/Gimson)
EVERYMAN'S FRENCH-ENGLISH AND ENGLISH-FRENCH DICTIONARY ... (Vinay
    et al.)
(THE) GAGE CANADIAN DICTIONARY (Barnhart/Avis)
LONGMAN DICTIONARY OF CONTEMPORARY ENGLISH (Procter et al.)
NBC HANDBOOK OF PRONUNCIATION (Bender)
(A) NEW CRITICAL PRONOUNCING DICTIONARY OF THE ENGLISH LANGUAGE ...
    (Coxe)
(A) NEW GENERAL ENGLISH DICTIONARY ... (Dyche/Pardon)
(A) PHONETIC DICTIONARY OF THE ENGLISH LANGUAGE (Jones/Michaelis)
(A) PHONOGRAPHIC PRONOUNCING DICTIONARY OF THE ENGLISH LANGUAGE
    (Bolles)
(A) PRONOUNCING DICTIONARY OF AMERICAN ENGLISH (Kenyon/Knott)
RANDOM HOUSE DICTIONARY OF THE ENGLISH LANGUAGE (Urdang/Stein)
(THE) SHORTER OXFORD ENGLISH DICTIONARY (Little/Onions)
A TABLE ALPHABETICALL ... (Cawdrey)
THORNDIKE-BARNHART HIGH SCHOOL DICTIONARY (Thorndike/Barnhart)
UNIVERAL AND CRITICAL DICTIONARY OF THE ENGLISH LANGUAGE ...
    (Worcester)
(AN) UNIVERSAL ETYMOLOGICAL ENGLISH DICTIONARY ... (Bailey)
WAR WORDS see WORLD WORDS
WEBSTER'S NEW WORLD DICTIONARY ... (Guralnik)
WEBSTER'S NINTH NEW COLLEGIATE DICTIONARY (Mish)
WEBSTER'S (SECOND) NEW INTERNATIONAL DICTIONARY (Neilson)
WEBSTER'S THIRD NEW INTERNATIONAL DICTIONARY ... (Gove)
(THE) WORLD BOOK DICTIONARY (Barnhart)
WORLD WORDS (Greet)

Other literature:

Allen, Harold B. (1973-76) The Linguistic Atlas of the Upper
    Midwest, Volumes 1-3. Minneapolis: U. of Minnesota P.
Bailey, Charles-James N. and Shuy, Roger W. eds. (1973) New Ways of
    Analyzing Variation in English. Washington DC: Georgetown U.P.
Chomsky, Noam and Halle, Morris (1968) The Sound Pattern of English.
    New York: Harper & Row

Congleton, James E. (1979) "Pronunciation in Johnson's Dictionary"
    in Papers on Lexicography in Honor of W.N. Cordell ed. by James
    E. Congleton et al. for DSNA. Terre Haute: Indiana State U.
    59-81
Halle, Morris (1964) "On the basis of phonology" in The Structure of
    Language ed. by Jerry A. Fodor and Jerry J. Katz. Englewood
    Cliffs NJ: Prentice-Hall 324-333
Jakobson, Roman et al. (1952) Preliminaries to Speech Analysis. Cam-
    bridge MA: M.I.T. Press
Jones, Daniel (1909/17) The Pronunciation of English. Cambridge:
    U.P.
Kenyon, John S. (1924) American Pronunciation. Ann Arbor MI: George
    Wahr Publishing
Kurath, Hans (1949) A Word Geography of the Eastern United States.
    Ann Arbor: U. of Michigan P.
Kurath, Hans and McDavid, Raven I. Jr. (1961) The Pronunciation of
    English in the Atlantic States. Ann Arbor: U. of Michigan P.
Labov, William (1966) The Social Stratification of English in New
    York City. Washington DC: C.A.L.
Lounsbury, Thomas R. (1904) The Standard of Pronunciation in
    English. New York & London: Harper
McDavid, Raven I. Jr. (1980) "The social role of the dictionary" in
    Varieties of English. Essays by Raven I. McDavid Jr. (ed. by
    Anwar S. Dil). Stanford CA: Stanford U.P. 296-309
Pederson, Lee (1977) "Studies of American pronunciation since 1945"
    American Speech 52: 163-261
Shopen, Tim and Williams, Joseph. M. (1980) Standards and Dialects
    in English. Cambridge MA: Winthrop
Starnes, DeWitt T. and Noyes, Gertrude E. (1946) The English Dic-
    tionary from Cawdrey to Johnson, 1604-1755. Chapel Hill: U. of
    North Carolina P.
Stewart, William A. (1965) "Urban Negro speech" in Social Dialects
    and Language Learning ed. by Roger W. Shuy. Urbana IL: N.C.T.E.
    10-18
Wolfram, Walter and Christian, Donna (1976) Appalachian Speech.
    Washington DC: C.A.L.
Wolfram, Walter and Johnson, Robert E. (1982) Phonological Analysis:
    Focus on American English. Washington DC: C.A.L.

A BRIEF HISTORY OF CHINESE BILINGUAL LEXICOGRAPHY

David Chien & Thomas Creamer

Introduction

The history of Chinese bilingual lexicography reflects two
recurring themes in Chinese history. The first is the interaction
between Han Chinese (native speakers of Chinese) and their non-Han
neighboring peoples and the Chinese minority nationalities. The second
theme is foreign, especially missionary, interest in China. Buddhist
missionaries took up residence in China during the second century A.D.,
while Christian missionaries arrived in force during the sixteenth
century. On the one hand, the early missionaries in their zeal to
translate their scriptures into Chinese and spread their beliefs
realized the importance of bilingualism. On the other hand, Chinese
officials and scholars, in the course of executing diplomatic relations
and in their interest in foreign sciences, also began to encourage
foreign language acquisition. As a result, numerous bilingual
dictionaries were produced by foreign and native Chinese scholars. The
purpose of this paper is to briefly describe the history of Chinese
bilingual lexicography from earliest times to the nineteenth century,
and to highlight the influence of bilingual lexicography on Chinese
monolingual lexicography.

Buddhism and Bilingual Lexicography

Buddhism was introduced to China during the Western Han Dynasty
(25-220). Buddhist missionaries, aside from the problems of introducing
an alien religion to China, were faced with the difficulty of
translating their scriptures into Chinese. Early translations were
crude as the monks struggled to render Buddhist concepts from Sanskrit
and Pali into Chinese. By fits and starts, translations gradually
improved as translation bureaus were established, reference works
developed and translators trained. A significant breakthrough in the
quality of translations occurred during the Tang Dynasty (616-907) after
Chinese Buddhist monks such as Xuan Zhuang (玄 奘 , 602-664) and Yi
Jing (义净 , 635-713) made pilgrimages to India to study Buddhism and
the Buddhist languages. Yi Jing compiled what might be the first
reliable Sanskrit-Chinese glossary, entitled SANSKRIT ONE-THOUSAND
CHARACTER TEXT (梵语千字文, FAN YU QIAN ZI WEN) (Watters 1889).

In addition to glossaries, Buddhist monks began compiling
dictionaries. One of the earliest dictionaries is THE SOUND AND MEANING

OF THE TRIPITAKA (一切经音义 , YI QIE JING YIN YI), a twenty-five
chapter (卷 , juan) work compiled by Xuan Ying (玄应). Little is
known about Xuan Ying. He is said to have been a contemporary of Xuan
Zhuang, and like Xuan Zhuang, was a monk at the Da Ci En Monastery
(大慈恩寺) in Chang'an, the capital during the Tang Dynasty.
Under the patronage of Empress Zhen Guan (贞观 , r. 627- 649), Xuan
began the work of compiling his dictionary by collecting 454 Mahayana
and Hinayana sutras and arranging them in a series starting with the
Avatamsaka sutra (华严经 , Hua Yan Jing) and ending with the
Abhidharma Naya Anusara sutra (顺正理论, Shun Zheng Li Lun). His
purpose in compiling the dictionary was to define difficult words, both
Sanskrit and Chinese, that appeared in the Chinese translations of the
sutras. At the beginning of each chapter of the dictionary is a listing
of the sutras from which the headwords are selected. The headwords are
then arranged and numbered according to the chapter of the sutra in
which they appear. The basic structure of each definition is first to
give any variant renderings of the headword, then the definition, the
pronunciation of difficult characters in the headword combination and an
explanation of any unusual character that appears in the definition.

    The dictionary is not bilingual in the sense that it contains
Sanskrit or other Buddhist-language scripts for its headwords. All
headwords are given in Chinese characters that transliterate the foreign
Buddhist words. However, the dictionary can be considered an early
attempt at bilingual lexicography in the sense that it collects, for the
most part, non-Chinese words and defines them in Chinese. By translit-
erating the foreign words with Chinese characters, the dictionary is a
valuable reference tool for monks in their reading of the scriptures,
and, just as important, for those learning the sound of the Buddhist
words. The dictionary is not without its problems, though. Because it
is arranged according to the sutras, look-up is difficult. Also, there
are numerous cryptic or incomplete definitions and repetitions. In any
case, THE SOUND AND MEANING OF THE TRIPITAKA is the first Buddhist
dictionary of its kind and the first, albeit crude, attempt at bilingual
lexicography.

    Buddhism has had a profound and lasting impact on Chinese culture
and the Chinese language. In addition to the myriad of terms adopted
into the language from Buddhism, Buddhist monks, with their knowledge of
Sanskrit grammar and phonology, may be considered among the first to
scientifically study Chinese. They introduced the idea of consonants
and vowels, a thirty-six character (字母 , zimu) scheme of initial
consonants and popularized the fanqie (反切) system of indicating
the pronunciation of a Chinese character. In the fanqie system, the
pronunciation of a character is demonstrated by selecting two familiar
characters, demonstrated by selecting two familiar characters, the first
representing the initial consonant of the character in question and the
second representing its vowel and tone. For centuries, the fanqie

system has been popular with Chinese lexicographers. One of the
earliest dictionaries to use the system is the JADE CHAPTERS (玉 篇 ,
YU PIAN), compiled by Gu Yewang (顾野王) of the Southern Dynas-
ties/Liang period (502-557). Other dictionaries that have employed the
fanqie system are the KANGXI DICTIONARY (康熙字典, KANG XI ZI
DIAN), compiled in 1716 and the revised edition of CIYUAN (辞源)
published by the Commercial Press, Beijing in 1979.

Chinese-Minority Language Lexicography

China is a multinational country. The main nationality is Han
(汉) Chinese, but there are more than fifty minority nationalities
comprising more than forty million people dwelling mostly in the
Northwest and Southwest. Linguistically, the minorities span the
Sino-Tibetan, Altaic, Austro-Asiatic and Indo-European language
families. Relations between the Han Chinese and the minorities have
generally been friendly, although at times the intercourse has been
marred by invasions and wars. In fact, the Khitan, Mongol and Manchu
national minorities, established three of China's major dynasties,
namely, the Liao (916-1125), the Yuan (1271-1368) and the Qing
(1644-1911). In the dealings among the nationalities, the need for
bilingual translators and reference works has been keenly felt.

Tangut (西夏 , Xi Xia) dictionaries occupy a prominent position
in the history of Chinese bilingual lexicography because of their
variety and their rather sophisticated levels of compilation. The first
Tangut dictionary and one of the earliest minority language (hereafter
ML) bilingual dictionaries was compiled by Yuan Hao (元昊), the first
emperor of the Western Xia (Tangut) Kingdom (1038-1227). Yuan was a
member of the Dangxiang (党项) nationality, an ethnic group long
since assimilated into other minorities. In the early 1030's he created
the Tangut language of approximately 6,000 characters based on the form
of Chinese characters. The language was officially adopted in 1036 and
continued in use as late as the Ming Dynasty (1368-1644). As part of
the effort to standardize the language, Yuan, in cooperation with Yeli
Renrong (野利仁荣) compiled FOREIGN ER YA (番尔雅, FAN ER YA),
a Tangut-Chinese dictionary in twelve chapters. The dictionary is
modeled after ER YA (尔雅), an important lexicon compiled sometime
before the second century B.C. Unfortunately, FOREIGN ER YA is no
longer extant.

FAN HAN HE SHI ZHANG ZHONG ZHU (番汉合时掌中珠, literally
"FOREIGN-CHINESE (GLOSSARY) AS TIMELY AS A PEARL IN THE PALM") is
another Tangut-Chinese dictionary produced during the Western Xia
period. Gule Maocai (骨勒茂才), a Dangxiang ethnic, completed
the dictionary in 1190. Originally, it was printed on thirty-seven

numbered sheets in the traditional Chinese method called "butterfly"
(蝴蝶蝶 , hu die) binding. In the preface, Gule describes the glossary
as an attempt to foster better relations between the two peoples through
the understanding of each other's language. The glossary lists 824
entries and is divided into three major sections concerning Heaven,
earth and man. The main sections are further divided into three
subsections. Each entry contains the Tangut headword, the Chinese
equivalent, the transcription of the Tangut headword in Chinese
characters, and the transcription of the Chinese equivalent in Tangut.
Because of its dual phonetic notations, the dictionary is a valuable
tool for scholars engaged in reconstructing the ancient Tangut language
(Nevsky 1928 and Shi 1980).

A number of other bilingual dictionaries were produced between the
eleventh and early fourteenth centuries. Some of the more noteworthy
include TRANSLATION OF THE TIBETAN LANGUAGE (西 番 译 语 , XI FAN
YI YU), a Tibetan-Chinese glossary. It is divided into twenty sections
and contains between 200 and 300 entries. Each entry is divided into
three parts. First is the Tibetan headword, then the Chinese equivalent
and the Tibetan pronunciation transliterated in Chinese characters.
Other important works include HEN GROVE ANALOGIES (鸡林类事 , JI LIN
LEI SHI), a Korean-Chinese glossary by Sun Mu (孙穆) of the Song
Dynasty (960-1279); EXPLANATIONS OF THE LIAO LANGUAGE (辽国语解 ,
LIAO GUO YU JIE), a Liao-Chinese glossary compiled by Tuoketuo (托克托),
a Mongol ethnic of the Yuan Dynasty; and EXPLANATIONS OF THE MONGOLIAN
LANGUAGE (蒙 古 译 语 , MENG GU YI YU), a classified
Mongolian-Chinese glossary also from the Yuan.

A CHINESE-FOREIGN GLOSSARY (华 夷 译 语 , HUA YI YI YU) is one of
the few bilingual dictionaries produced during the Ming Dynasty. The
glossary was compiled in 1382 by Huoyuanjie (火 原 洁   ) and
Mayichihei (马懿赤黑) , both Mongol ethnics and members of the
Imperial Academy (翰林院, Han Lin Yuan). The work was commissioned
by the first Ming emperor, Hong Wu (洪 武 , r. 1368-1398) and was
intended to bridge the communication gap between Mongol and Han Chinese
officials. Based on the Secret History of the Mongols (元朝秘史 ,
Yuan Chao Mi Shi), the glossary is in nine chapters, is topically
arranged and covers a variety of subjects ranging from astronomy to
geography to food. Under each Mongolian headword is the Chinese
equivalent followed by the fanqie transcription. The glossary contains
a number of errors, however (Ma 1983). Later, a two chapter work
entitled A REVISED CHINESE-FOREIGN GLOSSARY (增 订 华 夷 译 语 ,
ZENG DING HUA YI YI YU) appeared that corrected many of the mistakes in
the original edition.

Chinese-ML and ML-Chinese dictionaries compiled during the Qing
Dynasty account for a large portion of the early bilingual works.

During the early and middle Qing period, the Manchu language was
particularly influential because the ruling class were Manchus. As a
result, approximately 100 Manchu dictionaries appeared, of which a
majority were bilingual (Ji 1982). Many of the Manchu works are
impressive not only for their quality, but also for their size. For
example, there is A COMPREHENSIVE COLLECTION OF THE MANCHU LANGUAGE
(清 文 总 汇 , QING WEN ZONG HUI), a Manchu-Chinese dictionary by
Zhikuan (志 宽) and Zhipei (志 培). This twelve-volume
dictionary was completed in 1897 and contains more than 20,000 entries.
Even today the dictionary is still deemed an indispensable reference
work by scholars of Manchu studies because of its large collection of
lexical items. Another example is THE ENLARGED IMPERIAL MANCHU
LANGUAGE SURVEY (御制增订清文鉴, YU ZHI ZENG DING QING WEN JIAN), a
Manchu-Chinese classified encyclopedic dictionary compiled under the
editorship of Fu Heng (傅恒). Printed in 1771, the dictionary is in
forty-one main volumes and five supplementary volumes and contains more
than 18,000 headwords, including about 1,600 ancient or rare entries.
Significantly, each entry is defined in both Manchu and Chinese. The
uniqueness of the dictionary is that the pronunciation of Manchu
explanatory words is transcribed in _fanqie_, while the Chinese
explanatory part is rendered in Manchu phonetic symbols. This feature
greatly facilitates the use of the dictionary by speakers of either
language.

     No survey of Manchu-Chinese dictionaries is complete without mention
of A COMPREHENSIVE DICTIONARY OF THE GREAT QING DYNASTY (大 清 全 书 ,
DA QING QUAN SHU). The dictionary was written by Shen Qiliang (沈启亮),
a Han Chinese, and encompasses twelve volumes and includes 12,000
entries.   The dictionary is divided into twelve parts, based on the
twelve head-character system, a specially designed system of symbols and
syllables for Han Chinese to learn Manchu. Shen states in the preface
that he intends his dictionary to be exhaustive and to act as a "ladder"
for those learning Manchu. He goes to great lengths in describing the
importance to Han Chinese in studying Manchu and how a knowledge of both
Manchu and Chinese promotes understanding between the two cultures. A
typical entry in the dictionary lists the Manchu headword followed by
variants or example sentences. Definitions are given in Chinese as
either equivalents or explanations. A few Manchu words are simply
transliterated into Chinese.

Chinese Government and Bilingual Lexicography

     Although there had been officially appointed interpreters since as
early as the Zhou Dynasty (11th century B.C. - 221 B.C.), the Chinese
government did not become active in translation and lexicography until
the Ming Dynasty with the establishment of the Bureau of Translators
(四 夷 (译) 馆 , Si Yi (Yi) Guan). The bureau was founded in 1407 to

deal with foreign tribute-bearing nations. One reason for the
establishment of the bureau was that the Chinese government felt it lost
face if a memorial was sent by a foreign government and no one could be
found to translate it into Chinese (Wild 1945). The bureau was divided
into eight departments concerned with Tartar, Mongolian, Tibetan, the
languages of India, Moslem, Shan, Uygur and Burmese. Other bureaus such
as Thai were added later. During the Qing Dynasty the Bureau of
Translators was combined with the Hui Tong Academy (会 同 馆 , Hui Tong
Guan). The new academy produced a number of manuscript dictionaries,
but most were taken out of China and lost (Li 1982).

   Beginning with the Treaty of Nanjing (Nanking) in 1842 that ended
the Opium War between China and England, China was forcibly "opened" to
the West by a series of treaties that have come to be know as the
"unequal treaty system." These treaties represented the first time in
Chinese history that a foreign country was allowed legally recognized,
permanent settlements in China. The opening of China not only led to an
influx of Western diplomats, merchants and missionaries, but also to the
introduction of Western science. The Chinese government sought to learn
from Western advances, while maintaining China's integrity. Many
officials were skeptical, and rightly so, of the aggressive Westerners,
but realized the importance of learning the Western languages.

   In response to the upsurge in Western scholarship the government
established the Tongwen Academy (同 文 馆 , Tong Wen Guan), sometimes
called the Interpreters College. The main academy was in Beijing, with
branches in Shanghai, Fuzhou and Guangzhou. Besides producing dictionaries and glossaries, the Academy also involved itself in standardizing
Chinese equivalents for foreign words. In 1901, in a related event, an
Editing and Translation Department (编 译 局 , Bian Yi Ju) was created
at the Beijing Academy (京 师 大 学 堂, Jing Shi Da Xue Tong). Chapter
seven of the department's charter entitled "Language Dictionaries" laid
out the ground rules for bilingual dictionaries with a view toward
standardizing terminology. The charter called for the compilation of
English-Chinese, French-Chinese, Russian-Chinese, German-Chinese and
Japanese-Chinese dictionaries and glossaries (Li 1982). Other
institutions such as the Jiangnan (江 南) Arsenal near Shanghai also
were actively involved in dictionary-making. The arsenal was
established in 1865 as an effort to modernize China's military. With the
help of foreign advisers, the arsenal shortly became one of the most
modern of its time. One way the engineers were able to keep abreast of
the latest Western scientific advances was through translations provided
by the arsenal's translation bureau. The bureau produced numerous
glossaries as well. Some of the early bilingual dictionaries include a
chemistry glossary in 1870, a metallurgy glossary in 1872, a medicine
glossary in 1887, a steam engine glossary in 1890 and a glossary of
weights and measures in 1891 (Li 1982).

The West and Bilingual Lexicography

Like their Buddhist counterparts, early Christian missionaries concentrated on learning Chinese and on developing bilingual reference materials. The two most important missionaries who compiled bilingual dictionaries are Matteo Ricci and Robert Morrison. By the middle of the nineteenth century, as the western diplomatic and commercial presence grew in China, secular scholars had become involved in bilingual lexicography. The most noteworthy non-missionary dictionary-maker is Herbert A. Giles.

Matteo Ricci, an Italian Jesuit missionary, reached China in 1583. His two important linguistic achievements were a romanization scheme for Chinese based on Portuguese and Italian orthography and a system of marking tones which, with some modification, is the same system used today in Chinese dictionaries. Perhaps Ricci's most significant contribution to the development of bilingual lexicography was his DIZIONARIO PORTOGHESE-CINESE compiled with fellow Jesuit Michele Ruggieri. The dictionary is in 189 folios and collects Portugese words arranged in alphabetical order from "aba da vestidura" to "zunir." Ricci's dictionary is the first western language Chinese dictionary (Yang 1960).

Thanks to the efforts of Ricci and his colleagues, Jesuits and Catholic missionaries took the lead in compiling bilingual Chinese dictionaries. The Polish Jesuit Michael Boym (1612-1659) compiled a CHINESE-LATIN DICTIONARY and a CHINESE-FRENCH DICTIONARY, which were printed in 1667 and 1670 respectively in the popular magazine China Illustrata (Szczesniak 1969). These two works, more vocabularies than dictionaries, may be the first of their kind published in Europe. Another important Jesuit was the Frenchman Nicolas Trigault (1577-1628) who compiled AN AUDIO AND VISUAL GUIDE FOR FOREIGN SCHOLARS (西儒耳目 資 , XI RU ER MU ZI), a massive vocabulary to help Chinese learn Latin. Trigualt's work, when combined with Ricci's, set the stage for the introduction of the romanization of Chinese and for modern phonological studies in China (Yang 1960). The Jesuits also developed an alphabetic dictionary and what is generally referred to as the manuscript dictionaries, a series of dictionaries in several Western languages that contain between ten to thirteen thousand Chinese entries. The manuscripts were used by M. deGuignes for his DICTIONNAIRE CHINOIS, FRANÇAIS ET LATIN (Paris, 1813), sometimes called the first dictionary of the Chinese language printed in Europe (Anonymous, 1815), and by Robert Morrison in his DICTIONARY OF THE CHINESE LANGUAGE.

To Robert Morrison (1782-1834) goes the distinction of being not

only the first Protestant missionary to China, but also the author of
the first Chinese-English dictionary. The London Missionary Society
sent Morrison to China in 1807 with three specific goals. He was to
establish residence in China or on an adjacent island, learn Chinese and
translate the Bible into Chinese (which he completed in 1819). In
addition to achieving these goals Morrison, during his more than
twenty-five years in China, also founded the Anglo-Chinese College at
Malacca and was the official translator for the British East India
Company.

     Morrison's most significant lexicographic accomplishment was his
DICTIONARY OF THE CHINESE LANGUAGE published from 1815 to 1822. Morrison
began working on a dictionary soon after he arrived in China. He
brought with him a transcribed copy of a Latin-Chinese dictionary lent
to him by the Royal Society in London and also obtained a copy of the
Jesuit's manuscript dictionaries. In addition, he amassed a library of
almost 10,000 Chinese books that served as sources for the examples he
included in the dictionary. The dictionary itself is based on the
KANGXI DICTIONARY. In all, the dictionary took Morrison sixteen years
to complete and was published in three parts by the East India Company
at a cost of £12,000. Part one is organized Chinese to English and is
arranged according to the 214 Kangxi radicals. Part two is also Chinese
to English but arranged alphabetically according to the Chinese rhyme
dictionary WU JU YUN FU (五车韵府). Part three is organized English
to Chinese and arranged alphabetically. The dictionary was published in
six large quarto volumes, contains 4,595 pages and defines more than
40,000 Chinese expressions.

     In 1828 Morrison published VOCABULARY OF THE CANTON DIALECT , the
first bilingual Chinese dialect dictionary in a Western language.
Following Morrison's lead, missionaries and other foreigners became
active in Chinese dialectology. A few of the early dialect dictionaries
include: William H. Medhurst's A DICTIONARY OF THE HOK-KEEN (FUJIAN)
DIALECT OF THE CHINESE LANGUAGE, 1832; S. Wells William's A TONIC
DICTIONARY OF THE CHINESE LANGUAGE IN THE CANTON DIALECT, 1856; Joseph
Edkins' A VOCABULARY OF THE SHANGHAI DIALECT, 1869; and George Carter
Stent's A CHINESE AND ENGLISH VOCABULARY IN THE PEKINESE DIALECT, 1871.

     The nineteenth century ended on a high note in Chinese bilingual
lexicography with the publication of Herbert A. Giles' A CHINESE-ENGLISH
DICTIONARY. Giles (1845-1935) began his career in China in 1867 as an
interpreter for the British Consular Service, returned to Ningbo as
Consul in 1891 and in 1897 was named Professor of Chinese at Cambridge
University. Perhaps the most respected sinologist of his time, Giles
wrote more than two dozen books on China. His crowning achievement was
his CHINESE-ENGLISH DICTIONARY, first published in 1892 and revised in
1912. The dictionary is still useful today, especially to students of

Imperial China and of Chinese literature and formed the basis for Robert H. Mathews' CHINESE-ENGLISH DICTIONARY (1931, 1943), perhaps the most popular Chinese-English dictionary in use until the 1970s.

Giles' dictionary was published in two volumes in London by Bernard Quaritch and in Shanghai by Kelly and Walsh, Ltd. The dictionary contains 13,848 head characters arranged in alphabetical order by the Wade-Giles romanization system and approximately 80,000 character combinations. Each head character entry includes its standard pronunciation, plus pronunciation in nine Chinese dialects and in Japanese, Vietnamese and Korean. Character combinations are listed under each head character using the head character in either the initial position or elsewhere in the character string.

Besides its overall usefulness, Giles' dictionary is the authoritative source for the Wade-Giles romanization system. The system was first devised by Sir Thomas Wade in his Zi Er Ji (自邇集), a handbook for the Beijing dialect. Until the advent of pinyin, the official romanization of the People's Republic of China adopted in 1958, the Wade-Giles system was the most popular romanization scheme in English-speaking countries for Chinese. The system continues to be used today in dictionaries such as Wen-shun Chi's CHINESE-ENGLISH DICTIONARY OF CONTEMPORARY USAGE (University of California Press, 1977) and by institutions such as the Library of Congress.

Summary

The history of Chinese bilingual lexicography is the history of foreign interest in China and of China's concern for its non-Chinese neighboring peoples and national minorities. With glossaries such as SANSKRIT ONE-THOUSAND CHARACTER TEXT and dictionaries such as THE SOUND AND MEANING OF THE TRIPITAKA, the Buddhists pioneered the practice of bilingual lexicography in China. Later, Chinese-ML lexicographers produced impressive reference works in Tangut, Mongolian and Manchu. The Chinese government became involved in bilingual lexicography during the Ming Dynasty with the Bureau of Translators and during the Qing Dynasty with the Tongwen Academy and the Jiangnan Arsenal. Finally, Western missionaries such as Matteo Ricci and Robert Morrison and diplomats such as Herbert Giles were among the most active Chinese bilingual lexicographers. Chinese monolingual lexicography was greatly influenced by Chinese bilingual lexicography. From the Buddhists came the study of linguistics, a phonetic alphabet and the fanqie system of indicating the pronunciation of a Chinese character. From Western lexicographers came the modern method of marking the tone of a Chinese character, romanization schemes such as Wade-Giles, and the phonetic arrangement of dictionaries.

References

Cited dictionaries (see Appendix):

(A) CHINESE AND ENGLISH VOCABULARY IN THE PEKINESE DIALECT (Stent)
(A) CHINESE-ENGLISH DICTIONARY (Giles)
(A) CHINESE-ENGLISH DICTIONARY (Mathews)
CHINESE-ENGLISH DICTIONARY OF CONTEMPORARY USAGE (Chi)
CHINESE-FRENCH VOCABULARY (Boym)
CHINESE-LATIN VOCABULARY (Boym)
CIYUAN (Lu et al.)
DA QING QUAN SHU (Shen)
DICTIONARY OF THE CHINESE LANGUAGE (Morrison)
(A) DICTIONARY OF THE HO-KEEN (FUJIAN) DIALECT (Medhurst)
DICTIONNAIRE CHINOIS, FRANÇAIS ET LATIN (DeGuignes)
DIZIONARIO PORTOGHESE-CINESE (Ricci/Ruggieri)
FAN ER YA (Yuan/Yeli)
FAN HAN HE SHI ZHANG ZHONG ZHU (Gule)
FAN YU QIAN ZI WEN (Yi Jing)
HUA YI YI YU (Huoyuanjie/Mayichihei)
JI LIN LEI SHI (Sun)
KANG XI ZI DIAN (Zhang)
LIAO GUO YU JIE (Tuoketuo)
MENG GU YI YU
QING WEN ZONG HUI (Zhikuan/Zhipei)
(A) TONIC DICTIONARY OF THE CHINESE LANGUAGE IN THE CANTON DIALECT
    (Williams)
(A) VOCABULARY OF THE CANTON DIALECT (Morrison)
(A) VOCABULARY OF THE SHANGHAI DIALECT (Edkins)
WU JU YUN FU (Chen/Hu)
XI FAN YI YU
XI RU ER MU ZI (Trigault)
YI QIE JING YIN YI (Xuan)
YU PIAN (Gu)
YU ZHI ZENG DING QING WEN JIAN (Fu et al.)
ZENG DING HUA YI YI YU see HUA YI YI YU
ZI ER JI (Wade)

Other literature:

Anonymous (1815) "Dictionnaire Chinois" Quarterly Review April 1815:
    56-76
Ji Yonghai (1982) "Manwen cishu sihhua (The history of Manchu lexi-
    cography)" Cishu Yanjiu No. 2: 148-156
Li Nanqiu (1982) "Zhongguo shuangyu cidian shihua (A history of
    Chinese bilingual lexicography)" Cishu Yanjiu No. 1: 166-172
Ma Zuyi (1984) Zhongguo Fanyi Jianshi (A Brief History of Trans-
    lation in China). Beijing: China Translation Press

Nevsky, Nicholas (1928) "Concerning Tangut dictionaries" in Kano
    Kyoju Kanreki Kinen Shinagaku Ronshu. Kyoto: Kobundo
Shi Jinbo (1980) "Jianlun xixiawen cishu (A brief discussion on
    Tangut dictionaries)" Cishu Yanjiu No. 2: 246-260
Szczesniak, B. (1969) "The first Chinese dictionary published in
    Europe" in American Oriental Society Middle West Branch Semi-
    Centennial Volume ed. by Denis Sinor. Bloomington: Indiana U.P.
    217-227
Watters, T. (1889) Essays on the Chinese Language. Shanghai: Pres-
    byterian Mission Press
Wild, N. (1945) "Materials for the study of the Ssu I Kuan" Bulletin
    of the School of Oriental and African Studies (University of
    London) 11,3: 617-640
Yang, Paul (1960) "The Catholic missionary contribution to the study
    of Chinese dialects" Orbis 9,1: 158-185

HOW ABSTRACT IS THE ENGLISH DICTIONARY?

Frederic Dolezal

I was first attracted to the history of lexicography while undertaking a linguistic analysis of John Wilkins' Essay towards a Real Character and a Philosophical Language (1668); the more I studied the Essay the more I realized that the text that I was reading could not be adequately described, explained, or appreciated by appealing to the intentions which produced it. In fact, it seemed clear to me that the work had disappeared into some sort of scholarly dark abyss precisely because previous analyses consigned it to the never-never land of failed artificial language projects (e.g. Starnes and Noyes 1946). Those who are familiar with my work (Dolezal 1983, 1984, 1985) know the arguments detailing the importance of the Essay in the history of lexicography. Simply put, my analysis began and ended with the text as given.

The uncertainty surrounding what constitutes a lexicographic text in the academy is countered by the dictionary-buying and -using public who normally refer to their alphabetically ordered word lists, of whatever origin, as 'the dictionary' (as in "Look it up in the dictionary"). Perhaps the people understand the issue intuitively; even so, one is apt to hear from a speaker of some Language L that if a word is not in the Dictionary, then it is not a word of Language L.

I propose to present evidence from the early history of English lexicography that will show the extent to which the 'tradition' (be it mildly labelled as influence or harshly labelled as plagiarism) can be adequately described as a series of edited and revised texts. I will support my claims with data from a selection of major English dictionaries. The evidence I present will lend substance to the hitherto intuitive notion we commonly refer to as the English Dictionary; my argument turns on the textual question of uniformity among a plurality of texts, and the theoretical implications of the concept 'author'.

The early evolution of the English Dictionary has been considered as: 1) an example of received and passed along tradition; 2) a tangled chain of influence and borrowing; 3) a loose conglomeration of word lists waiting for the imprimatur of authority from Samuel Johnson; and even 4) a sequence of clever and no-so-clever plagiarists. A reading of the works on the history of English lexicography (see Hayashi 1978; Osselton 1979; Sledd and Kolb 1955; Starnes and Noyes 1946) finds all of these attitudes stated to one degree or another. It is not my purpose here to delineate and summarize the scholarship on the history of English lexicography (see Dolezal 1983, 1985). Rather, I would like to suggest another approach, which I hope might bring a unified vision of the development of the English dictionary. Namely, if we viewed the English dictionary as a single text, then the different 'authors' of successive dictionaries would more felicitously be called 'editors'. The common practice in modern English dictionary publications is to have an Editor-in-Chief and varying numbers of special editors; however, one suspects the title 'editor' in these cases underlines the particular dictionary's brand-name genealogy (e.g. Webster's, Funk and Wagnalls) which has as its origination an author (Noah Webster, for instance).

The history of lexicography is the history of a succession of printed texts. We would do well to consider this history in the manner in which one would approach the history of, say, printed editions of Shakespeare's tragedies. That is to say, we should consider each particular dictionary as a variant form of an un-available text. 'Variant' entails 'sameness'; it is in the uni-formity between texts that we judge genealogy. Thus, I restricted my study to four types of textual occurrences: 1) title page composition; 2) notational devices; 3) vocabulary selection; and 4) construction of definitions.

The limitations of space require that I confine my discussion to points 3) and mainly 4); however, we note that from the earliest English dictionary to the present there is a general format for title pages which depends on varying the size and type of the font used on a multi-layered succession of printed lines. Generally, ENGLISH DICTIONARY is most prominently rendered on the page; dictionaries which do not follow this style are usually special kinds of dictionaries (dialect, terminology, learner's). An interesting question that I cannot consider here examines the re-lation of dictionary title pages and other kinds of printed texts synchronically and diachronically. The notational devices used (italics, abbreviations, brackets, page format, etc.) also need to be studied in the context of the general history of printing. We might want to consider what other texts outside of the Judeo-Christian Bible have had the same long and continued printing tra-dition as the texts we know as dictionaries.

The scholarship on the early history of English lexicography which appeared before my work on Wilkins' and Lloyd's ALPHABETICAL DICTIONARY (1668) established two main trends of development: 1) the inclusion of only so-called 'hard words' of English in the first hundred years or so and 2) the heavy borrowing of terms and defini-tions from a varied number of dictionaries, glossaries, and word books covering the broad range of the vocabulary in succeeding years

We can only maintain these propositions by ignoring Wilkins' and
Lloyd's dictionary. The most widely published claim gives the lexicographer J.K. the credit for introducing the 'ordinary word' into
the English dictionary. My research (Dolezal 1985) argues for a
reevaluation of this point. Sidney Landau provisionally set aside
my assertions (Landau 1984), because he was not at that time convinced of the dictionariness of the ALPHABETICAL DICTIONARY.
Evidently, he based his decision on the stated intentions behind both
texts. However, when we try to trace the genealogy of a dictionary
we cannot afford to overlook texts which the public may not use yet
which the dictionary compiler may, and probably would, use. A
cursory glance at the ALPHABETICAL DICTIONARY shows a preponderance
of the 'ordinary' words. Furthermore, J.K. in his preface tells us
that "the main design . . . is to instruct Youth, and even adult
Persons . . . in the *Orthography* . . . of their own Mother-tongue."
His spotty and primitive definitions would seem to bear this out.
Thus, one might more pertinently question the lexicographical nature
of A NEW ENGLISH DICTIONARY (1702) by J.K.

The studies comparing the constructions of definitions (e.g.
Starnes and Noyes 1946) are used in tandem with the studies on the
lexicon. Influence from Latin-English dictionaries is noted in these
works. Osselton (1979), on the other hand, points to the English-
Latin dictionaries and English-French dictionaries as a probable
source for the 'ordinary words' which appear in J.K. (1702). In
Littleton's LINGUAE LATINAE LIBER DICTIONARIUS QUADRIPARTITUS (1678),
he finds evidence that J.K. used this bilingual source. Osselton,
as the scholars preceding him, overlooks the substantial list of
English words in the ALPHABETICAL DICTIONARY; as a consequence he
partially uncovers the line of influence in English lexicography.
In Littleton's dictionary, he finds this definition under **arm:**

Arm

       Littleton: A man's Arm. Brachium, laceratus
       (1678)   An Arm of the sea. Sinus Maris, aestuarium
                  An Arm of a tree. Ramus, ramale.

       J.K.:   An Arm of a man's body, of a tree, or of the
       (1702)   sea.

Now look at the entry as it appears in the ALPHABETICAL DICTIONARY
(1668).

    Wilkins and Lloyd:

Arm

   ___of Man. PG.V.I.
   ___of the Sea. [Bay]
   ___of a Tree, [Branch]
   to ___ Arms.

Since the publication of the ALPHABETICAL DICTIONARY precedes Littleton by ten years we cannot say with certainty which, if either, text
J.K. was looking at. I would not be surprised to learn of an entry in
a bilingual dictionary predating both Littleton and Wilkins which
bears close resemblance to their definitions. The question that
prompted my initial investigation still remains only partially answered: namely, where did Wilkins and Lloyd gather their extensive
list of words? I can show with some confidence that Wilkins and
Lloyd deserve a place in the genealogy by tracing parallel occurrences in succeeding dictionaries, but have not found a source, or
sources, previous to their work. However, even if the texts were all
known and available, the problem of deciding influence and/or coincidence of entries, definitions, notational systems, and title pages
would not be solved conclusively without an objective standard of
measure. The establishment of such a standard, I suggest, should be
a primary desideratum of the history of lexicography.

The following data (first collected in Dolezal 1985) are entries
taken from the major dictionaries published from 1604-1721; a dictionary is listed only when the entry word occurs in it.

Bacon

        Wilkins: Condited Hogs-flesh
        J.K.:   as a flitch of bacon.
        Bailey: Hog's flesh salted and dryed.

Bait

        Wilkins: [Refresh] sp. with Sustenance in Journey.
                  [Allure] sp. with Sustenance
                  as Hook or Trap [make allure(aptitude]
                  [Provoke]

        J.K.:   for fish, etc.
                  To bait a hook
                  To bait a bear, Bull, etc.
                  The hawk baits, or shakes her wings.

Kersey: to allure or entice, to set Beasts a
            fighting together; also to take some
            Refreshment on a journey: In Falconry
            A Hawk is said to Bait when she claps
            her wings, or stoops at her prey.

Bailey: to allure or intice, to set Beasts a
            Fighting together.
            to take some refreshment on a journey.

Clod

Wilkins: [Lump]
Bailey: a Lump.

Felter

Wilkins: [Entangle]
Bailey: to entangle.

Effeminate

Cawdrey: Womanish, delicate, wanton.
Bullokar: Womanish, nice.
Cockeram: Womanish, nice.
Wilkins: [Woman-like]
            [Tender]
            [Nice]
J.K.:   woman-like
Kersey: Woman-like, delicate, nice.
Bailey: Woman-like, tender, delicate, nice.

Dysury

Wilkins: [Disease of pissing (def]
Kersey: A Difficulty of making Water.
Bailey: a difficulty of Urine.

Fast

Wilkins: Adj.
              Fixed.
              ___and loose   (Light)
              ___asleep   )asleep ( )intensive]
              hold___   )hold   (
              tie___   (tie   )

<pre>
                    Firm.
                    [Swift]
                    Substantive.
                    [absteining from feeding] Religious.
          J.K.:   firm, close, or swift.
          Kersey: A Rope to fasten a Ship, or Boat.
          Bailey: to Abstain from food.
                    firm, sure.
</pre>

There is really no reason to stop with Bailey (1721), except that
after that date the proliferation of dictionaries and definitions
increases to a not easily manageable corpus. However, let us trace
the first entry up to the twentieth century.

Bacon

<pre>
          Johnson: 1. The flesh of a hog salted and dried.
                       2. To save the bacon...

          O.E.D.:   1. The back and sides of the pig, 'cured' by
                          salting, drying, etc. Formerly also the
                          fresh flesh now called pork.

          Century: 1. Hog's flesh, especially the back and
                          sides, salted or pickled and dried,
                          usually in smoke.
</pre>

From the data available it is clear that Wilkins' and Lloyd's 'hogs-
flesh' stands at the beginning of one transmission of the text;
since I have not looked at all precursors to the O.E.D., I cannot say
that they stand at the beginning of the 'back and sides' transmission
('back and sides' occurs in some form in WEBSTER'S THIRD and the
AMERICAN HERITAGE). There is enough uniformity between Wilkins,
Bailey, Johnson, and the CENTURY DICTIONARY to claim a textual history
for the definition of bacon.

   It is only an accident of printing and publishing history that
causes us to view particular dictionaries as discrete texts. Modern
English dictionaries normally have editors, but what text is being
edited? The apparent answer is THE ENGLISH DICTIONARY. This holds
as true for the so-called authors such as Johnson as it does for editors such as Philip Gove. THE ENGLISH DICTIONARY, however, occurs
only fragmentedly as particular and discrete texts published over a
period of more than 300 years. In this sense THE ENGLISH DICTIONARY
is nothing more nor less than the lexicon of the (allusive) ideal
speaker (whether the ideal knowledge of semantic content includes its
derivational history is a theoretical problem which cannot be broached

here). Any particular dictionary is a partial expression of this
lexicon.

Dictionaries are treated as authorities, yet, they have no traditional author-ship. As in other textual analyses, authority in a
dictionary is established upon the judgement and common sense of an
editor or group of editors. Indeed, when we look at the history of
English lexicography we can see that the task of the editors is to
decide upon the appropriate points for recension and emendation of
the text. For example, in defining bacon does one choose 'back and
sides of pig', 'hog's flesh', both or neither? To choose neither
would mean only that evidence from other texts suggests a different
analysis. The history of lexicography is not just a succession of
printed texts as I said earlier, but it is also the history of the
transmission of textual authority.

Particular and concrete dictionaries generally base their authority on the number of citations collected from recognized texts. One
might want to question the authority of the cited text; what relationship does a cited passage form Shakespeare's Hamlet have to the
understanding of the target word if the citation itself may be suspect?
One of the problems inherent in citing texts to establish authority is
indirectly expressed in this passage from Bowers (1966).

It should matter to us whether the thirteenth of
John Donne's Holy Sonnets ends triumphantly,

so I say to thee
To wicked spirits are horrid shapes assign'd,
This beauteous forme assures a pitious minde

as in Grierson's alteration on manuscript authority,
or flatly, as in the printed texts,

This beauteous form assumes a pitious minde

It should matter to us that the very bases for
establishing the texts of such important Shakespeare plays as 2 Henry IV, and Hamlet, are still
undecided. (page 9)

Let us consider an hypothetical dictionary which uses the
assumes text of Donne's poem for its illustrative citation. Is it
only a curiosity of the textual history of this sonnet that assumes
probably doesn't belong in the text? At the very least we must
recognize that even evidence from printed texts of the 'best'
authors is really dependent not only upon the reliability of the

editor of the dictionary, but also upon the reliability of the process of transmission of the cited text. The situation is completely circular; the dictionary is the repository of all possible texts which at once defines any particular text while being defined itself by all existing texts.

We all know that people have a penchant for demanding more from a dictionary than can be delivered; by viewing THE ENGLISH DICTIONARY as a single edited and re-edited text, we can at least attempt to answer misbegotten demands for 'correctness' etc. with our own documented claims about the nature of the printed text. When confronted by the authoritarian "Is it in the dictionary?" we can clear a bit of breathing space, as it were, by a rejoinder: "Do you mean the dictionary of all possible occurrences that are recognized by the ideal speaker of Language L to be members of Language L; or, do you mean some particular, derivative, unabridged but somehow, nevertheless, limited dictionary?"

Note

An earlier version of this paper was presented before the Society for Textual Scholarship in April 1985 at New York City.

References

Cited dictionaries (see Appendix):

(AN) ALPHABETICAL DICTIONARY ... (in Wilkins)
(THE) AMERICAN HERITAGE DICTIONARY (Morris/Berube)
(THE) CENTURY DICTIONARY ... (Whitney et al.)
DICTIONARIUM ANGLO-BRITANNICUM ... (Kersey)
(A) DICTIONARY OF THE ENGLISH LANGUAGE (Johnson)
(THE) ENGLISH DICTIONARIE ... (Cockeram)
(AN) ENGLISH DICTIONARY ... (Coles) -
(AN) ENGLISH EXPOSITOR ... (Bullokar)
GLOSSOGRAPHIA ... (Blount)
LINGUAE LATINAE LIBER DICTIONARIUS QUADRIPARTITUS (Littleton)
(A) NEW ENGLISH DICTIONARY ... ('J.K.')
(THE) NEW WORLD OF ENGLISH WORDS ... (Phillips)
(AN) UNIVERSAL ETYMOLOGICAL ENGLISH DICTIONARY ... (Bailey)
WEBSTER'S THIRD NEW INTERNATIONAL ... (Gove)

Other literature:

Bowers, Fredson (1966) Textual and Literary Criticism. Cambridge: U.P.
Dolezal, Fredric (1983) The Lexicographical and Lexicological Procedures and Methods of John Wilkins. Urbana: University of Illinois Ph.D. dissertation

Dolezal, Fredric (1984) "The construction of entries in the Alpha-
    betical Dictionary (1668) of John Wilkins and William Lloyd" in
    LEXeter '83 Proceedings ed. by R.R.K. Hartmann (Lexicographica.
    Series Maior 1). Tübingen: M. Niemeyer 67-72
Dolezal, Fredric (1985) Forgotten but Important Lexicographers: John
    Wilkins and William Lloyd. A Modern Approach to Lexicography
    before Johnson (Lexicographica. Series Maior 4). Tübingen: M.
    Niemeyer
Hayashi, Tetsuro (1978) The Theory of English Lexicography 1530-1791
    (Amsterdam Studies in the Theory and History of Linguistic
    Science III.18). Amsterdam: J. Benjamins
Kolb, Gwin J. and Sledd, James H. (1953) "Johnson's Dictionary and
    lexicographical tradition" Modern Philology 50,3: 171-194
Landau, Sidney I. (1984) Dictionaries: The Art and Craft of Lexico-
    graphy. New York: Scribner
Mathews, Mitford M. (1933) A Survey of English Dictionaries. London:
    Oxford U.P.
Osselton, Noel E. (1979) "John Kersey and the ordinary words of
    English" English Studies 60, 4: 555-561
Sledd, James H. and Kolb, Gwin J. (1955) Dr. Johnson's Dictionary:
    Essays in the Biography of a Book. Chicago: U. of Chicago P.
Starnes, DeWitt T. and Noyes, Gertrude E. (1946) The English Dic-
    tionary from Cawdrey to Johnson, 1604-1755. Chapel Hill: U. of
    North Carolina P.
Wilkins, John (1668) An Essay towards a Real Character and a Philo-
    sophical Language. London: J.M. for Gellibrand and Martin

THE DEVELOPMENT OF THE BILINGUAL ENGLISH-ARABIC DICTIONARY
FROM THE MIDDLE OF THE NINETEENTH CENTURY TO THE PRESENT

Nawal El-Badry

Introduction

"Dictionaries first came into being in response to very practical needs" (Osselton 1983). This probably explains why prior to
the 19th century there was not much activity in the domain of
English and Arabic bilingual lexicography. However, with the growing
interest in oriental studies, this situation changed. A bibliography
of Arabic lexicography (Ghāli 1971) lists about 50 general and a
number of specialised English and Arabic bilingual dictionaries,
many with multiple editions.

This paper surveys seven Arabic-English and eight English-Arabic
dictionaries in order to trace the development of bilingual lexicography of these two languages in terms of the explicit or implicit
plans of their respective authors and the sources they draw on.

Arabic-English dictionaries

Edward William Lane's ARABIC-ENGLISH LEXICON (1862) is a most
comprehensive work on Classical Arabic in eight parts "derived from
the best and most copious of Eastern sources", chiefly from TĀJ AL-
'ARŪS, an exhaustive 18th-century work. The preface in Volume I
gives a 34-page survey of Classical Arabic and a chronology of lexicographical works and grammars as well as a guide to the use of the
dictionary. Lane's LEXICON comprises 4,596 pages, the entries
arranged in three columns, each containing English explanations and
translations interspersed with Arabic examples. No transliterations
are provided since the compiler supposes the "student who will make
use of this work to be acquainted with the general rules of
grammar". We can assume that the dictionary is aimed at providing
the non-native scholar of Classical Arabic interested in 5th- to
8th-century literature with a thorough and comprehensive translation
into English of all available linguistic evidence. To give an example of the degree of coverage, the article on alif, the first
letter of the alphabet, occupies almost three pages.

The second important work to be considered is F. Steingass'
STUDENT'S ARABIC-ENGLISH DICTIONARY of 1884. In the preface the
compiler says that his aim is "to provide the English student, at a
moderate price, with a dictionary which would enable him to read not
only Arabic books of a limited vocabulary (but also) other standard

works of a wider etymological range" such as pre-Islamic and early
Islamic literature.

The dictionary uses source material from several contemporary
bilingual dictionaries with French and German, "checked by, and
occasionally enlarged upon, from the MUḤĪṬ", a monolingual dictionary of Arabic. The dictionary is in one volume of 1,242 pages
arranged in two columns. The 40,000 entries are given in Arabic
script without diacritical signs, but with English transliteration.

The third in this group is Ḥ.A. Salmoné's ADVANCED LEARNER'S
ARABIC-ENGLISH DICTIONARY (1890). The compiler's aim was to produce
a dictionary "which is comprehensive, handy and cheap". His system
for saving space and expense was not to give "under each root the
various nouns, adjectives, etc., with their plurals, (but) refer by
figures to a table of model forms which will be found attached to
the dictionary ..."

Again Arabic-French and Arabic-English dictionaries as well as
MUḤĪṬ serve as sources for Salmoné. To achieve the above aims, he
splits the material into two volumes, the first containing all
Arabic entries and equivalents as well as a Table of Arabic Derived
Forms and abbreviations, the second an Index of the English words
with page and line references to their locations in Volume I.

Socrates Spiro-Bey's ARABIC-ENGLISH VOCABULARY OF THE COLLOQUIAL
ARABIC OF EGYPT (1895) is aimed at "oriental scholars in general and
Arabic scholars in particular". The VOCABULARY includes "a large
number of administrative, financial, engineering, mechanical and
military words (collated from) a mass of official publications". To
record a large number of idioms and slang phrases Spiro-Bey claims
to have read 'almost all' literature in colloquial Arabic and to
have listened 'carefully' to casual conversation.

The book consists of 661 two-column pages, containing about
5,000 entries. The 10-page front matter includes abbreviations, a
note on entry design, the Arabic alphabet, days of the week, names
etc.

The ARABIC-ENGLISH DICTIONARY FOR THE USE OF STUDENTS by the
Reverend Hava (1899) was meant "to meet the want of a classical
Arabic-English Dictionary, which would be comprehensive, yet might
be handy and cheap enough for practical use amongst the students
desirous of acquiring a thorough knowledge of Arabic literature and
poetry".

The 'standard work of Mr. Lane' is followed in the translations,
but original Arabic sources were also consulted. The compiler claims
to have taken particular care to translate scientific terms accur-
ately. An apparent effort is also made to include Syrian and
Egyptian regionalisms.

Next comes ELIĀS' MODERN DICTIONARY ARABIC-ENGLISH published in
1922 "to meet two urgent needs: that of the English-speaking student
of the living Arabic, for whom the more exhaustive and costly works
are unsuited, as well as that of the Arabic-speaking student of the
English language for whom no Arabic-English dictionary has, as yet,
been made".

Eliās reconciles the conventional arrangement of Arabic dictionaries "with the simple methods required by present-day students
(i.e. by inserting) most of the derivatives in small type, according
to their alphabetical order, followed by Arabic roots under which
they are to be found enclosed in plain brackets".

Obsolete and rare words are deliberately omitted, while "living
words and their different shades of meanings are amply dealt with".
While the author makes no claim to comprehensiveness (45,000 words),
the dictionary proved extremely popular, reaching 13 editions by
1981.

The last of the Arabic-English dictionaries to be mentioned here
is Hans Wehr's DICTIONARY OF MODERN WRITTEN ARABIC, first issued in
1960. It "is based on the form of the language which, throughout the
Arab world from Iraq to Morocco, is found in the prose of books,
newspapers, periodicals and letters. This form is also employed in
formal public address, over radio and television". It is expected to
be useful to those interested in writings that have appeared since
1900.

The dictionary follows a 'scientific descriptive' approach; "it
not only lists classical words and phrases of elegant rhetorical
style side by side with new coinages ... but it also contains neologisms, loan translations, foreign loans, and colloquialisms." The
author expected the dictionary to "be welcome not only to English
and American users, but to orientalists throughout the world".

To sum up the main stages in the development of Arabic-English
dictionaries, we note that they came into being in response to the
needs of orientalists who were mainly interested in the study of
Classical Arabic literature. Lane's LEXICON, the greatest of such
works, derived its Arabic text from the great monolingual Classical
Arabic dictionaries. Later dictionaries copied from Lane's LEXICON
as well as similar bilingual works of Arabic with French and German.

A new trend began with Spiro-Bey's DICTIONARY which concentrated
on colloquial Arabic. This dictionary exemplified another new
feature, viz. the way the source material was collected from a
contemporary discourse corpus. Interest in the modern language continued to affect later dictionaries, e.g. Hava's DICTIONARY introduced regionalisms from Syria and Egypt.

Eliās' DICTIONARY which reflected this trend in a more explicit
way also started a new interest in the Arabic native speaker as a
potential user whose needs, according to Elias, had not been catered
for in preceding works. The emphasis on contemporary language and
systematic compilation techniques is more apparent in Wehr's DIC-
TIONARY, even though it is addressed primarily to European and American rather than Arab users.

English-Arabic lexicography

The first dictionary in this section is AN ENGLISH-ARABIC LEX-
ICON by George Percy Badger (1881). The dictionary has a short preface in Arabic and a more detailed one in English. In the Arabic
preface the editor says that he had "long thought of translating the
English language into the Arabic tongue in order to help spreading
the knowledge of Arabic among the English and the knowledge of
English among the Arabs." In the English preface he writes about the
availability of Arabic-English dictionaries for students of Arabic,
especially English students. He cites various published Arabic-
English dictionaries, including William Lane's 'marvellous work'. By
contrast, he describes one representative contemporary English-Arabic dictionary as being at best "merely a compendious vocabulary,
forming a useful handbook for ordinary travellers in the East, but
utterly inadequate as an aid to the English-speaking student or
writer..." Badger utilised the KĀMOOS and other linguistic and literary works of Classical writers as well as Lane's LEXICON, Bus-
tāni's MUHĪT, and bilingual dictionaries of Arabic with French and
Turkish. He also obtained many modern expressions and idiomatic
usages from various newspapers. It is noteworthy that the key to
symbols and terminology used in the dictionary is given only in
English.

The second work is F. Steingass' ENGLISH-ARABIC DICTIONARY of
1882, intended mainly for English-speaking scholars and people
travelling and "resident in the East". The introductory and
explanatory material is in English. Similar dictionaries in English,
French and German as well as works by known Arab authors were used
as sources for this dictionary, later reprinted under the title A
LEARNER'S ENGLISH-ARABIC DICTIONARY.

The third dictionary is Spiro-Bey's ARABIC-ENGLISH VOCABULARY OF
THE MODERN AND COLLOQUIAL ARABIC OF EGYPT published in 1897. In the
preface the compiler expresses his intention to "help the foreigners
in Egypt to communicate intelligibly with the natives of this
country". The VOCABULARY therefore "includes only such words and
sentences as they may require".

SA'ĀDEH'S DICTIONARY (1911) is described as "A new practical and
exhaustive" dictionary that aims at "giving the English language a

much wider scope in the East than it has hitherto had, and of
raising Arabic into the dignity of a scientific language", thus
bridging the 'deep chasm' between the two languages.

Sa'ādeh meant to offer his dictionary to the "English student of
Arabic and the modern oriental student of English". He was not
"content to copy from (his) predecessors", but introduced many
technical and scientific terms as well as colloquial and slang
expressions by consulting the most celebrated English monolingual
dictionaries. Title page, introduction, prefatory note and list of
abbreviations are given in both languages.

ELIĀS' MODERN ENGLISH-ARABIC DICTIONARY (1913) comes next. It
was compiled "with a view to the needs of the Arabic speaking
students in their study of English" which, according to the author,
had not been catered for by previous reference works. At the same
time, he hoped "that English-speaking students of Arabic, who have
obtained a fair degree of proficiency in that language, (would) find
it more useful than any other English-Arabic dictionary".

The sixth dictionary in this survey is Munīr Ba'albaki's AL-
MAWRID (1967). Having experienced the kind of frustration felt by
educated Arabs when English-Arabic dictionaries fail to meet their
needs, the editor wanted to produce a comprehensive dictionary of no
less than 100,000 entries on modern lines.

To this end, Ba'albaki had recourse to English and American
monolingual dictionaries, general and specialised bilingual works,
terminology lists published by the Cairo Academy of the Arabic
Language, and glossaries in numerous books recently translated into
Arabic. The introductory matter of the dictionary is in Arabic.

Hassan S. Karmi's AL-MANĀR (1970) is the seventh dictionary
considered in this group. It has a vocabulary of about 40,000 words
and is intended for students at colleges and secondary schools as
well as the general user.

For his English source material, Karmi relied on word frequency
lists and dictionaries published recently in the United States and
Great Britain. With reference to Arabic equivalents, he claims that
the "Arabic meanings of words are given for the English words as
they are used in practice". The introduction is in English, the
guide on how to use the dictionary is in English and Arabic, the key
to pronunciation is in English only.

The last of this group is THE OXFORD ENGLISH-ARABIC DICTIONARY
OF CURRENT USAGE by N.S. Doniach, published in 1972. It is intended
for both English-speaking and Arabic-speaking users. Its compilation
was carried out on the basis of a fresh appraisal of "what usage was
current in English (and what) relevant usage" was current in Arabic.

Doniach's dictionary broke new ground by giving the Arabic equivalents, as far as possible, "at the same level of usage". Care was
taken "to produce a representative English text so arranged on the
page that the specific usage was easy to find".

The CONCISE OXFORD DICTIONARY and Hornby's ADVANCED LEARNER'S
DICTIONARY were the main sources for the English text. In addition,
a panel of professional linguists were consulted for questions of
usage. Arabic equivalents were checked by native speakers in order
to ensure that the semantic scope of the entry in question was fully
conveyed and the layout was clear to the user.

To summarise we may say that English-Arabic dictionaries, just
as their Arabic-English counterparts, developed initially in response to the needs of Western orientalists. The earlier works again
drew on Lane's LEXICON and Bustani's MUḤĪṬ as well as on bilingual
French, German and Turkish dictionaries. Unlike the Arabic-English
dictionaries, English-Arabic dictionaries not only reproduced most
of the Classical language, but also consciously introduced aspects
of colloquial discourse, to help English users communicate in
Arabic. Again, Spiro-Bey's ARABIC-ENGLISH VOCABULARY was an important pioneer in this trend.

An interesting point emerges from this short survey. Although by
the beginning of the 20th century a number of English-Arabic dictionaries had become available, we find Eliās claiming in 1913 that
the needs of the Arabic-speaking student of English had not yet been
catered for. By 1922 an even greater number of Arabic-English dictionaries were on the market, but once more Eliās claimed that Arabic learners of English had not been provided with this type of
dictionary. Whether his claims were justified and whether his works
provided for this particular user group needs further investigation.

As in many other traditions of bilingual lexicography, direc-
tionality is inextricably bound to the purpose for which the dictionary is intended: in both directions, Arabic bilingual dictionaries follow the universal pattern of meeting the needs of 'passive
comprehension' before those of 'active composition'. The first full-
fledged dictionary for English users (intended for comprehension)
was Lane's ARABIC-ENGLISH LEXICON (1862), followed 20 years later by
Badger's ENGLISH-ARABIC LEXICON (aimed at composition for English
and comprehension for Arab users). The first dictionary of significant size specifically aimed at composition for Arab users is
probably ELIĀS'S MODERN DICTIONARY (1922).

References

Cited dictionaries (see Appendix):

(AN) ADVANCED LEARNER'S ARABIC-ENGLISH DICTIONARY (Salmoné)
(THE) ADVANCED LEARNER'S DICTIONARY OF CURRENT ENGLISH (Hornby)
ARABIC-ENGLISH DICTIONARY FOR THE USE OF STUDENTS (Hava)
(AN) ARABIC-ENGLISH LEXICON (Lane)
(AN) ARABIC-ENGLISH VOCABULARY ... (Spiro-Bey)
(THE) CONCISE OXFORD DICTIONARY (Fowler/Sykes)
(A) DICTIONARY OF MODERN WRITTEN ARABIC (Wehr)
ELIĀS' MODERN DICTIONARY ARABIC-ENGLISH (Eliās)
ELIĀS' MODERN DICTIONARY ENGLISH-ARABIC (Eliās)
ENGLISH-ARABIC DICTIONARY (Steingass)
(AN) ENGLISH-ARABIC LEXICON (Badger)
(AN) ENGLISH-ARABIC VOCABULARY ... (Spiro-Bey)
(AL-) KĀMOOS ... (Al-Firūzābādī)
(A) LEARNER'S ENGLISH-ARABIC DICTIONARY (Steingass)
(AL-) MANĀR (AN) ENGLISH ARABIC DICTIONARY (Karmi)
(AL-) MAWRID (A) MODERN ENGLISH-ARABIC DICTIONARY (Ba'albaki)
MUHĪṬ AL-MUHĪṬ (Al-Bustāni)
(THE) OXFORD ENGLISH-ARABIC DICTIONARY OF CURRENT USAGE (Doniach)
SA'ĀDEH'S ENGLISH-ARABIC DICTIONARY (Sa'ādeh)
(THE) STUDENT'S ARABIC-ENGLISH DICTIONARY (Steingass)
TĀJ AL-A'RŪS (Al-Zabīdī)

Other references:

Collison, Robert L. (1982) A History of Foreign-Language Dic-
    tionaries (The Language Library). London: A. Deutsch
Darwish, Abdallah A. (1956) Al-Ma'ājim al-'Arabiya (Arabic
    Dictionaries). Cairo: The Anglo-Egyptian Bookshop & Printers
Ghāli, Wagdi R. (1971) Arabic Dictionaries: An Annotated Com-
    prehensive Bibliography. Cairo: Al-Hay'a al-Misriyyeh al-'Āmmeh
Hayashi, Tetsuro (1978) The Theory of English Lexicography 1530-1791
    (Amsterdam Studies in the Theory and History of Linguistic
    Science III.18). Amsterdam: J. Benjamins
Haywood, John A. (1960) Arabic Lexicography: Its History and Its
    Place in the General History of Lexicography. Leiden: E.J. Brill
Nassār, Husseīn (1956) Al-Mu'jam al'Arabi: Nash'atuhu wa Tatawwuruhu
    (The Arabic Dictionary. Its Origin and Development). 2 volumes.
    Cairo: Dār Misr lil Tibā'ah
Osselton, Noel E. (1983) "The history of English-language diction-
    aries" in Lexicography: Principles and Practice ed. by R.R.K.
    Hartmann. London: Academic Press 13-22

THE BEGINNINGS OF LEXICOGRAPHY IN CROATIA

Rudolf Filipović

THE BEGINNINGS OF LEXICOGRAPHY IN CROATIA

Introduction

Glosses found in manuscripts, interlinearly and marginally, in
the 11th and the 12th centuries are regarded as precursors of
Croatian lexicography. They belong to the Radon Bible and it is
believed that they were written in Zagreb during the period of
office of the first bishop of Zagreb. Among them there are some
glosses with examples of the local Zagreb kajkavic dialect. These
glosses are (some scholars believe) among the oldest non-Romance
lexicography in the Middle Ages. Other Croatian glosses were found
later in some Zagreb medieval Latin codices, especially in school
manuals. In the Pauline monastery at Remete near Zagreb, in
Johannes Balbus's CATHOLICON, there are Croatian kajkavic glosses
from the 16th century (Franolić 1983). It is a fact that before the
15th century no lexicographical work was preserved in Croatia.

Lexicography in Croatia began during Humanism and the
Renaissance: the former stimulated the use of Latin both in
literature and official life in Croatia; the latter shows the rise
of the Croatian language in literature. Since Latin was the
official language in Croatia both in administration and in education
as well as in scientific works, bilingual and multilingual dictionaries which appeared in great number at that time incorporated
Latin and vernacular languages. The other classical language,
Greek, was another language very often used in multilingual dictionaries. The first multilingual dictionary preserved in manuscript form in which Croatian is used is LIBER DE SIMPLICIBUS,
compiled in Zadar (on the Croatian coast of the Adriatic) in the
middle of the 15th century by the physician Niccolò Roccabonella.
Every entry is illustrated by a picture of a plant, thus it is also
the first Croatian pictorial dictionary. The LIBER is an Arabic-
Greek-Latin-Croatian dictionary of botanical and pharmacological
terms. In this specialized encyclopedic dictionary objects as well
as words are explained.

Printed lexicographical material

During the following hundred or so years several other
manuscripts of lexicographical works appeared each containing a
number of Croatian words. Then comes the period when the first
dictionaries or lexicographical works were printed. The earliest
printed Croatian dictionary we know of appeared in Italian, entitled
OPERA NUOVA CHE INSEGNA A PARLARE LA LINGUA SCHIAVONESCA ALLI

GRANDI, ALLI PICOLI ET ALLE DONNE, printed in 1527 (in all likelihood in Ancona). Its author is (probably) a Spanish Jew, Pietro
Lupis (Lópes) Valentiano who fled from Spain in 1492 and afterwards
settled in Italy. From the Introduction and the rest of the book we
learn that he was a merchant and that he wanted to help other
merchants and travellers to learn the language spoken and understood
not only in Croatia but also in other neighbouring countries such as
Serbia, Albania, Turkey, Hungary, etc., in many cities and trade
centres. His book is intended to enable merchants to sell their
goods, to make purchases and to calculate in those languages. But
he also wanted to help Croats to learn Italian, and even to learn
how to read it.

His instruction to the reader is very interesting, particularly
when he tells him how to learn the language. One should start from
things which are easy and progress to the more difficult items.
That is why he begins with words, and later introduces phrases. He
instructs the reader on how to find a Croatian equivalent for an
Italian word, i.e. to follow the alphabetical order in the
dictionary.

From the linguistic point of view Valentiano's dictionary gives
a mixture of Croatian dialects and a mixture of Italian dialects.
The form of Italian used in the dictionary is the 16th-century
Italian spoken in the areas of Florence, Siena, Udine linked with
the district of Venice and Trento containing typical local dialectal
characteristics. The Croatian used in the dictionary is a combination of čakavian i-dialect and štokavian ije-dialect spoken in
the part of Croatia he travelled through and traded in, i.e. most
parts of the Croatian littoral of the Adriatic. Three of the best
developed trading centres of the period may be mentioned according
to the language used in the book, Dubrovnik, Zadar and Senj.

Valentiano's dictionary represents the first bilingual printed
dictionary of Croatian and fixes the beginning of lexicography in
Croatia at 1527, 68 years before the first major printed lexicographical work in Croatia, Vrančić's dictionary. Valentiano's OPERA
NUOVA has eight pages: the front page, the second page with the
author's introduction to the aim of the dictionary and the first
instruction to the reader on how to use the dictionary; then follow
three pages, with two columns each, containing 196 Italian entries
explained by 328 Croatian equivalents, and then two pages of 38
bilingual dialogues, and on the last (eighth) page a model letter in
Italian and its Croatian translation. The book OPERA NUOVA is kept
in the Bayerische Staatsbibliothek in Munich in a fascicle under the
shelf mark 4 Polygl. 27[a]. It was discovered by a Czech scholar, Jan
Petr. The name of the author is not printed on the front page of
the booklet, but somebody has added the name in pencil. Petr has
demonstrated quite convincingly that the work was indeed written by
the man named Pietro Lupis Valentiano.

Another book, printed in the 16th century, deserves our
undivided attention. It is De afflictione ... by Bartholomaeus
Georgievič (Djurdjevič) who supplemented his book with the first
Croatian-Latin dictionary and some additional material. This
dictionary had been regarded for some time as the first lexicographical work in Croatian until Valentiano's booklet was
discovered.

Bartholomaeus Georgievič, a Croat born near Zagreb, had been
taken prisoner by the Turks in 1526 in the great battle between the
Turks and the Christians at Mohácz and spent nine years as a slave
in Turkey where he learned Turkish. After escaping from Turkish
captivity he devoted his life to writing popular books in Latin
about the Turks and the Ottoman empire.

In one of his works entitled De afflictione tam captivorum quam
etiam sub Turcae tributo viventium Christianorum (Antwerp 1544) he
printed, as a supplement, a systematic analytical Croatian-Latin
dictionary called VOCABULA SCLAVONICA containing 52 words and
phrases. The VOCABULA are preceded by a brief dialogue in Croatian
with an interlinear Latin translation. The VOCABULA SCLAVONICA are
grouped analytically under five headings: 'Coelestia' (12 units),
'Terrena' (19 units), 'Fructuum' (8 units), 'Verbal phrases' (8),
'Nomina vestimentorum' (5). When De afflictione ... was translated
into French, Dutch and English, the Croatian-Latin dictionary was
transformed into the first interlingual Croatian-French, Croatian-
Dutch and Croatian-English dictionary. The Latin part of the
dialogue which accompanies the dictionary was also translated into
the three above-mentioned languages.

The Croatian part of the dictionary and the added dialogue were
written in čakavian i-dialect, one of the three main Croatian
dialects in literary use before the single modern Croatian standard
was established at the beginning of the 19th century. It is worth
mentioning that Djurdjevič added his Croatian-Latin dictionary to
other works of his. He himself gives the reasons. Since he uses
several Turkish and oriental words in his books he supplements them
with Croatian examples to show the European reader that Croatian is
entirely different from Turkish.

In the same volume there are: the Lord's Prayer, Hail Mary and
the Apostle's Creed in the čakavian dialect. Croatian numerals from
one to one hundred and one thousand with their equivalents in Latin,
French, Dutch and English are also added.

The First major printed dictionary

Croatian lexicographical material appears in various other works
of this period with a greater or smaller number of Croatian words.
And then at the end of the 16th century, in 1595, a five-language

dictionary by Faust Vrančić was printed in Venice under the title of
DICTIONARIUM QUINQUE NOBILISSIMARUM EUROPAE LINGUARUM LATINAE,
ITALICAE, GERMANICAE, DALMATICAE ET UNGARICAE in which Croatian
(under the name Dalmatica) is one of the five languages.

By its form and its size, in terms of number of words, this
multilingual dictionary must be regarded as the first major
dictionary of the Croatian language and its author Faust Vrančić as
the founder of Croatian lexicography. This dictionary is also the
first attempt to write an etymological dictionary, since in it there
is a list of Hungarian words of Slavonic origin (Slavicisms). It is
in this dictionary that the Croatian language is presented for the
first time in its totality with a direct lexicographical intention.
Vrančić's dictionary has only 128 pages, each containing five
columns, one for each language. It comprises 5467 Latin lexical
items explained by 3581 Croatian words. Although it is by its size
a small dictionary, it is packed with lexical material. Equivalents
are arranged in five columns: Latin, Italian, German, Croatian and
Hungarian. "The basic assumption underlying such an effort is that
there exist certain syntactic and semantic invariants which make
linguistic comparisons of this nature both possible and fruitful"
(Franolić 1983).

The DICTIONARIUM QUINQUE ... LINGUARUM stimulated similar
efforts by other linguists. It was used by the Czech Benedictine
monk Peter Loderecker as a basis for his own dictionary of seven
languages: DICTIONARIUM SEPTEM DIVERSARUM LINGUARUM, VIDELICET
LATINE, ITALICE, DALMATICE, BOHEMICE, POLONICE, GERMANICE ET
UNGARICE, published in Prague in 1605. Loderecker's dictionary is
essentially Vrančić's dictionary revised and expanded by the
inclusion of Czech and Polish and the addition of indices in Latin
for each language. Vrančić himself wrote a preface in Croatian for
this dictionary. In Loderecker's dictionary the terms 'Dalmata',
'Dalmatia', 'Dalamatice' are explained as 'Harvat' (Croat),
'Harvatska zemlja' (Croatian land), 'Harvatski' (Croatian), which
entitles us not only from a linguistic but also from a historical
point of view to refer to the 'lingua dalmatica' of this dictionary
as Croatian, Dalmatian being a geographical and not an ethnic
designation (Franolić 1976).

Some years ago the Croatian lexicographer V. Putanec prepared a
photostatic edition of Vrančić's dictionary and compiled an index of
Croatian-Latin lexical equivalents contained in it. The index is an
inventory of all Croatian lexical units found in the DICTIONARIUM,
indicating their frequency. He also studied the Croatian words
recorded in the dictionary from the point of view of the place and
time in which the dictionary was written.

In spite of the immense philological importance of Vrančić's
dictionary, it has some imperfections. The first is that due to the

great number of languages (five), the number of word-entries is
small and they have not been given full lexical elaboration, but are
cited in their fundamental forms only. The choice of languages was
the result of the author's views being limited to the Croatian
Mediterranean area and directed only to the neighbouring Italy and
Central European lands. Therefore he used Italian and Hungarian
instead of French and English (or even Spanish), the languages which
were by the end of the 16th century already considered 'nobilissimarum Europae linguarum'. Still, in assessing Vrančić's work one
has to take into account the time when he was active. For the
Croatian literary language this was the period of many unsettled
problems: the Croatian version of Old Slavonic was coming to an end,
the Glagolitic script was in decline and the Latin script was not
yet fully mastered. Vrančić's intervention in orthography is very
important for the historical development of the Latin script in
Croatia. By defining, for instance, the pronunciation of the Latin
letter c based on four diffent orthographies in Croatian cz, cs, ch,
k, he considers the four possible types of pronunciation only as
'ways' behind which the idea of consonantal phonemes of the Croatian
language is hidden.

    If we consider only three ways of pronouncing   the Latin
letter c, we can conclude that Vrančić distinguishes two norms:
orthographic and orthoepic. According to him, Croatian has three
orthographies cz, cs, ch and three different pronunciations /c/,
/č/, /ć/. This is the first time that the orthoepic norm of
Croatian was explicitly defined. In the matter of orthography he
attempted to overcome discrepancies in the use of the Latin script
in the south and in the north, thus making way for the imple-
mentation of a Latin script which would be based on the phonetic and
phonological requirements of the Croatian language (Vončina 1979).
In defining the geographical area covered by the Croatian language
as being "from the Adriatic to the Drava and the Danube rivers" he
remained faithful to the tradition of exposing čakavian to other
dialects (especially štokavian but also kajkavian). Vrančić's
language is based on the čakavian i-dialect, the dialect spoken in
his birthplace, Šibenik in Dalmatia.

    On the last four pages (118-122) under the title of VOCABULA
DALMATICA QUE UNGARI SIBI USURPARUNT there are printed 304 Hungarian
words which Vrančić regards as being of Croatian origin. This shows
Vrančić's interest in the etymology of borrowings from one language
to another resulting from the long cultural and linguistic contacts
between Hungary and Croatia. This is, according to our present
knowledge, the first analysis and classification of borrowed words -
loanwords. The list of borrowings compiled in Vrančić's time shows
that there must have been quite a number of Croatian loanwords in
Hungarian, and not a much smaller number of Hungarian words in
Croatian.

Vrančić's DICTIONARIUM has further great importance for the
history of the Croatian language. On the last six pages of his book
Vrančić recorded the complete Croatian text of the Ten Commandments,
the Lord's Prayer, the Apostle's Creed and Ave Maria in the Croatian
vernacular spoken in Dalmatia during the 16th century.

Faust Vrančić was not only a distinguished lexicographer. He
was also known as an inventor and philosopher. In the international
world of science he became renowned for his inventions and dis-
coveries described in his book Machinae novae (Venice 1595). As a
philosopher he is remembered by his philosophical works Logica nova
(Venice 1616) and Ethica Christiana (Venice 1616), and as a
historian he left two unpublished manuscripts, Illyrica historia and
Statuta civitatis Sibenicensis.

Conclusion

In our attempt to establish the beginnings of Croatian
lexicography we have stated that glosses, found in many Latin
manuscripts and later in printed codices and manuals, are the
precursors of the earliest lexicographical works, some of which are
preserved in manuscript form and others printed as parts of
published books on various subjects or as independent dictionaries.
Thus we have classified as the earliest of them a 15th-century (ca.
1445) manuscript dictionary in which Croatian appears as one of the
languages dealt with, LIBER DE SIMPLICIBUS, a four-language
botanical and pharmacological pictorial dictionary. Then, after a
period rich in other manuscript dictionaries, comes the first
printed dictionary, the bilingual Italian-Croatian OPERA NUOVA ...
(1527) which contains an Italian-Croatian glossary. Seventeen years
later a book was printed, entitled De afflictione ..., which was
supplemented by a Croatian-Latin glossary. When it was translated
into other European languages, the Croatian-Latin glossary was
turned into Croatian, one of the other major languages mentioned,
thus enriching the series of the earliest Croatian bilingual
dictionaries. Many more glossaries and lexicographical material in
Croatian appeared in the period betwen 1544 and 1595 when the first
major dictionary was printed. This is Faust Vrančić's DICTIONARIUM
QUINQUE ... LINGUARUM. In the following two centuries Croatian
lexicography flourished by producing a number of bilingual and
multilingual dictionaries, which shows that Croatian lexicographers
were developing more and more into competent linguists. That modern
trend led towards the period in the 19th century when a comprehensive historical monolingual dictionary of Croatian was conceived
and a team started to work on it. When the Yugoslav Academy of
Sciences and Arts was founded in Zagreb in 1866, the scheme of a
completely new Croatian dictionary was converted into the Academy's
first working programme in 1867. Soon after that work on a new
historical RJEČNIK HRVATSKOGA ILI SRPSKOGA JEZIKA began, and its
first volume appeared in 1882.

We can conclude that Croatian lexicography from its rather modest but stable beginnings in the 16th century and through the very productive period of the 17th and the 18th centuries, developed into a well-established lexicography in the 19th century of a modern European type.

References

Cited dictionaries (see Appendix):

CATHOLICON (Balbus)
DICTIONARIUM QUINQUE NOBILISSIMARUM EUROPAE LINGUARUM ... (Vrančić)
DICTIONARIUM SEPTEM DIVERSARUM LINGUARUM ... (Loderecker)
ENGLESKO-HRVATSKE KNJIŽEVNE VEZE (Filipović)
LIBER DE SIMPLICIBUS (Roccabonella)
OPERA NVOVA ... (Valentiano)
RJEČNIK HRVATSKOGA ILI SRPSKOGA JEZIKA
VOCABULA DALMATICA ... (in DICTIONARIUM QUINQUE ...)
VOCABULA SCLAVONICA (Georgievič)

Other literature:

Baudouin de Courtenay, Jan I. (1888) "Das Slavische in den Werken
    von B. Georgievics" Archiv für Slavische Philologie 11: 343-354
Filipović, Rudolf (1953) "Anglo-Croatian literary relations in the
    19th century" The Slavonic and East European Review 78: 92-107
Franolić, Branko (1976) "Was Faust Vrančić the first Croatian lexi-
    cographer?" Annali Istituto Universitario Orientale (Napoli)
    19: 177-182
Franolić, Branko (1983) "An historical outline of Croatian lexico-
    graphy" Die Welt der Slaven 7,2: 286-306
Musulin, Stjepan (1959) "Hrvatska i srpska leksikografija" Filo-
    logija 2: 41-63
Petr, Jan (1973) "Italsko-čakavská jezyková příručka z r. 1527"
    Slavia 42: 44-67
Putanec, Valentin (1952) Francuska leksikografija na hrvatskom ili
    sprskom i slovenskom jeziku do 1914.g. Zagreb: Sveučilište
Putanec, Valentin (1962) "Leksikografija" in Enciklopedija Jugo-
    slavije Vol. 5: 503-511
Putanec, Valentin (1971) "Apostile uz 'Dictionarium quinque nobi-
    lissimarum Europae linguarum' (1595) Fausta Vrančiča" Čakavska
    rič 1,2: 5-18
Putanec, Valentin (1979) "Talijansko-hrvatski i hrvatsko-talijanski
    rječnik Petra Lupisa Valentiana (Ancona 1527)" Filologija 9:
    101-138
Vončina, Josip (1979) "Vrančićev rječnik" Filologija 9: 7-36

Vončina, Josip (1984) "Joakim Stulli i starija hrvatska leksiko-
    grafija" Filologija 12: 245-263

OPERA NVOVA CHE
INSEGNA A PARLARE LA LINGVA SCHIAVONESCHA ALLI GRANDI ALLI PICOLI ET ALLE DONNE.

ET SIMILMENTE LA DITTA OPERA
Insegna alli Schiauoni A parlare bono et corretto Italiano.

ANCORA LA DITTA OPERA INSEGNA
A legere a chi non sa, et a quelli che sano vno poco legere Lo ditto ammaistramento li sara di molta vtilita, per caxon delle parole et silabe scritte in Schiauonescho

Con Gratia et Priuilegio.

M. D. XXVII.

AFRIKAANS LEXICOGRAPHY

Rufus H. Gouws

Introduction

A review of the history of Afrikaans lexicography has to refer to certain aspects of the history of Afrikaans and the position of Afrikaans
in the Republic of South Africa.

Afrikaans is a young language. Although it primarily developed from
17th century Dutch, the Afrikaans vocabulary accommodates a lot of
words originating from French, German, English, Malay and several native
languages. During the 19th century Afrikaans had to compete with
English when an Anglicisation policy was enforced by the British colonial government. The recognition of Afrikaans as an official language had to wait till the twentieth century. In 1925 Afrikaans became
one of the official languages to be used in the House of Parliament.
Since then Afrikaans and English have been the two official languages
of the R.S.A.

In South Africa Afrikaans has to survive alongside the international
language English. The average South African has a reasonable to good
command of both languages. The South African speech community is
subjected to language contact. This contact situation does not only
have an influence on Afrikaans and English but it also affects
Afrikaans lexicography. Being a young language Afrikaans still has to
be fully accommodated in a dictionary and Afrikaans lexicographers
have to bear the position of Afrikaans in mind.

This paper gives a brief discussion of some of the early lexicographical work and the underlying principles. Attention is also drawn to
the present-day lexicography. Objective definitions and bilingual
dictionaries are discussed. The effects of the two official languages
on bilingual dictionaries and some semantic and morphological aspects
in monolingual dictionaries receive attention.

Early lexicographical work and principles

The earliest lexicographical work in Afrikaans was a list of 400 words,
PROEVE VAN KAAPSCH TAALEIGEN, included in a publication by Changuion in
1848. This 'dictionary' was not aimed at the improvement of Afrikaans,
but at the vindication of Dutch in South Africa. Shortly after this
list several other dictionaries were published, but none of them
reached any high lexicographical standards.

The first major breakthrough came in 1902 with the publication of the
bilingual PATRIOT WOORDEBOEK/DICTIONARY. This dictionary had more or

less 16,500 entries and its editors had a few definite aims with this
publication. It was an attempt to reach spelling uniformity because
Afrikaans had not yet been established as a written language. It was
also an aid for both Afrikaans and English speaking South Africans to
master the other language. This dictionary was published shortly
after the Anglo-Boer War (1899-1902). Its principal aim was not linguistic but cultural and political. In the preface to this dictionary
the authors said they wanted to promote co-operation between English
and Afrikaans speaking South Africans.

The most comprehensive lexicographical project in South Africa was
initiated in 1926 with the establishment of the WOORDEBOEK VAN DIE
AFRIKAANSE TAAL (The Dictionary of the Afrikaans Language) (hereafter
WAT). This overall-descriptive dictionary was also the product of its
circumstances. Because of the incipient lack of other Afrikaans dictionaries and encyclopedias the WAT included more than the usual
amount of non-linguistic and technical information. It also provided
pragmatic information on the usage of its entries. In the course of
time a stronger linguistic approach was to be adopted.

The WAT is a long-term project. Since 1926 seven volumes, from $\underline{A}$ to
korvynael, have been published. But in this time there was a considerable expansion in the Afrikaans dictionary family. A number of
standard dictionaries have been completed and, normative in their
approach, they were immediately aimed at the linguistic needs of the
language community. Meaning discrimination and correct spelling
received precedence. A major shortcoming in these dictionaries is
insufficient information on pronunciation. Although primary stress,
an orthographic respelling in some cases, and syllabification are
indicated, there is a definite need for a phonetic transcription. Only
then the attempted syllabification can be successful because at present
it is only valid in those cases where it coincides with hyphenation.

Due to the work done by the Terminology Bureau as well as some other
contributions there exists a wide range of technical dictionaries today.
The publication of these dictionaries had an influence on the character
and extent of the WAT's entries and led to a more definite linguistic
approach in this comprehensive dictionary.

Objective definitions

For the average language user dictionaries remain an authoritative
source of reference and this attitude compels the lexicographer to be
objective and unbiased in his definitions. A review of Afrikaans
dictionaries confirms a change towards an impartial and objective
definition. This change corresponds with a major shift in the focus
from a cultural to an encyclopedic and pragmatic to a linguistic basis.

The objectivity covers a wide range of areas. It includes religion,
politics and social behaviour. In the first edition of the
VERKLARENDE HANDWOORDEBOEK VAN DIE AFRIKAANSE TAAL (hereafter HAT) the
lemma **doop** (baptise) had the following entry as one of its senses
      "2. Met water besprinkel as simbool van die afwassing van sondes."

(To sprinkle (someone) with water as a symbol of the
purification from sin.)
In the second edition this definition was altered:
  "2. Met water besprinkel of in water dompel ..."
    (To sprinkle someone with water or to immerse someone in
    water ...)
This second definition satisfies more church denominations than the
first one.

In the fifth edition of NASIONALE WOORDEBOEK (hereafter NW) **apostolies**
(apostolic) was defined as
  "2. van, betreffende 'n Wederdopersekte"
    (regarding an Anabaptist sect)
The sixth edition defines this sense as
  "2. van, betreffende 'n Apostoliese kerk"
    (regarding an Apostolic church).
This type of redefining represents definite progress in Afrikaans
lexicography. Similar progress is seen with regard to words with a
derogatory meaning. The best examples of this improvement can be
found in the above-mentioned standard dictionaries and the TWEETALIGE
WOORDEBOEK/BILINGUAL DICTIONARY (hereafter BD).

Although it is an accepted lexicographical practice to define a compound in terms of its components, Afrikaans dictionaries often renounce
this definition type when one of the components is a derogatory word.
Instead an unstigmatised synonym or a paraphrase is given. This is
done in such a way that the syntactic and semantic relations between
the components are still explicated.

NW defines **kafferpot** (kaffirpot) as "1. kleipot deur Swartes
gemaak." (clay pot manufactured by Blacks). This is a definite improvement on the definition given in the WAT: "1. ... kleipot ...
gemaak deur Kaffers ..." (clay pot manufactured by Kaffirs ...).

BD translates the derogatory <u>Koeliewinkel</u> (Coolie store) as "Indian
store (shop)". One of the translation equivalents of <u>koelie</u> is <u>coolie</u>.
<u>Koeliewinkel</u> could have been translated with <u>Coolie store</u>. Then both
source and target language would have had the same derogatory value.
The present translation is not aimed at social equivalence but at a
non-derogatory equivalent. The lexicographer deviates from the
principle of translation equivalents with the same connotation in
favour of a non-offending entry. BD proves its sensitivity regarding
derogatory words by an excellent use of labels to mark these forms.
The extensive application of labels in the present-day Afrikaans
lexicography contributes to the above-mentioned progress.

Bilingual dictionaries

According to Al-Kasimi (1977:1) "Dictionaries have developed not as
theoretical instruments but as practical tools ... Each culture
fosters the development of dictionaries appropriate to its characteristic demands." This also applies to Afrikaans bilingual dictionaries.
The co-existence of two official languages puts its own characteristic
demands on lexicography. Bilingual dictionaries in S.A. can be

divided into two distinct categories: Afrikaans/English dictionaries
and Afrikaans/X dictionaries where X is a language other than English.

This second category includes target languages like German, French,
Italian, Portugese, etc. These dictionaries are aimed at the speakers
of the source language. They are learners' dictionaries for the
benefit of Afrikaans-speaking persons and their entries are typical
examples from the written rather than from the spoken language. The
category Afrikaans/X also includes dictionaries where X is one of the
native African languages, e.g. Zulu, Venda, Northern and Southern
Sotho, Xhosa. Although some of these languages have many speakers,
these dictionaries are primarily learners' dictionaries. This causes
concern and was identified as a major problem at a seminar on the
needs and crucial problems in S.A. lexicography recently hosted by
the Human Sciences Research Council.

Afrikaans/English dictionaries dominate the scene of bilingual lexicography and the history of this section of Afrikaans lexicography prod-
uces more than enough proof of a sound linguistic development.

Where the PATRIOT WOORDEBOEK/DICTIONARY fostered the relations between
the speakers of Afrikaans and English, dictionaries like BD try to
serve both languages on an equal basis. According to Al-Kasimi
(1977:21) it is impossible to serve the speakers of both languages
equally in one dictionary. In earlier bilingual dictionaries preference was given to Afrikaans. But this has changed. The average South
African has a reasonable knowledge of both Afrikaans and English.
Al-Kasimi (1977:21) wants the lexicographer to decide from the very
beginning whether X-speakers or Y-speakers are going to use his dictionary. This decision will determine the way in which he compiles his
dictionary. Contrary to this view it is not possible for the lexicographer of an Afrikaans/English dictionary to ascertain beforehand
whether the majority of his users will be English or Afrikaans.
Thanks to the development in Afrikaans lexicography the bilingual
dictionaries, with BD the superior member of this class, became authoritative sources of reference for speakers of both languages.

Accommodating two official languages a dictionary has to give more
than just a translation equivalent. Where the earlier bilingual dictionaries sufficed with a few translation equivalents the present-day
dictionaries give an adequate treatment of lexical semantics by providing a profound exposition of e.g. polysemy and synonymy. Equivalents
for the different polysemous senses of a lemma are provided with the
necessary context to eliminate the other polysemous senses.

In an attempt to serve the speakers of both languages, bilingual dictionaries utilise the reversibility principle better than their earlier
counterparts did. Previously one often found that a translation
equivalent did not appear as a lemma in the other half of the dictionary. This may be permissible if the dictionary is written for the
speaker of the source language but not if both languages are supposed
to have equal treatment. The application of the reversibility principle has significance where there is no direct equivalent for a lemma.

The lexicographer of a bilingual dictionary must be able to cope with
lexical gaps that may exist in either of the languages. Afrikaans,
for example, has no direct equivalent for pup(py). It takes no major
lexicographical effort to give a description as klein of jong hondjie
(small or young dog) as an equivalent. However, according to the
reversibility principle pup(py) must also be included as a translation
equivalent. In the entry for hond (dog) there has to be room for
jong - : pup(py) (young -). The correct application of this principle
is one of the results of attention given to bilingual lexicography in
S.A.

Bilingual dictionaries lack sufficient information about pronunciation.
Only an indication of the main stress is given. This needs rectific-
ation because Afrikaans and English show major pronunciation differences even with regard to words with the same spelling and meaning,
e.g.

	English	Afrikaans
hand	[hænd]	[hant]
in	[in]	[ən]
water	[wɔter]	[vAtər]

Common cultural values of Afrikaans and English speaking South Africans
lead to a more comprehensive vocabulary of the speakers' second language being either Afrikaans or English. This results in an extended
collection of dictionary entries. The entries substantiate the view
that Afrikaans/English bilingual dictionaries expanded to something
more than learners' dictionaries. Bilingual dictionaries also give
evidence of the bilateral influence of Afrikaans and English on each
other. Where earlier lexicographers avoided the inclusion of loanwords the present-day bilingual dictionaries reflect the reality of
the co-existence of Afrikaans and English by including the results of
the languages in contact.

Monolingual dictionaries

This section of the paper deals with the WAT as overall-descriptive
dictionary and HAT and NW as standard dictionaries. Attention is
drawn to semantic and morphological aspects.

Meaning discrimination is of vital importance in a monolingual dictionary because meaning is the type of information most commonly looked
for in a dictionary. Therefore a lexicographer needs a sound semantic
training. Afrikaans dictionaries could not always produce proof of
the necessary semantic input and this evoked severe criticism. This
criticism has often been directed at the failure to distinguish between meaning and non-meaning.

As mentioned earlier the WAT was initially more than just a dictionary;
it was a source of technical reference and often used as encyclopedia.
This is clearly stated by a previous editor, P. C. Schoonees, regard-

ing WAT III: "The farmer can obtain reliable facts about his farm
animals, plants and trees, the housewife about food and clothes, the
stampcollector about his postage stamps, the student in mathematics,
zoology, geology, etc. also his technical terms" (Schoonees 1958:110).
The WAT was dominated by a utility principle. This approach was also
adapted by Snijman who succeeded Schoonees. At this stage there was
no need for such a policy because terminology lists and encyclopedias
had already been published.

The domination of encyclopedic detail decreased the WAT's linguistic
status and threw doubt upon the lexicographers' semantic competence.
Especially in Volumes five and six of the WAT little distinction is
made between meaning and usage. The knowledge and application of
componential analysis would have rendered a far better product because
of the necessary discrimination between meaning, usage and encyclopedic
detail that must be excluded from a definition where meaning is
superior.

This encyclopedic approach was not only detrimental to the WAT but it
also had a backlash in the standard dictionaries which resulted in an
insufficient account of semantic information there. Contrary to the
WAT the standard dictionaries tried to give as little information as
possible in an attempt to avoid the much disapproved encyclopedic
trap. NW defines geelbek (Cape salmon) as: "soort vis" (a kind of
fish). This definition applies equally unsatisfactorily to any other
fish. Yet, the lack of sound meaning description was less obvious in
the standard dictionaries than in the WAT.

Another reason for the early volumes of the WAT's poor semantic performance could be attributed to a lack of interest among other linguists in theoretical lexicography and insufficient training opportun-
ities for lexicographers. But this position has changed. A number of
prominent linguists are working actively in the field of theoretical
lexicography and several universities offer postgraduate courses in
lexicography.

This interest in theoretical lexicography resulted in a few pungent
academic reviews of WAT VI. The criticism of WAT VI contributed to a
reformulation of the WAT's policy.

In May 1981 Dr. Snijman was succeeded by Mr. D. C. Hauptfleisch as
editor in chief and in the new editorial policy it has been made clear
that meaning discrimination will be prominent in the future volumes of
the WAT.

Compounds in monolingual dictionaries

As in German and Dutch the vocabulary of Afrikaans includes many compounds. According to the editorial policies of the leading monolingual
dictionaries not all compounds have to be included in the dictionary.
The meaning of many compounds can be obtained by combining the senses
of their components. Where such self-explaining compounds are included,
they are not provided with definitions but only entered in list form.

In Afrikaans this principle was first formulated by the WAT but a
number of standard dictionaries also apply the same method. Although
it is an accepted lexicographical method its application in Afrikaans
dictionaries has not always been plausible. This is to a large extent
due to the above-mentioned semantic insufficiency.

The history of Afrikaans lexicography shows that there has been a
change in the approach towards these 'self-explaining' undefined
compounds.

Formally the WAT still has the same approach to these compounds. In
Volumes I and VII it is stated that the meaning of these compounds can
be easily derived. The unexplained compounds are contrasted with those
that are defined. The meaning of those explained compounds are not
easily derived from the senses of the different components.

This view is stated in the preface of the WAT and compels the lexicographer not only to maintain this principle but also to abide by its
semantic implications. The HAT uses the same system without explaining it. It is stated in the preface that HAT has been compiled in
accordance with the principles followed in the WAT.

From a semantic point of view the treatment of unexplained compounds
in the WAT and HAT is disappointing. The stated principle leads to
major problems for both explained and unexplained compounds. In many
cases there is no difference in the transparency of meaning between
these two types of compounds. Many examples prove a higher degree of
intransparency among the unexplained compounds than among their explained counterparts. The WAT has an unexplained lemma **kiemomstandigheid** (germcircumstance (?)) but it explains the lemma **kiemvry** (germ-
free) as "free of germs". Kiemvry is a self-explaining compound;
kiemomstandigheid by no means. This type of problem is illustrated by
a lot of examples proving the semantic insufficiency. In a number of
these examples the same syntactic relation holds between the components of the explained as well as the unexplained compounds. Yet,
they are treated differently.

Afrikaans dictionaries display a thorough treatment of polysemy. But
polysemy does not only concern a lexical item's occurrence as simplex.
It is of the same importance for that item's occurrence as component
of a compound.

In a dictionary a polysemous word must be described in such a manner
that it can be disambiguated in a given context. The lexicographer
has to treat a polysemous component of a compound in the same way. A
compound with one or more polysemous components may not be entered
unexplained if the dictionary states that unexplained compounds have
no semantic problems because of their transparency.

The word ketting (chain) has seven polysemous senses in the WAT. A
number of unexplained compounds with ketting as the first component
are listed. No indication is given as to which sense of ketting is
applicable in each compound. The lexicographer has to give the

necessary disambiguating guidance.

Progress has been made. NW did not fall into the same trap. This
dictionary clearly states which sense applies when there are polysemous components. The lemma **poeier** (powder) has two senses. The unexplained compounds are marked for the applicable sense: "poeiermelk,
-suiker (by 1); -doos, -kwas (by 2)". With some adjustments a
higher degree of lexicographical practice is imminent. A review of
Afrikaans lexicography shows that the progress that has been made
must be expanded to other dictionaries.

In its preface the NW explains its treatment of unexplained compounds.
This treatment gives evidence of an important new approach to this
type of entry. This approach has actually already been put into practice by the leading Afrikaans dictionaries although they have not
stated it explicitly. NW says that these compounds are listed to show
that they are part of the lexicon and to help with spelling problems.
In a few instances reference is made to semantic problems. With
regard to unexplained compounds this indicates a shift away from
semantics as the basis for inclusion.

A review of the WAT's entries shows a definite increase in the amount
of unexplained compounds. WAT VII contains 10,000 explained and 3,000
unexplained entries. According to Hauptfleisch (personal communication) the WAT includes unexplained compounds mainly for two reasons.
By including these words the dictionary gives evidence of their existence but it also includes these words to indicate the combinatorial
valence of the lexical item as the first component in a compound.
This approach indicates a shift from semantics (as stated in the WAT's
preface) to morphology and this is a positive development in the
history of the WAT.

Unexplained compounds included merely because of their semantic transparency should be omitted. Where there are spelling difficulties the
compounds may be included.

Afrikaans compounds quite often contain link phonemes, for example
werk + bevrediging = werksbevrediging (job satisfaction). Some components in a compound demand a link phoneme while other components
reject such a link phoneme. In some compounds these link phonemes are
optional. With regard to link phonemes the inclusion of unexplained
compounds is important. It gives valuable linguistic information because the occurrence of the link phoneme is not systematically predictable (Botha 1968:183). Morphologically the link phoneme constitutes part of the preceding component. Initially the WAT's unexplained
compounds gave implicit evidence to the contrary: atoomgewig ...
sbepaling, skaal (atomic weight, determining, scale); asemhaling ...
sbelemmering, sgeluid, smoeilikheid, sproses (breathing ... impediment,
sound, trouble, process); beuk ... ebas, eblaar, eboom (beech ... bark,
leaf, tree). However, in later volumes this was rectified and this
improvement leads to sound linguistic guidance: kontrakteurs bedryf,
firma (contracting industry, firm).

Conclusion

The history of Afrikaans lexicography reflects the growth of the
language and the awakening and expansion of a linguistic approach
towards dictionaries, in spite of a number of misconceptions and
errors which need to be rectified. Encouraging progress has been
made to substantiate these dictionaries as authoritative sources of
reference.

References

Cited dictionaries (see Appendix):

NASIONALE WOORDEBOEK (De Villiers et al.)
PATRIOT WOORDEBOEK/DICTIONARY ... (Du Toit)
PROEVE VAN KAAPSCH TAALEIGEN (in Changuion)
TWEETALIGE WOORDEBOEK/BILINGUAL DICTIONARY (Bosman et al.)
VERKLARENDE HANDWOORDEBOEK VAN DIE AFRIKAANSE TAAL (Schoonees/
    Odendal et al.)
WOORDEBOEK VAN DIE AFRIKAANSE TAAL (Schoonees/Snijman/Hauptfleisch)

Other literature:

Al-Kasimi, Ali M. (1977) Linguistics and Bilingual Dictionaries.
    Leiden: E.J. Brill
Botha, Rudolf P. (1968) The Function of the Lexicon in Transform-
    ational Generative Grammar. The Hague: Mouton
Changuion, Anthoni N.E. (1848) De Nederduitsche taal in Zuid-Afrika
    hersteld. Rotterdam: J. van der Vliet
Schoonees, P.C. (1958) Rondom die Woordeboek. Kaapstad: Nasionale
    Boekhandel

THE 'DUDEN RECHTSCHREIBUNG' 1880-1986:

DEVELOPMENT AND FUNCTION OF A POPULAR DICTIONARY

Glyn Hatherall

My justification for presenting the DUDEN RECHTSCHREIBUNG (DR
or DUDEN) at this conference is firstly that it appeared to me to be
a dictionary model specific to the German-speaking world but worthy
of evaluation as a potential tool for other dictionary-using
language communities, and secondly that its longevity (nineteen
editions since 1880 and still going strong) was of interest to the
historical lexicographer in its own right. I see the DUDEN,
controversially, as a serious alternative model for a general one-
volume desk dictionary for native-speakers of languages other than
German, and, non-controversially, as a rich digging-ground for the
'lexicographic archaeologist' in Robert Ilson's sense (this volume).
A comparison of monolingual French and German dictionaries (Hausmann 1983:134) concluded: "Es ist immer wieder überraschend festzu-
stellen, wie wenig die Wörterbuchmacher und -forscher der einzelnen
Länder über die Wörterbücher anderer Sprachen wissen...Erst der
europäisch-amerikanische Blick auf die ganze Wörterbuchvielfalt des
Abendlandes in Geschichte und Gegenwart, einsprachig wie zweisprach-
ig, wird uns lehren, das Phänomen Wörterbuch richtig einzuschätzen."
This paper is a small but hopefully productive contribution to such
enlightenment. (During the conference two interesting parallels
with the tradition the paper describes were pointed out: the treatment of 'transparent' compounds in Afrikaans dictionaries, as out-
lined in Gouws's contribution to this volume, and a dictionary-
using tradition in Poland, noted in discussion by Piotrowski, that
is very similar to and probably copied from the German one.)

In connection with the paper's first justification above, an
important, if unoriginal, claim is made that, where dictionaries are
involved, the theoretician, however valuable as a potential source
of innovatory ideas, must be subservient to the user. An intellect-
ually satisfying construct that generates dictionary entries which
only other lexicographers read and appreciate is not wholly convinc-
ing. Popular dictionaries in particular which fall outside the
prevailing paradigm(s) may have a very useful therapeutic function
to perform. It is well worth asking, for example, how an 'unortho-
dox' dictionary such as CHAMBERS TWENTIETH CENTURY DICTIONARY
satisfies its many supporters in the market place. It does not, for
instance, do this by including seventy-three lines of information on
the English definite article such as are offered within the pages of
the CONCISE OXFORD DICTIONARY (1976). A 'standard' dictionary for
native-speakers is in my experience judged by 'normal' users not on
how exhaustively common words are treated but on whether or not the
desired low-frequency items are to be found within it. Fast access

to brief (and comprehensible) information on what a word (roughly)
means, or even on no more than how it is spelt, is arguably what
most native-speaker users most frequently want. Robert Ilson, elsewhere in this volume, comments on abridged dictionaries thus: "The
first question in producing an abridgment is deciding what to leave
out. Nowadays the choice is almost always to leave out the hard
words, though lexicographers have protested (tirelessly but fruitlessly) that the result is a small dictionary that tells us only
what we already know, not what we need to look up." The definite
article entries in the most successful of German dictionaries, the
DUDEN (latest edition), contrast markedly with the equivalent entry
in the CONCISE OXFORD. Note in particular that only the das entry
contains any contextual/usage information. 'R66' is a cross-
reference to a spelling rule in the introductory section of the
dictionary:

| das; ↑ R 66 (*Nom. u. Akk.*); vgl. der; alles das, was ich gesagt ha- be | der (↑ R 66), die (vgl. d.), das (vgl. d.); des u. dessen (vgl. d.), dem, den; *Plur.* die, der, deren u. derer (vgl. d.), den u. denen, die | die (↑ R 66); *Gen.* der u. deren (vgl. d.); *Plur.* vgl. der |

Whatever else it now contains, the Rechtschreibe-DUDEN is in
origin first and foremost a spelling dictionary, and this primary
function has been documented in its changing titles: 1880-1905 (1st
to 8th editions) = ORTHOGRAPHISCHES WÖRTERBUCH DER DEUTSCHEN SPRACHE
(the designation VOLLSTÄNDIG (complete) was dropped after the sixth
edition); 1915-1986 (9th to 19th editions) = DUDEN RECHTSCHREIBUNG
DER DEUTSCHEN SPRACHE UND DER FREMDWÖRTER; since 1957 in East
Germany = DER GROSSE DUDEN, WÖRTERBUCH UND LEITFADEN DER DEUTSCHEN
RECHTSCHREIBUNG. Each edition has contained a preface or, in East
Germany, an appendix listing mostly spelling rules, and since 1941
individual entries have been cross-referenced, where the compilers
have deemed this potentially useful, with the rules section. This
section can attract considerable attention from reviewers (e.g.
Standop 1982), public debate about spelling and indeed spelling
reform in the German-speaking countries being active and on-going
(Drewitz/ Reuter 1974; Nerius/ Scharnhorst 1980; Küppers 1984). The
prefaces of popular British dictionaries, on the other hand, make
cursory reference to orthography: acceptable alternative spellings
might be mentioned, and perhaps deviant American spelling behaviour.
It is 'meanings', 'definitions', 'explanations' and, in varying
quantities, 'usage' that English general dictionaries declare themselves to be primarily about - which is not, of course, to say that
these dictionaries, too, are not used for spelling information more
often than for anything else.

It is ironic that, although overall German spelling is more
predictable than e.g. English or French, tolerance of deviations
from the norm is less widespread in Germany than in Britain or
France (Petitjean 1985). Certainly, application of the 'phonemic
principle' by German schoolchildren (for whom a good performance in
dictation exercises constitutes an important yardstick of educational
attainment) will help them to get a lot of German words right, but
an admixture of other principles (Keller 1978:543) ensures that mistakes are made. Foreign borrowings, too, cause problems when they
are not fully integrated into the German (largely phonemic) spelling
system (cf. der Streik :[ʃtʀaɪk] but die Pipeline :['paɪplaɪn]),

and idiosyncratic and complicated capitalisation rules provide
another incentive for Germans to consult a dictionary for spelling
information.

It might also be argued that definitions are less important, in
quantitative terms, in German than in English dictionaries, resulting partly from the fact that compounding of high-frequency elements
(e.g. an-, auf-, durch-, mit-, nach-, zu- + machen) usually
renders meanings 'obvious'. Germans certainly do not normally need to
look up such items as allwissend (omniscient) or Kinderarzt (paed-
iatrician); however, not all such compounds reveal their meaning that
readily, and foreign borrowings are not always calqued as per 'Fern-
sehen' (television). Even when they are, the opaque 'foreign' form
may persist beside the (often less popular) transparent calque (cf.
Telefon / Fernsprecher , Fragment / Bruchstück , äquivalent /
gleichwertig , Diphthong / Zwielaut , or indeed Orthographie /
Rechtschreibung). Spelling information in the DUDENs has therefore
increasingly been supplemented with definitions, albeit very select-
ively (see below for examples from the 1986 DR).

Politics interacts with language development in the birth of
the first DUDEN (1880), and the late date for the emergence of a
popular and authoritative German dictionary points to a political/
linguistic situation that again contrasts strongly with the situation in England and France.   Before 1871 and the founding of the
German Empire, the equivalent area had consisted of a remarkable, if
steadily decreasing number of more or less independent states, a few
of them large (e.g. Prussia, Bavaria), many of them small (e.g.
Mecklenburg-Strelitz). Linguistic norms were therefore slow to
emerge. It might even be argued that the German particularist, or
at least 'pluricentric' (Kloss 1978:66), tradition is reflected in
the fact that West Germany today, as a federation, has no central
Ministry of Education. (However, on matters of common concern agreement is sometimes sought between the education ministers of the
federal states ('Länder'): in 1955, for instance, they jointly
declared the DR arbiter in matters of German spelling, and occasionally since then, as indeed regularly before World War II, the DR
has used the term 'amtlich' (official) in its sub-titles, e.g.
"Auf der Grundlage der amtlichen Rechtschreibregeln" (1986).)

In the first half of the nineteenth century there were, "auf
deutschem Boden", no generally 'valid' guidelines on matters of
spelling, either within the individual states or even within
individual schools, where until the appearance of spelling rulebooks (the Kingdom of Hanover led the way in 1855 (Grebe 1968:11))
each individual teacher might be free to make his own selection
from a variety of current spellings. Nevertheless, in spite of the
political fragmentation, movement towards recognised spelling norms
was taking place, an important contribution coming from Johann
Christoph Adelung, a linguistician and lexicographer whose publications included a VOLLSTÄNDIGE ANWEISUNG ZUR DEUTSCHEN
ORTHOGRAPHIE NEBST EINEM KLEINEN WÖRTERBUCH FÜR DIE AUSSPRACHE,
ORTHOGRAPHIE, BIEGUNG UND ABLEITUNG (1788). Subsequently, however,
the impressive achievements of German historical linguistics during

the Romantic period led ironically to new insecurity on the spelling
front; the search for cultural identity in a common past, prior to
achieving political unity, began to tear the German-speaking
'nation' orthographically apart. Jacob Grimm advocated, in the
cause of German scholarship, a spelling system consonant with the
historical development of words rather than with their current
pronunciation: "In der grammatik habe ich dargestellt, wie unrichtig,
barbarisch und schimpflich die heutige schreibung ist, es wäre fast
allen übelständen abgeholfen, wenn sich, in der hauptsache, zu dem
mittelhochdeutschen brauch zurückkehren ließe, wodurch auch die
scheidewand zwischen gegenwart und vorzeit weggerissen und das
lebendige studium unseres alterthums unsäglich gefördert würde"
(1849) (Grebe 1968:10). Grimm's rejection of upper-case letters was
also a return to the Middle High German past. Operation of what
came to be called the 'historical principle' for spelling would have
required e.g. Mand for Mond (Middle High German mān(e)) and
Leffel for Löffel (Middle High German leffel) regardless of
the fact that the more modern spellings gave a clearer indication
of current pronunciation (Wurzel 1979:57).

    Significantly, Konrad Duden's first publication on the subject
of spelling was produced for his school in Schleiz in Thuringia in
1871. It was contained in his, the headmaster's, annual report.
His second, a more ambitious publication, was published by Teubner
in Leipzig in 1872 under the title: Die deutsche Rechtschreibung –
Abhandlung, Regeln und Wörterverzeichnis mit etymologischen Angaben.
Für die oberen Klassen höherer Lehranstalten und zur Selbstbelehrung
für Gebildete. The recent achievements of German historical linguistics are acknowledged in this publication (the "Schleizer DUDEN")
in the prominence given to etymology; subsequent DUDENs are not
totally devoid of basic etymological information such as language of
origin for more recent foreign borrowings (see below), but they no
longer seek to improve the educated in matters etymological. Unlike
the proponents of the historical principle (these were dubbed the
"Leffel-Partei"), Duden, as a practising teacher, was wedded to the
concept of spelling reform according to the, for learners more
manageable and therefore more democratic, 'phonemic principle'. The
most distinguished upholder of the "Schreibe, wie du sprichst!"
approach was the Erlangen Germanist, Rudolf von Raumer, and it was
Raumer's work which inspired the first "Orthographische Konferenz",
called by the Prussian Minister of Education, Falk, in Berlin in
1876, five years after the Empire had been founded. Although the
participants, among whom was Konrad Duden, considered their suggestions for spelling reform to be "das Minimum...das den Schulen und
durch die Schulen dem Volke...geboten werden kann" (Duden 1876), the
proposals were not accepted, the most notable opponent being the
Prussian Chancellor, Bismarck. Lacking a general agreement on
spelling norms for the whole of Germany, many of the larger
states (but also Mecklenburg-Strelitz) issued or continued to issue
their own guidelines for school use. Since Prussia, however, was
the mainspring of the Empire it was almost inevitable that the
Prussian rulebook (the work of Wilhelm Wilmanns) should become the
basis for the first DUDEN proper (1880). This aimed at a greater

degree of explicitness than either the Prussian or Bavarian rulebooks
which it closely followed, in order to provide not only the schools
but also the general public with a much-needed guide to German orthography. After a second "Orthographische Konferenz" in Berlin in
1901, proposals for common spelling norms and limited spelling
reform were accepted by all the German and German-speaking states,
and in 1902 the seventh edition of Duden's ORTHOGRAPHISCHES WÖRTER-
BUCH appeared, incorporating the agreed changes and establishing
'the' DUDEN as the popular and apparently unassailable authority it
remains today (Veith 1985).

The first twelve editions (1880-1941) were published in Leipzig
(the second edition was only a reprint). The thirteenth edition was
printed under licence in Austria, Switzerland, West Germany (Wiesbaden 1947) and East Germany (Leipzig 1949: "ein leicht überarbeitet-
er Nachdruck"). All subsequent editions have appeared either in
Leipzig or in Mannheim, and although the shared heritage is plain to
see, Mannheim and Leipzig editions have differed significantly from
each other since 1954, stemming as they do from different publishers,
different editorial boards, and different "Gesellschaftssystemen".
The DUDEN publisher in Leipzig in the German Democratic Republic is
today a nationalised concern ("Volkseigener Betrieb"), the
publisher in Mannheim in the Federal Republic of Germany, on the
other hand, is a joint stock company ("Aktiengesellschaft") - which
is one reason why eyebrows were raised when the Federal German Post
Office provided the Mannheim Institute with a free advertisement in
1980, DUDEN's centenary year, in the form of a postage stamp (see
below). In 1985 Leipzig issued an eighteenth edition, in 1986
Mannheim a nineteenth.

There follows a brief look at some of the features of the DR as
illustrated by the entries listed under the head-words **W** to **Wanze**
over the many editions from 1880 to 1986, Mannheim lineage only.
Here I ignore spelling features and look at ways of comparison which
are potentially of interest not only to Germanists but also to
lexicographers in general.

By focusing not on the whole dictionary but on a limited section
it is still possible to obtain a fairly accurate measure of growth
in the quantity of information listed. The aforesaid postage-stamp
is, to my knowledge, the first to indulge in 'lexicographic archaeology', reproducing parallel texts from the 1880 and 1980 editions:

The equivalent section which starts in 1880 with **Thal** and finishes
with 'thätig' (left-hand column above) covers 476 lines in the 1986

DUDEN1   In 1986 between **Tat** and **tatenlos** fourteen items intervene
(**That** and **thatenlos** are adjacent in 1880). The following
diagram, based on the **W** to **Wanze** word-stock, gives an edition-
by-edition indication of growth using two different measures. The
broken line indicates the increase in words in absolute terms, revealing a steady increase until 1905 and a spectacular increase in
1915. Duden died in 1911 but was still largely responsible for the
1915 edition which amalgamated the standard DUDEN with his so-called
"Buchdruckerduden", an edition specially designed for the printing
trade and containing, among other things, many more proper names
than the standard DUDENs before it (Wurzel 1979:76). On the
evidence of the figures below there was a quite significant drop in
the number of entries in the first DR published after World War II,
and possibly also a drop in the overall number of words listed in
1980. The baseline of 0 constituted in fact about 140 entries in
1880, the latest (1986) Mannheim figure being about 610 (the latest
Leipzig figure (1985) is about 330). The other method indicated of
comparing quantity is the non-cumulative one (unbroken line). Here
each edition is compared only with the previous one (figures in
parenthesis show overall gain or loss in word-stock). Such a
comparison clearly shows that some editions constitute much more
substantial revisions than others, and on this basis the editions of
1915, 1954 and 1973 were particularly good buys:

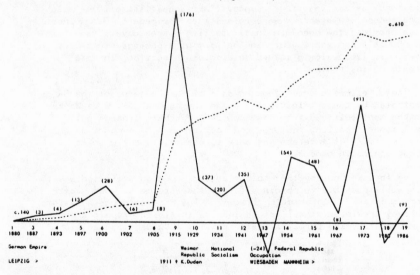

Additions to the corpus across all the DUDEN editions cannot
be handled here even on the small scale of the sample chosen.
Additions are , however, what most DR reviewers, usually unsystemat-
ically, look for above all in new editions. The total list, 1986
only, for the section in question is given below and I have included
all additional information listed other than genders and inflections.
It will be noted that there are some definitions, some style labels,

some usage/register markers, and one indication of language of
origin, in other words much more than might be expected in a spelling dictionary as such (see Kühn/ Püschel 1982 for the strength of
users' views on this point):

    wachstumsfördernd
    Wackelpudding (ugs.)
    Wafer <eng.> (kleine runde Scheibe für die Herstellung von Mikro-
    Waffenlager   chips)
    Wahlbenachrichtigung
    Wahlhelfer
    Wahlparty
    Wählton (beim Telefon)
    Wahnsinnstat
    Wahrheitsfindung (bes. Rechtsspr.)
    Wahrheitsgehalt
    Währungsreserven
    Währungsschlange (Verbund der Währungen der EG-Staaten zur
    Waldohreule   Begrenzung der Wechselkursschwankungen)
    Waldorfsalat (Gastr.)
    Waldsterben
    Waldvögelein (eine Orchidee)
    Walkman (Wz) (kleiner Kassettenrecorder mit Kopfhörern)
    Wandelung (bes. Rechtsspr.)
    Wanderweg
    Wandteller

    Rather less attention is generally paid by reviewers to items
omitted. Until the eighth edition in 1905, in the section under
consideration there were no omissions, only additions. Notable in
the following specimen list from the eighth to the eleventh editions
are not only the disappearances but also the reappearances:

    out 1905 Waldloch (After des Wildes) - in since 1897
        1915 wachsam - in since 1880, back 1934 et seq.
              wahrscheinlich - in since 1880, back 1934 et seq.
        1929 Wahuma (Volk)   ⎫
              Wajao (Volk)   ⎪
              Wakuafi (Volk)   ⎬ in since 1915
              Wanjamwesi (Volk) ⎭
              Wallrafmuseum, Wallraf-Richartzmuseum - in since 1915
        1934 wahn - in since 1887
              Waisengericht - in since 1915, out 1934, in 1954, out
              (+ thirteen other items)   1986

Overall in the sample the record for instability is held by **Wäh-
rungspolitik** and **Wandschrank**, both of which have an in-out-in-
out-in pattern, the latter achieving this over no more than seven
editions: in 1934, out 1947, in 1954, out 1967, in 1973 et seq. (the
former requires nine: 1929 to 1980). Especially ephemeral items (in
one edition, out the next, like the "Völker" above) could of course
constitute a study on their own, but the slower demise of an item
has the advantage of sometimes being documentable by an interesting
sequence of glosses from within the dictionary itself, as with:

         wahn (adj.)
    1880 Ø
    1887 ziemlich veraltet
    1893 ziemlich veraltet   ⎫
    1897   fast veraltet   ⎬ leer,
    1900   fast veraltet   ⎪ unverständig
    1902   fast veraltet   ⎭
    1915   veraltet, noch mundartlich ⎫ leer,
    1929   veraltet, noch südhannov. ⎬ fehlerhaft,
    1934 Ø   ⎭ unverständig

From the 1986 DUDEN (W to **Wanzenvertilgungsmittel**)   the following
items were omitted:

entered 1961	Wagehalsigkeit
1941	Wahrscheinlichkeitsbeweis
1973	Währungskonferenz
1954	Währungsschnitt
1961	Währungsstabilität
1915	Waisengericht
1915	waldaus
1961	Waldbestand
1954	Wandbewurf
1880	wanstig
1934	Wanzenvertilgung

As every learner of the language knows, compounds in German are
both common and initially daunting. They have, however, a useful
spin-off effect on the amount and kind of linguistic information
that German dictionaries 'automatically' provide: such compounds
equate in English terms with certain categories of collocational
or usage information. In the section under consideration here,
there have been since 1880 no less than sixty-two different wahl-/
Wahl- compounds listed in the DR, forty-two of which have appeared
since 1954: the 1986 Mannheim DUDEN has fifty-two, the 1985 Leipzig
DUDEN eighteen.   It is intriguing to attempt to relate changes in
word-stock to changes in social conditions/structures: why, for
instance, did Wahllokal (polling-station) appear in 1915, then
disappear for five editions until 1961, or Wahlzelle (polling-
booth) appear in 1934 and disappear after 1973 (it is still the
official term in Federal Electoral Law, although Wahlkabine is the
only version attested in the Frequenzwörterbuch der deutschen
Zeitungssprache (Rosengren 1977)?   Whether any clear correlation
between the number of Waffen- (weapons, armaments) compounds listed and military activity, either current or pending, can be established is a moot point: the following, however, gives a possible
presentation of the DUDEN data for further deliberation:

	1880	1887	1893	1897	1900	1902	1905	1915	1929	1934	1941	1947	1954	1961	1967*	1973*	1980*	1986*	Leipzig	1957	1967	1976	1985
Waffe	+	+	+	+	+	+	+	+	+	+	+	+	+	+	+	+	+	+		+	+	+	+
Waffenschau	+	+	+	+	+	+	+	+															
-stillstand	+	+	+	+	+	+	+	+	+	+	+	+	+							+	+	+	+
-platz							+	+		+	+	+	+	+	+	+	+			+	+	+	+
-tanz								+	+	+	+	+	+	+	+	+							
-übung							+	+	+														
-fähig							+	+	+	+	+	+	+	+	+	+				+	+	+	
-gang									+	+		+	+	+	+	+							
-gattung									+		+	+	+	+	+	+							
-meister									+														
-gewalt													+	+	+	+	+						
-kammer													+	+	+	+							
-recht													+	+									
-rock													+	+									
-ruhe													+	+		+	+	+					
-saal													+	+									
-student													+	+	+								
-muster													+	+									
-bruderschaft													+										
waffenlos													+		+	+	+						
Waffenschein													+		+	+	+						
-schmied													+	+	+	+							
-system														+	+	+	+						
-besitz															+	+	+						
-bruder															+	+	+						
-brüderschaft															+	+	+						
-lieferung															+	+	+						
-stillstandslinie															+	+	+						
-lager																		+					

(* = + 'atomare, konventionelle, nukleare Waffen')

In addition to the collocational information of the kind
indicated above, for a limited number of entries the DUDENs have
long since provided brief but typical contextual information. In
the 1986 DR, in the chosen sample, the number of such entries is
fifteen, viz.:

W, w	wachrufen	während
wabbeln	wachrütteln	wahrhaben
wach	wackelig	wällen
Wache	wäg	walten
wachhalten	wahr (vs. war)	Wank

Two examples of contextual information are:

wabbeln (ugs. für: hin u.
her wackeln); der Pudding wab-
belt

wallten (gebieten; sich sorgend einer Sache annehmen); Gnade ·
lassen; (↑R 68:) das Walten der
Naturgesetze

Finally, as the changing entries for **wahn** indicated, it is
possible in the DUDENs to observe definitions moving with the
times. From 1929 to 1961 **Wahnfried** is defined as 'Wagners Heim in
Bayreuth'; in 1967 the Heim becomes a Haus , something more than
a stylistic shift, as is that contained in the definition of
Wallach (gelding) which in 1880 was given as 'Pferd', from 1887 to
1973 (and by Leipzig still thus) as 'verschnittener Hengst', but
since 1980 (Mannheim only) as 'kastrierter Hengst'. On a political
note I cannot but applaud the West Germans for the use of Groß-
britannien in the following, where the East Germans, clearly less
attuned to Celtic sensitivities, sing the old misleading song:

Wales	1880-1915	Land
	1929	westengl. Halbinsel
	1934-1941	südwestengl. Halbinsel
	1947	Halbinsel und Fürstentum in Südwestengland
	1954-1967	südwestengl. Halbinsel
	1973-	Halbinsel im Westen der Insel Großbritannien

but Leipzig 1985: Halbinsel im Westen Englands

It would be remiss of me not to mention here in passing that
comparisons of Mannheim and Leipzig post-1947 DUDENs have provided
much data for discussions of, among other things, a putative East-
West German language divide (Hellmann 1984). A comparison of W to
Wanze (Leipzig 1985 and Mannheim 1986) is, however, more revealing
for the similarities than the differences, at least in terms of the
Leipzig stock as listed in the Mannheim edition (the latter contains
very much more). One of the few Leipzig items in this section that is
not in the Mannheim word-stock is, significantly but not alarmingly,
Waldaihöhen(n) (im W der UdSSR); and **Wallstreet**, notably and
predictably, is seen in differing lights:

Wallstreet ['ɔːlstriːt] die; - (ame-
rik.) (Geschäftsstraße in New
York [Bankzentrum]; übertr. für:
Geld- u. Kapitalmarkt der USA)

Wall|street ['wɔːlstriːt], die, - (die
Finanzoligarchie der USA) (nach
der Straße in New York)

I have sought to demonstrate that the DUDEN RECHTSCHREIBUNG is a
dictionary of special interest for two reasons. Firstly, its numerous
editions from 1880 onwards provide a wealth of data on aspects of the
development of modern German. Secondly, the DR is an interesting
model for other dictionary-using cultures because it appears to
satisfy the general needs of a linguistic community in a succinct
and manageable form by omitting, or rather not including, a

considerable amount of linguistic information that is part and
parcel of the average native speaker's competence and therefore
deemed, under normal dictionary-using circumstances, not to require
checking in a book (Kühn/ Püschel 1982:14). The DR can be seen as
a 'bottom-up' rather than 'top-down' dictionary: it provides an
enormous word-stock for its size, with, as a baseline, spelling
information and thereafter other categories of information depend-
ing on perceived user demand. It is partly compiler intuition
that perceives which items the user is likely to need or to need
additional assistance with, but user demand is also established via
data resulting from a free answering service on linguistic
questions relating to German that the Bibliographisches Institut
in Mannheim provides (Müller 1968).

On the whole, it has to be said, German academic commentators
on lexicography are reluctant to bestow plaudits on the dictionary in
question: "ein Buch, das, von der Orthographie abgesehen, nicht mehr
ist als ein Mini-Wörterbuch der 'schweren Wörter'" (Hausmann 1983:
20); "das zwergwüchsig-autoritative Wörterbuch" (Weinrich 1976);
"hauptsächlich ein Vorzimmer-Requisit. Er ist nicht so sehr ein
Buch als vielmehr ein Gerät und gehört zur Büroaustattung wie die
Schreibmaschine und das Diktiergerät" (Weinrich 1985). What under
other circumstances might be viewed as positive statements tend to
lose their strength in the context of lamentations over the lack in
the German 'dictionary-landscape' of standard vegetation such as the
one-volume "dokumentierendes Wörterbuch" as represented in Britain by
the CONCISE OXFORD DICTIONARY. In particular, Gerhard Wahrig's
DEUTSCHES WÖRTERBUCH (³1980) and the DUDEN UNIVERSALWÖRTERBUCH (1983)
have recently enriched the (West) German scene; there is nothing,
though, yet to suggest (Kühn/ Püschel 1982) that the DUDEN RECHT-
SCHREIBUNG will ever be ousted from its very firm place in the
German dictionary best-seller tables.

The reasons for this are surely not wholly culture-specific; they
also relate to the general usefulness of the artefact. Patrick Hanks
once wrote (1982) of his regret at the demise in CHAMBERS TWENTIETH
CENTURY DICTIONARY of the idiosyncratic definition of éclair as a
'cake, long in shape but short in duration' (the definition was subsequently restored!). I am reminded (Leech 1974:205) of another
refreshingly singular definition from the 1901 edition of CHAMBERS,
that for horse , viz. 'a well-known quadruped'. A line-drawing was
also provided. In the second edition (1952), horse , the animal,
minus drawing, became: a solid-hoofed ungulate (*Equus*
caballus) with flowing tail and mane: any member
of the genus Equus (horse, ass, zebra, &c.) or the
family Equidae: a male adult of the species

This does not necessarily constitute an improvement. In a general
dictionary for the native-speaker there is something to be said for
e.g. glossing 'horsepower' (DR 1986) as "mechan. Leistungseinheit =
745,7 Watt, nicht gleichzusetzen mit PS = 736 Watt", but equally
(and especially in a one-volume dictionary) for listing, as Duden
did in 1880 and, with only a change in type-face, the DUDEN RECHT-
SCHREIBUNG still does today, 'horse' as just plain

Pferd, das; _[e]s, _e

References

Cited dictionaries (see Appendix):

CHAMBERS TWENTIETH CENTURY DICTIONARY (Davidson/Kirkpatrick)
(THE) CONCISE OXFORD DICTIONARY (Fowler/Sykes)
DEUTSCHES WORTERBUCH ... (Wahrig)
DUDEN. DEUTSCHES UNIVERSALWÖRTERBUCH (Drosdowski et al.)
DUDEN. RECHTSCHREIBUNG (Klien et al.)
DUDEN. RECHTSCHREIBUNG ... (Dudenredaktion)
DUDEN. (VOLLSTÄNDIGES) ORTHOGRAPHISCHES WÖRTERBUCH ... (Duden)
VOLLSTÄNDIGE ANWEISUNG ZUR DEUTSCHEN ORTHOGRAPHIE ... (Adelung)

Other literature:

Drewitz, Ingeborg and Reuter, Ernst eds. (1974) vernünftiger
    schreiben. reform der rechtschreibung. Frankfurt: Fischer
Duden, Konrad (1876) Die Zukunftsorthographie nach den Vor-
    schlägen der zur Herstellung größerer Einigung in der
    deutschen Rechtschreibung berufenen Konferenz erläutert und
    mit Verbesserungsvorschlägen versehen. Leipzig: Teubner
Grebe, Paul (1968) "Geschichte und Leistung des Dudens" in
    Geschichte und Leistung des Dudens. Mannheim & Zürich:
    Bibliographisches Institut/Dudenverlag 9-22
Hanks, Patrick (1982) "Coining it" Times Educational Supplement
    (London) 15 October
Hausmann, Franz J. (1983) "Wörterbücher in Frankreich und Deutsch-
    land. Ein Vergleich" Germanistische Linguistik 1-4/82: 119-152
Hellmann, Manfred W. ed. (1984) Ost-West-Wortschatzvergleiche
    (Forschungsberichte des Instituts für deutsche Sprache 48).
    Tübingen: G. Narr
Keller, R.E. (1978) The German Language. London: Faber and Faber
Kloss, Heinz (1952/78) Die Entwicklung neuer germanischer Kultur-
    sprachen seit 1800 (Sprache der Gegenwart 37). Düsseldorf:
    Schwann
Kühn, Peter and Püschel, Ulrich (1982) "'Der Duden reicht mir'.
    Zum Gebrauch allgemeiner einsprachiger und spezieller Wörter-
    bücher des Deutschen" Germanistische Linguistik 3-6/80:
    121-151
Küppers, Hans-Georg (1984) Orthographiereform und Öffentlichkeit.
    Zur Entwicklung und Diskussion der Rechtschreibreformbe-
    mühungen zwischen 1876 und 1982 (Sprache der Gegenwart 61).
    Düsseldorf: Schwann
Leech, Geoffrey N. (1974) Semantics. Harmondsworth: Penguin Books
Müller, Wolfgang (1968) "Sprachwandel und Spracherfassung ..." in
    Geschichte und Leistung des Dudens. Mannheim & Zürich: Biblio-
    graphisches Institut/Dudenverlag 54-88
Nerius, Dieter and Scharnhorst, Jürgen eds. (1980) Theoretische
    Probleme der deutschen Orthographie (Sprache und Gesellschaft
    16). Berlin: Akademie-Verlag

Petitjean, G. (1985) "Les Français malades de l'orthographe" Le
    Nouvel Observateur (Paris) 6-12 September
Rosengren, Inger (1977) Frequenzwörterbuch der deutschen Zeitungs-
    sprache. Lund: Gleerup
Standop, Ewald (1982) "Duden 1980" Linguistische Berichte 77/82:
    80-88
Veith, Werner H. (1985) "Die Bestrebungen der Orthographiereform
    im 18., 19. und 20. Jahrhundert" in Sprachgeschichte. Ein Hand
    buch zur Geschichte der deutschen Sprache und ihrer Erfor-
    schung ed. by Werner Besch et al. Berlin: W. de Gruyter:
    1482-1495
Weinrich, Harald (1976) "Die Wahrheit der Wörterbücher" in Pro-
    bleme der Lexikologie und Lexikographie ed. by Hugo Moser
    (Sprache der Gegenwart 39). Düsseldorf: Schwann 347-371
Weinrich, Harald (1985) "Eine deutsche Wörterbuchlandschaft"
    Frankfurter Allgemeine Zeitung (Frankfurt) No. 125, 1 June
Wurzel, Wolfgang U. (1979) Konrad Duden. Leipzig: VEB Biblio-
    graphisches Institut

Vollständiges

Orthographisches Wörterbuch

der

deutschen Sprache

1st edition: Leipzig 1880

Vollständiges

Orthographisches Wörterbuch

der deutschen Sprache

mit zahlreichen kurzen Wort- und Sacherklärungen und
Verdeutschungen der Fremdwörter

5th edition: Leipzig 1897

Duden,

Rechtschreibung der deutschen Sprache
und der Fremdwörter.

9th edition: Leipzig 1915

Der Große Duden

Rechtschreibung
der deutschen Sprache und der
Fremdwörter

10th edition: Leipzig 1929

Der Große Duden

Rechtschreibung
der deutschen Sprache und der
Fremdwörter

11th edition: Leipzig 1934

Der Große Duden

Rechtschreibung der deutschen Sprache
und der Fremdwörter

12th edition: Leipzig 1941

DUDEN

Rechtschreibung
der deutschen Sprache und der Fremdwörter

13th edition: Wiesbaden 1947

DUDEN

Rechtschreibung
der deutschen Sprache und der
Fremdwörter

19th edition: Mannheim 1986

Der Große DUDEN

Wörterbuch und Leitfaden der deutschen Rechtschreibung

18th edition: Leipzig 1985

LEARNED LEXICOGRAPHERS OF THE NORTH: SEVENTEENTH-CENTURY VIGNETTES

Einar Haugen

It is part of the lore of lexicography that Samuel Johnson loftily described us (and himself) as 'harmless drudges'. If we are harmless, it is not necessarily our real intention. Many lexicographers have written their works with the purpose of arousing nations and even of promoting the cause of minorities (Haugen 1985).

But there is no doubt that much drudgery is involved in preparing complete lexica. The history of lexicography, like the bottom of the ocean, is littered with sorry shipwrecks. A Danish verse, in my translation, poignantly and amusingly describes the lexicographer's fate:

At the dictionary's letter A

Mr. Brandt is young and gay.

But when at last he reaches Zed,

He's in his wheelchair, nearly dead.

(Gullberg 1964:x)

This slightly mocking verse reflects in some degree my own feelings while producing a NORSK-ENGELSK ORDBOK, though I happily survived the ordeal. My wife also survived the even more chastening ordeal of preparing a bibliography of Scandinavian dictionaries from the sixteenth century to 1980, recently published (E. L. Haugen 1984). Her work enabled me to write a survey of Scandinavian lexicography, which appeared as an introduction to her book (pp. 1-61). My present paper draws heavily on that work.

There were two factors that cooperated in creating a tradition of dictionary-making in Scandinavia. One was the new nationalism that swept Europe from the time of the Renaissance. The other was the opportunity that the printing press offered for multiplying literacy at the time of the Reformation. Popular reading went hand in hand with national self-assertion. While

the new nationalism sprang up in the sixteenth century, its
lexicographic effects did not reach Scandinavia until the
seventeenth (Marcu 1976; Paludan 1887; Haugen 1976: 394-5).

        In 1500 Scandinavia was still held together in an uneasy
dynastic union extending from Greenland in the west to Finland in
the east, with Copenhagen as its political center. By 1600
Scandinavia was split down the middle, with a Dano-Norwegian
kingdom on the west, governed from Copenhagen, and a
Swedo-Finnish kingdom on the east, governed from Stockholm.(Scott
1977)

        Denmark-Norway was ruled by a strong and enlightened
monarch, Christian IV, and was still the dominant power in the
North. But Christian would shortly be eclipsed by Gustavus
Adolphus of Sweden, her greatest military genius, who threw
himself and his country into the Thirty Years' War. Even though
he fell, he became the savior of Lutheranism. In the period from
1600 to 1660 Sweden not only drove the Danes out of the
Scandinavian peninsula, but also achieved hegemony over the
entire Baltic Sea (Skautrup 1947: 293-299).

        This brief sketch of Scandinavian political history is a
possibly needful reminder of the brief period when Scandinavia
played a more decisive role in European history than at any time
before or since.

        The roots of Scandinavian lexicography, like those of most
European nations, go back to the Middle Ages, when
Latin-to-native glossaries were prepared for the benefit of Latin
scholars. In spite of the radical Protestant insistence on
producing native versions of the Bible, Latin remained the
language of learning. From the sixteenth century we have two
Latin-to-native glossaries associated with the translators of the
Bible. It is significant that one of them is Danish (1510) and
the other Swedish (1538) (E. L. Haugen 1984: 5). Christiern
Pedersen was the author of VOCABULARIUM AD USUM DACORUM, while
Swedish Olaus Petri is reputed to be the author of VARIARUM RERUM
VOCABULA CUM SUECA INTERPRETATIONE. These works reflect the
first great cleavage of the Scandinavian area in modern times.

        One result was a certain rivalry between the Danes and the
Swedes in asserting their respective glories. They set to work
creating dictionaries of their mother tongues, once the idea had
filtered into the North. Models were available in Italy and
France, and above all in Germany, where the Fruchtbringende
Gesellschaft was founded in 1617. Here, too, the poet Martin
Opitz (1597-1639) wrote his Aristarchus(c. 1618) in praise of
German as a poetic medium, illustrated by his classic Buch von
der deutschen Poeterey (1624) (Skautrup 1947: 308-9; NEW CENTURY
CYCLOPEDIA OF NAMES 3.3027).

We shall now present some of the 'firsts' of Scandinavian
lexicography in the form of vignettes to throw light on the
motivations and the accomplishments of these early word
processors.

Povl Colding, the author of the first (bilingual) Danish
dictionary, taught at the classical school of Herlufsholm, for
which reason his book is known as the DICTIONARIUM HERLOVIANUM
(1626). Although the target language is Latin, he uses his
introduction (also in Latin) to attack writers who regard Danish
with contempt and mix it with Latin and other foreign languages.
"What is there in Latin or any other language that cannot just as
readily be expressed in Danish? Do the objects of daily life
lack expressions, or has nature created us as dumb as fish? What
do foreign languages have either in their characters or in their
beauty over our mother tongue?" (Skautrup 1947:308).

An anonymous Swede who taught at the Linköping Latin
School was not to be outdone. His Swedish-Latin dictionary
appeared in 1640 and was affectionately known as 'Linkopensen'.
Although both books were for Latinists, they were also the first
attempts to assemble the native lexicon in a single alphabet (E.
L. Haugen 1984: 9).

Although the revolt against Latin was imminent and
inescapable, there was still little understanding of the
relationships between the newly established norms or of their
dialects or their historical backgrounds. The goal was rather
the glorification of the state than the making of contributions
to knowledge, which could often be merely serendipitous. This
appears from the preface to an unpublished manuscript of the
early 1630's by the Swedish man of letters Ericus Johannis
Schroderus (c. 1608-1639). His works have been called "almost
modern", since he wishes "to present the vocabulary (of Swedish)
purely and clearly, without a superfluous admixture of foreign
words" (Hesselman 1929:xi).

In his unpublished DICTIONARIUM QUADRILINGUE columns of
Swedish are followed by German, Latin, and Greek. He actually
published a LEXICON LATINO-SCONDICUM (1637); here the significant
innovation was a column of Finnish, the first glossary of that
language, resulting from his visit to Finland in 1636. Although
the Bible had been translated into Finnish by Mikael Agricola
(1548) in the first fervor of Lutheran enthusiasm, Finnish
remained a highly neglected language. It was dominated and
overlooked by the Swedes. Schroderus was deeply influenced by
the well-known Czech scholar Comenius, whose JANUA LINGUARUM he
rendered into Swedish (1640)   (Hesselman 1929:xi; Ahokas 1973).

The Swedes were eager to bolster their newly-won military
success by providing themselves with a glorious past. They found
it in old manuscripts, most of which were actually Icelandic, but

were popularized under the name 'Gothic'. The most renowned
figure in this exploration was Georg Stiernhielm (1598-1672),
also called "the father of Swedish poetry".(Gustafson 1961:83).
He started a lexicon entitled 'A Storehouse of the Ancient
Swedish and Gothic Tongues' (1642). This was a grand mixture of
Old Swedish and Icelandic; but he happily gave it up after
completing the letter A (Swedish title: GAMBLA SWEA OCH GöTHA
MALES FATEBUR). In his preface he asserted the poetic power of
the Swedish language and urged his countrymen to rescue it from
"an unhappy neglect" by reviving old terms that would enrich the
language and free it from excessive dependence on foreigners
(Gustafson 1961: 87).

        In Denmark the corresponding champion of the national
honor was Ole Worm, in Latin Olaus Wormius, antiquarian and royal
historiographer (1588-1654) (E. L. Haugen 1984: 10-11). Thanks
to the incorporation of Iceland in the Danish realm, he had
better access to the Old Norse past than the Swedes, largely
because of the coming of Icelandic students to the University of
Copenhagen. He turned his entries into runic characters,
followed by equivalent Roman letters, mistakenly thinking that
the epigraphic runic writing was the original manuscript hand of
the Old Scandinavians.

        He gave his learned dictionary the title of LEXICI RUNICI
(1650). As the title suggests, the text and the translations
were in Latin. The Icelandic is drawn from old manuscripts, but
the orthography (possibly due to Magnus Olafsson) is based on
Danish practice. There are many obvious errors, for example the
derivation of ass 'god' from 'Asia', in allusion to the supposed
origin of the mythical Norse gods from Troy. Whatever the
divagations from present-day opinion, the work is an impressive
contribution from the infancy of Old Norse studies.

        Denmark also sponsored a first attempt at a comprehensive
collection of the entire native lexicon. This was done under the
leadership of Matthias Moth, medic and royal secretary
(1649-1719) (Skautrup 1947:282; Henriksen 1976: 31-34). With a
royal prerogative Moth set as many as possible of the local
clergy in Denmark and Norway to work gathering the vocabulary of
their parishioners. Under promise of promotion he urged the
clergymen to collect not just what he called 'usable words',
meaning words from the literary language, but also "those which
are not used except by ordinary folk", such as "the names that
sailors, artisans, farmers etc. use for their tools". He may
have heard of the French Academy, but he was far from embracing
the 'academy principle'.

        In the words of Skautrup, historian of Danish, "in his
inclusion of words from the lowest spheres of language, even the
vulgar and the obscene, he surely suffered from no inhibitions"
(Skautrup 1947: 283). Although only a modest number of pastors

responded, the materials returned fill sixty volumes of
manuscript, and Moth's own final redaction runs to twenty
volumes. It has been an invaluable source for the language of
the seventeenth century, mined by Scandinavian lexicographers
ever since.

   One Scandinavian language has so far been set aside,
namely Norwegian. In principle there was no longer any such
language, since Norway had been officially incorporated into a
union with Denmark, and Danish had become its only written
language. But the tradition of its actual existence in the past
persisted and was called attention to from time to time, most
recently by the translation by Peder Claussøn of Snorri
Sturluson's <u>History of the Kings of Norway</u> (1633) (Skautrup 1947:
277).

   In 1646 there appeared in Copenhagen a little book
entitled DEN NORSKE DICTIONARIUM ELLER GLOSEBOG (The Norwegian
Dictionary or Glossary) (Hannaas 1915). The author was one
Christen Jenssøn, a pastor in the parish of Askevold (now written
Askvoll), on the west coast of Norway a short distance north of
Bergen. Inspection of its contents reveals that it is in fact a
glossary of the local dialect, and as such the first published in
Scandinavia. But the author had ambitions far beyond the Askvoll
dialect. He not only called his language 'Norwegian', but he
complained that "our good, old Norwegian speech is particularly
and increasingly mixed with many tongues snd foreign languages"
(Hannaas 1915: xix).

   He does not reveal any knowledge of Old Norwegian,
although his isolated dialect had many features in common with
it. But he declared that "in order that it may more clearly come
to light and be distinguished from others, with which it is
involved, I have wished to have this work of mine appear in print
for the benefit of all good Norsemen (<u>Norbagger</u>)". Instead of
dedicating it to some 'highly placed persons', as most writers
do, he dedicates "this my humble work" to "all good Norsemen, who
are my dear countrymen and agreeable good friends, whether noble
or common, clerical or secular, high or low". While his book
seems to have been largely ignored in its own day, it has been an
inspiration to later students of Norwegian, and most especially
to the advocates and supporters of Norway's alternate language,
the Landsmål or Nynorsk. By interesting coincidence, Ivar Aasen,
creator of the latter, was born and raised in a west Norwegian
community a short distance up the coast from Jenssøn's, and with
a similar dialect (Hannaas 1915:xv).

   The problem that faces us is to explain why this obscure
clergyman in a remote, isolated parish would write and publish
such a pioneering lexicon. He was apparently the son of his
clerical predecessor, and the precision of his information about
the dialect reveals him as a native speaker. His father must

have been a Dane, but his mother may have been a local woman. He
was educated at the Latin school in Bergen, the so-called
Cathedral school, and then went on to Copenhagen for his
theological training. His entire schooling was in Latin, but his
DICTIONARIUM had entries of the local dialect, with definitions
in Danish. The words are richly illustrated by sentences from
daily speech, including proverbs and even anecdotes. It gives
one a vivid picture of life in a Norwegian fishing and farming
community in the early seventeenth century.

        We can only attempt an explanation. Bergen was then
Norway's largest and most prosperous city. The school he
attended was founded by Bergen's first Lutheran bishop (Bull
1924: 2.31). There was here an interest in Norwegian history
going back to the preceding century. At the same time the city
was an outpost of the North German Hanseatic League, so that the
country boy would here come up against a different culture and
language, sharpening his sense of being Norwegian. From there he
went on to Copenhagen, where Norwegian students tended to band
together. He must have observed the publication of Snorri's
History, mentioned above. He was probably bilingual in Danish,
through his father, and in the local dialect, through his
childhood contacts. Beside using Colding's Danish-Latin
dictionary with its nationalistic introduction, he may have heard
reports of the German movement in favor of adopting the native
language in place of Latin.

        In summary, I hope to have shown that in the seventeenth
century Scandinavia had both the means, through the printing
press, and the motivation, through learned contacts, to
participate in the movement towards national liberation that
began spreading through Europe at the time of the Renaissance and
the Reformation. The universal Latinity of the Middle Ages was,
for better or worse, yielding to the native languages.
Lexicographers were not merely symptomatic of this development:
they helped to furnish the means by which it eventually
triumphed. New nations were born, and the learned men of
Scandinavia acted as their midwives. This applied not only to
the dominant Danish and Swedish, but also to the marginal
languages of Finland, Iceland, and Norway. By deepening the
historical perspectives they laid the foundations of the great
lexicographic enterprises of modern times.

References

Cited dictionaries (see Appendix):

DICTIONARIUM HERLOVIANUM ... (Colding)
DICTIONARIUM QUADRILINGUE ... (Schroderus)
GAMBLA SWEA OCH GOTHA MÅLES FATEBUR (Stiernhielm)
JANUA LINGUARUM RESERATA ... (Comenius)
LEXICI RUNICI ... (Wormius)
LEXICON LATINO-SCONDICUM ... (Schroderus)
(THE) NEW CENTURY CYLOPEDIA OF NAMES (Barnhart et al.)
(DEN) NORSKE DICTIONARIUM ELLER GLOSEBOG (Jenssøn)
NORSK-ENGELSK ORDBOK/NORWEGIAN-ENGLISH DICTIONARY (Haugen)
SVENSK-ENGELSK FACKORDBOK (Gullberg)
VARIARUM RERUM VOCABULA CUM SUECA INTERPRETATIONE (Petri)
VOCABULARIUM AD USUM DACORUM ... (Pedersen)

Other literature:

Ahokas, Jaakko (1973) A History of Finnish Literature. Bloomington:
    Indiana U.P.
Bull, Francis (1924) Norges litteratur fra Reformationen til 1814
    (Bull og Paasche: Norsk Litteraturhistorie 2). Kristiania:
    Aschehoug
Gustafson, Alrik (1961) A History of Swedish Literature. Minne-
    apolis: U. of Minnesota P.
Haugen, Einar (1976) The Scandinavian Languages: An Introduction to
    Their History. London: Faber & Cambridge MA: Harvard U.P.
Haugen, Einar (1985) "Lexicography and language planning" in Fest-
    schrift for Robert Lado ed. by Kurt Jankowski. Amsterdam/Phil-
    adelphia: J. Benjamins 571-580
Haugen, Eva L. (1984) A Bibliography of Scandinavian Dictionaries.
    White Plains NY: Kraus International Publications
Henriksen, Caroline C. (1976) Dansk Rigssprog: En beskrivelse fra
    1700-tallet. København: Akademisk Forlag
Marcu, Eva D. (1976) Sixteenth Century Nationalism. New York:
    Abaris Books
Paludan, Julius (1887) Fremmed indflydelse paa den danske national-
    literatur i det 17. og 18. aarhundrede. København: W. Priors
    Hofboghandel
Scott, Franklin D. (1977) Sweden: The Nation's History. Minneapolis:
    U. of Minnesota P.
Skautrup, Peter (1947) Det danske sprogs historie. Vol. 2. Køben-
    havn: Gyldendal

THE ENTRY IN MEDIEVAL ARABIC MONOLINGUAL DICTIONARIES:
SOME ASPECTS OF ARRANGEMENT AND CONTENT

John A. Haywood

Between the 8th and 15th centuries more than a dozen
comprehensive Arabic dictionaries were compiled: and though the
order of entries varied, the entry unit was, from the first, the
root. Arabic being a Semitic language, most roots consist of three
radicals (i.e. consonants/letters), though biliteral, quadriliteral
and even quinquiliteral roots are found in considerable numbers.
Except for quinquiliterals, which cannot normally form verbs, the
root is most conveniently represented by the 3rd person masculine
singular of the perfect tense of the simple verb, giving most often
the meaning of a past or completed action/state. Arabic does not
have an infinitive of regular pattern such as is found in Indo-
European and some other language families. True, every verb has at
least one noun of action, often rather loosely called the 'verbal
noun' by orientalists, but this is not standardised, save for
derived-form verbs. Thus we commonly call the root q-t-1 qatala (=
he killed), and bilingual dictionaries will - perhaps rather
illogically - translate it as 'to kill'.

From any given root, derivations are formed, either merely by
varying the vowelling of the radicals, or - more commonly - by the
addition of prefixes, infixes and suffixes. Such derivations may
number a hundred or more for such common roots as 'alima (= to
know), or as few as 2 or 3 from rarely-used or quinquiliteral roots.
Further, though some Arab scholars postulated a single basic meaning
area - in some instances two - for each root, when we look up a root
like 'alima in a large-scale dictionary, we find a wide and varied
semantic spectrum. There are at least 15 'semantic bands', including words for a high mountain, a split lip, a flag, a road-sign,
the Universe, a hawk, henna, a copious well, a frog and a breast-
plate, plus compound expressions and proper names. In additon to
these nouns, many of the meaning bands also afford appropriate
epithets and verbs (intransitive, transitive, causative etc.).

The dictionary compiler faced a daunting task. First he had to
decide where to start an entry, and how to arrange the various
derivations. Secondly he had the problem of how to define meaning,
both for common and rare words. Thirdly he had to justify some of
his statements by citations from reliable authorities or literary
texts. The present paper is no more than a preliminary study of
this neglected subject - how the lexicographers approached these
three problems. It is based, for convenience, on necessarily
limited evidence from eight famous dictionaries:

(1) [al-] Khalīl's 'AIN (8th century);
(2) Ibn Duraid's JAMHARA (9th century);
(3) [al-] Azharī's TAHDHĪB (10th century);
(4) [al-] Jauharī's ṢAḤĀḤ (10th century);
(5) Ibn 'Abbād's MUḤĪṬ (10th century);
(6) Ibn Sīda's MUHKĀM (11th century);
(7) Ibn Manẓur's LISĀN (13th century);
(8) [al-] Firūzabadī's QĀMŪS (14th century);

All were designed to be exhaustive – at least as regards the root
entries. But numbers (5) and (8) are comparatively short, the
MUḤĪṬ being sparing in citations, the QĀMŪS almost completely
dispensing with them. Even so, the latter's 4 volumes and 1600
pages would be doubled or trebled, if the time-honoured Cairo
edition were replaced by a new one set out in the modern manner. As
for the LISĀN (7), it is comparable in scope and size to the OXFORD
ENGLISH DICTIONARY. The Beirut edition is in 15 volumes.

Let us consider the first of the three problems mentioned – how
to arrange an entry. One might expect it to start with the 3rd
person masculine perfect root-form verb already mentioned. This
might be followed by the varous derived-form verbs. These are
important as they add shades of meaning by adding letters before,
after or inside the root. Such additions may therefore be regarded
as morphemes as well as phonemes, and these derived-form verbs are
associated with meaning patterns, yet these are not sufficiently
steriotyped to make definition superfluous. Such derived-form verbs
may number at least 14, though the last four are rare, and many
roots have fewer than ten. We are referring here only to triliteral
roots. Biliteral roots may behave more or less like triliterals, by
doubling the second radical, as in marra and tamma; alternatively,
or additionally, they may form reduplicative quadriliterals, like
tamtama and marmara. Quadriliterals may form up to three derived
verbs, though most form only one.

Assuming our lexicographer listed verbs beginning with the root
(I), followed by derived forms (II – XV for triliterals, II – IV for
quadriliterals), defining each in turn, he might be expected to
follow with the various nouns and adjectives derived from the root
in ascending order of length, ending with those having a prefixed m
(mu-, ma-, mi-). Unfortunately, while Arab lexicographers did see
the logic of starting with the simple root, it was European Arabists
who ultimately established the sequence of derivations we have come
to expect in an Arabic dictionary. Credit is particularly due to
G.W. Freytag (LEXICON ARABICO-LATINUM, Halle 1830-37) and E.W. Lane
(ARABIC-ENGLISH LEXICON, London 1863-93). It is above all the lack
of such a stereotyped arrangement within root-entries which proves
the 'last straw' to non-Arabs who try to make practical use of the
Medieval dictionaries. There are, perhaps, some compensations for

the time consumed, for lovers of rare words and those with a taste
for all facets of desert life. How charming it may seem, when
searching through the entry raja'a (= to return) to discover that
rāji', applied to a she-camel, implies that her owner was expecting
her to foal, but all she produced was a shower of urine!

Detailed examination of the entries 'alima and raja'a in all
eight dictionaries, plus random check of numerous other entries, has
only served to confirm the author's impressions in many years of
browsing: not only was it impossible to elicit any single system
common to all, but there was no consistency in any. Certainly root
verbs tend to precede derived forms, but the latter are not arranged
according to the number of letters of increase, as is done today.
Moreover, many entries do not even begin with a verb. Beginning
with the root verb is most common in the JAMHARA and MUHĪT, but rare
in the TAHDHĪB. Entries often begin with a noun or even an epithet.
No consistent reason could be found for this variation. Equally
strange is the fact that many entries begin with the 'verbal noun'
of the root verb, even though there are over 20 possible forms, most
of them containing letters of increase. Many verbs have several,
with or without variation in meaning.

There appears to be one possible explanation why certain entries
may open with a noun or epithet: that is, where such words have
Islamic religious connotations. This might, for example, apply to
epithets of God (Allah), in particular the '99 most beautiful
names'. Such words mostly belong to the category of 'epithets
resembling the active participle' (in meaning) or intensive forms of
them. This occurs in the entry 'alima in the MUHĪT and LISĀN. In
the TAHDHĪB, Azharī precedes them with the (verbal) noun 'ilm,
because he wishes to demonstrate that this word's original meaning
was not so much 'knowledge' as 'fear of God'. He adds that though
the epithets 'ālim, 'alīm and 'allām are qualities of God, they can
be used of a man 'given knowledge by God'. Another type of entry
liable to open with a noun is one which includes the name of a well-
known animal, such as asad (lion) and faras (horse). In such cases
the verbs might be regarded as denominal. It must, however, be
stressed that inconsistency was the order of the day, and no
lexicographer felt the need to justify his arrangement of
derivations in an entry.

There is scope for much more research here. There is some
evidence that the lexicographers were more interested in having a
meaning sequence than a derivation one. Thus, if a word has several
distinct meanings, it may occur several times, once for each
meaning. This might seem inconvenient, assuming that dictionaries
were used as we use them today - for looking-up words. But in fact,
few could afford the price of a manuscript, and almost throughout
the Middle Ages, dictionaries, like other forms of literature, were
learned by heart, and we often read that some scholar learned or

studied a certain dictionary under the actual author or under some
teacher who had done so. Only with the QĀMŪS did copies proliferate
to the extent that it might be called a best-seller. And so it has
remained, both before and since the advent of printing in the Arab
world.

However nouns and adjectives were arranged in an entry, plurals
had frequently to be given. This is because, in addition to 'sound
plurals' formed by the addition of standard masculine and feminine
suffixes, Arabic has a wide range of what are called 'broken
plurals'. These are formed on a large number of patterns, by
prefixes, infixes and suffixes, or a combination of them. Many
nouns have several plurals. An extreme case is the noun 'abd (=
servant, slave, man), for which LISĀN and QĀMŪS give 15 plurals.
The varied 'broken plural' forms are not, of course, unique to
Arabic. Among Indo-European languages, German, and more
particularly Welsh, spring readily to mind. But surely few
languages can rival Arabic's lexical embarras de richesses.

When we turn to the second problem, that of definition, we find
general agreement among Arabic lexicographers on the range of
methods open to them. First there was the single-word antonym, much
favoured at first, nor was it abandoned as late as the 18th century.
The formula was al- 'ilm naqīd/didd/khilāf al-jahl (= knowledge is
the opposite of ignorance), three different words being used for
'opposite'. Secondly there was definition by a single-word synonym
or near-synonym. Thus QĀMŪS defines 'alima as 'arafa: and it is
true that they both do mean 'to know', though they have different
nuances. Thirdly there was the more precise definition consisting
of at least a phrase or sentence. These were at times unavoidable,
even in the shorter dictionaries; but they came into their own in
the later and larger ones, especially the LISĀN, in which verbosity
and digression became almost an obsession. An example of a clear
yet succinct definition is that of du'th in the MUHIT: awwal al-mard
yabdu (= the beginning of an illness that appears, i.e. the first
symptoms). Fourthly, there were various sorts of definition by
implication. For example, a verb might be provided with a subject
or object, to suggest its meaning; or an adjective might be applied
to a masculine or feminine noun, the reader being expected to deduce
its meaning from the root verb, or from some other derivation
already given. Again, a citation from literature might be used to
clarify the meaning. But if all else failed, there remained a final
possibility - to give no real definition at all. In its extreme
form, this could be complete omission - though here the copyist
might be to blame. An example of this is the failure of the 'AIN to
define raja'a (= to return). Perhaps Khalil felt that so common a
verb required no defining: in any case, the meaning might emerge
from what followed. A common word could also be described as ma'rūf
(= well-known). Then again, we find such explanations as that of
batt (= duck) in JAMHARA: "and as for the bird called batt, this is

a well-known foreign word Arabicised". The SAḤĀḤ contains several
examples of bogus definitions in which a noun is 'defined' by being
given its broken plural, such as dawā' wāhid al-adwiya (= medicine -
the plural of medicines)! One cannot commend Jauhari for this!

Once the Arabs emerged from their desert homeland, and through
their conquests came into contact with other cultures, they adopted
meticulous and logical attitudes towards their sciences: they expected important statements of fact to be substantiated by reference
to reliable authorities and supporting evidence. This applied to
lexicography, though the length and scope of a particular dictionary
imposed practical limitations. There were at least five types of
citation, of which there are numerous examples in the eight dictionaries under discussion', the QĀMŪS being the exception. These types
are: (a) reference to or quotation from grammarians and other lexicographers; (b) the Koran, and less frequently other religious
texts, especially the Ḥadith (Traditions of the Prophet); (c)
quotation from poetry; (d) reference to spoken Arabic in various
dialects; and (e) proverbs or proverbial expressions.

Khalīl's 'AIN was often quoted in later dictionaries, as was
also the first full grammar composed by his pupil Sibawaih. Subsequent lexicographers quoted from their predecessors' dictionaries
and from a vast array of linguistic monographs. These included
vocabularies specialised and general, the latter including some
exhaustive works which differed from dictionaries chiefly in their
arrangement. But the Koran, and how doctors of religion and
language explained various verses, was of great importance to the
lexicographer. On the one hand, the Sacred Volume was considered a
peerless model of Arabic; as such, it could be quoted to substantiate some word or usage. On the other hand, it contains
passages susceptible of different interpretations, and there were
even different 'readings'. Of these, the lexicographer must at
least provide information, and if he were bold enough, he might even
give his own opinion. The TAHDHĪB is particularly rich in Koranic
references and discussion of them.

The Arab love of poetry goes back to at least a century before
Islam, but the earlier poetry was not committed to writing until
after the 'revelation' of the Koran. It was virtually the only pre-
Islamic literature. Even after prose literature developed in
various forms, it did not command as much respect as poetry, and
probably still does not. The major Koranic commentators did not
hesitate to quote poetry to clarify and even justify their explanation of ambiguous or rare vocabulary in the Koran. It is not,
therefore, surprising that lexicographers should cite poetry to
support word-definition - in moderation at first, but later to
excess, as in the LISĀN. And if the earlier dictionaries, like the
'AIN, sometimes failed to name the poet, their successors were only
too willing to fill the gaps. In this short paper no poetical

examples need be given. Suffice it to say that all the major and
many of the minor poets were quoted: indeed, for some of the latter,
the dictionaries are at times a major – or even a sole – source.

As the lexicographers were concerned first and foremost with the
literary language, it may seem surprising that they should cite the
spoken language here and there. And there seems little doubt that
even a millennium ago, the written and spoken forms of the language
were nearly as far apart as they are today. However, in Arabic, as
in other languages, dialectal variants had an awkward habit of in-
filtrating the standard written language. There was also a sort of
mystique surrounding the desert; and lexicographers liked to record
usages peculiar to different tribes, some of which they considered
to be repositories of 'pure Arabic'. For example, in the JAMHARA,
under **raja'a**, Ibn Duraid tells us that the Hudhail tribe used the
words **raj'** and **raji'** to mean water. The TAHDHĪB tells us that the
Salīm tribe used the root verb to mean 'to make an impression, be
effective,' as in the sentence: qad raja'a kalāmī fī l-rajul (= what
I said made an impression on the man). It also tells us that the
verb **naja'a** could be substituted for **raja'a**, thus giving an example
of rhyming pairs of synonyms, which occur in Arabic as in many other
languages. The SAHĀH defines **birqish** (= finch) as 'a small bird
like the sparrow, which the people of Hedjāz call **shurshūr**'. The
dictionaries also admit, from time to time, that certain words are
foreign, or Persian, and Arabicised (**mu'arrab**). In this respect,
later lexicographers had the benefit of al-Jawalīqi's specialised
dictionary of such words, KITĀB AL-MU'ARRAB, compiled around 1100
A.D.

Finally, these Arabic dictionaries are rich in proverbs and
proverbial expressions. No doubt al-MAIDĀNI drew on them in writing
his great MAJMA' AL-AMTHĀL (Collection of Proverbs), also dating
from c.1100. Considering its size, the MUHĪT has many proverbs. A
sample count would suggest that it may well contain over a thousand.
In many cases, a proverb is not merely repeated and explained – its
origin is also given.

From what has been said, it can be seen that despite some short-
comings, the Arabs (or more properly, the compilers of Arabic dictionaries, as they were not all Arabs) showed considerable expertise
in marshalling their material. They were fired by a love of the
language and pride in its copiousness. Successive compilers of
dictionaries added to the total lexical content, bringing the works
of their predecessors up to date. The vocabulary of philosophy and
the sciences was added; some of it was formed from Arabic roots,
some by taking over Greek and other foreign words. It must be borne
in mind that an increasing number of dictionary users were non-
Arabs, of whom most were Muslims. For them, Arabic was a second
language, essential for religion, commerce and official business.
They required more exact definitions. At the same time, they

brought foreign words into Arabic, and these often formed derivations on Arabic patterns. The lexicographer could no longer take
so much for granted. This may explain why, for example, under the
root 'alima, there are only two derived-form verbs in the 'AIN, as
against six in the QĀMŪS.

References

Cited dictionaries (see Appendix):

(AL-) 'AIN see KITĀB AL-'AIN
ARABIC-ENGLISH LEXICON (Lane)
(AL-) JAMHARA FI-L-LUGHA (Ibn Duraid)
KITĀB AL-'AIN (Al-Khalīl)
KITĀB AL-MU'ARRAB (Al-Jawālīqī)
LEXICON ARABICO-LATINUM (Freytag)
LISĀN AL-'ARAB (Ibn Manẓur)
MAJMA AL-AMTHĀL (Al-Maidani)
(AL-) MUHĪṬ FĪ-L-LUGHA (Ibn 'Abbād)
(AL-) MUHKAM WA L-MUHĪṬ AL-A'ẒAM (Ibn Sīda)
(THE) OXFORD ENGLISH DICTIONARY (Murray et al.)
(AL-) QĀMŪS AL-MUHĪṬ (Al-Firuzabadi)
(TĀJ AL-LUGHA WA-) ṢAHĀH (Al-Jauhari)
TAHDHĪB AL-LUGHA (Al-Azhari)

Other literature:

Haywood, John A. (1960/65) Arabic Lexicography: Its History and Its
    Place in the General History of Lexicography. Leiden: E.J. Brill
Szegin, F. (1982) Geschichte des arabischen Schrifttums (Band 8:
    Lexikographie). Leiden: E.J. Brill

THE PARADIGM OF JOHN WILKINS' THESAURUS

Werner Hüllen

Paradigms in history

The linguistic investigation to be presented here depends on a basic
assumption about the nature of intellectual history and the ensuing
methods of researching into it (Cohen 1977: XI-XXV).
Analyses of historical developments have long aimed at establishing and
describing what can be called 'continuity' within the flow of time. Such
analyses try to prove that a particular kind of linguistic thinking can
be accounted for by developments in its past, which themselves find an
explanation again in their past, and so on backwards in time. If, in
this way, we consider continuity to be the essential feature of historical development, innovatory ideas are looked upon as links in a chain,
but not as beginnings.
The names Thomas S. Kuhn and Michel Foucault stand for a more recent
way of historical thinking which assumes that our intellectual history
is more thoroughly characterized by breaks and turnovers than by continuity, much in the same way as political history is more characterized by
revolutions than by evolution. According to this theory, scientific thinking periodically assesses its own assumptions and foundations and in
doing so establishes a new paradigm which serves as a pattern for explanation till it is done away with in the same manner. Intellectual history
thus takes on the shape of a succession of paradigms (Kuhn 1964,
Foucault 1970, Said 1974).
We wish to use this theory (in an adapted version, but without further
discussion) as an instrument of analysis with reference to thesauri. In
order to do this, we assume that a linguistic paradigm brings forth certain products such as grammars, textbooks, monographs which, however, do
not vanish or become ineffective when the paradigm itself changes, but
which go on living and exercising influence even if no longer in the
focus of linguistic discussion. Such products which are typical of a
certain paradigm adopt a life of their own. Although their reception
undergoes certain changes in the course of linguistic history because
it suffers the influence of new paradigms, the original paradigm is nevertheless kept alive. This is supposed to be the case because such products
answer certain needs of language users outside linguistic thinking proper.
A certain grammar theory (e.g. universal grammar) may go on living in
schoolbooks long after it has ceased to be recognized in academic circles.
The universal language scheme (another example) lost its linguistic and
philosophical attraction towards the end of the 17th century, but this
did not prevent many people outside the discussions of linguistic experts
from trying to invent artificial languages for their own practical
purposes.
In this way we assume that the idea of a thesaurus was conceived within
the framework of a certain linguistic paradigm and then went on living
after this paradigm had stopped being really influential. Once this type
of word collection was in the world, it went on attracting the attention
of people because it could serve some of their practical needs.

'Dictionary' vs. 'thesaurus'

In order to open the discussion, a definition of what a thesaurus is in
comparison to a dictionary is needed. It will be given in abstracto,

which means that we describe lexicological ideas rather than lexicographic
reality (Schildt and Viehweger 1983).
Definitions of 'dictionary' and 'thesaurus' might run like this
(Baldinger 1956):

i. A dictionary is an inventory of words of one particular language (in
the left column) with matching definitions of their meanings (in the
right column). The arrangement within entries moves from the word to
its meaning, which means from the (complex) sign to what it signifies.
This arrangement is generally called semasiological. The dictionary
allows users to find hitherto unknown meanings of words which they
already know. In order to spot a specific word, the arrangement between
entries follows the alphabet.

ii. A thesaurus is an inventory of definitions of meanings (in the left
column) with matching words (in the right column). The arrangement
within entries moves from the meaning to its word, which means from
the signified to its (complex) sign. This arrangement is generally
called onomasiological..The thesaurus allows users to find hitherto
unknown words corresponding to meanings which they already know. In
order to spot a specific meaning, the arrangement between entries
must follow a system in such a way that the user can anticipate where
an entry is to be found.

The two definitions given make the dictionary and the thesaurus appear to
be two versions of one thing, which are symmetrically related to each
other. This means that the one actually cannot exist without the other.
This relation is for example envisaged in Comenius' ORBIS SENSUALIUM PICTUS
QUADRILINGUIS where pictures with their descriptive sentences are followed
by an alphabetical word list, so that both can be used in both directions.
There are, however, good reasons why such ideal symmetry can never become
reality. They lie in the problem of equality between the left and the
right column of the dictionary and the thesaurus alike.
The left column of a dictionary consists of decontextualized words,
given as formatives in abstracto. The right column of a dictionary,
however, consists of definitions in various textual patterns. They are
typically marked by two important features: the first is their drawing on
world knowledge in different degrees. Every definition includes information
which is necessary for understanding the word but which is outside its
semantic compass. The relation between this information and the word
itself is determined by language use which, ultimately, is identical
with the habits of thinking and the conventions of acting in a given
culture. The order in which this world knowledge is introduced in
dictionary definitions is given by the words to be explained. It is an
order that depends on the alphabet, but is totally arbitrary for world
knowledge itself. The area which is cut out from the total mass of world
knowledge available, in order to find a word, is called a 'frame'
(Beaugrande/Dressler 1981).
This means that whereas there is a strict order in the serial arrangement of words - the order of the alphabet -, there is no such order in
the serial arrangement of frames. The definition side of a dictionary is
an encyclopedia, and an encyclopedia - according to   Eco (1984:46-86) - is
a labyrinth of meanings, an assembly of units of information without a
centre and without a unifying system.
The second feature of definitions in dictionaries is that they can
never be exhaustive. It is an axiom of semantics that words adopt their

THE PARADIGM OF JOHN WILKINS' THESAURUS   117

meanings from the context of situation, i.e. by fusing their own meaning
potential with the meaning potential of other words within a frame which
is interpreted as meaningful by its users. Strictly speaking, therefore,
a word has as many meanings as there are frames in which it can be used.
The range of use for a given word thus always exceeds the number of
possible definitions, and this not only due to lack of space but because
of the mechanics of meaning constitution in the language sign.
Dictionary and thesaurus are not, therefore, merely interchangeable. It
is possible to write a dictionary in which users find what they want to
know, though the semantic information offered is never exhaustive. It is,
however, not possible to write a thesaurus with the same qualifications
unless an order can be conceived which could be called an 'onomasiological
alphabet', and even then users find that such a thesaurus is 'full of
holes'.
In spite of such difficulties, there is a general linguistic interest in
creating integrated dictionaries which combine the usefulness of alphabetical order with the fact that language in performance shows a meaningful (but never an alphabetical) arrangement of words which is determined
by the reality of our world and the way in which language users see it.
Such integrated dictionaries would, in their arrangement, reproduce the
fact that every single word has many meanings and that all words stand
in semantic relation to each other. This means that a dictionary lists
the vocabulary of a language per se, whereas a thesaurus lists synonyms,
that is words with more or less overlapping meanings (Henne 1977).

Wilkins' thesaurus

When Wilkins published An Essay towards a Real Character and Philosophical
Language in 1668 (Asbach-Schnitker 1984), dictionaries in alphabetical
order were quite popular (Hayashi 1978). His book is the first collection
of words that in our understanding deserves the name 'thesaurus'. However, Wilkins' thesaurus does not give definitions at all but simply
lists words in a certain arrangement. It is our hypothesis that Wilkins
endeavoured to replace definitions by arrangement, i.e. the meaning of
a word is mirrored in the very location it is assigned to within an all-
embracing system of meanings which ideally covers everything that can
be expressed in language. This is an attempt to overcome the difficulties
of sequencing definitions mentioned. In a non-defining thesaurus, as
Wilkins' word list can be called, world knowledge - otherwise encapsu-
lated in the frames of word definitions - is expressed in the system of
concepts that provides a slot for each single word. Whoever wishes to
understand a word must take this entire system into account.
It is well-known that John Wilkins did not plan to collect a thesaurus
as such but thought of it as a first step towards a universal language
and a universal character. Nothing will be said about this here (Slaughter
1982, Large 1985). The important thing in our context is that he published
an enormous list of words/synonyms and arranged them in a certain way.
This way is determined by long deductive chains which, starting from the
most abstract conception 'things and notions' continually narrows meanings down until they fit into an existing lexeme. Consequently, the
meaning of each of these lexemes/words is mirrored in the very location
it is assigned to within the overall system of concepts. All the concepts
that occur between 'things and notions' and the last members of each
deductive chain can be looked upon as semantic markers of each of the

entries of the thesaurus. So each word/synonym could be given a paraphrase which would have to contain the respective deductive chain as
(part of) frames.
The tables in which these deductive chains are embedded follow the
traditional and well-known procedure of breaking down a genus into
species by their differentiae specificae. This leads to chains of varying length, which means that entries in the thesaurus occur on different
hierarchical levels in the system.
The specific differences which distinguish logically higher and lower
classes are taken from quite different areas of reality. They may for
example be philosophical/logical, classificatory (in the way in which
this is typical, for instance, for botany), functional, or social. As
it is actually these differentiae specificae which determine such tables,
they (the tables) are structured by a host of widely differing features
which are collected with encyclopedic fullness and then arranged from
the abstract to the more concrete.
This procedure does not in all cases lead to the same 'end'. At least
two different results of deduction can be defined. The first is a taxonomic terminology as typically used in the sciences. In this case, the
location of the word at the end of the deductive chain is its definition,
and there is only one word given. The second does not yield such clear-
cut and unequivocal meanings. If at all, the deductive chains end in a
pseudo-taxonomic terminology where words need further clarification by
synonyms or neighbouring words from comparable frames, which means that
the definition of their word meaning is not entirely expressed in their
location in the system. Of course, it is the nature of word meanings that
ultimately accounts for this difference. The classes of plants, animals,
etc. are examples of the first case; highly abstract word meanings, but
also words from social contexts are examples of the second case. Obviously the replacement of definition by arrangement is most successful in
areas of vocabulary which lack   clear relations and hierarchies. For
all words, however, taxonomy seems to be the model of arrangement which
Wilkins used.

The paradigm of Wilkins' thesaurus

A more systematic linguistic description of the paradigm which Wilkins
obviously followed can be given under four headings (Slaughter 1982):
The first and most eminent feature of this paradigm is its concentration
on words. Language is first of all approached as a nomenclature, as a
store of designations/names which can be bound together into sentences
by (secondary) grammatical devices.
The reason for this word-centred linguistic view is obviously the new
scientists' preoccupation with concrete things. In opposition to the
Medieval and Renaissance tradition, Bacon had founded the primacy of the
concrete, i.e. objects of reality, before the general, i.e. ideas. The
linguistic corollary to this epistemological view is the primacy of words
before grammatical structures. This idea was common to people such as
Bacon, Hobbes, Locke, and Wilkins.
As Wilkins is in many respects a classical syncretiser, he does not
subscribe to this concentration on words to the exclusion of other
linguistic approaches. There is indeed a chapter on universal grammar
in his Essay and he devises graphematic means to express syntagmatic
relations in his universal characters (Salmon 1974). However, the fact

that the thesaurus is the first step towards his universal language is
itself telling.
The second outstanding feature of the linguistic paradigm that underlies
Wilkins' thesaurus is the assumption of a rational organization of words
as signs. This entails that they are clearly opposed to each other and,
by this opposition, unambiguously denote their meanings. Another entail-
ment is that words consist of elements – just as for the new scientists
matter consisted of elements – and that analysing and teaching them demands
their identification. Proving that words as complex signs are rationally
organized focusses the linguist's attention as much on the physical side
of language as on meaning, because the rationality of language can only
apply to the relation between the sign itself and the signified.
The third important feature of the linguistic paradigm under discussion
is Aristotelian logic. Though in the wake of Bacon, the authors of the
17th century almost unanimously – and certainly John Wilkins as a founding
member of the Royal Society – strove to replace Aristotelian logic with
its primacy of the general by their scientific method with its primacy
of the individual, Wilkins' enumeration of words depends on the basic
works of Aristotelian logic. Wilkins shares with this tradition the basic
notion of essence as the necessary and permanent condition of everything
real and as taking the first position in the hierarchy of terms. Furthermore, he shares the notions of substance and accidence. In his tables,
he organizes reality according to genus, species, difference, property
and accident as was customary in the Porphyrian variant of the Aristotelian
tradition (Aarsleff 1982).
Wilkins' tables attempt to give everything in this world a location in
the categorial system set up according to the logical principles mentioned.
Words, which are the names of these things, thus define the places in which
their objects exist in an orderly fashion. The definition of a thing is
given by the hierarchy which is 'above' it. The perfect language which
Wilkins wants to invent would have to replicate this system in the morphology of its signs in such a way that a specific combination of this
morphology in one word would designate its place in the overall system.
This means that reality and language form two isomorphic systems. There
is "the nature of things and common notion of them, wherein mankind does
agree" which makes a system of word meanings possible "wherein mankind
does agree" (Wilkins' Essay: To the Reader).
The most important assumption of this third feature of the linguistic
paradigm then is that this world order exists and can be expressed in a
language, provided it keeps to the strict rules of signification.
The fourth important feature of the linguistic paradigm that underlies
Wilkins' thesaurus is taxonomy. It expresses itself most clearly in the
chapters which enumerate classes of minerals, plants and animals, but
can also be traced in other chapters – if only in the observation that
such chapters are unsuccessfully modelled on the idea of a taxonomy
(Slaughter 1982).
Scientific classification, e.g. in botany, is, of course, an offspring
of the analytical procedures of formalized Aristotelian logic. The immediate consequence of such taxonomies, as they became popular during the
16th & 17th centuries in words and pictures, is what we can call 'decon-
textualization'. This means that plants etc. were no longer described
as something that existed in an ecological connection with other plants
or answered the needs of men or bore allegorical meanings given to them

by the Scriptures and by theological tradition, but that they were
described as objects isolated from their surroundings and based on
nothing but their own physical characteristics. Description of plants
is stripped of everything except information about their size, shape,
colour, etc.
In summary, we can say that Wilkins'thesaurus, collected on his way to
a universal language, depended on four outstanding linguistic features:
i. the concentration on words as the primary and most important units
   of language,
ii. the assumption of the rational organization of words as signs, i.e.
    the clearly demarcated and constant relation of signs (and elements
    of signs) to meanings (and elements of meanings),
iii. the assumption that there is an order in reality on which all man-
     kind agrees and which is the foundation of a possible parallel
     order in language, i.e. vocabulary,
iv. taxonomy with its special effect of decontextualizing word meanings
    and rearranging them in a new system.

Scientific nomenclatures

Wilkins' Essay marks the climax and simultaneously the end of primarily
linguistic discussion of the paradigm thus described. However, there
are at least two paths of historical development on which it can clearly
be found to be influential in later centuries. Such paths are the development of scientific nomenclature, and the further development of thesauri.
Both cannot be followed here in any detail, but at least some linguistic
affinities can be hinted at.
The evolution of early folkloristic language into a systematically
patterned terminology is most conspicuous in botany and chemistry and,
due to the enormous expansion of both branches of sciences, started at
the very time when Wilkins worked on and published his Essay. Earlier,
mythological and allegorical meanings, colour symbolism, taste and smell,
names of persons and of places, medicinal properties and many other
features had served as a basis for coining terms (Flood 1963, Crosland
1978). But this procedure proved not adaptable to expanding knowledge.
What simultaneously happened from the beginning of the 17th century in
several European countries is, of course, first of all an intrinsic part
of the development of these sciences, but it has a linguistic component
derived from the kind of terminological thinking which we encountered
in Wilkins.
In chemistry, folkloristic terminology was slowly replaced by definition
and then by nomenclature which shortened the long descriptive phrases
of definitions, yet kept their message, i.e. the description of the
compound nature of substances seen within a unified system. One of the
most influential innovations in this respect was the introduction of
binominal names (in Latin) for salts, which had slowly come into use
during the 16th and 17th centuries and was in 1775 strongly advocated
by T. O.Bergman, the Swedish chemist. From there it found its way into
botany as well as into chemistry. Linnaeus' universal fame, for example,
does not depend so much on the validity of his classification which, on
the contrary, was strongly doubted by other botanists, but on his consistent use of binominally defining terms. In particular the sequence
of a generic name and a trivial specific name won universal approval.
Moreover he adopted Bergman's principle that similar word endings should
be used for similar substances.

For chemistry, Bergman's ideas influenced L. B. Guyton de Morveau who, in a memoire of 1782, laid down the principles of chemical terminology. He stated that descriptive phrases could not be regarded as names, which, consequently, have to be newly coined. They should, as much as possible, be in conformity with the nature of things. This means that a simple substance should be denominated by a simple name and that the denomination of a chemical compound must give its constituents.

Guyton's belief in the meaningfulness of names went as far as the suggestion that when chemists lack knowledge as to the exact ingredients of a chemical compound, a name which expresses nothing, i.e. a dummy, was preferable to a name which might convey a wrong idea.

The most influential publication in this area is of course Lavoisier's Méthode de nomenclature chimique of 1787 which included his famous address to the Académie des Sciences on 18 April of that year, in which he stated that language is a means of analysis, not just a means of giving names to things. Therefore the perfection of language was the beginning of the perfection of sciences (a thought which like a red thread had run through philosophical and scientific thinking from Bacon on).

There is no space here to follow the development any further or to give details. Of linguistic importance is the fact that the scientific language which grew out of such thinking followed - and still follows - the four basic features of the paradigm that shaped Wilkins' thesaurus: It concentrates more on words than on any other element of language because it is occupied with identifying reality. It assumes a rational organization of words as signs and demands a morphological and compositional regularity which is meant to express identical meanings with identical structural signs. It assumes an order in reality which is paralleled by an order of terminology. This order of reality may not have - or may gradually lose - the philosophical underpinnings that Wilkins gave it and that has had its own tradition. In the place of an epistemological apriorism, such as Wilkins put forth, sciences gradually developed their own conceptual network for describing reality. But this does not preclude nomenclature here serving the same linguistic function which language as a whole was meant to serve in Wilkins' book. Finally, taxonomy is the general principle of order. Plants, just like chemical substances, are decontextualized from life or their use by men, and are allocated systematic places in their own scientific systems. Thus, the vast terminological systems of the sciences which developed during the centuries and are in use today are the true paradigmatic successors to Wilkins' thesaurus.

Practical thesauri

There is as yet no satisfying history of thesauri. So it is only the few odd case studies which can show the affinity of their groundwork to Wilkins' thesaurus and the growing concern with their practical use.

In Johann August Eberhard's VERSUCH EINER ALLGEMEINEN DEUTSCHEN SYNONYMIK (1795) word meanings are thought of exclusively in terms of a logical system of concepts. This results in a hierarchy where words on the same logical level are differentiated by distinguishing features, but where they share all other higher ranking features of their meanings. This is exactly the principle of Wilkins and of chemical nomenclature as planned by Lavoisier. Synonyms, the entries of thesauri, are defined as expressions for concepts are as close to each other as is semantically possible without becoming identical in meaning. Like Wilkins, Eberhard views the existence of such

synonyms as a signal for the state of imperfection into which our language
has developed in the course of history. A perfect language would only
contain word meanings which are morphologically expressed and, thus, need
no explanation with the help of more general, hierarchically arranged
meanings. This shows that Eberhard indeed believed ultimately in the
rational organization of the language sign, but saw it distorted in
historical reality.

Wilkins' thesaurus was part of his plan to construct a universal character
and a philosophical language. Eberhard envisages a fourfold use for his
work: exact differentiation of concepts, avoidance of mistakes because of
wrongly used concepts, avoidance of unnecessary controversy between
scholars, and stylistic adaptation of language form to matter. Such
aims would fit into Wilkins' universal language plans as well as into
the nomenclatures of scientists. In this context it is interesting to
note that Eberhard expressly compares the good that his dictionary can
do for the education of people with the good that chemical nomenclature
did for the progress of this branch of science. A corollary of this way
of thinking is his postulate for a perfect language which has exactly
as many words as there are concepts in the human mind. This, of course,
calls up many similar postulates in the 17th century by Hobbes, Locke,
Wilkins, Sprat, etc.

Roget's THESAURUS is the most famous contemporary book of the kind under
consideration. Its author confesses to following practical aims and no
others. In comparison to Eberhard's rational, high-flown educational aim,
Peter Mark Roget's ambitions sound rather pedestrian. He writes his
compilation for all those "who are unpractised in the art of composition"
and wants to give them a means for improving their style. Users of the
thesaurus have the choice among the abundance of words given and "an
instinctive tact will rarely fail to lead him [the user] to the proper
choice." (Introduction to the original edition, 1852).

The understanding of stylistic perfection is obviously far removed from
Wilkins' philosophical and epistemological considerations on language
or from Eberhard's rationalistic ideas of stylistic and intellectual
education. Style is understood in the fairly simple sense of 'proper
words in proper places' without any further analysis. Its norm is accuracy,
perspicuity and correctness. Style is instrumental, and nothing but
instrumental, to clear thinking.

With such views and the needs of those people in mind who want to avoid
repetition in their letters, who do translations or crossword puzzles,
P. M. Roget still used some of the philosophical underpinnings of Wilkins
for his own book which he acknowledged to be of influence on his own
work. He speaks of "the more obvious characters of the ideas" which come
from reflexion and experience and which are obviously universal. This
is why the classification of the English vocabulary according to these
ideas could also be used for other langues or even for a polyglot
thesaurus. Such belief in classification has even here its scientific
roots, because P. M. Roget explains that the sectional divisions of his
thesaurus correspond to the natural families in botany and zoology
(Introduction to the original edition, 1852).

Concluding remarks

There does not seem to be any need for expressly relating Eberhard's
and Roget's thesauri to the paradigm underlying Wilkins' book. Our focus

of interest lies on the fact that a special paradigmatic way of approach-
ing language appears under different conditions and at quite different
times. For Wilkins it serves the construction of a universal language;
for the chemists and botanists of his time and of later centuries it
served the perfection of their scientific work; for Eberhard it served
the education of mankind in terms of enlightenment and rationalism, and
for Roget it served the very practical needs of inexperienced language
users. But basically it is the same linguistic thinking that took its
origin from 17th-century scientific and philosophical thinking. Comparing
thinkers and books who (and which) are so widely apart from each other
in time is of course only permissible here in order to prove the
life of a paradigm under differing conditions. No attempt is made at
finding and describing direct influences.

References

Cited dictionaries (see Appendix):

(AN) ALPHABETICAL DICTIONARY ... (in Wilkins)
ORBIS SENSUALIUM PICTUS QUADRILINGUIS (Comenius)
THESAURUS OF ENGLISH WORDS AND PHRASES ... (Roget)
VERSUCH EINER ALLGEMEINEN DEUTSCHEN SYNONYMIK ... (Eberhard)

Other literature:

Aarsleff, Hans (1982) "John Wilkins" in From Locke to Saussure.
    Essays on the Study of Language and Intellectual History ed. by
    Hans Aarsleff. London: Athlone 239-277
Asbach-Schnitker, Brigitte (1984) "The Works of John Wilkins" in
    (Introduction to) Mercury: Or the Secret and Swift Messenger
    (by John Wilkins, reprint of third edition). Amsterdam: J.
    Benjamins lxxxi-cix
Baldinger, Kurt (1956) "Grundsätzliches zur Gestaltung des wissen-
    schaftlichen Wörterbuches" in Deutsche Akademie der Wissen-
    schaften zu Berlin 1946-1956 ed. by J. Irmscher and W. Radig.
    Berlin: Akademie-Verlag 379-388
Beaugrande, Robert de and Dressler, Wolfgang (1981) Introduction to
    Text Linguistics. London: Longman
Cohen, Murray (1977) Sensible Words. Linguistic Practice in England
    1640-1785. Baltimore: The Johns Hopkins U.P.
Crosland, Maurice P. (1978) Historical Studies in the Language of
    Chemistry. New York: Dover
Eco, Umberto (1984) Semiotics and the Philosophy of Language.
    London: Macmillan

Flood, Walter E. (1963) The Origin of Chemical Names. London: Old-
 bourne
Foucault, Michel (1970) The Order of Things: An Archaeology of the
 Human Sciences. New York: Panther Books
Hayashi, Tetsuro (1978) The Theory of English Lexicography 1530-1791
 (Amsterdam Studies in the Theory and History of Linguistic
 Science III.18). Amsterdam: J. Benjamins
Henne, Helmut (1977) "Nachdenken über Wörterbücher: Historische
 Erfahrungen" in Nachdenken über Wörterbücher by Günther Dros-
 dowski et al. Mannheim: Bibliographisches Institut 7-49
Kuhn, Thomas S. (1964) The Structure of Scientific Revolutions.
 Chicago: U. of Chicago P.
Large, Andrew (1985) The Artificial Language Movement. Oxford:
 Blackwell
Morveau, L.B. Guyton de et al. (1787) Méthode de nomenclature
 chimique. Paris
Said, Edward W. (1974) "An Ethics of Language" Diacritics 3: 28-39
Salmon, Vivian (1974) "John Wilkins' Essay (1668). Critics and
 commentators" Historiographia Linguistica 1,2: 147-163
Schildt, Joachim and Viehweger, Dieter eds. (1983) Die Lexikographie
 von heute und das Wörterbuch von morgen. Analysen - Probleme -
 Vorschläge (Linguistische Studien Reihe A, Arbeitsberichte 109).
 Berlin: Akademie der Wissenschaften
Slaughter, Mary M. (1982) Universal Languages and Scientific Tax-
 onomy in the Seventeenth Century. Cambridge: U.P.
Wilkins, John (1668) Essay towards a Real Character and a Philo-
 sophical Language. London: J.M. for Gellibrand and Martin

AN
ALPHABETICAL DICTIONARY,

Wherein all

ENGLISH WORDS

According to their

VARIOUS SIGNIFICATIONS,

Are either referred to their Places in the

PHILOSOPHICAL TABLES,

Or explained by such Words as are in those

TABLES.

LONDON,

Printed by *J.* M. for *Samuel Gellibrand* and
John Martin, 1668.

LEXICOGRAPHIC ARCHAEOLOGY: COMPARING DICTIONARIES

OF THE SAME FAMILY

Robert F. Ilson

Lexicographic Archaeology (calqued on 'Industrial Archaeology')
is one of the component disciplines of lexicography. It consists in
the comparison of different editions of the same dictionary, of
different dictionaries derived from a common source, or different
dictionaries from the same publisher. It is an especially manageable instance of the more general enterprise of comparing
dictionaries critically. Lexicographic Archaeology can reveal facts
about the language itself, can cast light on important problems of
dictionary-making, and can play an important role in the training of
lexicographers and dictionary reviewers.

Facts about the language

What Collignon and Glatigny (1978:20) call 'le renouvellement
constant des dictionnaires' provides a rich source of information
about general movements in the vocabulary of a language over time.
The classic study using this information, summarised in Collignon
and Glatigny, is that for French of Dubois et al. (1960), who
compared two editions of the PETIT LAROUSSE ILLUSTRE, those of 1949
and 1960. They conclude (Dubois and Dubois 1971:113) that in those
11 years "près de 25% du vocabulaire du dictionnaire est modifié" --
a figure representing additions and deletions of headwords and
senses. These changes in vocabulary reflect changes in society
(Collignon and Glatigny 1978:21):

> L'évolution des techniques au cours de la décennie apparaît en
> filigrane derrière ces modifications : c'est la biologie et la
> médecine, ainsi que les sciences économiques et politiques
> qui, avec les techniques industrielles, fournissent le plus
> grand nombre d'additions, alors que les suppressions portent,
> le plus souvent, sur le vocabulaire non technique, dit souvent
> "général" (ex. accusable, considérément, etc.) ou sur des
> pratiques artisanales dépassées (attisonoir-aoûtage, etc.)

An assessment of changes in the vocabulary of English from the
late 1950's to the mid-1970's is to be found at the beginning of
Merriam-Webster's 6,000 WORDS (1976), a supplement to WEBSTER'S
THIRD NEW INTERNATIONAL DICTIONARY of 1961 (WIII). Unfortunately,
no statistics are provided, and, of course, there is no discussion
of items that might deserve deletion from WIII.

Valuable as such studies are (and there should be more of
them), their validity as a picture of changes in living languages
depends on the representativeness of the sources of vocabulary
investigated in the making of the dictionaries. The reluctance of
dictionary publishers to use recorded spoken language, or even to
tap the rich resources of printed advertisements, remains a
serious weakness, as is shown in 6,000 WORDS by Merriam-Webster's
poignant account of mayo 'mayonnaise': "Mayo has probably been
heard at lunch counters for forty years or more, but it was only
in the early 1960s that we began to see it in print". And even
though mayo was included in 6,000 WORDS, it has not made the pages
of WEBSTER'S NINTH NEW COLLEGIATE DICTIONARY (W9, 1983).

In addition to information about the vocabulary as a whole, a
family of dictionaries can tell us much about the shifting status
of individual items: about what, following Hausmann (1977, Chapter
8), may be called their 'diasystematic' status. For example, the
adjective trendy is labelled chiefly Brit by WEBSTER'S (EIGHTH)
NEW COLLEGIATE DICTIONARY (W8) of 1973. In 6,000 WORDS of 1976 it
is unlabelled, and in W9 of 1983 it is not only unlabelled, but
has acquired a second sense. Sadly, however, the noun use of
trendy, recorded as a run-on in 6,000 WORDS, has not been retained
in W9, suggesting that its integration into American English may
still not be complete. Conversely, by comparing different
editions of CHAMBERS TWENTIETH CENTURY DICTIONARY (TCD) and the
CONCISE OXFORD DICTIONARY (COD) we may chart the vertiginous rise
in British English of billion in its originally American sense of
'thousand million'. The 1975 edition of the TCD says of billion:
'in Britain, France (since 1948), etc., a million millions... : in
U.S.A. one thousand millions...' The 1983 edition keeps the first
part of the entry unchanged, but the second part now reads 'in
U.S., often now in Britain, one thousand millions'. As for the
COD, its fourth edition (1951) says of billion: 'A million
millions; (in U.S. and France) a thousand millions'. Its sixth
edition (1976) says: '// A million millions; *a thousand
millions'. Here // means '... usu. U.K. and Commonwealth' whereas
* means 'chiefly U.S. ...'. Its seventh edition (1982) says: '//
A million million; a thousand million'. Thus the wheel has come
full circle: in COD4 'million millions' was unmarked, 'thousand
millions' marked; in COD6 both were marked; in COD7 'million
million' is marked, 'thousand million' unmarked. These examples
show what Hausmann would call the changing 'diatopic' status of
items.

An area of particular interest for the sociolinguist is what
Hausmann would call the 'diaconnotative' status of items. Thus
ethnic slurs like nigger and Yid have long been marked as pej-
orative (or omitted from dictionaries entirely), but it is only
recently, in response to changing social attitudes, that slurs of

other types have come to be marked similarly. In W8 (1973) <u>queer</u>
in its (male) homosexual sense was unmarked; in W9 (1983) it is
marked '--usu. used disparagingly'. In W8 <u>boy</u> 'a male servant'
was marked '--sometimes taken to be offensive' but <u>girl</u> 'a female
servant or employee' was unmarked, as was <u>girl</u> 'a single or
married woman of any age' (for which there is no corresponding
sense of <u>boy</u> in W8 or W9). In W9 both these senses of <u>girl</u> bear
the same marking as the 'servant' sense of <u>boy</u> still does.

Problems of dictionary-making

The up-dating of a dictionary to produce a new edition is
typically a 'diachronic' task, though new editions of existing
dictionaries can also offer new features or dispense with old
ones. Thus W9, in contrast to W8, dates many of its entries,
provides usage essays as well as synonym essays, and has trans-
ferred its abbreviations from the A-Z text to an appendix; and W8
had already eliminated the appendices of common Christian names
and of rhymes to be found in W7 (1963).

However, dictionaries of the same family can differ in many
other ways even if they are 'synchronically' similar; that is,
produced at roughly the same time. The most typical synchronic
dictionary family is one in which a relatively large dictionary
has been the progenitor of successively smaller ones: dictionary
families usually go from larger to smaller, though it would in
principle be sounder to build the family up than to 'build it
down'. The first problem in producing an abridgment is deciding
what to leave out. Nowadays the choice is almost always to leave
out the hard words, though lexicographers have protested (tirelessly but fruitlessly) that the result is a small dictionary that
tells us only what we already know, not what we need to look up
(cf. for example, Zgusta 1986:141-142). Rather than focussing on
the problem of deletion, however, I should like to examine the
differences in explanation associated with abridgment. Here is
how everyday <u>water</u> is explained in three successively smaller
dictionaries of the Collins family:

1. a clear colourless tasteless odourless liquid that is
essential for plant and animal life and constitutes, in impure
form, rain, oceans, rivers, lakes, etc. It is a neutral substance, an effective solvent for many compounds, and is used
as a standard for many physical properties. Formula: H_2O.
Related adj.: **aqueous**. Related combining form: **hydro-**.
(COLLINS ENGLISH DICTIONARY 1979)

1. a clear colourless tasteless odourless liquid that is
essential for plant and animal life and consititutes, in

impure form, rain, oceans, rivers, lakes, etc. Formula: H_2O.
Related adj.: **aqueous**. (NEW COLLINS CONCISE ENGLISH DICTIONARY
1982)

1. transparent, colourless, odourless, tasteless liquid,
substance of rain, river, etc. (NEW COLLINS COMPACT ENGLISH
DICTIONARY 1984)

The second definition is simply a truncation of the first by the
excision of the 'second sentence' and (alas) the related combining
form. The third definition, however, not only excises further
information but also has been reworked substantially: note,
besides the changed wording, the adoption of a telegraphic style
and the introduction of commas (perhaps to compensate for the
extreme concision). Perhaps the most important point is that the
information lost at each stage is essentially 'synthetic' or
'encyclopaedic': information about the use of water rather than
about its nature (see Geeraerts 1985 and Geeraerts forthcoming).

These Collins dictionaries differ greatly in size, but they
are all intended for essentially the same public: adult native
speakers. Quite different problems are presented when a dictionary is adapted to a different public; for example, when an
adults' dictionary is adapted for children or vice versa. Here
two competing forces interact: the desire to make the dictionaries
different because of their different users (or uses), and the
desire to keep the dictionaries similar in order to maintain the
unity of the family and encourage users to 'graduate' from one
member of it to others.

The American Thorndike-Barnhart family is a particularly
interesting case in point, not only because of the vast lexicographic experience embodied in the family but also because the
children's dictionaries of the family seem actually to have
preceded the adult dictionaries. In the most elementary
dictionary of the family the entry for everyday water is:

1. the liquid that fills the ocean, rivers, lakes, and ponds,
and falls from the sky as rain. We use water for drinking and
washing. (SCOTT, FORESMAN BEGINNING DICTIONARY 1976: a
revision of the THORNDIKE-BARNHART BEGINNING DICTIONARY first
published in 1952)

In an adult dictionary of the same family, the corresponding entry
is:

1. liquid that constitutes rain, oceans, rivers, lakes, and
ponds. Perfectly pure water is a transparent, colorless,
tasteless, scentless compound of hydrogen and oxygen, H_2O,
freezing at 32 degrees F. or 0 degrees C., and boiling at 212

degrees F. or 100 degrees C. (THORNDIKE-BARNHART COMPREHENSIVE
DESK DICTIONARY 1967: first published in 1951)

The children's definition uses simpler language. But more
interesting perhaps are the two 'second sentences'. The adult
'second sentence' is both encyclopaedic and analytic: it gives
encyclopaedic information about the nature of water. The
children's 'second sentence' is both encyclopaedic and synthetic:
it tells how we use water. This accords well with the finding of
developmental psycholinguistics that children themselves explain
things in terms of their function ('a broom is for sweeping')
before they begin explaining things in terms of their physical
appearance or characteristics (see Crystal 1986: Discussion
Summary, point 2). In addition, the use of we helps to establish
rapport. I have maintained elsewhere (cf. Ilson 1985:3 and Ilson
1986:69-70) that children's dictionaries are an important area of
lexicographic innovation (especially in America), and it is
interesting to see how a subsequent Thorndike-Barnhart dictionary
intended 'to be useful to all members of the family and to
students of various ages', the magnificent WORLD BOOK DICTIONARY
(1979: first published in 1963), combines both the children's
definition and the adult one, while expanding the latter:

1. the liquid that fills the oceans, rivers, lakes, and ponds,
and falls from the sky as rain. We use water for drinking and
washing. Pure water is a transparent, colorless, tasteless,
odorless compound of hydrogen and oxygen. It freezes at 32
degrees Fahrenheit or 0 degrees centigrade (Celsius), boils at
212 degrees Fahrenheit or 100 degrees centigrade (Celsius),
and has its maximum density at 39 degrees Fahrenheit or 4
degrees centigrade (Celsius), one cubic meter weighing one
gram. Formula : H_2O

Yet another set of problems -- 'diatopic' problems -- must be
faced when the varietal basis of a dictionary is changed; as when
an American dictionary gives rise to a British one or vice versa.
A classic example is the AMERICAN COLLEGE DICTIONARY (Barnhart et
al., first published in 1947), which gave rise to the British
ENCYCLOPEDIC WORLD DICTIONARY (Hamlyn 1971), which in turn gave
rise to the Australian MACQUARIE DICTIONARY (1981). The general
problems of such varietal transmutations have been discussed
elsewhere (cf. Burchfield 1984, Urdang 1984, Ilson 1986). Here I
should like to limit myself to one case not previously discussed,
and of special relevance for dictionaries that do not use historical ordering. To North Americans, the most 'disponible' or
psychologically salient referent of buffalo is the bison, whose
noble bust adorned the 'buffalo-head' nickel. North Americans
tend to call bison buffaloes. To other English-speakers, the most
salient referent of buffalo is the Cape buffalo or the water
buffalo, and such English-speakers are far less likely to call a

bison a buffalo. In the LONGMAN DICTIONARY OF CONTEMPORARY
ENGLISH (LDOCE 1978), an EFL learners' dictionary, the entry for
buffalo has two senses: the first covers the African and Asian
buffaloes, the second is a cross-reference to bison. In 1983
LDOCE gave rise to two smaller learners' dictionaries, the LONGMAN
ACTIVE STUDY DICTIONARY OF ENGLISH (LASDE) for those learning
British English and the LONGMAN DICTIONARY OF AMERICAN ENGLISH
(LDAE) for those learning American English. Here are the entries
for buffalo and bison in these three dictionaries:

> buffalo...1. any of several kinds of very large black cattle
> with long flattish curved horns, found mainly in Africa and
> Asia -- see picture at RUMINANT 2 BISON (LDOCE)

> bison...any of several large wild cowlike animals formerly
> very common in Europe and North America, with a very large
> head and shoulders covered with lots of hair -- see picture at
> RUMINANT (LDOCE)

> buffalo...(same as above, but without the illustration)
> (LASDE)

> bison...a large wild cowlike animal formerly very common in
> Europe and North America (LASDE)

> buffalo...1. a large wild cowlike animal formerly very common
> in North America and Europe with a very large head and
> shoulders covered with lots of hair; BISON
>   2. (same a LDOCE buffalo 1) (LDAE)

> bison... → BUFFALO (LDAE)

Note in particular how the American LDAE transfers the definition
of bison/buffalo to buffalo, re-orders the senses of buffalo,
artfully changes LDOCE's 'Europe and North America' to 'North
America and Europe', and retains LDOCE's information about the
bison/buffalo's noble appearance, so basic to its stereotype in
the North American mind. The differences between LASDE and LDAE
are appropriate for their different publics.

The discussion so far has concentrated on aspects of
Lexicographic Archaeology that should interest anyone generally
interested in language. For those with a more particular interest
in the craft of lexicography, the discipline is a valuable source
of information about lexicographic strategy and tactics.

Consider, for example, the treatment of John Hancock in the
Merriam-Webster COLLEGIATE Dictionary:

John Hancock...An autograph signature;--from the legibility of
the handwriting of John Hancock (W5 1941)

John Hancock...[John Hancock; fr. the prominence of his
signature on the Declaration of Independence] (1846) : an
autograph signature (W9 1983)

W5 has incorporated etymological information into the explanation
in the form of a usage note. W9 presents essentially the same
information in an explicit etymology. (For further information
about the synchronic role of etymological information, cf. Ilson
1983.) This case demonstrates powerfully that dictionary entries
should be viewed as wholes, with the closest possible co-operation
between definer, etymologist, and even pronunciation editor --
when those roles are separated: in some dictionary projects the
lexicographers are responsible for the complete entry.

A second example concerns the treatment of the verb fly in its
baseball sense. Its treatment is identical in W8 (1973) and W9
(1983):

3. fly vi flied; fly.ing (...) : to hit a fly in baseball

But in WEBSTER'S NEW STUDENT'S DICTIONARY (WNSD 1974) -- for those
in secondary education -- the treatment is as follows:

1. fly...vb flew...; flown...; fly.ing... 6. past or past part
flied... : to hit a fly in baseball

This treatment is like that in WIII (1961). Thus W8 and W9 make it
a separate homograph (without etymology), while WIII and WNSD have
a single entry for all verbal senses of fly. Like LDOCE, Merriam
homograph by etymology and part of speech; unlike LDOCE (or the
Larousse DICTIONNAIRE DU FRANÇAIS CONTEMPORAIN and LEXIS), Merriam
do not homograph by morphology alone. Why then have the Collegiate dictionaries homographed baseball fly? The answer is
probably that there are etymological grounds for doing so. The
general verb fly was probably converted into the noun fly, which
developed the baseball sense of 'fly ball' and was then, as it
were, re-converted into a new verb fly with regular inflexions (as
is typical in such cases). A similar process of re-conversion
took place when another sense of the noun fly, referring to types
of horse-drawn vehicle, was converted into a now archaic regular
verb fly glossable as 'to transport or travel in a fly', which is
homographed in WIII (with etymology) but is not entered in later
Merriam-Webster dictionaries. Thus, Merriam seem not to have a
consistent policy about whether word-formation processes 'count'
as etymological differences for purposes of homography.
Dictionary users cannot be expected to appreciate the

considerations underlying the treatment of <u>fly</u> in different
Merriam-Webster dictionaries, and lexicographers cannot make
informed decisions about the macrostructure of their dictionaries
without the same close co-operation with etymologists (and other
specialists) as was needed for the evolution of the treatment of
<u>John Hancock</u> between W5 and W9. A dictionary cannot be 'user-
friendly' unless it is 'lexicographer-friendly'!

The training of lexicographers and reviewers

The features common to dictionaries of the same family help to
emphasise the differences revealed by Lexicographic Archaeology
and thus alert reviewers to what are really important differences
of content, by contrast with 'notational variants' or differences
of form. As for lexicographers, most of them will spend most of
their time preparing different editions of the same dictionary, or
adapting pre-existing dictionaries to the needs of different types
of user. Even those lexicographers lucky enough to be allowed to
create dictionaries <u>de novo</u> will make use of the 'secondary
sources' that are the dictionaries already produced by their
colleagues, and can profit from the insights gained by an
introduction to the discipline of Lexicographic Archaeology. In
the in-house training programme I established for Longman
lexicographers, Lexicographic Archaeology was an important
component, whose success made me realise how much an understanding
of past dictionaries can contribute to the improvement of future
ones.

References

Cited dictionaries (see Appendix):

AMERICAN COLLEGE DICTIONARY (Barnhart et al.)
CHAMBERS TWENTIETH CENTURY DICTIONARY (Davidson/Kirkpatrick)
(THE) CONCISE ENGLISH DICTIONARY (Fowler/Sykes)
DICTIONNAIRE DUE FRANÇAIS CONTEMPORAIN (Dubois)
ENCYCLOPEDIC WORLD DICTIONARY (Hanks)
LEXIS (Dubois)
LONGMAN ACTIVE STUDY DICTIONARY (Summers)
LONGMAN DICTIONARY OF AMERICAN ENGLISH (Gray et al.)
LONGMAN DICTIONARY OF CONTEMPORARY ENGLISH (Procter et al.)
(THE) MACQUARIE DICTIONARY (Delbridge et al.)
MERRIAM-WEBSTER'S (FIFTH) COLLEGIATE DICTIONARY
(THE) NEW COLLINS COMPACT ENGLISH DICTIONARY (McLeod)
(THE) NEW COLLINS CONCISE DICTIONARY ... (McLeod)
9,000 WORDS (WIII Supplement)
PETIT LAROUSSE ILLUSTRÉ

SCOTT, FORESMAN BEGINNING DICTIONARY (Barnhart)
6,000 WORDS (WIII Supplement)
THORNDIKE-BARNHART BEGINNING DICTIONARY (Thorndike/Barnhart)
THORNDIKE-BARNHART COMPREHENSIVE DESK DICTIONARY (Barnhart)
WEBSTER'S (EIGHTH) NEW COLLEGIATE DICTIONARY
WEBSTER'S NEW STUDENT'S DICTIONARY
WEBSTER'S NINTH NEW COLLEGIATE DICTIONARY (Mish et al.)
WEBSTER'S (SEVENTH) NEW COLLEGIATE DICTIONARY
WEBSTER'S THIRD NEW INTERNATIONAL DICTIONARY ... (Gove)
(THE) WORLD BOOK DICTIONARY (Barnhart)

Other literature:

Burchfield, Robert W. (1984) "Dictionaries, new & old" Encounter
    63,3: 10-22 and "Robert Burchfield replies [to Laurence
    Urdang]" Encounter 63,5: 73
Collignon, Lucien and Glatigny, Michel (1978) Les dictionnaires:
    initiation à la lexicographie (Collection Textes et Non
    Textes). Paris: CEDIC
Crystal, David (1986) "The ideal dictionary, lexicographer and
    user" in Lexicography: an Emerging International Profession
    (The Fulbright Papers 1) ed. by Robert F. Ilson. Manchester:
    U.P. 72-81
Dubois, Jean and Dubois, Claude (1971) Introduction à la
    lexicographie: le dictionnaire. Paris: Larousse
Dubois, Jean et al. (1960) "Le mouvement général du vocabulaire
    français de 1949 à 1960 d'après un dictionnaire d'usage" Le
    Français moderne April 1960: 86-105; July 1960: 196-210
Geeraerts, Dirk (1985) "Les données stéréotypiques, prototypiques
    et encyclopédiques dans le dictionnaire" Cahiers de
    Lexicologie 46,1: 27-43
Geeraerts, Dirk (forthcoming) "Types of semantic information in
    dictionaries" in The Spectrum of Lexicography: Papers from
    AILA Brussels '84 ed. by Robert F. Ilson
Hausmann, Franz J. (1977) Einführung in die Benutzung der neu-
    französischen Wörterbücher (Romanistische Arbeitshefte 19).
    Tübingen: M. Niemeyer
Ilson, Robert F. (1983) "Etymological information: can it help our
    students?" English Language Teaching Journal 37,1: 76-82
Ilson, Robert F. (1985) "Introduction" to Dictionaries,
    Lexicography and Language Learning (ELT Documents 120) ed. by
    Robert F. Ilson. Oxford: Pergamon Press 1-6
Ilson Robert F. (1986) "British and American lexicography" in
    Lexicography: an Emerging International Profession (The
    Fulbright Papers 1) ed. by Robert F. Ilson. Manchester: U.P.
    51-71
Urdang, Laurence (1984) "'To plagiarise, or to purloin, or to
    borrow'? A reply to R.W. Burchfield" Encounter 63,5: 71-73

Zgusta, Ladislav (1986) "Summation" in Lexicography: an Emerging
    International Profession (The Fulbright Papers 1) ed. by
    Robert F. Ilson. Manchester: U.P. 138-146

THE HUMANIST PERIOD IN RENAISSANCE BILINGUAL LEXICOGRAPHY

Douglas A. Kibbee

John Palsgrave's LESCLAIRCISSEMENT DE LA LANGUE FRANCOYSE (1530) and Robert Estienne's THESAURUS LINGUAE LATINAE (1531) and DICTIONAIRE FRANCOISLATIN (here I consider only the editions of 1539 and 1549) are roughly contemporaneous bilingual lexicons. At first glance, they would appear to be quite different. The first relates two living languages, and does its best to keep its examples lively. It is tied to a lengthy grammar and makes frequent references to that grammar. With a goal of helping the English student survive and thrive in France, it must include the vocabulary of everyday life. The second group, Estienne's dictionaries, is more concerned with correcting the Latin of the medieval dictionaries, and thus providing a tool with which the French student can write good, i.e., classical, Latin. Taking a close look at the entries – their scope, their format, and their content – of these Humanist dictionaries of the first half of the sixteenth century, we find many similarities in lexicographic goals and technique. Relating their native languages to the literature of another language, each author, sometimes consciously, sometimes unconsciously, lays the foundation for the description of his own vernacular.

A first necessary step is to see what goals Palsgrave and Estienne express in their introduction and other lexicographic commentaries. By combining the grammar and the dictionary, with the stated intent that each help the other, Palsgrave hopes to have provided the complete instructional program for students of French. In his introduction to the third book, Palsgrave claims to have included all the words of English, and promises to add a French-English dictionary ('vocabulyst') upon the completion of the English-French tables:

> After every of which partes [of speech] so completely
> entreated of/ shall folowe certayne tables/
> contayning all the wordes in our tong/ after the
> order of a/b/c/ with the frenche wordes ioyned unto
> them/ To thentent that after the lernar can by the
> helpe of the sayde first boke/pronounce this frenche
> tong truely/ and by meanes of the seconde/ with the
> frenche vocabulyst (whiche shall folowe whan the
> thirde boke with his tables is completely finisshed)
> understande any authour that writeth in the sayd tong
> by his owne study/ without any other teacher.
>
> He maye also by the helpe of this thirde boke and
> tables therunto belongyng/ knowe how to speke any
> sentence/ or truely and parfitely to endyte any mater
> in the same tong. (III i r)

Somewhat later, he seems to be claiming that he is providing all the French nouns, as well as all the English:

> And nowe that I have here in this thirde boke
> declared at length/ what accidentes and properties
> belong unto all the substantyves in the frenche tong/
> I shall here consequently set forthe/ what and howe
> many substantyves there be in that same tong...(III
> xvi r)

Much later, after completing the lengthy section on the verbs, and we
must keep in mind that it took Palsgrave seven years to compile his
dictionary, he wearily concedes that some words might be missing:

> I beseche all maner persones whiche shall take
> pleasure or delyte in these my poore labours to
> consyder the ample largenesse of the mater whiche I
> here entreate/ and the great diffyculte of myne
> entrepryse/ whiche if I have for the chefe effecte
> brought to passe that is to say redused the frenche
> tonge under a rule and grammer certayne/ the wantynge
> somtyme of a worde is nat of so great importance/ for
> it may soone be gotten/ and ones had/ maye easyly be
> set in his dewe place... (III cccclxi v) (emphasis
> added)

Estienne, although he wrote some grammatical works, did not combine
grammatical treatises directly with these dictionaries. The separa-
tion of the two tasks may represent a step towards the production of
consultable reference works, to be used outside the context of the
classroom. In his preface to the 1539 DICTIONAIRE he states that he
has composed that work (and the Latin-French version which appeared
the year before), to help students of all ages. He realizes that many
words may have been omitted, and in the 1549 edition he addresses that
problem:

> Oultre la premiere impression de ce present livre,
> saches Lecteur qu'il a esté en ceste seconde, augmen-
> té d'infiniz motz, lesquelz autant que possible a
> esté, on a tourné en Latin, fors aucuns ausquelz on
> n'a point encores trouve es autheurs mots Latins
> respondans. Pour lesquelz te prions si tu leur
> trouves propres dictions Latines, de nous en adver-
> tir. Mesmes aussi d'autant de mots que tu trouveras
> es Rommans & bons autheurs Francois, lesquelz aurions
> omis... (1549, Préface)

In spite of his call for words from 'bons autheurs francois', he makes
no references to French authors in these two works, although he does,
in the 1549 edition, make reference to 'aucuns' who spell or pronounce
French words differently than he.   Those direct and attributed citations will be a major step forward for French lexicography, but must

await the efforts of Nicot (1573 and especially 1606). He has expur-
gated Latin words which have no classical citation to back them up.

The goals expressed have a direct effect on the choice of sources.
As noted above, Estienne includes no French sources, and Palsgrave
cites few English sources. But this is not to say that the authors
were unaware of the needs of their source languages. Indeed, they
were, in effect, establishing the standard lexicon of their language.
In the grammar Palsgrave cites many authors, all French: Octavien de
Saint-Gelais (often referred to as L'Evesque d'Angoulême), Jean Lemaire de Belges, Gaston Phoebus, Alain Chartier, Jean Meschinot,
Froissart and Jean de Meung. In the dictionary, French authors are
extensively cited in the sections on adverbs and conjunctions, and in
these sections the examples used are frequently not translated. Many
examples in the verbs smack of a literary source (references to Troy,
for example, or stylistic devices such as repetition: "soft softe the
chylde is a slepe.."), without any author being cited. Two English
authors are mentioned - Chaucer on a very few occasions, and Lydgate
quite regularly, although many of those references are simply notations of spelling variants. English sources are not used for examples, as far as I can tell.

Can one assume then that Palsgrave made a detailed analysis of the
above-mentioned French authors, and listed English equivalents for
those words, and then turned his lists around? English translations
of many of the cited authors appeared in the first decades of the 16th
century, and the comparison of the translations with the original
French texts would have provided Palsgrave with a ready-made dictionary. It is true that he includes some English paraphrases simply
to accommodate an idea expressed by a single French word:

babe that chyldren play with, pouppee s fe.
ball that is greatter and softer than a tennes ball, plotte s fe.

Yet Palsgrave includes few of the words which Humpers (1921) cited as
rare, new, or in some other way distinctive in the works of Jean
Lemaire de Belges. If he has used the French sources as the basis for
his word-list, he has selected the words with care, weeding out words
he felt were not in common enough usage.   Moreover, Palsgrave also
includes a number of English words with no French equivalent, particularly among the nouns and adjectives. If Palsgrave has used the
French sources to choose the vocabulary he will include, why does he
have a number of English words in all parts of speech with no French
equivalent (e.g., dint of swerde, dogge brere, dorneckes, plonkette, I
newefangell, I multe)? In some cases, this may be explained by a difference in the societies, as Palsgrave himself explains in this
example:

I indyte a man by indytement/ they have no suche processe in their lawe.

But geese are certainly as well known in France as in England, and
Palsgrave gives no French equivalent to:

I gagyll as a goose dothe.

Perhaps he started from an already established word-list, an English-
Latin list for example, and tried to find French equivalents for all
the words on that list. However, a lexicographic source of the
ESCLAIRCISSEMENT is hard to determine. It is hard to imagine Palsgrave compiling all this work himself, but it is also clear that if he
used the major available word lists (English-French or English-Latin)
he revised them so drastically and added so much to them that his
indebtedness must be deemed minimal. A likely source would seem to be
the PROMPTORIUM PARVULORUM, an English-Latin dictionary often paired
with the CATHOLICON to provide students with a bidirectional bilingual
dictionary. However, Palsgrave's additions to the English included,
and the differences in the phrasing of the head-words makes it clear
that any relationship between the two works is quite distant.   Furthermore, the English words which lack French equivalents in LESCLAIR-
CISSEMENT are frequently not to be found in the PROMPTORIUM either (at
least in the editions available to me). For his sources, then, Palsgrave relied primarily on French literature, and on some unknown
English text or texts.

Estienne has as a primary goal cleaning up the Latin dictionaries
of his medieval predecessors, ridding them of the medieval barbarisms
by substituting classical sources for medieval sources, and expunging
medieval usages for which no classical examples can be found. He
cites as his sources a fairly standard list of classical Latin authors
- Cicero, Aulus Gellius, Pliny, Terrence, Plautus, etc. Even though
it is a French-Latin dictionary, the improvement of the sources (of
the citations) is solely in the target language, as a result of Bude's
work.

Estienne is more straightforward about his sources,so we find no
French words without Latin equivalents. Like Palsgrave, he does include, in his French-Latin dictionaries, long paraphrases as a head-
word, in order to represent an idea expressed by a single Latin word:

Qui s'abbaisse devant ung autre comme on fait devant Dieu quand on le
     prie, Supplex. (1539, 1549)

Quand aucun accuse ou desprise ung autre & me dit de luy a force,
     Infectatio. (1539, 1549)

The obvious explanation for this practice, that Estienne has simply
reversed earlier dictionaries in composing their later dictionaries,
is tempting but does not stand up to rigorous investigation. Estienne
substantially rewrote the dictionary of 1531 in composing his bilingual works of 1538 and 1539. Starting from the French-Latin dic-

tionary of 1539 one finds a lack of concordance between it and the
1531 THESAURUS. The article convoiter, convoitise, convoite, convoitant, convoitement lists a number of Latin equivalents which are not
listed as equivalents of those words in the earlier Latin dictionary:

une ardente convoitise, fax corporis
convoitise mauvaise et difficile a supporter, dura domina cupiditas
estre abusé par la convoitise, prolabi cupiditate
engendrer une convoitise aux hommes, cupiditatem iniicere hominibus
convoitise de regner le tient grandement pensif, versat animum cupido
     regni
resister aux convoitises, cupidinibus responsare
estre puni de sa convoitise, cupiditatis ac saevitiae poenas luere
avec grande convoitise, sitienter
convoitement, appetitio
convoiter par avarice, appetere per avaritiam
convoiteux, percupidus
convoitant, expetens
qui n'est point convoiteux, a cupiditate remotus

Moreover, several Latin words drawn from the 1531 THESAURUS which list
as a French equivalent some form of convoiter are not included as
equivalents of the French word in the 1539 DICTIONAIRE FRANCOISLATIN:

appetentia, appetit, convoitise, desyr.
avide, affectueusement, ardamment, convoiteusement, de grand desir.
avare, avaritieusement, par convoitise. Terent in prologo Heaut. Si
     nunquam avare pretium statui arti meae, Si iamais ie ne mis pris a
     mon art par convoitise d'avoir argent.

Certainly Estienne used the THESAURUS as a source for the DICTIONAIRE,
but the latter is not simply a reversal of the former.

    The primary written sources for both dictionaries are clearly in
the target language, and this significantly changes the scope of the
dictionary. Both authors try to include all the words of the target
language, whatever the effect may be on the head-words, a practice
which certainly does not help the consultability of their works.

    The organization of the works, too, affects the nature of the
entries and the ways in which the works may be consulted. Palsgrave
lists the words alphabetically by part of speech, i.e., all the nouns
are listed in alphabetical order, then all the adjectives, etc. Each
word-list follows a section of commentaries on the rules of grammar
(relating to each part of speech) presented in the first two books of
LESCLAIRCISSEMENT. For the lexicographer/grammarian, this approach
has clear advantages. The listing of grammatical rules in the first
two books permits him to avoid listing all the variants and derivatives in the dictionary (xv verso). Palsgrave regularly makes cross-
references to points of grammar discussed in the sections preceding

the dictionary. Indeed, nearly all the pronoun entries are accompanied
by references to specific rules. The listing of all the words by
part of speech permits him to make rules which take into account the
lexicon, as in his distinction of the conjunctions as/that/than: if
they are preceded by several words and are not listed among the adverbs, they are conjunctions (e.g., 'all be it that').

    For the user, this approach has certain disadvantages. The listing
of words by part of speech requires a knowledge of the grammar before
one can find the word sought. Even if one has a good idea, the
results are sometimes surprising. Past participles and even present
participles are frequently listed among the adjectives. Adjectives
combined with the verb être are frequently listed among the verbs.
This makes sense if a different syntactic or semantic structure is
used to represent the idea in the target language (e.g., I am a
hongred, j'ai faim), but frequently this is not the case (e.g., I am
astonysshed, ie suis estonné). Listing all the words by part of
speech thus leads to much repetition, participles/adjectives, adverbs/
prepositions, adverbs/coonjunctions, etc., a fact which Palsgrave
recognizes:

          Notyng first that for so moche as that prepositions
          in bothe our tonges maye waxe somtyme adverbes and
          somtyme be used as coniunctions I shall gyve exemple
          of al their dyversytes...(III ccccxv r)

    If that manner of organization requires a knowledge of the grammar,
Estienne's requires a knowledge of derivation. Some of the entries
list rather broad word families - debonnaire is listed under aire. In
the 1539 edition all the derivatives are usually listed in the heading, but in the 1549 edition they are not. Past participles are
regularly included in the heading, but present participles are not,
even if the examples include uses of the present participle as an
adjective. Sometimes these are given separate status, and not included in the word-family: ars the past participle of ardre, to burn,
has its own entry, as does ayant, the present participle of avoir, to
have.

    How has the way these two lexicographers used their announced and
unannounced sources affected the nature of the entries? Sometimes the
emphasis on the target language leads to head words that we would not
recognize as such. Some head-words read more like explanations of the
target language equivalent, even almost encyclopedic entries, particularly in Estienne. Some have definitions of the head word, in the
source language. Others present multiple head-words for a single
equivalent. Still others present some type of specification of the
head-word, either limiting its scope or classifying it. These practices represent a step in the development of a monolingual dictionary
of each of the source languages. Having listed parfaire and achever
both as equivalents for absoluere, it is only natural that he should

provide these two together in a listing of his French-Latin dictionary, paving the way for one to define the other later in the development of a French monolingual dictionary (such as Nicot 1606).

One type of information which is frequently included in the source language is the classification of certain types of nouns, particularly as herbs, spices, rocks, or other categories of nature.

Estienne 1539   aspic, herbe ou serpent
                 aspic, herbe, pseudonardum
                 serpent nommé aspic, aspis, aspidis

                 ung pierre pretieuse nommée amathysite, Amethystes.

Palsgrave   crapaude a precious stone crapaudine s fe.

                 monkey, a beest broutique s fe. marmot z ma.

A second type of information provided is the specification of the head-word, limiting it to a particular range, or showing the common use of a noun:

hoory as meate that is kepte to longe ma. fleury s fe. fleurye s
hoory as a man or beestes heare is ma. chaneu s fe. chaneue s.
wrest for a harpe broche de harpe s fe.
yoke for an oxe ioug a beuf z ma. collier a beuf s ma.

A third type of information provided in the source language are synonyms of the head-word, a first step towards the definition of the head-word.

Estienne (1539)   abastardir et corrompre, adulterare
                   annales et chroniques annales
                   abaisser et amoindrir le loy et honneur d'aucun,
                       gloriam alicuius refringere.

Palsgrave   hydyouse terryble or fearfull, ma. hideux fe,
                       hydeuse s.
                   craker a boster vanteur s ma.
                   I am confused/ amased or abasshed/ Ie suis estonné

Sometimes Palsgrave elaborates upon the synonymy, stating directly that one word can replace the other:

> Upon, as upon Ester daye/ upon Christmasse
> daye: Le iour de pasques, le iour de nouel, so that
> all the examples whiche I have gyven of of[sic. =
> on]/here byfore maye also be used with upon/ for we
> in our tonge use on and upon byfore our feestes
> indifferently.

Finally, we reach the ultimate stage of information provided about the
source language, the definition of the head-word in the source language:

Estienne: Avoine,[1549: Aucuns dient Avene] Avena, Bromos. Une herbe
croissante communément es murailles & parois nouvelles, semblable a
l'herbe appelée yvroie, vulgairement dicte, Avoine sterile, Murinum
hordeum.

Abhorrir ou abhorrer une chose, c'est a dire, l'avoir en horreur,
abhorrere, exhorrere, abominari

Abiect, de quoy on ne tient compte, de quoy on ne fait point d'es-
timer, abiectus.

Palsgrave: courfewe a ryngyng of belles towarde evenyng couvrefeu x
ma.

cressent the newe mone as long as it is nat rounde cressant s ma.

pecunyall/ belongynge to money ma. pecunial aulx fe. pecunialle s.

Sometimes the definitions are expanded to provide a full encyclopedic
entry, as in these examples from Estienne:

Argentier, office ou estat anciennement usité, consistant en faict
d'argent baillé & prins a interest & usure, & autres contractz conse-
cutifz. Tellement que par le papier des argentiers plusieurs contractz estoyent expediez, & estoyent lesdicts papiers authentiques &
faisoyent foy comme les instruments passez par devant les notaires
aujourd'huy, Argentarius.

Asseurance que le peuple, ou celuy qui ha l'administration de la chose
publique donne a quelqu'ung pour faire ou dire quelque chose, l'as-
seurant qu'il n'aura nul mal, Fides publica.

    In the 1549 edition, Estienne includes a number of etymologies,
relating the French word back not just to Latin but also to Greek, in
the tradition of Jean Lemaire de Belges' CONCORDE DES DEUX LANGAGES
(1510) and paving the way for Henri Estienne's DE LA CONFORMITÉ DU
LANGAGE FRANÇOIS AVEC LE GREC (1565).

    Palsgrave is less likely to provide such long explanations, and
includes no etymologies (although he does note language change by recording words which were more common in Old French than in the modern
(i.e., sixteenth-century) language, and language variation in both
French and English) but he does include some notations of the differences between the two societies, as noted above in the example with no
French equivalent (I indyte), and in this explanation of the possible

answers to the question 'how farre forthe':

myle thre myle. etc. they reken by lieues as/ une lieue, deux lieues,
troys lieues, etc. Of whiche every lieue contayneth two englysshe
myles.

What do these three elements, the sources, the structure of the
dictionary, and the information provided about the source head-word
tell us about the lexicographic principles used by the authors, and
about the ultimate goals of their works? Both use the target language
as the primary source for the words in their lists, but do so carefully, eliminating or at least taking note of outdated or uncertain words
in both languages. As a result, the source language is provided a
description that far surpasses any previous effort, and the the position of the source vernacular is strengthened.   The goal of edifying
the source language, through comparison with the target language,
reveals itself when we note that in the 1549 edition Estienne adds
French words, clearly taken directly from the Latin, which he had not
found previously, and also comments upon the spelling and pronunciation of French words.   In general, his comments are designed to latin-
ize the orthography, so that the derivation of the word is clearly
seen from the spelling, e.g.:

adiancer. Semble qu'on doibve escrire Adgencer, pour Adgenter, c'est
a dire, faire gent. Aptare, Decorare, Componere, Concinnare.

Sometimes, however, the changes are suggested strictly according to
the logic of French, as when he corrects aisné:

aisné. Primogenitus, Primigenius. Il semble mieux d'escrire Ainsné,
comme qui diroit Ains né, c'est a dire, devant né, ainsi le monstre
son contraire, qui est Puisné.

Furthermore, by the edition of 1549, Estienne is adding words to the
French lexicon so that paraphrases are no longer required to represent
single Latin word:

1539: qui abbaye, latrator

1549: Qui abbaye, ou abbayeur, latrator.

Palsgrave too is correcting his native language, when he casts aside
dialectal variations (particularly northern dialects) and Lydgate's
deviant spelling, and is enlarging its horizons when he provides
English translations for words recently borrowed from French with
which he feels the reader may not yet be acquainted:

fonnell to fyll a bottell or vessell with, autonnoyr s ma.

The word fonnell (funnel) had entered English, probably from southern

France, in the fifteenth century. By explaining the meaning and
specific use, Palsgrave adds the vocabulary to the everyday usage of
his fellow countryman. Similarly, he specifies the use of popet (pup-
pet): for childre to play with poupee s fe. For dissolute he specifies the sixteenth-century meaning of the word (incontynent of lyv-
ynge), replacing the earlier meaning of 'weak'. Thus the inclusion
of definitions and specifications in the source language concerning
the source language head-word is used to bring the source language
under the same control he is proposing for the target language, and
serves as a basis for the beginning of English monolingual lexicography.

These two Humanist lexicographers, by their concern for the propriety of usage in their own language, and the enrichment of their
native languages by borrowing from other languages, are an integral
part of the movement in both of their countries to fix and improve the
level of language. Both show clear Humanist tendencies in their
preference for written to spoken sources, their acceptance of etymolo-
gizing spelling, and their rejection of dialect. Although Estienne's
influence was destined to be far greater than Palsgrave's, each must
be considered a key figure in the founding of his country's lexicographic tradition.

References

Cited dictionaries (see Appendix):

CATHOLICON (Balbus)
(LA) CONCORDE DES DEUX LANGAGES (Lemaire de Belges)
(DE LA) CONFORMITE DU LANGAGE FRANÇOIS AVEC LE GREC (Estienne)
DICTIONAIRE FRANCOISLATIN (Estienne)
DICTIONAIRE FRANÇOIS-LATIN (Nicot)
LESCLARCISSEMENT DE LA LANGUE FRANCOYSE (Palsgrave)
PROMPTORIUM PARVULORUM ...
THESAURUS LINGUAE LATINAE (Estienne)
THRESOR DE LA LANGUE FRANÇOYSE (Nicot)

Other literature:

Humpers, Alfred (1921) Etude sur la langue de Jean Lemaire de
     Belges. Liège: H. Vaillante-Carmanne

LÁSZLÓ ORSZÁGH, THE LEXICOGRAPHER

Tamás Magay

Introduction

László Országh's oeuvre was not that of a
lexicographer. It was he who insisted on being called
a philologist, and vigorously refused to be restricted
to the status of a 'linguist'. First of all he was a
teacher, a teacher of the English language and literature. Then, a literary historian (he wrote a history
of the American literature, first in Hungary). Then,
a lexicologist taking care of words of English origin
in the Hungarian language. Was it an eccentric claim
not to rank himself among lexicographers? - no one
can tell. But his achievement in terms of figures speaks
for itself: 7,400 pages of English and Hungarian
bilingual dictionaries and 7,400 pages of a Hungarian
monolingual dictionary - an unparalleled achievement
superseding all lexicographers in the history of Hungarian lexicography, and one that won him a name
among the noted lexicographers of the world.

But even greater, indeed a unique achievement it
was if we consider the fact that Crszágh's lexicographic
activities both in monolingual and bilingual lexicography
were carried out simultaneously and on an equally high
level.

A brief survey of Hungarian lexicography

As in most European languages, in Hungarian too,
recording of the facts of the mother tongue followed
in the wake of Latin language studies. Thus, it is the
first Hungarian-Latin dictionary that marks the beginning
of Hungarian lexicography. Albert Szenczi Molnár's
DICTIONARIUM UNGARO-LATINUM, published in 1604, can be
compared, mutatis mutandis, with PROMPTORIUM PARVULORUM,
first published in 1499 (cf. Starnes 1954).

The linguistic result of post-medieval social
and scientific development was the compilation in the
15th and 16th centuries of great bilingual dictionaries
taking stock of the mother tongue and interpreting

headwords in a foreign language. Later, parallel with
the consolidation and standardization of the national
language, the 16th and 17th centuries witnessed the
birth of dictionaries with definitions in the mother
tongue.

The systematic collection of the Hungarian national
vocabulary became possible around the turn of the 18th
and 19th centuries when Hungarian—as against German—
was reinstated in its rights and the compilation of the
long-desired comprehensive dictionary of the Hungarian
language commenced. The Hungarian Academy of Sciences,
founded as late as 1825, was responsible for the compilation of the first dictionary of the Hungarian language, Gergely Czuczor and János Fogarasi's six-volume
A MAGYAR NYELV SZÓTÁRA (A Dictionary of the Hungarian
Language) published between 1862 and 1874. This great
academic dictionary reflected the state of the Hungarian
language in the first half of the 19th century. "It is
a curious fact—writes Országh (1960, 215)—that by
the beginning of the 20th century, when the struggles
of the language reform had bequeathed a renewed and re-
fined Hungarian language...still rapidly developing,
living, standard Hungarian vocabulary and phraseology
were, so to speak, unclaimed property as far as lexicographers were concerned." In the absence of Hungarian
monolingual dictionaries a growing number of bilingual
dictionaries were the only works, even as late as the
50s of the present century, that recorded to a certain
extent the Hungarian vocabulary. No wonder then that
up to the appearance of Országh's work the word
'dictionary' itself had acquired the primary meaning
of a bilingual dictionary unlike the French dictionnaire
or the English dictionary whose primary meaning is,
on the other hand, still a dictionary of the mother
tongue (i.e. a monolingual one) . Thus, it was through
the good offices of Országh that the very concept of
'dictionary' has changed radically in the Hungarian
mind to mean two basic types of dictionaries: the
monolingual explanatory as well as the bilingual.

Monolingual dictionary-making

With the widening of public education in the years
following 1945 the need for a descriptive, synchronic
dictionary of the Hungarian language was felt greater
than ever before. The task was urgent, though aggra-
vated by the lack of previous spadework. It had to be
started from scratch, and one man was chosen to organize
and conduct all operations — L. Országh. Unfortunately
for the English studies in Hungary which, in Debrecen,
had to be terminated in 1949 for political reasons, and

very fortunately for Hungarian linguistics—and indeed
the entire Hungarian cultural life—Országh could
concentrate all his time and energy on lexicography
during the fifties, that otherwise rather shocking
decade in the history of Hungary. After ten years of
hard work of a 35-strong editorial team the first volume came out in 1959 and the seventh in 1962.

Of Országh's role—methaphorically that of a mid-
wife—at the birth of this monumental work he himself
gave a short account pencilled in his own copy of the
A MAGYAR NYELV ÉRTELMEZŐ SZÓTÁRA (An Explanatory
Dictionary of the Hungarian Language, henceforth referred to as the Dictionary), donated together with his
brilliant library to the University of Debrecen. A free
translation of his words runs as follows:

The work on the Dictionary began at the beginning
of 1950...To begin with it was planned to be a one-
volume popular dictionary. The head of the editorial
staff from 1950 to 1962, the appearance of the seventh
volume, was L. Országh. His role as the head of the
editorial staff was this: he raised the financial
basis and means for the compilation of a dictionary many
times bigger and far more scholarly than originally
planned. By winning over the Hungarian Academy of
Sciences and its publisher he employed 35 experts instead of the planned 5 editors; - wrote a draft
policy which was then to come into and remain in force
to the end; - compiled the list of headwords single-
handed; - introduced the partial marking of pronunciation, first in Hungarian monolingual lexicography;
- won a battle for the inclusion of run-on entries; -
organized a thorough cross-reference system; - fought
for the inclusion of taboo words; - edited and supervised alone three quarters of the manuscript; - urged
and enhanced the number of literary quotations; - fought
out the idea of an overall consistency throughout the
Dictionary; - and, finally, published a scholarly
introduction on the history and methods of editing the
Dictionary, as a separate volume (cf. Országh 1962).

The first step in organizing the work was the
launching of a gigantic data gathering. The only material available were dictionaries of past centuries and
a collection for the Academic Dictionary (i.e. the
OED of the Hungarian language which started in the
80s of the last century). Tens of thousands of slips
were gathered representing the written and spoken
language of contemporary Hungarian from a great number
of sources, mostly literary. No word-frequency diction-

ary had been available for the selection of headwords,
yet the principle underlying the selection had to be
the same as the one applied to modern word-frequency
dictionaries: the importance of the word in communication, its frequency in both spoken and written
language, its weight and function in the life of the
speech community. The sources yielded some 150,000
entries which then boiled down to some 60,000. For,
the scope of the Dictionary was to treat the words
entered intensively rather than extensively, vertically
rather than horizontally. The very concept of word
had to be redefined to include every lexeme, i.e. every
commonly adopted, socially valid and consequently widely
established and constant, naturalized linguistic symbol,
derived by abstraction from the generalization of the
moments of reality as reflected in our consciousness,
and expressing an independent, condensed meaning
irrespective of whether the carrier of this
content is a single word or a combination.

The inclusion of words was considered upon four
criteria: lexicological, morphological, grammatical,
and semantic.   Országh's firm stand and unswerving insistence on making his decisions always on the basis of
sound principles saved him and his team a lot of difficulties and even political involvement. For, it was a
period when words were labelled according to their
political connotations and overtones. Insert a word
between bolond (meaning'fool') and bolsevik ('Bolshevik'),
the lexicographer was instructed by some higher authority just because this awkward neighbourhood reflects
a reactionary mind which would give offence to the user,
should he read the list of headwords in continuity. Thus,
a peaceful plant name had to be coined to put in between
'fool'and 'Bolshevik'. Országh, on strictly theoretical
grounds, could and did refuse such intervention from
the non-linguist, and included all kinds of taboo words,
even the political ones, on the principle that his duty
was "to give a balanced and unbiased picture of the
language of a period... The registration of the tabu
[sic!] words... is the task of the lexicographer just
as much as the indication in due form of the stylistic
value of such words" (cf. Országh 1960, 225). In other
words this dictionary has to be descriptive and not prescriptive.

An elaborate study preceded the selection of peri-
pheral material both temporally and socially: archaic
or obsolete words and neologisms on the one hand, and
dialectal words and technical terms on the other.

We cannot go into detail with all the criteria
(lexicological, morphological, grammatical and semantic),
suffice it to say here that whatever decision was made
in any of these questions it was considered as part of
a system. It cannot be overemphasized that Országh was
always thinking—and made his collaborators think—in a
system. He never failed to see the whole, therefore he
was never lost to particulars. This was the basis of
that desired consistency, a merit very often wanting
in lexicographers and one that was carried out in all
aspects of lexicography and phases of dictionary-making
by Országh. To pick out just two from among the numerous points of consistency we might refer to the principle
of making a dictionary entirely self-contained, i.e.
to use in the definitions only such words as figure as
headwords themselves in the dictionary, thereby avoiding
circularity. Then, another point from the desiderata is
the uniform treatment of the various conceptual classes
such as the names of nationalities, zoological or botanical terms, measurements, notions from everyday life
such as food, clothing, colours, days of the week, or
grammatical categories as, for example, numerals etc.
Thinking out and carrying into effect the work of co-
ordination within the conceptual sphere was done and
supervised throughout by Országh. And it was because he
knew and had learned from the works of the old masters.
"A glance at the divergences—he noted once—in the
definitions of spring, summer, autumn, winter in
Johnson's dictionary will show that the problem did
not yet exist two centuries ago" (cf. Országh 1960,
249).

Bilingual dictionary-making

It was jokingly said of Országh: in the morning
he worked on the monolingual, and in the afternoon,
well into the night, he busied himself with the bilingual dictionary. And when asked which of the two was
easier or harder—defining in the native language or
finding target-language equivalents in a foreign
language—he voted for the latter. For, although the
monolingual dictionary is said to require a greater
amount of scholarship than the bilingual often regarded
—quite undeservedly—as a commercial rather than
scholarly undertaking, the latter has an unquestionable
difficulty over against the monolingual: it has to
compare (and contrast) not only two languages but
two—often widely—different cultures and civilizations.

In the post-1945 years, parallel with the great
economic and social transformation in Hungary, a great

upswing was seen in the learning of languages, especially of English. The need for a new, up-to-date dictionary
was at once felt and was fully satisfied by Országh's
A CONCISE DICTIONARY OF THE ENGLISH AND HUNGARIAN
LANGUAGES (Part I English-Hungarian, 1948) marking
a new era in Anglo-Hungarian lexicography.

Statistics again: while within forty years (1908
to 1948) 12,000 copies of Yolland's HUNGARIAN AND ENGLISH
DICTIONARY (First, English-Hungarian Part, 1908) were
sold, 7,000 copies of Országh's dictionary were sold
within two years (1948 to 1950), and in 1982 the total
output of his other English/Hungarian dictionaries was
somewhere around one million and 300 thousand (for
comparison: the population of Hungary is ten million).

Space is far too limited here to describe Országh's
bilingual dictionaries; I have done that in my unpublished thesis in Hungarian for my "candidate's"
degree (cf. Magay 1979). What I try to highlight in
this paper are the new features or, more precisely,
the qualitative changes that made Országh's dictionaries
strikingly superior to their predecessors.

An overall merit of Országh's dictionaries was, what
much later here in Exeter was postulated, that they were
user-oriented. Országh realized as far back as the
1940s that a dictionary is meant to cater for its users,
and that it is their demands that have to be considered
in the first place. This—I should say—democratic
attitude was reflected first and foremost in his selection of vocabulary. He was fully aware that there can
be no such thing as a complete or all-inclusive dictionary of the living, ever-growing and ever-changing
language (cf. Ruttkay 1977). What he did endeavour and
achieve, however, was a relative completeness. In a
letter to the publisher, in 1946, he wrote these words:
"In the selection of vocabulary I avoid, as a rule, the
inclusion of rarities, since the average user of this
relatively small dictionary rarely encounters them.
And although I am rather selective in the field of
technical terms, yet trying to keep abreast of the
times, I did, of course, include such terms as clutch,
radio broadcast and the like, hitherto not registered
in English-Hungarian dictionaries. Generally I record
the more important words of the past 10-15 years, among
others, the new words relating to war and peace, technology, politics, economics etc " (cf. Magay 1977). We
may add to the list of new words: air-conditionong,
atomic fission, electronics, income brackets, jeep,
jet-plane, nylon, plastics, radar, walkie-talkie etc.

all duly recorded by Országh. And, what followed in
the new editions, viz. the idea of constant and regular
updating, was, so to speak, a mania with Országh all
through his general editorship. And finding the right
and adequate proportion of the elements (units) of
standard (general) and technical vocabulary, was another. The meticulous care with which Országh selected
material from the various registers was duly appreciated
by experts who ever so often preferred Országh's general dictionaries to bilingual technical dictionaries.

As mentioned already, the monolingual dictionary-
maker Országh could rely only on Országh, the bilingual
lexicographer. For, prior to compiling the vocabulary
of the A MAGYAR NYELV ÉRTELMEZŐ SZÓTÁRA, Országh was
the first to collect the Hungarian word stock of the
fifties of the present century and—indeed—of the era
between and after the two world wars. In his great
bilingual dictionary, the HUNGARIAN-ENGLISH DICTIONARY
(1953), which contained 122,000 headwords and 116,000
multiword units (i.e. examples, phrases, idioms, proverbs etc.) , just as in the ENGLISH-HUNGARIAN DICTIONARY
(1960)which was even larger in size and depth, the terminology of a radically changed society as well as the
vocabulary of all the fields of knowledge and the various
registers of the language have duly been covered.

Meaning discrimination was based on semantic analysis
in all of his dictionaries. Meanings and shades of
meaning of the source-language words were matched with
carefully selected target-language equivalents. The
functional aspect prevailed, i.e. translation equivalents were chosen and discriminated and labelled
so as to function in the target-language context. Országh
laid great stress on the substitutability of equivalents
or, in a more cautious wording, synonyms in/of the
target language. He realized the importance of the relation between meaning and context, and their interde-
pendence. Words were broken down—as it were— to
their meanings, and all the meanings were shown in
ample context from example sentences to set phrases and
idioms or proverbs. Special emphasis was given as early
as his first English-Hungarian dictionary (1948) to
phrasal verbs which had not even been commonly called
as such in those days (cf. Kennedy 1920). Országh knew it
well right at the outset that with their highly idiomatic
content this type of verbal collocation represents
an important element of the developing and changing
present-day English language, lexicographically treated
in full, among the first, by HARRAP'S STANDARD FRENCH

AND ENGLISH DICTIONARY. "While all these phrasal
illustrations contribute to a more subtle discrimination of meanings—says Ruttkay—they give us more
than lexical information by presenting words function-
ing in their syntactical medium, restored, as it
were, to their organic, natural environment " (cf.
Ruttkay 1977).

Országh was quite early sensitive to a major
dilemma of bilingual lexicography, viz. the existence
of culture-bound elements found mainly among names of
institutions, terms of administration, jurisdiction,
education, folklore, names of dishes etc. And while
he was unable to solve problems offered by these
phenomena of language, just as any other lexicographers
up to the present day are faced with the same problem,
Országh offered correct explanations by way of compen-
sation. "This is not to say—to quote Ruttkay once
again—that, having consulted his dictionaries, we could
foot a morris-dance with choreographical perfection,
or that an English cook would run no risks if she were
to prepare túróscsusza, taking the respective entry for
a recipe. What is evident is that, to his mind, meaning
is more than a semantic question...and...his interest
in the possibility or impossibility of bilingual verbal
correspondence is not purely lexicographical, as indeed
his interest in language and languages is not purely
linguistic. In registering the similarities and differences in communication...he is always aware of the two
cultures...or,rather, it is three cultures, since
American data are so numerous (more numerous, perhaps,
than in any other standard English dictionary) that it
would be wrong not to notice them specially" (cf.
Ruttkay 1977).

And, last but not least, we might mention as one
of the chief merits of Országh the introduction into
his 1948 dictionary—and into Hungarian lexicography
as well as into English language teaching and much
later into general linguistics in Hungary—the IPA-
system for marking the pronunciation of English words.
As early as 1939 Országh employed the IPA-notation in
the first volume of his English readers for Hungarian
grammar schools, putting an end to the various individual
transcriptions bound to be casual and highly inconsist-
ent. A brief survey of the lexicography of the first third
of the present century will show that in monolingual
as well as in bilingual dictionaries the IPA-notation
was employed relatively late (cf. Magay 1977, note 18).
Thus, in his textbooks and dictionaries Országh was
internationally among the first to introduce the IPA-

system of transcription.

In conclusion yet another of his merits deserves
to be mentioned. Országh was decades ahead of his time
in realizing the difference between the two-way character
of bilingual dictionaries, the difference between a
dictionary of comprehension and production. Especially in
L1 - L2 direction Országh went into depths in differentiat-
ing the various stylistic values and registers by means of
a fair selection of usage labels and indicators to help the
Hungarian user find the proper equivalents when translating
from his native language into English.

By writing on the theoretical aspects of lexicography
Országh became internationally known and recognized. One only
wonders how this came to pass when most of his lexicographical
writings appeared in Hungarian only. It must have been the
radiation of his mind that broke through the barriers of
languages.But apart from poesy, however little he produced
quantitatively in English, his message was important and
qualitatively rich.

In a brilliant essay (also in Hungarian) on his great
predecessor, Samuel Johnson, one can easily recognize or identify Országh's 'ars linguistica' expressed by a quotation
from that other great eccentric: "I am not yet so lost in
lexicography, as to forget that words are daughters of earth,
and that things are the sons of heaven." Indeed, he was not
lost to any one branch of learning, his scholarly interest
covered a wide range of literary and linguistic studies.
This may be one of the main reasons why he was an eminent
lexicographer, one among the few who indeed created a school
in lexicography.

References

Cited dictionaries (see Appendix):

(A) CONCISE DICTIONARY OF THE ENGLISH AND HUNGARIAN LANGUAGES
     (Országh)
DICTIONARIUM UNGARO-LATINUM (Szenczi Molnár)
ENGLISH-HUNGARIAN DICTIONARY (Országh)
HARRAP'S STANDARD FRENCH AND ENGLISH DICTIONARY (Mansion)
HUNGARIAN AND ENGLISH DICTIONARY (Yolland)
HUNGARIAN-ENGLISH DICTIONARY (Országh)
(A) MAGYAR NYELV ERTELMEZŐ SZOTÁRA (Barczi/Országh)
(A) MAGYAR NYELV SZOTÁRA (Czuczor/Fogarasi)
(THE) OXFORD ENGLISH DICTIONARY (Murray et al.)
PROMPTORIUM PARVULORUM ...

Other literature:

Kennedy, Arthur G. (1920) The Modern English Verb-Adverb Combinations. Stanford CA: Stanford U. Publications Vol. 1 No.1

Magay, Tamás (1977) "A chapter in the history of English lexicography in Hungary" Hungarian Studies in English 11: 19-27

Magay, Tamás (1979) A kétnyelvű szótárírás törvényszerűségei: Országh László szótárai (The Principles of Bilingual Lexicography: The Dictionaries of L. Országh). Unpublished Cand. thesis, Hungarian Academy of Sciences, Budapest

Országh, László (1960) "Problems and principles of the new dictionary of the Hungarian language" Acta Linguistica (Budapest) 10: 211-273

Országh, László ed. (1962) A szótárírás elmélete és gyakorlata a Magyar Nyelv Ertelmező Szótárában (Theory and Practice in the Explanatory Dictionary of the Hungarian Language) (Nyelvtudományi Ertekezések 36). Budapest: Akadémiai Kiadó

Ruttkay, K. (1977) "Look it up in Országh" The New Hungarian Quarterly 18: 128-131

Starnes, DeWitt T. (1954) Renaissance Dictionaries, English-Latin and Latin-English. Austin: U. of Texas P.

THEMATIC LEXICOGRAPHY

Tom McArthur

There is more to the story of lexicography than dictionaries - if by
'dictionaries' one means no more and no less than alphabetically
organized books that list words and their definitions. Nowadays,
most people think of wordbooks in terms of ABC ordering, and by and
large most lexicographers see themselves as engaged in the creation
of such books. Both of these related views of what lexicographers
do, however, may be a limited perspective on what lexicography in
fact is.

Generally speaking, the historians of lexicography have tended
to buttress these views, in which one can contrast 'monolingual' with
'bilingual' dictionaries, 'unabridged' with 'concise' dictionaries,
and 'academic' with 'popular' or 'commercial' dictionaries. Murray
in 1900, Mathews in 1933, Hulbert in 1955, Whitehall in 1985, Matoré
in 1968, Read in 1976 and others have all tended to see lexicography -
their area of reference technology and taxonomy - as essentially
covering the invention and evolution of the alphabetic wordbook. It
is only the occasional maverick like Starnes in 1946 who has sought to
divert attention out of this rather closed-off view of things.

My own argument here is that there is a 'micro-lexicography' in
which the positions of Murray and the others can be justified, but that
there is also a 'macro-lexicography' in which lexical reference materials
can look rather different. Certainly, if one deals only with standard
dictionaries and looks only at their history, it is easy to argue that
only they matter. This, however, is to select from the data of history
only that material which supports a position already (explicitly or
implicitly) held. A more panoramic examination of the history of
reference technology and taxonomy suggests that lexicography - the
art and craft of marshalling and relating words, etc. - consists of not
one strong tradition-cum-format plus some occasionally fascinating
fragments of other approaches, but <u>two</u> distinct and complementary
traditions.

These traditions are <u>alphabetic lexicography</u> on the one side and
<u>thematic lexicography</u> on the other. As a format the alphabetic mode
was practised rather haphazardly and hesitantly until the invention of
the printing press in the 15th century, but thereafter - and particularly
from around 1600 -it consolidated itself into the dominant tradition, in
a line of development that has been well delineated by such historians
as those mentioned above. The thematic mode, however, is the older,
broader tradition, with its roots in the classical traditions of Plato,
Aristotle and Pliny, and with strong foundations in the world of
medieval Scholasticism. It is hardly a spent force today. Indeed, it

is a covert influence on much of current reference-book practice,
and is enjoying a modest overt renaissance among 'print' dictionaries.
It could also have a useful future as lexicography moves on into the
electronic era.

My detailed review of the nature of thematic lexicography and
its relationship with alphabetic lexicography, set within a broad
framework of reference materials through some five millennia of
human history, can be found in Worlds of Reference (Cambridge, 1986).
I do not wish to duplicate that review here, but the core argument is
worth a summary: Lexicography is part - and an important part - of
that interplay of technology and taxonomy which has helped our species
find means of storing information beyond the brain, our first and for
an enormous length of time our only container of knowledge. The
invention of writing systems and adequate writing surfaces, the development of storage and presentational systems, the growth of techniques for
classification (etc.) have all combined to provide us with a wide range
of options in the kinds of product or artifact we create, the kinds of
layout that will animate them, the kinds of formats available for use,
and the kinds of information poured into those formats. Crudely - in
terms of the macro-lexicography of secular reference books - the broad
options can be shown by means of the device below, which I would like
to call 'the reference rectangle':

the 'encyclopedic' option   the 'wordbook' option
producing artifacts that   producing artifacts that
handle 'things in the world',   handle 'words' (etc.),
marshalled for 'easy' reference   marshalled for 'easy' referenc

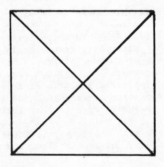

the thematic option   the alphabetic option
formats which present   formats which present
information of any kind   information of any kind via
via themes, classes, topics,   the alphabet as an invariant
contents lists, menus, etc.   series

The six lines in the diagram bring the four points of the
rectangle together in various combinations, within which many further
minor permutations are possible. They cover, for example, alphabetic
encyclopedias like the traditional BRITANNICA, thematic encyclopedias
like the CAMBRIDGE ENCYCLOPEDIA OF ARCHAEOLOGY, conventional dictionaries
like the OED, COD, Webster's COLLEGIATE, CHAMBERS 20th CENTURY (etc.),
thematic wordbooks such as Roget's THESAURUS, a pictorial DUDEN or my
own LEXICON, and an indefinite range of mixed alphabetic-cum-thematic
compilations such as the READER'S DIGEST GREAT ILLUSTRATED DICTIONARY
and the Petit Robert DICTIONNAIRE UNIVERSEL DES NOMS PROPRES, which
also mix the ideas of 'encyclopedia' and 'dictionary' in interesting
ways. There is in fact very little in the world of reference materials -
including library catalogues and telephone directories - which does
not fit comfortably into the model as shown.

It is necessary to stress, however, that the model is independent
of such words as 'encyclopedia' and 'dictionary'. Such words are
historically and culturally volatile; there may be a broad consensus
about what they can and should mean, but in practice that consensus
tends constantly to be violated. Thus, in the 18th century such
encyclopedists as Ephraim Chambers, Denis Diderot and the Edinburgh
Society of Gentlemen who created the BRITANNICA called their works
'dictionaries'. Many a work that is called a 'dictionary' could just
as easily be called an 'encyclopedia' - the Petit Robert title mentioned
above for example, or a Penguin 'Dictionary of Saints'. In Tudor times,
John Withals brought out a 'dictionarie' for young students of Latin
which was entirely thematic in layout, while at the present time my
own LEXICON OF CONTEMPORARY ENGLISH is often loosely referred to by
its publisher Longman and others as 'a semantic dictionary'. Roget's
original THESAURUS was entirely thematic - without even an index - but
nowadays there are many works which call themselves thesauruses and are
entirely alphabetic. The key generic terms of macro-lexicography are
therefore inherently fuzzy in strict referential terms, and should be
accepted as such; they have been referentially fuzzy since they first
came into use in the Middle Ages. This is one reason why I prefer to
talk about 'wordbooks' for generic purposes, rather than 'dictionaries'.

With the macro-lexicographic perspective, however, one can place
books, however they are named, somewhere in the reference rectangle;
that is, one can see where they are 'located' in terms of the
historically and culturally significant interaction among the genres
and formats available to us. And this is as true of the French, German
and other traditions as it is true of English-language lexicography.
Indeed, using such a model as the rectangle, one can talk about where
the French tradition tends to locate itself, and show how, for example,
the Scottish lexicographical tradition differs from the English, and
where the American differs from the British as a whole. Without such a
model, one's statements may tend to remain diffuse and unfocussed. Within
such a model, it may be possible to demonstrate succinctly ways in which
the French tend towards encyclopedic dictionaries and crypto-thematic
'analogical' presentations of words, while the Oxford tradition enshrined
in the COD eschews the encyclopedic connection and the Merriam-Webster
tradition - highlighting the American approach to lexicography - embraces
it, with an emphasis on thematic appendices of all kinds to the main
alphabetic list.

Despite all this, however, it is true to say that in the immediate
world of wordbooks people do not readily think of thematic works. If
invited to do so, they will probably mention Roget, shortly followed
perhaps by comments on the arcane and idiosyncratic quality of his
conceptual scheme. Roget was first published by Longman in 1852 and
the work has been one of the great publishing successes of the English-
using world, but its taxonomy is highly Latinate and academic and most
of the people who use the book get to its lists via the index. Additionally, as I have indicated above, there have been many re-castings of
Roget in straight alphabetic form, and both these points - index and
re-casting - inevitably suggest the primacy of alphabetization over
thematization.

At first sight this looks daunting, but I would suggest that it
conceals one of a number of pseudo-problems that arise in minds conditioned to think alphabetically about lexis. The core of the problem
is to assume (a) that a thematic layout promotes eccentricity, and
(b) that an alphabetic layout inhibits eccentricity. The thematic
compiler is seen as having one - idiosyncratic - view of the world,
foregrounded by his or her conceptual schema, and users are seen as
having their own schemas, inevitably at odds with the compiler's. In
quasi-Whorfian terms, it may not be possible to map one schema onto
any other, or in broad philosophical terms there may not exist any
Platonic 'true' list from which a thematic work could be derived.

I belong among those who consider that it is impossible to find
an ultimate true schema for ordering things and words in the world; in
Popperian terms, there can only be better or worse schemata for any
purpose, whether it is Roget's plan or the Yellow Pages. Even where
such schemata are created by committee or consensus rather than by one
compiler, they will still be culture-bound, period-bound, place-bound
and, say, Anglocentric or Francocentric. And this is where the pseudo-
problem comes in: All this is just as true of alphabetic wordbooks -
except that the alphabet helps shuffle the material in such a way that
the limitations, relativism and idiosyncrasy of such books is not
immediately or panoramically obvious. However, as one retreats in time
and style from such works, the 'failings' of time, place, culture and
personality increasingly display themselves. This is amply demonstrated
by looking at commentaries on, for example, the idiosyncrasies of the
great alphabeticist himself, Samuel Johnson in 1755, every bit as
eccentric as Peter Mark Roget a century later. It could therefore be
said that a thematic format has the virtue of being more patently
limited than an equally but covertly limited alphabetic format.

Additionally, to judge thematic compilations in terms of one such
work - Roget's THESAURUS - is no more an argument against the genres
involved than would be a judgement against dictionaries because of
deficiencies in - well, choose the present-day dictionary that you like
least. Once one chooses to look beyond the restrictions imposed by an
alphabet-centred view of lexicography, it becomes apparent that there
are many varieties and instances of thematic presentation, and not just
among encyclopedias, where the tradition flourishes. Some of these are:

o   the tradition   of travellers' phrase books, epitomized for
    example by the Berlitz booklets. These tend to be small 200-
    page handbooks with colour-coded themes whose topical pre-
    sentation goes back to the vocabularia of the Middles Ages and
    the vulgaria of the Renaissance. They are structured in diverse
    ways, but often use alphabetic sublists within their themes.

o   the tradition of pictorial wordbooks, of which the DUDEN
    Bildwörterbücher of Germany are outstanding examples. These
    are standard dictionary size, with an alphabetic index attached to
    thematically organized lists whose antecedents were the radically
    successful pedagogical works of John Comenius, the Moravian
    bishop, in the 17th century.

o   specialized vocabulary lists arranged in topics or classes
    within a wide range of standard language textbooks, a lexico-
    graphical sub-tradition, especially where organized bilingually,
    which dates back not just to the vocabularia but through classical
    times to the scribal schools of ancient Mesopotamia.

o   individual innovative works in this century, such as WHAT'S WHAT:
    A VISUAL GLOSSARY OF THE PHYSICAL WORLD (Fisher & Bragonier,
    Hammond, New Jersey, 1981) and my own LONGMAN LEXICON OF CONTEMPORARY
    ENGLISH (also 1981).

o   as already touched on, elements within or behind alphabetic works
    which are either overtly thematic or covertly thematic. Overt
    examples are grouped appendices of various kinds in many standard
    works, or whole volumes of classified glossaries, as for example
    Don Ethan Miller's THE BOOK OF JARGON (Macmillan, New York, again
    1981), which consists of six theme groupings divided into 24
    sub-theme glossaries, each glossary alphabetic. Covert examples
    are legion, among them for example the analogical background to the
    varied listings of related words in the DICTIONNAIRE LE PETIT
    ROBERT.

    Behind all of these recent works lies a traceable tradition going
back at least to the Scholastics, if not to classical and remoter times.
One could draw attention to a variety of conceptual schemata for presenting the entire cosmos in thematic form (for some examples of these,
see Worlds of Reference). I shall content myself here, however, with
noting that such orderings do indeed vary with the personality of the
compiler and the time and place in which the compiling was done, while
also containing a surprisingly consistent 'core' of thematic ideas which -
if not culturally universal - is evidence of the shared interests of all
literate communities and also of a continuous tradition. To illustrate
this point let me juxtapose two such orderings. The first is a condensed
version of an 11th century list from England (based on the work of Aelfric,
Abbot of Eynsham near Oxford); the second is the list used in my LEXICON.
They are:

Aelfric (11th century)	Tom McArthur (1981)
1 God, heaven, angels, sun, moon, earth and sea	1 Life and living things
2 Man, woman, parts of the body	2 The body, its functions and welfare
3 Kinship, professional and trades people; diseases	3 People and the family
4 Abstract terms	4 Buildings, houses, the home, clothes, belongings and personal care
5 Times of the year, the seasons, the weather	5 Food, drink and farming
6 Colours	6 Feelings, emotions, attitudes and sensations
7 Birds, fishes, beasts, herbs, trees	7 Thought and communication, language and grammar
8 House furnishings, kitchen and cooking utensils, weapons	8 Substances, materials, objects and equipment
9 Parts of the city	9 Arts and crafts, science and technology, industry and education
10 Metals and precious stones	10 Numbers, measurement, money and commerce
11 General terms, both concrete and abstract	11 Entertainment, sports and games
	12 Space and time
	13 Movement, location, travel and transport
	14 General and abstract terms

Aelfric's list could have been cut up differently; it is by no means as neat as the above groupings suggest. By the time I finalized my own set of themes I was aware of Aelfric's (and a variety of other) lists, but was hardly likely to base a 20th-century compendium for foreign learners of English upon a vocabularium of Latin and Anglo-Saxon terms a thousand years earlier. It is, however, worth noting that the two pedagogues in question have produced markedly similar schemes, and also that my 20th-century needs have dictated a set of themes closer to the medieval than to the 19th-century Roget.

Aelfric's schema is representative of his time. The Schoolmen
were well disposed to the idea of classifying the cosmos, of catching
the omne scibile ('all that is knowable') in a thematic net. Aelfric's
is the tradition of the vocabularium, the (usually bilingual) word list
by means of which the young cleric could acquire Latin, his passport to
religious and cultural elevation. That tradition remains fundamental
to the growth of thematic reference materials, but is only one of two
powerful medieval trends in this direction. The other relates to the
proto-encyclopedic inclinations of such theologians and scholars as
Thomas Aquinas with his Summa theologiae (uncompleted when he died in
1274) and Vincent de Beauvais with his Speculum triplex of 1244. These
were philosopher-compilers, each with a three-fold conceptual frame
for the universe running from God and his angels through to the broad
(and nefarious) doings of 'man'.

All such medieval views were hierarchical and hyponymic, with
the higher subsuming the lower until all 'nature' was included. Although grounded in theology and Catholic Christian dogma, they were
also fed with a rationalism derived through the seven liberal arts from
the secular tradition of ancient Greece. They possessed as a consequence an inner tension between faith and reason, which became tenser
still with the advent of first the Renaissance and then the Reformation.

Both the pedagogic tradition typified by Aelfric and the philosophical tradition typified by Aquinas continued through this turbulent
period into the early 17th century, the time when alphabetic wordbooks
were firmly establishing themselves in Western Europe. This was also
a period of seminal activity for the thematic mode, initiated by two
key figures, the first a pedagogue, the second a philosopher.

The pedagogue was the Irish Jesuit William Bathe who, in 1611,
brought out his thematic IANUA LINGUARUM, a Latin-to-Spanish manual
that in 1615 acquired in London its Latin-to-English equivalent.
This 'Gate of Tongues' was religiously oriented, had twelve great
themes, and some 5,000 items accompanied by 1,200 illustrative
sentences. It was in the Aelfric tradition, a straightforward
vocabulary-builder, and was a commercial success.

The philosopher was Sir Francis Bacon, who at about the same time
in his INSTAURATIO MAGNA ('Great Renewal') created a taxonomy of knowledge descended from the work of the Scholastics but defined in secular
and proto-scientific terms. It was also tripartite, but its divisions
covered first nature, then 'man', then man acting upon nature. Within
the schema, the great areas had sub-areas, and the sub-areas sub-sub-areas
until - it was assumed - everything worth talking about could be covered.
It was both the basis for an encyclopedic compilation that was never
written and a blueprint for the scientific revolution, in which power
to change our circumstances was given into the hands of human beings.
This taxonomy (Cf. McArthur, 1986: 111) has had a profound and fully
acknowledged influence on many taxonomists since, including the encyclopedists Diderot in France in the 18th and Samuel Taylor Coleridge
in England in the 19th century.

There were, however, more immediate repercussions than these, in
the work of Bishop John Wilkins of the Royal Society of London and

of John Comenius, the Moravian bishop and educator. Wilkins in 1668
produced an erudite work - another master plan for scientists and
logicians - entitled Towards a Real Character and a Philosophical
Language. This contained, among other things, a conceptual scheme
for the organization of words which has links with the tradition of
Aelfric and Bathe as well as of Aquinas and Bacon. Meanwhile, in
1631, Comenius brought out his wryly entitled IANUA LINGUARUM RESERATA
('The Gate of Tongues Unlocked'), intent upon improving upon the
system offered by Bathe (a Protestant improving upon a Catholic and a
Jesuit). This was followed by the radical ORBIS SENSUALIUM PICTUS
('The Illustrated World of Things we can Feel') in 1657, which was not
only also thematic, but made use of vivid pictorial aids in which
numbers linked elements of the pictures with words on the printed page.

These men either knew each other or knew of each other. For
example, when Comenius studied in Heidelberg he read the works of
Bacon, and (in the words of the commentator John Sadler, 1976) 'returned
home convinced that the millennium could be obtained with the aid of
science'. Additionally, the influences of these men on later thematic
compilers is as traceable as, say, the influence of Nathaniel Bailey
on Samuel Johnson and of Samuel Johnson on Noah Webster in the complementary alphabetic tradition. Bishop Wilkins was, for example, a
founder of the Royal Society. Peter Mark Roget in the 19th century was
for 22 years secretary of that society and acknowledges the influence
of Wilkins in the introduction to his THESAURUS. Furthermore, in his
younger days Roget wrote articles for the short-lived ENCYCLOPAEDIA
METROPOLITANA, planned and started by Coleridge who in his turn had
been influenced by Bacon's INSTAURATIO.

These then are some of the historical elements in the development
of thematic lexicography, which has lacked until now nothing as a
lexicographical tradition except a label. Like most people who have
found themselves working in this field, I have to confess both a
pedagogical and a philosophical interest in the format - plus a more
modern linguistic-cum-semantic interest which arises directly from
the work of de Saussure, Sapir, Whorf, the structural semantics of
John Lyons and the cognitive anthropology of Stephen Tyler and Harold
Conklin. Separately - and apparently with little or no knowledge of
the history of the thematic mode - modern linguists with interests in
lexis and ethnology have proposed that alternatives to the alphabet be
sought out as a means of usefully handling the systemic aspects of
the vocabularies of the world's languages (Cf. in particular Tyler, 1969).
Indeed, it was the influence of Lyons's description of structural
semantics in 1968 together with the enthusiasm of David Crystal for
the potential of 'conceptual wordbooks' that conspired to launch me into
this area, when I became the researcher for Longman in the early 1970s
whose spadework in due course became the LEXICON. The group which commissioned me to explore this area was not in the least interested at
the time in my diggings into the history of the subject; they were
focussed on modern linguistics, not ancient Scholastics and Reformation
'scientists'. In my own view, however, having spent quite a lot of time
in the area subsequently, I feel that the two cannot reasonably be
separated and, if anything, I owe more to the ancient tradition than to
the relatively programmatic developments in the modern science.

Effectively, however, they fuse in the late 20th century into one
organically developing tradition. That tradition - which I have elected
to call 'thematic lexicography' - has great potential in the electronic
era, either on its own or in combination with the currently more
powerful alphabetic tradition. My own expectation is that lexicographers
with alphabetic bents will steadily - almost willy-nilly - be nudged
into looking at the thematic options available to all of us, particularly
because of the exigencies of computerized lexicography. This hardly
seems pernicious, allowing for all sorts of judicious blends of the
two formats, enriching the profession in the process.

The two modes need not be seen as rivals, but as complementary
approaches to the same deeply intractable material - the lexis of any
natural language. It is possible to foresee compilations in the not-
too-far-distant future where material from the same data core (however
arranged there) will be presented to the user (on demand, on a monitor
or in a printout) in either of the formats - a service that may well
help make the mass of material less intractable. I look forward to that
possibility.

References

Cited dictionaries (see Appendix):

(AN) ALPHABETICAL DICTIONARY ... (in Wilkins)
(THE) BOOK OF JARGON (Miller)
CAMBRIDGE ENCYCLOPEDIA OF ARCHAEOLOGY (Sherratt)
CHAMBERS TWENTIETH CENTURY DICTIONARY (Davidson/Kirkpatrick)
(THE) CONCISE OXFORD DICTIONARY (Fowler/Sykes)
(A) DICTIONARY OF THE ENGLISH LANGUAGE (Johnson)
DICTIONNAIRE LE PETIT ROBERT
DICTIONNAIRE UNIVERSEL DES NOMS PROPRES (Robert)
DUDEN BILDWORTERBUCH (Solf)
ENCYCLOPAEDIA BRITANNICA
(THE) ENCYCLOPAEDIA METROPOLITANA (Coleridge et al.)
IANUA LINGUARUM (Bathe)
IANUA LINGUARUM RESEARATA (Comenius)
INSTAURATIO MAGNA (Bacon)
LONGMAN LEXICON OF CONTEMPORARY ENGLISH (McArthur)
MERRIAM-WEBSTER'S (FIFTH) COLLEGIATE DICTIONARY
ORBIS SENSUALIUM PICTUS QUADRILINGUE (Comenius)
(THE) OXFORD ENGLISH DICTIONARY (Murray et al.)
READER'S DIGEST GREAT ILLUSTRATED DICTIONARY (Ilson et al.)
THESAURUS OF ENGLISH WORDS AND PHRASES ... (Roget)
WHAT'S WHAT: A VISUAL GLOSSARY OF THE PHYSICAL WORLD (Fisher/
     Bragonier)

Other literature:

Collison, Robert L. (1964) Encyclopaedias: Their History Throughout
     the Ages. New York & London: Hafner
Collison, Robert L. (1976) "Encyclopaedia" in Encyclopaedia Brit-
     annica (15th ed.) Macropaedia 6: 781-799

Hulbert, James R. (1955) Dictionaries: British and American (The Language Library). London: A. Deutsch

Lyons, John (1968) Introduction to Theoretical Linguistics. Cambridge: U.P.

Matoré, Georges (1968) Histoire des dictionnaires français (La langue vivante). Paris: Larousse

McArthur, Tom (1986) Worlds of Reference: Lexicography, Learning and Language from the Clay Tablet to the Computer. Cambridge: U.P.

Murray, James A.H. (1900) The Evolution of English Lexicography (The Romanes Lecture). Oxford: Clarendon

Read, Allen Walker (1976) "Dictionary" in Encyclopaedia Britannica (15th ed.) Macropaedia 5: 713–722

Sadler, John E. (1976) "John Amos Comenius" in Encyclopaedia Britannica (15th ed.) Macropaedia 4: 967–969

Starnes, DeWitt T. and Noyes, Gertrude E. (1946) The English Dictionary from Cawdrey to Johnson, 1604-1755. Chapel Hill: U. of North Carolina P.

Tyler, Stephen A. ed. (1969) Cognitive Anthropology. New York: Holt

Whitehall, Harold (1958/71) "The development of the English dictionary" in The Play of Language ed. by Leonard F. Dean et al. Oxford: U.P.

Wilkins, John (1668) An Essay towards a Real Character and a Philosophical Language. London: J.M. for Gellibrand and Martin

FOUR REMARKS ON THE PREHISTORY OF HISTORICAL LEXICOGRAPHY

Reuven Merkin

The famous historical dictionaries (Grimm's DEUTSCHES WÖRTERBUCH, Littré's DICTIONNAIRE DE LA LANGUE FRANÇAISE, the WOORDENBOEK DER NEDERLANDSCHE TAAL and the NEW ENGLISH DICTIONARY ON HISTORICAL PRINCIPLES) began to appear only in the second half of the 19th century, but the idea of a dictionary on historical principles originated early in that century (Merkin 1984).

a

The comparison of the title page of Samuel Johnson's English Dictionary (1755) with that of John Jamieson's Scottish one (1808) shows great similarity, yet also a difference between the authoritative principle of Johnson on selecting illustrative quotations (Kolb 1972), on the one hand, and the descriptive – and more historical – principle of Jamieson, on the other:

Johnson	Jamieson
A Dictionary	An Etymological Dictionary
of the English Language	of the Scottish Language
in which the Words are	
deduced from their Originals	
and illustrated in their	illustrating the words in their
different Significations	different significations
by Examples from	by examples from
the best Writers,	ancient and modern writers,
to which are prefixed	to which is prefixed
a History of	a dissertation on the origin of
the Language	the Scottish Language
and an English Grammar	
by Samuel Johnson, M.A.	by John Jamieson
in Two Volumes....MDCCLV	in two volumes....1808

In his Preface Jamieson writes: "On every word, or particular sense of a word, I endeavour to give the oldest printed or MS. authorities....I am not so fastidious, however, as to reject every word that cannot be supported by written authority. In this case, many of our most ancient and expressive terms would be for ever buried" (p. V).

168   REUVEN MERKIN

A.J. Aitken, Editor of the DICTIONARY OF THE OLDER
SCOTTISH TONGUE, was kind enough to inform me that
"Jamieson accompanied each entry or sub-section of an
entry with one, two, occasionally three, but rarely more,
quotations, arranged in chronological then in text order,
with exact references and, for variously dated works,
dates" (in a private letter, 30 January 1981).

Jamieson's Scottish Dictionary was perhaps the first
British dictionary worthy of the title 'a dictionary on
historical principles' (Aitken 1971:38).

b

In 1817 the eminent poet and philosopher Samuel Taylor
Coleridge (1772-1834) initiated the publication of a new
"Methodological Compendium of Human Knowledge" - THE
ENCYCLOPAEDIA METROPOLITANA - the first part of which
appeared in January 1818. A Prospectus written by Coleridg
and Dr. (later Sir) John Stoddart had been issued some time
earlier (Snyder 1929:36, 1934:X). Paragraph SIX of the
Prospectus states: "an Encyclopaedia is a History of human
knowledge .... and we here give our public pledge that the
Encyclopaedia Metropolitana shall be so far historical in
all respects, that only what has been established .... and
to be found in the records of Science and Literature, shall
form the main body of every article" (Snyder 1934:75).

According to the original plan the ENCYCLOPAEDIA
METROPOLITANA should have consisted of four main divisions:
"The first .... comprises the Pure Sciences; and the second
.... the Mixed and Applied Sciences. The third .... is
devoted to Biography chronologically arranged .... and the
concluding or Miscellaneous part .... will have the unique
advantage of presenting to the public, for the first time,
a Philosophical and Etymological Lexicon of the English
Language; the citations selected and arranged chronological
ly, yet including all the purposes of a common Dictionary"
(Snyder 1934:76).

Alice Snyder (1934:71) writes: "Unfortunately no copy
of this Prospectus can be found .... but there is good
reason to think that the thirteen paragraphs printed below,
which open the rare Prospectus of the 1849 cabinet edition,
are taken almost bodily from the original document."
Nevertheless, even if the above-quoted paragraphs are not
taken word for word from the original Prospectus which
appeared prior to 1818, still we have the original plan
as published in the first edition of the ENCYCLOPAEDIA
METROPOLITANA: "Fourth Division .... containing ....
Philosophical and Etymological Lexicon of the English

Language, or the History of English Words; - the citations
arranged according to the Age of the Works from which they
are selected, yet with every attention to the independent
beauty or value of the sentences chosen" (Snyder 1934:
facing p. 71;   ENCYCLOPAEDIA METROPOLITANA,   Volume I (Pure
Sciences, Vol. I), London 1845, unnumbered page between
the "General Introduction or, Preliminary Treatise on
Method by S.T. Coleridge"   and the   "Grammar by Sir John
Stoddart").

According to his original intention Coleridge was to
have contributed the English Lexicon. He failed, however,
to keep to the timetable and the Lexicon was compiled
instead by Dr. Charles Richardson.

Richardson writes on the   "Advantages of Chronological
Citations" (ENC. METROPOLITANA,   ed. 1845, Vol. XIV, p. IV):
"By the arrangement of the citations chronologically, some
view may be taken of the progressive changes of the
language".

A similar view was first expressed in 1812 by a young
German classical scholar, Franz Passow, in his book "Über
Zweck, Anlage und Ergänzung Griechischer Wörterbücher"
("On the purpose, design and supplementation of Greek
dictionaries") in which he laid down "the canons by
which the lexicographer should be guided, amongst which
the most important was the requirement that citations
should be chronologically arranged in order to exhibit
the history of each word and its uses" (Jones 1925).

Several years later the 'chronological' - or, the
'historical' - principle in lexicography was fully
extended to English lexicography by Charles Richardson.

One of the editors of the ENCYCLOPAEDIA METROPOLITANA,
H.J. Rose, spoke with great enthusiasm about Richardson's
work: "The plan of giving the quotations of each word
chronologically has the advantage of embodying in a
Philosophical Lexicon a history of our own language.
They are full of interest; but the labour of searching
them out and arranging them is one of which those who have
never engaged in any similar occupation can form no
adequate notion. Once achieved, the work is performed for
ever; and Dr. Richardson may be contented to think that
he has here left a κτῆμα ἐς ἀεί   of infinite value
to his countrymen" (ENC. METROPOLITANA,   ed. 1845, Vol. I
p. XX).

c

When the term 'historical dictionary' (or its equivalents in other European languages) was coined in the
sense we mean today, is difficult to say.

The original title of the OED was A NEW ENGLISH
DICTIONARY ON HISTORICAL PRINCIPLES. Only in 1897, when
the third volume was dedicated to Queen Victoria, it was
called "....this Historical Dictionary of the English
Language".

In 1863 Emile Littré, in the Preface of his DICTIONNAIRE
DE LA LANGUE FRANÇAISE, describes Grimm's DEUTSCHES WÖRTER-
BUCH as "un dictionnaire historique".

In Jacob Grimm's Preface to the DEUTSCHES WÖRTERBUCH
of 1854 the term "historical dictionary" does not appear.
There is "historischer Sprachforschung" (p. IV 'historical linguistics'), "das Wörterbuch .... ein wissenschaft-
liches" (p.XIV 'the dictionary .... has to be a scholarly
one'), "alles nur geschichtlich erläutern" (p. XXXVIII
'but to explain everything historically') - nothing
like 'historical dictionary'.

Two years later, in 1856, Leopold Zunz (1794-1886),
the founder of "Wissenschaft des Judentums" (modern Jewish
scholarship in Europe), published an article "Wünsche für
ein Wörterbuch der hebräischen Sprache" ('Plea for a
dictionary of the Hebrew language'). Zunz concluded his
article saying that "Ein Wörterbuch, sprachvergleichend,
vollständig, authentisch, ausfürlich und geschichtlich,
würde demnach noch immer eine Leistung seyn, einer
Akademie der Wissenschaften würdig" ('a comparative,
complete, authentic, detailed and historical dictionary
would still be a worthy undertaking for an Academy of
Science') (Zunz 1854:512).

d

In March 1875 Rev. George Wheelwright, sub-editor for
letter F of the NEW ENGLISH DICTIONARY projected by the
Philological Society, published an "Appeal to the English
speaking Public on behalf of a New English Dictionary".
The first four pages of that Appeal contain an account of
the progress of the Dictionary in the period between 1860
and 1872, based mainly on Reports of the Editor (first
Herbert Coleridge till his death in April 1861 and then
Frederick James Furnival). Another eight pages of three
columns each contain a specimen of the Dictionary for
letter F from FA to FACE.

Each entry and each sense are accompanied by quite a large number of illustrative quotations arranged - more or less - chronologically. At the end of every quotation - in square brackets - a full reference of the source is given, the first item being the <u>date</u>. For example, the lemma facade is accompanied by eight quotations as follows:

FAÇADE', få-säd (Fr. *facade*; It. *facciata*; Sp. *fachada*). The face, front, or any principal elevation of a building, or of a natural object. * I.

'*Facade*; f. The forefront, forepart, outside, or representation of the outside, of a house.'—[1632. Cotgrave, Dict.]

'Those that belong to the European factors, are built on a fine quay, having a regular *facade* of two stories towards the river.'—[1772-84. Capt. Cook, Voyages, vol. vi. p. 2220, ed. 1790.]

'*Facade*; facciata, It.; hauptfasade, Ger.; a term adopted from the French for the exterior face or front of a building.'—[1850. J. H. Parker, Glossary of Architecture, vol. i. p. 200, 5th ed.]

'The duomo of Ancona, a building, it is supposed, of the end of the tenth century, is very interesting both within and without. The *façade* is of white marble, the porch Lombard, supported by slender pillars, resting on lions couchant.'—[1847. Lord Lindsay, Christian Art, vol. i. p. 65.]

'The pointed arches with quaintly-designed capitals, on the supporting pillars at the basement, and the stringing-courses, and labellings, and turrets, compose a *façade* well worth transferring by pencil or photography, to paper.'—[1861. G. M. Musgrave, By-Roads, and B. F. p. 201.]

'Shaded by a ledge of rock, beneath a *façade* of columnar lava, we ate our dinner.'—[1852. Darwin, Naturalist's Voyage, ch. xviii. p. 407.]

'In the finest and richest west front with which I am acquainted . . . there is no sham *façade*, but the gable rises honestly at its own height.'—[1861. A. Beresford Hope, The English Cathedral, p. 246.]

'That there is only one street of a single row, with a Janus *façade* looking towards the forest and the sea, may formerly have been true of all the village, or town, or city, whichever it is—and I shall say something an that delicate point anon—but is true only of a past now.'—[1866, July 13, Evening Standard, p. 3.]

As a result of Wheelwright's Appeal Frederick Furnival, the unofficial Editor of the Philological Society's projected Dictionary, made efforts to find a new Editor and Publisher for the Dictionary. In April 1876 a young member of the Society, James Murray, 39-year old Schoolmaster at Mill-Hill, was approached both by Alexander Macmillan, head of the well-known publishing firm, and by members of the Philological Society, concerning the publication of the proposed Dictionary (Murray 1979:133).

In a few months Murray prepared samples for letter C of which two MS. drafts and nine printed proofs have survived in the possession of his granddaughter K.M. Elisabeth Murray (Murray 1979:142). I was most lucky to enjoy Dr. Murray's hospitality at her house in West Sussex and had the opportunity to inspect James Murray's Papers.

In the earlier - marked "rough" - MS. draft (11 pages) each quotation is written separately and references come <u>after</u> quotations, as in Wheelwright's Appeal but without brackets:

carpetless (Kahr'pet-less) adj. Having no carpets

Carpetless but highly polished mahogany floors.

1837 Michael Scott, Cruise of the Midge,
Ed. 1859. p. 344.

Rooms .... curtainless, carpetless, comfortless
throughout.
1862 H. Aidé, Care of Carrl. v.2. p. 171.

In the second MS. draft (50 pages) all quotations for
a given entry constitute a single block and each reference
comes in front of the quotation, so that the date —
a year — is the first piece of information for each
source:

carpetless (Kaar'pet-less) adj.(from sb.) Having no carpets

1837 M. Scott. Cruise of the Midge, Ed. 1859.
344. Carpetless but highly polished mahogany
floors. —— 1862 H. Aidé. Care of Carrl.
vol. 2. 171. Rooms curtainless, carpetless,
comfortless throughout.

This practice, which was adopted later on in the NEW
ENGLISH DICTIONARY and has since become one of the most
common features of historical dictionaries, was therefore
introduced for the first time by James Murray in 1876, two
years before he became the Editor of the NED and 7-8 years
before the first Part of it was published in January 1884.

References

Cited dictionaries (see Appendix):

DEUTSCHES WÖRTERBUCH (Grimm)
(A) DICTIONARY OF THE ENGLISH LANGUAGE (Johnson)
DICTIONARY OF THE OLDER SCOTTISH TONGUE ... (Craigie/Aitken)
DICTIONNAIRE DE LA LANGUE FRANÇAISE (Littré)
(THE) ENCYCLOPAEDIA METROPOLITANA ... (Coleridge et al.)
(AN) ETYMOLOGICAL DICTIONARY OF THE SCOTTISH LANGUAGE ...
    (Jamieson)
(A) GREEK-ENGLISH LEXICON (Liddell/Scott)
(A) NEW ENGLISH DICTIONARY ON HISTORICAL PRINCIPLES see OXFORD
    ENGLISH DICTIONARY
(THE) OXFORD ENGLISH DICTIONARY (Murray et al.)
WOORDENBOEK DER NEDERLANDSCHE TAAL (De Vries et al.)

Other literature:

Aitken, Adam Jack (1973) "Le dictionnaire d'ancien écossais:
aperçu de son histoire" in Table ronde sur les grands dic-
tionnaires historiques (Florence, 3-5 mai 1971). Firenze:
Accademia della Crusca 37-44
Jones, H.S. (1925/40) "Preface" to Liddell/Scott's GREEK-ENGLISH
LEXICON. Oxford: Clarendon P. ix-xii
Kolb, Gwin J. and Kolb,Ruth A. (1972) "The selection and use of
the illustrative quotations in Dr. Johnson's Dictionary" in
New Aspects of Lexicography ed. by Howard D. Weinbrot.
Carbondale: Southern Illinois U.P. 61-72
Merkin, Reuven (1983) "Historical dictionaries" in Lexicography:
Principles and Practice ed. by R.R.K. Hartmann. London: Aca-
demic Press 123-133
Merkin, Reuven (1984) "Historical dictionaries and the computer -
another view" in LEXeter '83 Proceedings ed. by R.R.K. Hart-
mann (Lexicographica. Series Maior 1). Tübingen: M. Niemeyer
377-384
Murray, K.M. Elisabeth (1979) Caught in the Web of Words: James
A.H. Murray and the Oxford English Dictionary. Oxford: U.P.
Snyder, Alice D. (1929) Coleridge on Logic and Learning, with
Selections from the Unpublished Manuscripts. New Haven: Yale
U.P.
Snyder, Alice D. (1934) S.T. Coleridge's Treatise on Method as Pub
lished in the Encyclopaedia Metropolitana. London: Constable
Zunz, Leopold (1856) "Wünsche für ein Wörterbuch der hebräischen
Sprache" in Zeitschrift der Deutschen morgenländischen Gesell-
schaft 10: 501-512

THE FIRST ENGLISH DICTIONARY? A SIXTEENTH-CENTURY COMPILER AT WORK

Noel E. Osselton

Little is directly known about the practical working methods of early dictionary makers. Dr. Johnson's use of an interleaved copy of Bailey is well established, as is also his marking-up of books which were laid under contribution (McCracken 1969; Clifford 1978: 46-51). We know that Benjamin Martin instructed his amanuenses to place Ainsworth's Latin dictionary in front of them so as to force upon themselves the different senses that English words could bear (Starnes and Noyes 1946, p.152). For visual evidence of early practices, we have an elegant engraving dating from 1727 showing the Dutch lexicographer Willem Sewel, pen in hand in his library, with reference books propped up all around him (Osselton 1973, frontispiece). But such incidental bits of direct evidence are few, and any general impression of how the first compilers set to work must be gained by inference from their completed works. Historical study of the early English dictionaries has produced fairly detailed conclusions about sources: for instance, we know that Edward Phillips used Bullokar, Cockeram and Blount, and threw in items from Cowell too (Starnes and Noyes 1946: 48-54); but his actual procedures for marrying up the word lists remain obscure.

The chance survival in Bodl. MS Rawlinson Poet. 108 of an early and evidently abortive attempt at starting off an English-English dictionary (henceforward, 'the Rawlinson dictionary') is therefore of interest. The more so since, as I shall show, it is a very tentative effort, a mere initial draft for a dictionary text, with the false starts, gaps, corrections and duplications which are to be expected when a compiler is feeling his way in a hitherto unattempted mode.

The MS is of additional interest because of its date: the collection in which it occurs is dated by the Bodleian to c. 1570, and so the text may well antedate the earliest known English dictionary - that of Cawdrey in 1604 - by some decades. But we cannot be sure about this. The dictionary entries have been added on blank pages of a ready-existing MS some time after the original compilation it contains. Evidence for dating from handwriting will probably remain inconclusive, and no firm terminus ante quem can plausibly be established. Nevertheless, nothing has been found in the dictionary which would militate against a date in the last quarter of the sixteenth century. Furthermore, we know that once

monolingual English dictionaries do begin to be published, successive
compilers habitually draw upon their predecessors' efforts (Starnes
and Noyes 1946, passim). If the Rawlinson compiler had set to work
after Cawdrey and Cockeram, he would in all likelihood have used
Cawdrey and Cockeram. But there is no evidence of his having done so,
and there are therefore grounds for believing that this abruptly
terminated alphabetical list represents the earliest known attempt at
making an English dictionary. It is a text which therefore invites
comparison with the first such dictionary ever to be published,
Cawdrey's TABLE ALPHABETICALL and points of similarity and contrast
between the two will be offered in this preliminary report on its
contents.

Compiling procedures

The author of the Rawlinson dictionary drew up his text on sheets
already prepared by another hand for the compilation of a book-index.
The dictionary entries occur on the first three pages (each divided
into four columns) out of 35 which have been left blank for the
insertion of the index at the end of a manuscript medical treatise.
These 35 pages had previously been marked up in alphabetical blocks
with the headings Ab-, Ac-, etc., ready to receive the entries for
the foregoing text. Some medical items had been put in with their
page references; thus we find (in a different hand from that of the
dictionary entries) references such as 'Balsom 49.95.123' under Ba-,
'Belly great and hard 145' and '(Belly) ache 184' under Be-. But
there are very few of these. The medical indexer had evidently
quickly given up, leaving most of the page surface blank.

The intending lexicographer thus found here a convenient
receptacle for arranging his dictionary entries as he collected them:
a complete series of alphabetical slots or boxes already in some
measure proportioned to his needs. Be-, for instance, has been
allocated about 20 column inches, as against 9 for Ap- and only 3 for
Aw-. But by using these sheets the compiler of the Rawlinson
dictionary was accepting what may seem to us a surprising constraint
upon his activities: he was content to work within an alphabetical
framework set up by another man for an entirely different purpose.
This meant that he simply had to get everything in on the sheet in
front of him - all the words from abandon to amphibology on the first
page, those from analogy to azure on the next, and so on. I know of
no other evidence for such constraints on length accepted by or
imposed upon early lexicographers, though doubtless they will then
(as now) have had to accede to limits imposed by publishers.

The compiler's actual procedure may be illustrated from the
thirty MS entries under Ab-. These begin with a fully alphabetized
list of twenty entries (mainly verbs) as follows:

abandon - forsake

    abaleanate –
    Abase – humble
    abash.
    abate – diminish
    abbreviate ⎫
    abbridge   ⎬ – abstract
    abhomination – offence
    abhorre – loath
    abide – tarry
    abide – suffer
    abiect – forsake
    abiure – forsweare
    able – power
    abolish – destroy
    abound – plenty
    abrogate – destroy
    absolue – pardon
    absolutnesse – perfection
    absurdity – foolishnesse

Below the entry for _absurdity_ a single ink line has been drawn across
the whole column. There then follows a supplementary alphabetical
list of nine entries, this time consisting chiefly of nouns, with no
definitions and again with a terminal line:

    abbot
    abbey
    ablatiue case
    abortiue
    abricot appl
    absence
    abstinence
    abstract
    abuse

This total of twenty–nine entries fills up about three–quarters of
the space that was available for words beginning _Ab–_, and the rest is
left blank, except that to the right and immediately above the
section for _Ac–_, the single word _abstract_ has been scribbled in.

    All this gives us the impression of a compiler who is casting
about for an appropriate scale of entry, and a balance between word
types. The first trial list of twenty words fell short, so he had a
second alphabetical run, this time incorporating more nouns. At some
stage _abstract_ has been jotted down for inclusion, and it duly appears
in the second list. The column–to–column line after _absurdity_ would
presumably serve to warn a reviser or printer that a supplementary
list was being started, and that alphabetical incorporation was
therefore needed (though a division of verbs and nouns into two lists
had been an established tradition at least as early as the

PROMPTORIUM PARVULORUM). Evidently the compiler was content with the
total of 29 entries for Ab- (Cawdrey, we may note, has 27) because
the remaining space of some one and a half inches is left blank. But
he did not (or did not yet) go back to provide definitions for the
nine extra entries.

Under Ac- the same procedure is repeated, with 21 items in the
first list, and only 5 in the second (he seems to be getting better at
it). There is this time a total of five memorial jottings at the end
(accuse, acorne, acte, actiuity, action). Since they correspond (more
or less) to entries among the first 21, it is evident that the
compiler jotted down useful items before even starting on his
alphabetical list proper.

The Ac- items nicely fill the half column available for them, and
the dictionary-maker must have decided at this point that he had now
got the scale about right: at any rate from then on there are no more
double alphabetical lists.

The rest of the letter A is completed in the same manner and
seemingly with a roughly similar coverage of the vocabulary, giving
an effective total of 337 lemmata for the whole letter (as against
286 entries for the letter A in Cawdrey). Some of the ready-prepared
spaces on the pages remained partly unfilled - only three entries for
Aw-, for instance, with room for about eighteen. Under Ar- the
author overshoots badly: with the word arsnick he reached the bottom
of the page, and had no room for any more, so he continued with Art,
Artechoke, etc., written upside down above the beginning of the Ar-
words in a space which happened to have been left unused at the end
of Ap-. The device of finishing the entries upside down would
presumably have been intended to deter any unheeding printer from
setting them in the wrong place.

Only 81 consecutive entries have been filled in under the letter
B, and there, with the word baskett, the manuscript dictionary unfortunately comes to an end. A few memorial jottings further on in
the alphabet (besom, flattery, height) serve to indicate at least that
he had had plans to proceed further.

Projected length

The Rawlinson dictionary contains 337 entries for the letter A,
as against 286 in Cawdrey, a difference of over 17%. Projection of
these figures might lead us to believe that had it been completed the
dictionary would have had some 3000 entries, as against the 2560 in
Cawdrey. This total may however be misleading, because Cawdrey's
dictionary is noticeably skewed in its uptake of words through the
letters of the alphabet, with about 11½% of all entries falling under
the letter A, as against a normal expectation of about 6½%. A
calculation based on 6½% for the letter A would give the Rawlinson

dictionary a projected total of about 5000 entries, making it
comparable in size to Bullokar's ENGLISH EXPOSITOR of 1616.

Definitions

     Definitions or explanations have been provided for about half of
all the words entered under the letter A. There is however a notice-
able tailing off, as though the compiler was already wearying of his
task: under the initial list of Ab- 18 out of the 20 words have
explanations, but under An- only 12 out of 34, and for the letter B
not more than about one in six can be said to have anything that can
be called a definition.

     In general, one-word explanations are given (abandon 'forsake',
aduantage 'gaine'), though occasionally the compiler permits himself
a brace with multiple senses

                    assure   ⎰affirme
                                ⎱warrant

or gives successive entries for homographs (aray - 'apparell', aray -
'order'). Some definitions (alembick, artillery, ambiguity) appear
to have been added in another hand.

     One puzzling feature of the Rawlinson dictionary is that those
entries for which no definition has been provided are in general
(though not always) centred in the column. Yet it does not seem
likely that the compiler was envisaging a dictionary where (as happens
sometimes in spelling books) explanations are given only of selected
entries. As successive entries such as the following may show, some
centred entries do have definitions, and it is by no means the case
that only 'easy' words are left unexplained.

                    Amesse - robe
                  amity - friendship
                    Amphitheatre
                    amphibology.

The Rawlinson compiler is in general much inferior to Cawdrey in the
matter of defining. Sometimes their entries correspond exactly (both
give 'breathing' for aspiration), but Cawdrey normally provides fuller
explanations or lists of synonyms, having for instance 'cast away, or
yeelde vp, to leaue, or forsake' where Rawlinson has just the one word
'forsake' for the meaning of abandon. In addition to this, and to the
many gaps in his list of entries (though one may assume that the
intention was to go back and fill these in), the Rawlinson compiler
shows himself to be the less consistent in method. There are entries
where the 'explanation' is in fact a mere indication of the context
of usage ('ace - dice', 'Badger. for corne', 'barre where ye plead');
other items are given in the A or B formula ('bar - or bolt'); and

with some there is a failure to match word-class between entry and
definition (<u>aspire</u> 'ambition', <u>aschamed</u> 'bashfullness'). In some
cases, such as <u>anihilation</u> 'frustration', he shows a rather alarming
ignorance of the words he put in.

Deletions and corrections

There are as we might expect a number of deletions and
corrections in the MS. Mostly these are of no significance (repeated
entries, items out of alphabetical sequence, etc.) But there is some
evidence of the author having second thoughts about putting in an
item he had initially selected, as with the deletion of <u>adioyning</u> and
<u>askew</u> ('asquint'). There are also changes in the definitions:
'decree' has been crossed out and replaced by 'statute' for the
explanation of <u>act</u>, and 'chance' is deleted in favour or 'fortune' as
an equivalent for <u>aduenture</u>. On the whole, however, the MS evidence
suggests that the compiler proceeded with remarkably little
hesitation in making his selection of words.

Word selection

The differences between the Rawlinson dictionary and Cawdrey in
their approach to selection of words for entry may perhaps best be
illustrated by setting alongside each other the complete list of
entries for the letters words beginning <u>Ag-</u> and <u>Ai-</u> (erratic
alphabetisation has been adjusted):

Rawlinson dictionary	Cawdrey 1604
age	
agent	agent
	agglutinate
agrauate	aggrauate
agility	agilitie
	agitate
aglet	
agnaile	
agnition	agnition
agony	agony
agreement	
ague	
aide	
	aigre
aime	
aire	

It is a well-known fact that the first monolingual dictionaries of
English (Cawdrey, Bullokar, Cockeram and their successors) were
'hard-word' books, concentrating on the newly-acquired and unfamiliar
Latinate vocabulary of renaissance English, and that it is not until

the eighteenth century with the work of John Kersey (Osselton 1979)
that any systematic and serious attempt is made to cover the ordinary
or everyday words of the language. But it will be clear even from the
short selection given above that the Rawlinson dictionary, had it ever
been completed and published, would in this matter have been radically
different from the other dictionaries of its time. The compiler does
not ignore the learned words (agrauate, agility, agnition) though
(despite his longer list) he takes in fewer of them than Cawdrey does.
But in his decision to include common words such as age, aime and aire
(as well as, elsewhere, alehouse, apple, apron, arm, axe, barber,
barly and many others) he shows himself to be a century ahead of his
time in his view of what the monolingual dictionary should contain.

Source

Given that the Rawlinson text (however defective it may be)
represents the first known attempt at putting together an English
dictionary, the question of what source the compiler used is of
considerable interest. Even a cursory inspection of his vocabulary
suggests that it must have been a Latin one. We find, for instance, an
entry which reads band of souldiers. Now it is sensible enough to
have an entry for band (under B), and to have souldiers (under S).
But band of souldiers seems rather pointless, and its presence is
hard to explain until we note that the English noun phrase corresponds
to a simplex lexical item in Latin, namely, cohors. So also with
'bag and baggage' (that is, impedimenta) 'bay for shipps to be in'
(statio) and many others which point to some hidden Latin source.
Among them is an interesting group of phrasal verbs all listed under
back:

> put back - repulse
> keep back - reteine
> giue backe - recoile
> goe backe - returne.

These four suggest an original block of entries with re- in a Latin
source (e.g. repello, retineo, (pedem) referre, regredior). In any
case, one would hardly expect them to turn up in English under the
letter B.

By the time when the Rawlinson compiler set to work, a number of
English-Latin dictionaries had been produced (Starnes 1946, parts I
and II), and any of these could have provided a basic alphabetical
list of English words upon which the innovator of a monolingual
dictionary might build. If (as in this case seems likely) he were
working in the last decade of the sixteenth century the obvious choice
among such dictionaries would be the BIBLIOTHECA SCHOLASTICA by John
Rider. This was originally published in 1589 and went through
numerous editions and revisions during the next eighty years (Starnes
1946: 218-71).

A comparison of the Rawlinson text with the first edition of the
Rider dictionary shows that this could very well have been the main
source of the English word-list. At least three-quarters of the
hundred items from almes to aptness occur in Rider, and for many of
them, as with ambiguity 'doubtfulnes', appaire 'diminish', the compiler
would have been able to find his definition there too, since though
Rider is an English-Latin dictionary it will (as was then the custom)
frequently give an English synonym before the Latin equivalent, so as
to help out with polysemous words. Where (as under Ab- and Ac-) the
compiler took a second cull of words to extend his list, these too
appear to have come from Rider.

The Rider dictionary was able to provide learned as well as
common words (apostume, ancle), and the Rawlinson compiler has added
his own in both kinds (amphibology, applause), though he has been very
selective in the common words taken over - omitting, for instance,
alone, already, am and amorous (all of which are in Rider) and
preferring in general to keep to nouns and verbs. Comparison of
entries under the letter A suggests that he used Rider simply as some
kind of a browsing ground, picking up any suggestions for words which
suited his purpose at that point in the alphabet. Ambushment, for
instance, is not given an entry in Rider, but happens to occur in the
entry for ambush; Rider has 'An angling rodde' but Rawlinson prefers
angle-rod; ambrey, in Rider, is merely a cross-reference item ('vide
cupboard'), but the reference 'cupboard' becomes the explanation for
ambrey in the Rawlinson list.

It is of course almost impossible to prove a lexicographical
source, but the correspondences between the two works are sufficiently
close for us to infer that Rider was used, and we can in any case be
certain that the Rawlinson dictionary was heavily indebted to the
English-Latin tradition.

The Rawlinson MS dictionary and English lexicographical tradition

This manuscript dictionary is unfortunately only a fragment,
though it is a fragment big enough for us to know that the work, had
it been finished, would have been appreciably bigger than Cawdrey -
perhaps even twice the size.

We must also regret that the author never really advanced beyond
the vocabulary-selection stage, to tidy up entries, go back and
provide definitions for the many items which now stand as a single
word. Indeed, given the curiously haphazard and illogical nature of
some of his entries ('able - power', 'abound - plenty', 'accomplish -
perfection') one may even wonder whether he did not give up because
he saw that the task was too much for him.

The fact that this MS dictionary is located at the end of a
medical treatise provides a nice though somewhat fortuitous

confirmation for the view (Schäfer 1984) that historians of the early
English dictionary need to pay greater regard to all kinds of
glossaries appended to learned and technical books published in the
vernacular. More important than this are the limitations resulting
from the use of index pages. The acceptance of pre-defined blocks for
the insertion of dictionary entries, with only so many inches per
letter-combination, gives us a unique insight into what is (so far as
I know) a hitherto undocumented compiling method. The decision to
press into service the unfilled index pages may have been merely
opportunistic; but on the other hand what was felt to be an acceptable method for compiling a glossary might well have seemed a
serviceable technique for lexicographers as well.

The use of an English-Latin dictionary as a main source of
material is striking. The first English hard-word dictionaries have
been shown to derive their word-lists in large measure from Latin-
English (not English-Latin) dictionaries, by a process of wholesale
anglicisation of Latin items. By turning to an English-Latin source
the Rawlinson compiler provided himself with a much wider range of
lexical material to draw on. His decision to include 'ordinary'
words (which goes with the choice of source) was entirely at variance
with contemporary practice. Cawdrey has long been associated with
the establishment of a narrowly 'hard-word' tradition, and has even
been blamed for it (Noyes 1943). Even from this provisional account of
a fragmentary text now found in the Rawlinson MS it may be seen that
Cawdrey's choices were not self-evident even at the time: the English
dictionary might very well have been more balanced in its vocabulary
even from the start.

References

Cited dictionaries (see Appendix):

BIBLIOTHECA SCHOLASTICA ... (Rider)
(A) COMPENDIUOUS DICTIONARY OF THE LATIN TONGUE (Ainsworth)
(THE) ENGLISH DICTIONARIE ... (Cockeram)
(AN) ENGLISH EXPOSITOR ... (Bullokar)
GLOSSOGRAPHIA ... (Blount)
PROMPTORIUM PARVULORUM ...
(A) TABLE ALPHABETICALL ... (Cawdrey)

Other literature:

Clifford, James L. (1979) Dictionary Johnson. Samuel Johnson's
    Middle Years. New York: McGraw-Hill
McCracken, David (1969) "The drudgery of defining: Johnson's debt
    to Bailey's Dictionarium Britannicum" Modern Philology 66:
    338-341
Noyes, Gertrude E. (1943) "The first English dictionary, Cawdrey's
    Table Alphabeticall" Modern Language Notes 58: 600-605

Osselton, Noel E. (1973) The Dumb Linguists. A Study of the
    Earliest English and Dutch Dictionaries. Leiden: U.P.
Osselton, Noel E. (1979) "John Kersey and the ordinary words of
    English" English Studies 60: 555-561
Schäfer, Jürgen (1984) "Glossar, Index, Wörterbuch und Enzyklo-
    pädie: der Beginn einsprachiger Lexikographie zur Zeit Shake-
    speares" in Theoretische und praktische Probleme der Lexiko-
    graphie ed. by D. Goetz and T. Herbst. München: Hueber 276-299
Starnes, DeWitt T. (1954) Renaissance Dictionaries English-Latin
    and Latin-English. Austin: U. of Texas P.
Starnes, DeWitt T./Noyes, Gertrude E. (1946) The English Diction-
    ary from Cawdrey to Johnson, 1604-1755. Chapel Hill: U. of
    North Carolina P.

THE DEVELOPMENT OF THE GENERAL MONOLINGUAL DICTIONARY IN POLAND

Tadeusz Piotrowski

There are three large general dictionaries of the Polish language that make the history of monolingual lexicography in Poland. Other monolingual dictionaries are usually derivative. As the analysis that follows will show, a distinct lexicographical tradition developed in Poland to be later discarded in favour of a foreign tradition. This was perhaps due to external factors, which always had much influence on Polish life. A discussion of these factors would be far beyond the scope of this paper. Suffice it to say that Polish lexicography developed when Poland was under foreign rule.

The first monolingual dictionary of Polish was SŁOWNIK JĘZYKA POLSKIEGO by M. Samuel Bogumił Linde /1807 - 1814/ (henceforth SL). This is surprisingly late by European standards. Elsewhere in Europe monolingual lexicography began in the 17th c. Owing to the unusually high prestige of Latin in Poland all earlier Polish dictionaries were translational - bilingual (e.g. Mączyński 1564), or trilingual, with Greek (e.g. Cnapius 1621). But SL is not purely monolingual either: it provides a bridge between bilingual and monolingual dictionaries. Linde himself was a German-Polish bilingual, and SL is both definitional and translational - with German. It has been shown that SL may be used in translation very well (Jäger 1981). German was also employed as the language of description, thus it supplanted Latin in this function. The use of German could be propagandist: to make Polish better known in Europe, or it could be political: a large part of Poland had gone to Prussia and Austria.

Linde's work is also perhaps a bridge between Polish and German lexicography. Obviously, Linde used widely the existing Polish dictionaries. But in his ideas he seems to have been influenced by German lexicographers /this aspect is very underresearched/, esp. by J.C. Adelung and I.J.G. Scheller. As to Adelung (1774-86), Linde's debt is rather negative, as he thought it wrong to include only one dialect in preference to other ones, or to have only literary words. He seems to be more indebted to Scheller (1804), esp. in the format of entries and in citations.

At the time Linde began his work there was some mild controversy between him and some Polish scholars, who wanted an authoritarian dictionary - in the spirit of the 18th c., a dictionary that would set patterns on the level of individual entries, and which would help to invigorate the Polish language: with the loss of statehood, Polish was considered to be dying. Linde and the supporting aristocrats were strongly against any prescriptivism

of the dictionary. Though they, too, thought the Polish language
doomed, they wanted to preserve it for future generations in its
entirety, in a dictionary which was to be, then, a pattern again,
but on a grander scale - as a whole. Yet, though SL was not authoritarian in the least, Linde was influenced by some Polish linguists, a point I shall take up later on in the paper.

SL has more than 60,000 entries. Besides common words, there
are proper names /geographical, Christian, family, mythological,
etc.; c. 2,000 of them/, not very well selected (cf. Rzepka and
Walczak 1981), as well as prefixes. The dictionary was based on
citations from 400 writers /from 1500 to 1800/, from printed
sources only. The entry words - distinguished by full capitals -
are arranged alphabetically, but grouped in paragraphs, according
to etymology. The entries unrelated in etymology but which, for
the sake of alphabetical order, are inside such paragraphs, are
set off by brackets. The etymologies are obviously often absurd,
and rather backward even for Linde's times, as he still considered Hebrew the original language and based his etymologies only on
consonant changes. The entry itself contains the entry word, its
spelling variants, grammatical labels, Slavic equivalents, Polish
definition, German equivalent(s), senses with citations, and derivatives. The Polish definitions are either analytic, or synony-
mous. Quite often there is no definition proper, a citation having
the function of one, or else there is only a German equivalent.
Idioms and proverbs are inside the entries, and often their Slavic
equivalents are provided too. Senses are arranged on the logical
principle - first primary, concrete, then derivative, figurative,
and technical. The senses are numbered, or marked by letters, or
by other graphic signs, or not marked at all. Citations, which
span a period of three hundred years, are arranged only by meaning,
not chronologically. The entries are usually referenced to etymo-
gically related ones.

To all appearances SL is quite trustworthy. Many features,
however, make it very unusual but also very typical of the 18th
c., to which it really belongs in spirit. The selection of
entries is truly unauthoritarian /dialecticisms, colloquialisms,
taboo words/, though Linde was found not to have included all
words he had marked in texts (Pepłowski 1961), leaving out those
that were products of highly productive processes. Far more unusual is his inclusion of words he had coined himself - probably
c. 5,000 in number (Lewaszkiewicz 1980), on the basis of words
from other Slavic languages, most notably from Russian. The new
words were to fill up gaps in the structure of Polish vocabulary,
and, more importantly for Linde, to bring Polish closer to other
Slavic languages, and, with time, to make it the most important
language in the Slavic community. Linde, in fact, believed that
all Slavic languages are but dialects of one universal Slavic
language, Polish being the most important. Also because of this
he included an enormous number of Slavic equivalents, /c. 250,000/
(Lewaszkiewicz 1981:135), taken from other dictionaries /he

knew only the Polish language then/, the bulk of equivalents
being from Russian. The endeavour to make Polish the most important
Slavic language agreed perfectly well with wishful thinking of
Polish grammarians, like Kopczyński, who wanted to compensate in
this way for the loss of independence and its dreaded impact on
the Polish language. Of course, Linde's neologisms did not strike
root (Lewaszkiewicz 1980:152-157).

Linde's citations are perhaps most unusual. There are very
many of them, but their check-up has shown that he wrote them
himself on the basis of texts (Pepłowski 1961). He modernized
the spellings and inflection, again according to Kopczyński's
precepts, made them self-contained and more clear. His main
purpose was, it seems, to make the citations readable, and once
he had grasped the meaning in the text - though it was not always he managed to - to put as much emphasis on that meaning as
possible. Thus 4,500 pages of the dictionary with several hundred thousand citations can be said to be the work of one man.
This was also in agreement with aprioristic philosophy - what
was achieved by reason was more important than sensory data.
Moreover, though the citations span 300 years, Linde clearly paid
more attention to writers from the Golden Age of Polish literature /c. 1550-1630/ and to his near-contemporaries than to other
ones, which again was in accordance with the normative tendencies of the age.

SL was at least three dictionaries in one /Polish-Slavic-
German/ and it won great esteem. Faulty as it was, it was the
first comparative dictionary of Slavic languages, and the first
Slavic dictionary of such scope and, apparently, scholarship.
Linde had immediate followers, esp. Jungman in Bohemia (Orłoś
1981). In his dictionary Jungman not only modelled the entries
on SL, but also borrowed Polish words from SL to revive the
Czech language, which was in decline then. Perhaps SL was an influence on the Dal' dictionary (1863-66) of the Russian language,
but this would have to be studied in detail.

SL spawned a number of other dictionaries in Poland, and
was often followed blindly by lexicographers, e.g. by
Rykaczewski in the first Polish-English dictionary (1849). But
in the 1870s SL was felt to be inadequate. Perhaps this dissat-
isfaction was more due to the changes in Weltanschauung: the
19th c. was the age of evolutionism and of acute sense of history.
In lexicography that meant the historical principle started in
Germany by Passow in 1812 (Aarsleff 1967:253ff). German linguistics had certainly strong effect on Jan Karłowicz, who studied
in Germany. Karłowicz was a man of Renaissance abilities. In
Polish lexicography he has the position of Trench, Murray and
Wright combined. Indeed in his plan for a great dictionary of
the Polish language (1876) Karłowicz's views were similar to
Trench's, and, of course, to Passow's ideas. Karłowicz planned
two dictionaries: one great, the other abridged. The great dic-

188

TADEUSZ PIOTROWSKI

tionary should belong to pure scholarship, and be devoid of any
normative tendencies, in contrast to the smaller, handy dictionary, which would belong to applied linguistics. In some way this
division resembles the distinction into active:passive dictionaries /compare OED and COD, WEBSTER III and WEBSTER'S COLLE-
GIATE/. The smaller dictionary, however, was never produced. As
to the great dictionary, Karłowicz wanted it to be a pure inventory of words and their variants, inflection forms, etc. The
dictionary was to have histories of words, citations with exact
localization arranged chronologically. He was one of the early
advocates of studying collocability, and, in his view, the dictionary should include the most frequent open collocations, as
well as idioms, it should treat syntax, etc. In the century
which saw the big dictionary as basically an inventory of isolated
words, or word-histories, such an approach was rare indeed. An
influence of SL can be seen in Karłowicz's suggestion that headwords should be explained not only by definitions but by foreign
equivalents as well, though he gave no rationale for this sort
of treatment.

The dictionary that Karłowicz, together with Kryński and
Niedźwiedzki, set out to make in 1889 was far from the ideal he
had envisaged. SŁOWNIK JĘZYKA POLSKIEGO (1898-1927), often called
Słownik warszawski (henceforth SW), was meant to be practical,
not purely scholarly, as Karłowicz wrote in the preface to the
proof-sheet (Karłowicz et al. 1895; curiously enough SW has no
introduction at all), though its scope certainly precluded un-
sophisticated users from using it. The speed of compilation was
remarkable indeed but the lexicographic description was far
below the standards set by other great dictionaries of that time,
OED for instance. The structure of the entry was as follows:
head-word, its variants, the first sense had the basic definition,
and senses were arranged from concrete to metaphoric. The first
sense usually included also typical and frequent collocations
and idioms. Senses were also arranged in the order of increased
marking, the most technical being at the end. Some senses were
also distinguished by means of syntax. Citations, if any, had no
exact localization, only the writer's name. At the end there
were listed suffixal derivatives, which often had their own
entries as well. Very frequently a list of synonyms was at the
end of the entry. SW relied too heavily on SL, and included its
mis-quoted citations. Quotations from other sources are exact.
Not infrequently there was too little editorial work done and
the information SW included was not checked or evaluated, so it
was inaccurate.

Yet SW had great advantages, the chief being the still un-
surpassed number of lexical items - c. 280,000. SW included words
from the whole of Poland /in her pre-partition boundaries/ and
from all social strata: colloquialisms, slang /e.g. thieves'/,
four-letter words /there are even synonyms of them given/,
dialect vocabulary from Karłowicz's dialect dictionary (1900 -

1911). SW was completely unauthoritarian, the user was only
advised on some points, by means of exclamation marks / a word
to be avoided/, brackets /dialecticism/, cross /archaism/, etc.
Definitions were basically non-encyclopedic, though collocates
included often were encyclopedic. Very often there was no definition proper, only a string of synonyms - not because this
method was considered superior but because the dictionary in this
way immediately provided the users with synonymic expressions:
SW was to help the user enrich his vocabulary. Potential words
were included as entries - this gives excellent information on
word-formation system in the 19th c. On the other hand, many of
them were completely artificial. On the one hand, then, SW was
an all-embracing dictionary, but on the other it was a very
practical book.

    Obviously, SW shares some features with other great diction-
aries of that time, e.g. in the all-embracing attitude, or in non-
normativism. These features are also characteristic of positiv-
istic tendencies. The peculiarities of treatment in SW are, however, so great that it clearly belongs to another tradition. A
dictionary that SW can be usefully compared to is SLOVAR'
RUSSKOGO JAZYKA (Grot et al.; henceforth RAD). The 1st volume
came out in 1891, the project having been under way since the
1850s. In 1937, at the letter O, the work was stopped. The 1st
volume, when J.K. Grot was editor, was normative, mainly with
literary vocabulary. In 1897, when A.A. Sachmatov became chief
editor, in the first installment of the 2nd volume an editorial
change was announced: the dictionary was to be all-inclusive,
including dialecticisms, slang, and, as can be seen in the dictionary itself, obscene words. The dictionary was synchronic in
approach and very strongly anti-encyclopedic. It would be interesting to study whether there was any exchange of ideas between
SW and RAD. SW was also in a way similar to Dal's dictionary: both
had dialect, synonymic definitions, etc. Dal', however, wanted to
shape the language with his dictionary, and idea that the SW
editors were very far from.

    It appears, then, that in Poland a distinct lexicographic
tradition developed in the 19th c., though, paradoxically, it
originated to great extent thanks to the circumstances of Polish
life. Apart from SL and SW there were also other Polish dictionaries that belong to this tradition, but the two large dictionaries, being the most important, show the features of this tradition most clearly. The tradition can be described as absolutely
non-authoritarian, as regards spelling, word-stock, and description. Pronunciation was not included in any large Polish dictionary. Taboo-words were covered unabashedly, and inclusion of slang
rendered special dictionaries, like that by Farmer and Henley
(1890-1904) in Britain, unnecessary. The approach was basically
synchronic, the frequency and unmarkedness of senses being the
basis for their ordering rather than diachronic development. Defi-

nitions were not encyclopedic. And, finally, the dictionaries
attempted to show systematic relations across the lexicon: in SL
on the basis of etymology, and in SW on the basis of etymology,
word-formation, and synonyms. That these features were felt to
establish a tradition can be seen in the shorter, unfinished
dictionary (SŁOWNIK JĘZYKA POLSKIEGO, ed. Lehr-Spławiński), which
tried to unite what was best in SL and SW.

The comparison between SW and RAD will also prove useful in
my discussion of the third large Polish dictionary, SŁOWNIK
JĘZYKA POLSKIEGO PAN (1958-69, chief editor Witold Doroszewski;
henceforth SJPDor). The dictionary has c. 128,000 entries and was
made on the basis of 6,500,000 slips, collected mainly from 1950
to 1956. Only a minute fraction of the collected citations was
used in SJPDor. We have two pairs of dictionaries to compare in
fact: SW and SJPDor, and RAD and the Soviet Academy Dictionary
/BOL' ŠOJ AKADEMIČESKIJ SLOVAR' 1950-65, more than 120,000 entries,
henceforth BAS/. SJPDor, discontinuing the previous Polish lexicographical tradition, seems to be very similar both in execution
and function to BAS. For example, the number of entries is very
similar, and, in the case of SJPDor, it seems to have been established before the actual work began. The scope of both is analog-
ous: the end of the 18th c. to the 20th c. The format of entries
is very similar in both dictionaries: headword, without variants
usually, and numbered senses with citations. Senses usually proceed from general, concrete, i.e. those closest to reality, to
figurative and technical. Idioms are shown very similarly inside
particular senses. At the end of the entry there is etymology,
very scanty, or none at all, and an indication which previous
dictionaries included the entry-word. In SJPDor the latter is not
shown very faithfully. As regards citations, SJPDor is superior
over BAS, which does not have exact localizations. There are also
resemblances with regard to the defining procedures and to the
general aim of both dictionaries. These will be best shown by
comparison between earlier dictionaries and those discussed at
present. I will discuss SW and SJPDor, showing that similar relations obtain between RAD and BAS.

Doroszewski was strongly criticized after he had published
the initial project of the dictionary in 1951, and he felt ob-
liged to define his position in Polish lexicography, producing
a series of tendentious papers on its history (Doroszewski 1954).
He chose SL as his chief predecessor, praised its qualities and
did not mention its gross inadequacies /cf. SL citations, an
aspect well-known then/. In his biased criticism of SW he attacked
mainly its anti-normativist attitude. From this moment on SW has
been typically treated as an example of bad work in Polish lexicography. Also RAD, shortly before its discontinuation, was
accused of big political errors and of anti-normativism (cf.
Vinogradov 1941:236). In view of this criticism of SW it is in-

teresting that in SJPDor the large collected material is mostly
ordered by meaning discriminations and senses taken from SW.
SJPDor was compiled very quickly and apparently there was little
time to work on this aspect in detail. Two features of SJPDor,
however, were genuine improvements. One was the citations - for
the first time they are absolutely reliable and well-documented.
The other improvement was grammar in SJPDor. The most innovative
entries in it are those on function words, written by Jan
Tokarski, who also worked out a detailed inflection classification of Polish words, and keyed all entries to the classification.
This was an absolute novelty. Similarly BAS was using the resources of RAD - its citations and meaning discriminations. In
both SJPDor and BAS meaning discriminations taken from the
earlier dictionaries are changed in a very characteristic way. The
general direction of change is the same in both pairs. SW used
non-encyclopedic definitions, most often meaning is defined un-
sharply, without clear-cut boundaries between senses. RAD used
the same method /and it is far better than SW in this respect/.
The approach was linguistic. In RAD very generalized senses were
put first, the concrete, material ones following, though the gen-
etic relationship might be just the opposite /cf. oazis 'oasis'
in RAD: 1. sth good in the midst of sth bad; 2. a fertile place
in the desert/. SJPDor and BAS do not define the figurative senses
of 'oasis' at all, and the definition in SJPDor is clearly modelled
on that in BAS. The two dictionaries use encyclopedic definitions,
the definitions attempt to describe concrete entities in the real
world, rather than the fuzzy area that words cover, or than the
stable relation between a lexeme and its referents. On the other
hand, many senses, obtained by collapsing together several senses
from SW, are too general and vague. The boundaries between senses
in SJPDor and BAS are clear-cut. Quite often the senses give an
impression that they are separate homonyms. So, description of
referents is given as explanation of meaning. This may result from
materialistic ideology. For Doroszewski words are transparent
signs of real-world entities, the connection between them being
behavioural, so, according to him, it is the entities that should
be described, not the word meaning. Of course true explanation of
the real world can be given only by the sciences. Definitions in
SJPDor are scientifically worded, as a result they are often difficult to understand and cumbersome (the whole account of SJPDor
is based on Piotrowski 1985).

    Of course it is mostly nouns that can be given encyclopedic
definitions, in non-nominal entries the method of defining is
very much the same as in SW - by strings of synonyms, although
Doroszewski himself was strongly against such methods in his
theoretical writings. The synonyms that define are also frequently taken from SW. Often, because of the speed in compilation,
non-synonymic definitions were also adapted from SW, very often
becoming confusing in the process. In SJPDor there are fewer vari-

ants than in SW - it is the lexicographer that is to make the selection, not the users. The words that the lexicographer thinks
are wrong /bad borrowings, false coinages, etc./ are either not
included - some of them being admitted in the 1969 supplement -
or branded as "wrong", and the "right" words, or variants, are
suggested. Of course, nobody uses them. And, in contrast to previous dictionaries, SJPDor does not show systematic relations in
the lexicon: it is a collection of isolated entries. As a result
of these procedures, SJPDor is felt by many to be a very inadequate description of the Polish vocabulary.

The discussed lexicographis techniques result from the
function the dictionary was given - to be a link between the
sciences and man, and to help the user function in the world. It
is usually encyclopedias that are given that function. Like encyclopedias, the dictionaries were to be a component in the system of culture, which is state-controlled. For Doroszewski the
pedagogical function of the dictionary, its prescriptive power,
was more important than its descriptive value. The dictionary
should try to persuade the user to adopt certain attitudes, therefore the entries are very often heavily biased. The bias is again
the same in the Soviet dictionaries. The entries relating to
ideological key-words were very carefully edited, and they repeat
political slogans, current at the time of editing, after standard
textbooks. In such entries definitions are very biased /cf. aktyw
'the activists', kułak 'kulak'/ and citations are carefully selected, emphasizing the ideological aspects /cf. klasa 4 'class'/
or highlighting only negative aspects of words relating to those
facts of culture that should vanish in time /cf. kościół 2
'church'/.

This lexicographic practice is related to normativism. All
dictionaries should be highly normative, not excepting the unabridged ones. This means that the lexicographer should make a
very scrupulous selection of the material he has collected /cf.
SW: c. 280,000 entries; SJPDor: c. 130,000 entries on the basis
of 6,500,000 slips; OED: c. 420,000 entries, fewer slips/. What,
according to Doroszewski, should be, and was, omitted? These
were: colloquial expressions, slang, words considered taboo -
four-letter and political, and names of cultural items that should
find no future life in Polish society. These lexicographic methods
are similar in Polish and Soviet lexicography.

The ideological function of the dictionary is still considered very important, it seems, for, although a great many
lexicographers, both in Poland and in the Soviet Union, are
against lexicographic prescriptivism, the dictionaries aimed at
the general public continue the policies established in the 1950s.
In Poland this can be clearly seen in the dictionary edited by
Szymczak (SŁOWNIK JĘZYKA POLSKIEGO, 1978-81), which, despite the
claims of its editor, is an imperfect abridgement of SJPDor.

SJPDor is rather peculiar in its methods, but it might be
asked whether it shares some features with other dictionaries
made in the same period. For this end I will briefly compare
SJPDor with a product of a distinct and distant lexicographic
tradition: WEBSTER'S THIRD NEW INTERNATIONAL DICTIONARY (henceforth: WIII). The differences are clear: WIII includes most of
the contemporary English vocabulary. WIII is non-authoritarian,
but, although it was little affected by editorial whims and prejudices, it was affected by overliteral interpretation of the
function of the dictionary as a record of usage (cf. Barnhart
1978:105-106). SJPDor, on the other hand, was heavily affected by
whims and prejudices, and it was a product of an overliteral
interpretation of the function of the dictionary as a prescriptive guide. In a way SJPDor attempted to "fix" the language.
Another interesting difference related to this is the extent of
new vocabulary that both dictionaries cover. WIII has c. 22 %
of new words (Barnhart 1978:100), SJPDor has c. 10 %
(Smółkowa 1976).

And yet there are striking similarities. Also WIII was to
help the user move in the world (WIII:6a; that it was not the
average user cf. Barnhart, 113). The consequence was the wording of the definitions - beyond doubt many of them are encyclopedic /cf. the celebrated door: is it really possible to enumerate all referents, which the definition tries to do? I do not
think so/. SJPDor definitions were encyclopedic because of an
ideology. Encyclopedism in WIII definitions perhaps resulted from
American asemantic linguistics of the 1950s, which dealt with
relations and structures, putting semantics aside as extra-lin-
guistic /e.g. Hockett/. the lexicographer might think that, if
such was the case, meaning can be only explained as description
of real-world entities. More importantly, encyclopedic definitions may be regarded as instances of objectivist, scientist
attitude. Dictionaries made along such lines do not seem to be
made by human beings for other people - see, for instance, the
definition of man, which in various dictionaries usually uses
biological or anthropological terms. Is that the way we regard
ourselves? In both SJPDor and WIII the objectivist attitude can
be very clearly seen.

Dictionaries, apart from providing a lot of information on
languages, seem to be a human creation which throws much light
on the makers. Comparative studies of various lexicographic
traditions would provide valuable information on ideas underlying much of dictionary-making, and they would help to make
better dictionaries in future.

References

Cited dictionaries (see Appendix):

AUSFUHRLICHES ... LATEINISCH-DEUTSCHES LEXIKON ... (Scheller)
BOL'ŠOJ AKADEMIČESKIJ SLOVAR' see SLOVAR' SOVREMENNOGO RUSSKOGO
    LITERATURNOGO JAZYKA
(THE) CONCISE OXFORD DICTIONARY (Fowler/Sykes)
DOKŁADNY SŁOWNIK POLSKO-ANGIELSKI (Rykaczewski)
GRAMMATISCH-KRITISCHES WÖRTERBUCH DER HOCHDEUTSCHEN MUNDART ...
    (Adelung)
LEXICON LATINO-POLONICUM (Mączyński)
(THE) OXFORD ENGLISH DICTIONARY (Murray et al.)
SLANG AND ITS ANALOGUES ... (Farmer/Henley)
SLOVAR' RUSSKOGO JAZYKA (Grot et al.)
SLOVNÍK ČESKO-NĚMECKÝ (Jungmann)
SŁOWNIK GWAR POLSKICH (Karłowicz)
SŁOWNIK JĘZYKA POLSKIEGO (Doroszewski et al.)
SŁOWNIK JĘZYKA POLSKIEGO (Karłowicz)
SŁOWNIK JĘZYKA POLSKIEGO ... (Lehr-Spławiński)
SŁOWNIK JĘZYKA POLSKIEGO (Linde)
SŁOWNIK JĘZYKA POLSKIEGO (Szymczak)
THESAURUS POLONO-LATINO-GRAECUS ... (Cnapius)
TOLKOVYJ SLOVAR' ŽIVOGO VELIKORUSSKOGO JAZYKA (Dal')
WEBSTER'S NINTH NEW COLLEGIATE DICTIONARY (Mish et al.)
WEBSTER'S THIRD NEW INTERNATIONAL DICTIONARY ... (Gove)

Other literature:

Aarsleff, Hans (1967) The Study of Language in England 1780-1860.
    Princeton NJ: Princeton U.P.
Barnhart, Clarence L. (1978) "American lexicography, 1945-1973"
    American Speech 53,2: 83-140
Doroszewski, Witold (1954) Z zagadnień leksykografii polskiej.
    Warszawa: PIW
Jäger, Gert (1981) "Odpowiedniki niemieckie w słowniku Lindego"
    Prace Filologiczne 30: 73-79
Karłowicz, Jan (1876) "Przyczynki do projektu wielkiego słownika
    jęz. polskiego" Rozprawy i Sprawozdania Wydz. Fil. Akademii
    Umiejętności IV: 14-94
Karłowicz, Jan et al. (1895) Arkusz próbny. Słownik języka polskie-
    go. Warszawa: W Drukarni E. Lubowskiego i S-ki
Lewaszkiewicz, Tadeusz (1980) Panslawistyczne osobliwości leksykalne
    S.B. Lindego i jego projekt stworzenia wspólnego języka słowi-
    ańskiego (PAN Komisja Słowianoznawstwa. Monografie Slawistyczne
    42). Wrocław: Ossolineum

Lewaszkiewicz, Tadeusz (1981) "Słowiańskie materiały leksykalne w
   Słowniku języka polskiego S.B. Lindego /źródła-statystykazasady
   wprowadzania leksyku do artykułu hasłowego/" Prace Filologiczne
   30: 125-142
Orłoś, Teresa Z. (1981) "Linde a Jungmann" Prace Filologiczne 30:
   59-67
Pepłowski, Franciszek (1961) "O cytatach w słowniku Lindego" Pami-
   ętnik Literacki 52,4: 477-517
Piotrowski, Tadeusz (1985) "Leksykografia polska - teoria a prak-
   tyka" Język Polski 65, 2-3: 181-191
Rzepka, Wojciech R. and Walczak, Bogdan (1981) "Nazwy własne w
   słowniku jęz. polskiego S.B. Lindego" Prace Filologiczne 30:
   113-125
Smółkowa, Téresa (1976) Nowe słownictwo polskie. Badania rzeczow-
   ników. Wrocław: Ossolineum
Vinogradov, Viktor Vladimirovic (1941/77) "Tolkovye slovari russkogo
   jazyka" in Izbrannye trudy. Leksikologija i leksikografija.
   Moskva: Nauka

COMPETING LEXICOGRAPHICAL TRADITIONS IN AMERICA

Allen Walker Read

Dictionaries have played a distinctive role in the cultural
community of the United States. The chief basis of the special
American attitudes has been the colonial status of the people in
their early history. If London was the fountainhead of English-
speaking culture, then we should take our standards of speech from
there. A dependence on dictionaries was one result of this outlook,
and the history of American lexicography must be viewed in this
light.

The dominating figure in the history of such linguistic
attitudes has been Noah Webster, and he looms largest in American
lexicographical history. He established the 'Websterian tradition',
and I believe that it can rightly be called an 'institution', along
with other popular forces such as town meetings, the fostering of
public libraries, or 'bundling'. Through him, New England provided
the entire country with a structured means of dealing with some of
its linguistic problems. We might speculate that Noah Webster
himself would not have been averse to the notion that he founded an
'institution' (in the sociological sense that has grown up since his
time), for he had an exalted opinion of the value of his work. He
had a strong 'sense of mission'; and, as a result, controversy was
continually swirling around him.

The pervasiveness of his influence is indicated by the coinage
of the adjective Websterian as early as 1790. Ebenezer Hazard, the
historian and collector of documents, wrote in a letter of August
23, 1790: "I am vexed at the printer's Websterian division of words.
... This is perfectly puppyish." (Collections of the Mass. Hist.
Soc., 5th ser., III, 1877, p. 228)

Webster's career as a student of language began rather modestly,
with the spelling book of 1783, published when he was twenty-five
years old. But he chose a pretentious title, suggested by President
Ezra Stiles of Yale: A Grammatical Institute, of the English
Language, Comprising, an Easy, Concise, and Systematic Method of
Education. This was said to echo Calvin's Institutes, which had
established the fundamentals of Puritan religion.

The spelling book itself clearly followed the model of Thomas
Dilworth's New Guide to the English Tongue, originally published in
London in 1740 and very popular in the newly formed states — the
book that Webster was determined to supersede. In some ways Webster
was conservative, for he announced in his early pages: "In spelling
and accenting, I have generally made Dr. Johnson's dictionary my

guide; as in point of orthography this seems to be the most approved
authority in the language." (Webster 1783:11)

And yet in a letter of the next year, written July 22, 1784, he
gave another source. In denying his indebtedness to Sheridan,
Perry, Kenrick, and others, he said: "I was wholly unacquainted with
those authors, till after I had published the first edition --
Entick's Pocket Dictionary was the only work of the kind that I
consulted while I was compiling it." (Connecticut Journal, New
Haven, Dec. 15, 1784, p.1, col. 4)

Even in that first work, Webster's inquiring mind was wrestling
with the problem of language standard. In his own words in that
first edition: "The want of some standard in schools has occasioned
a great variety of dialects in Great-Britain and of course, in
America. Every county in England, every state in America and almost
every town in each state, has some peculiarities in pronunciation
which are equally erroneous and disagreeable to its neighbours. And
how can these distinctions be avoided?" (1783:5)

During the 1780s Webster gradually shed some of his Connecticut
provincialism as he travelled extensively throughout the country
giving lectures on language and pursuing copyright legislation. One
of the effects shows up in a letter that he wrote to Benjamin
Franklin on May 24, 1786. As he said: "The favorable reception my
lectures have generally met with encourages me to hope that most of
the Americans may be detached from an implicit adherence to the
language and manners of the British nation." (Letters of Noah
Webster, ed. Warfel, New York 1953:51)

When these lectures came to be printed in 1789 under the title,
Dissertations on the English Language ..., he was outspoken in his
championing of American autonomy in language. Consider the
following declaration: "As a nation, we have a very great interest
in opposing the introduction of any plan of uniformity with the
British language, even were the plan proposed perfectly unexcep-
tionable." (Webster 1789:171) One hundred thirty years later, H.L.
Mencken espoused the same position in his polemical book The
American Language of 1919, still much needed after that lapse of
time. Webster and Mencken differed remarkably in their person-
alities, but on this one issue they were in agreement.

Where did Webster find the standard that he felt to be suitable
for America? His answer was clear. He had faith in the New
Englanders around him -- those that he called the 'yeomanry'. He
thus described them in the Dissertations (1789:288)

Comparing the practice of speaking among the yeomanry of this
country, with the stile of Shakespear and Addison, I am
constrained to declare that the people of America, in particular

the English descendants, speak the most <u>pure English</u> now known
in the world.   There is hardly a foreign idiom in their
language; by which I mean, a <u>phrase</u> that has not been used by
the best English writers from the time of Chaucer. They retain
a few obsolete <u>words</u>, which have been dropt by writers, probably
from mere affectation, as those which are substituted are
neither more melodious nor expressive. In many instances they
retain correct phrases, instead of which the pretended refiners
of the language have introduced those which are highly improper
and absurd. Let Englishmen take notice that when I speak of the
American yeomanry, the latter are not to be compared to the
illiterate peasantry of their own country.

Other documents support him about the homogeneity and
historicity of these 'yeomen'. This was pointed out in 1793 when
the Massachusetts Society for the Information and Advice of
Immigrants was formed. In their Prospectus, speaking of conditions
in 1793, they rightly stated:

The inhabitants of New England, satisfied with the natural
increase of their population have, hitherto, rather discouraged
than countenanced foreigners from settling among them. Hence
few Europeans have come to us since 1640. The great body of the
present inhabitants are the offspring of about twenty-one
thousand persons, who came over previous to that period, driven
from their native land by persecution and oppression. This wise
policy has preserved a homogeneity of habits, manners, language,
government and religion. (Quoted by William Buel Sprague 1874:
137-138)

Webster's linguistic outlook continually underwent an evolution
throughout his long life, in general in the direction of
conservatism. It is fascinating to watch the changes as they
gradually took place. They are typified by the alteration of the
title of his great dictionary. On June 4, 1800, he announced that
he had in hand 'A Dictionary of the American Language', but when it
was completed, twenty-eight years later, it bore the title AN
AMERICAN DICTIONARY OF THE ENGLISH LANGUAGE.

His early enthusiasm for certain innovations, particularly in
spelling, dogged him for the rest of his life, and some critics
never forgave him. John Pickering, of Salem, Massachusetts, was one
of these. He was one of the most perceptive linguists America has
produced, especially in dealing with problems of recording Indian
languages. In the preface to a book about American English, he
said: "In this country, as is the case in England, we have thirsty
reformers and presumptuous sciolists, who would unsettle the whole
of our admirable language for the purpose of making it conform to
their whimsical notions of propriety." (Pickering 1816:vi)   Was
this an attack on Noah Webster? Probably. In the next year Webster

replied in a pamphlet of sixty pages, and he took note of the charge
in a lofty tone, saying: "Whether you number me with the thirsty
reformers and presumptuous sciolists, is a fact which I shall take
no pains to discover, nor if known, would the fact give me the
smallest concern." (A Letter to the Honorable John Pickering on the
Subject of his Vocabulary, Boston 1817, p. 31)

In the process of becoming a linguistic institution, the
Websterian interests had their most difficult tasks in the area of
pronunciation. Many Americans gave their allegiance to the English
orthoepist John Walker, whose CRITICAL PRONOUNCING DICTIONARY had
first appeared in London in 1791 and was widely reprinted. Webster
attacked it bitterly. In a letter of November 18, 1829, to the
New-England Magazine, he said: "I consider the use of Walker's
Dictionary as one of the greatest evils our language has ever
suffered." (Collection of the Mass. Hist. Soc., II, June 1832,
p.476) Then again in a letter of March 1, 1837, intended for
publication, he asserted: "As to Walker's being a standard with most
writers, you err most egregiously. Later British writers on
orthoepy pronounce his pronunciation, in some classes, ludicrous, in
others absolute absurdity & vulgarity; & one author says, that in
solemn discourse, it would be intolerable. His orthography, in some
classes of words, has been long rejected by every author whose works
I have seen." (MS letter from New Haven to the Rev. William
Twining, in the Pierpont Morgan Library, New York, N.Y.)

And yet John Walker had to be taken into account. Joseph
Emerson Worcester, later to become Webster's chief rival, began his
career as a lexicographer by bringing out an American edition of
Walker. He received advice from the John Pickering already
mentioned. Pickering's letter of October 24, 1827 (the year before
Webster's AMERICAN DICTIONARY appeared), is worth quoting, because
it represents the first recognition known to me in American lexicography of a distinction being made between a formal pronunciation
and a colloquial pronunciation. Pickering's letter, representing
his insight of 1827, is as follows:

One remark ought to be made, distinctly & fully, respecting the
daily colloquial pronunciation, & the more formal & exact
utterance which every man would use in public, for the double
purpose of being better understood & of performing his part with
all that exactness & finish, which the public would naturally
expect of him; just as they would expect every gentleman to
appear in society dresssed with care in his best apparel,
instead of his ordinary daily dress, & that too, put on in a
slovenly manner. Now Walker's pronunciation, as marked by his
mode of notation, is to be understood as the most exact
pronunciation that would be expected in public speaking, & not
as the ordinary colloquial utterance used in the common
intercourse of society, where no care is used in speaking; in

other words, he does not mean to designate all the little
aberrations from exactness, which occur at every moment in he
carelessness of conversation.

A little remark on this head will give the reader a more just
notion of the use to be made of the work & at the same time show
the reasonableness of Walker's opinions. ... It is highly
important, without appearing to take sides, that his authority
should be confirmed, in order to prevent every ignoramus from
setting himself up as a standard. (MS Letters to Worcester, V,
62, in Mass. Hist. Soc., Boston)

That both of the great rival dictionary traditions, that of
Webster and that of Worcester, represented New England speech,
caused trouble in other parts of the country. One American dialect
was accorded unfair prestige at the expense of others that had just
as sound historical roots.

Under such conditions a dictionary key was hard to interpret. A
good instance of this turns up in the Worcester correspondence. A
student at Oberlin College in Ohio had been selected to teach
elocution in the Preparatory Department but found that he disagreed
with the Professor of Rhetoric. In a letter to Worcester on
December 22, 1853, W.W. Woodruff told of his troubles:

In teaching Rhetorical Reading, my attention has been
particularly called to the matter of pronunciation; & I am so
unhappy as to be compelled to differ with our Professor of
Rhetoric as to what you mean by the sound of "A long before R,"
as in fare, pair, bear, & c. ... Although I have never failed
in satisfying a student who would sit down with me and examine
your Dictionary that I understood you correctly, yet the bad
habits of more than a thousand students backed by the authority
and example of the Professor is somewhat of an annoyance to me.
(MS Letters to Worcester, VI, 137)

We do not have Worcester's reply, but he evidently asked for
further information, and the student in a second letter, on January
16, 1854, explained again:

In regard to my inquiries, perhaps I can as well get my point
before your mind by stating what our difficulties are with our
Professor. He pronounces such words as parent, pair, bear, with
the sound of a in hat; and attempts to justify himself by
reference to common usage: & thinks that you must mean about
what he practices. Some of us, on the other hand, maintain that
by "the long sound of A before R," you mean the long sound as in
lame shortened a very little by being before r. We think that
this is your meaning because you have in Sec. 11 taken pains to
guard us against the error of thinking that the sound in
question is identical with the sound of a in late. (Ibid.)

Such misunderstandings must have been repeated time and again in areas outside New England.

Some uncertainties of pronunciation were not regional in nature. One very practical inquiry came from T.B. Hayward of Brookline, Massachusetts, in a letter to Worcester on January 7, 1854. He was superintending the publication of a hymnal, in which the accented syllables in the words had to be marked to be sung to the accented notes of the music. He stated his problem thus:

> I shall be obliged by your advice in regard to the pronunciation of two words. Thanksgiving, in all the English dictionaries, & in yours is accented on the first syllable. But in New England, & in all the U.S. so far as I am acquainted, it is accented on the second. Perhaps I am not accurately informed on this point. In several cases this word must be marked to be sung to the cadence measures of the music; & I will thank you if you will tell me which way you would advise to have it marked; whether with the accent on the first or second syllable. Is it to be expected that our people will ever change their pronunciation of the name of their time honored family gathering so as to accent it on the first syllable?
>
> Webster admits that upright is by many accented on the first syllable; but says that no one thinks of accenting its derivatives, uprightness, uprightly, in that manner. But I find them accented on the first syllable in your dictionary & in others. Do not the American people continue to accent all these on the second syllable? & what is your opinion with regard to the prevailing accentuation of these words, & also of thanksgiving, for twenty years to come? (MS Letters to Worcester, III, 72)

The principal support of the Websterian tradition as an institution is found in the popular attitudes that accepted its authority with pride. The hearty British seaman Captain Frederick Marryat, while traveling in America in the 1830s, reported: "I was once talking with an American about Webster's dictionary, and he observed, 'Well now, sir, I understand it's the only one used in the Court of St. James, by the king, queen, and princesses, and that by royal order." (A Diary in America [Part First], London 1839, II, p. 219)

As long as Noah Webster and Joseph Emerson Worcester both remained alive, personal loyalties to each of them were involved. The 'War of the Dictionaries', which began in 1834, was pursued on both sides by devotees with a crusading zeal. After Webster's death in 1843, his heirs arranged that the publishing interests should be

taken over by the George and Charles Merriam brothers and they
actively cultivated their commercial advantage. Webster's son-in-
law, Chauncey A. Goodrich, took over the editing, rather happy to be
freed from his father-in-law's crotchety demands.

Goodrich's modifications made it easier for the general public,
in its cry for a national standard, to accept the Websterian claims.
The trend can be documented by numerous letters in the files of the
G. & C. Merriam Company. A few typical ones may be quoted.

Here is a letter by Edward Beecher, a clergyman of Boston,
brother of Henry Ward Beecher, on April 2, 1855: "I approve,
therefore, the almost universal agreement to make it the standard of
our language. And since a standard is a universal necessity, why
should not all unite in this one whose merits & claims are so
unequivocal & unequalled?" (G. & C. Merriam MS Corresp.) In that
same week Daniel Kimball, who was principal of the Williams Academy
at Stockbridge, Massachusetts, wrote to the Merriams that he
regarded Noah Webster "... as the man who has done more to produce
stability, uniformity and elegance in the use of our rich and noble
language than any and all others, since the days of Johnson." He
closed with the hope "... that your efforts to flood the land with
copies of these Dictionaries, from the 'Common School' to the
'Unabridged', will meet with the encouragement they so richly
deserve." (G. & C. Merriam MS Corresp.)

A citizen of Wickford, Rhode Island, J.J. Leland, italicized the
phrase national standard authority when he wrote as follows in a
letter of September 29, 1855: "Its preeminent excellence as a
defining Dictionary, and its system of orthography, and its
principles of notation and pronunciation have deservedly given it
the high position it occupies of being the national standard
authority." (G. & C. Merriam MS Corresp.)

Of special interest are a number of letters that show a changing
allegiance towards the Webster series. The president of the
University of Rochester, in western New York, M.B. Anderson, voiced
his qualms in a letter of July 17, 1856, as follows:

... Though I cannot conscientiously speak in the unqualified
terms regarding the value of the work, which most scholars
adopt, I cheerfully bear testimony to the great excellence of
the definitions and to the value of the labors of the editors of
the edition now circulated, in modifying what some scholars have
thought the whims of the venerated author of the work. For good
or evil your Dictionary has obtained the suffrage of so great a
portion of the American public that it would savor of affectation for me to attempt to control the tide [of] opinion setting
so strong in its favor. (G. & C. Merriam MS Corresp.)

But twelve years later this same president was far less guarded,
writing in a letter of February 1, 1868:

> The original edition of Webster's Dictionary while marked by
> many excellencies, contained certain innovations in spelling and
> pronunciation which seemed to me uncalled for. Its Philological
> Introduction was in a great degree unsound and uncritical. Its
> etymologies were sometimes fanciful and not seldom clearly
> wrong. For these reasons I have not felt at liberty in past
> years to recommend it as a guide to our students in the study of
> English.
>
> But later editions have gradually remedied these defects and the
> present edition may justly be considered as an entirely new
> work. ... The complete revision which through a wise division
> of labor the whole work has undergone, compel[s] me in simple
> justice to say, that as a Dictionary of our Language your work
> now stands unrivalled in its excellence. (G. & C. Merriam MS
> Corresp.)

The later history of American lexicography was much influenced
by the commercial vitality of the various publishing companies.
Worcester's publishers became weaker, while the G. & C. Merriam
Company thrived, some thought by sharp dealing, including barratry.
The splendid CENTURY DICTIONARY AND CYCLOPEDIA, edited by the sound
scholar William Dwight Whitney, should have established a strong
competing tradition, but the agreement forced on it not to have a
small school-sized edition hampered it.

In the beginning years of the present century, the chief rivalry
was between the Webster series of the G. & C. Merriam Co., and a
dictionary series called the STANDARD ..., first edited in 1893 by
Isaac K. Funk. Its chief innovation was listing the meanings not in
historical order, but in the order of importance. It was brought
into disrepute by the maunderings of a later editor, a pseudo-
scholar named Frank Vizetelly; and its publishing company, Funk &
Wagnalls, allowed the work to falter beyond retrieval.

The rivalries among small dictionaries in recent decades would
require another paper.

I must allude to only one later episode -- the tremendous
popular outcry that followed the publication of WEBSTER'S THIRD NEW
INTERNATIONAL in 1961. The onslaught against that edition was, in
my opinion, highly unfair, engineered chiefly by a little coterie of
ideologues that won the backing of the literary establishment. A
whole volume, a 'casebook', on the controversy was assembled by
James Sledd and Wilma Ebbitt (1962).

I received much personal castigation for my own involvement in the affair. I was asked to give an evaluation by the American organization, Consumer's Union, and my favorable review of the dictionary was printed in Consumer Reports, Vol. 28, No. 10 (October, 1963), pp. 488-492. For this, I was attacked in a barrage of letters to the editor, as being "a standardless sociologist of language", a "wrong-side-up pedant", and a "dogmatist of linguistic democracy".

I will close by quoting my self-defense, printed in Consumer Reports (February, 1964, p. 97) as follows:

> The great danger in the use of dictionaries is that they may come to be thought of as straitjackets that prevent the swinging, free enjoyment of the mother tongue. Dictionaries are helpful if they are regarded as we regard atlases. An atlas does not tell us where a boundary ought to be; it records the information as to where the boundary has been found in the past. The best advice is that we should be so observant of the language used around us that we will carry our own dictionary in our heads, and most of us do just that. However, the language is so fearfully and wonderfully made that our personal dictionary sometimes needs to be supplemented. A dictionary serves to enlarge our language awareness and experience.

References

Cited dictionaries (see Appendix):

(AN) AMERICAN DICTIONARY ... (Webster)
(THE) CENTURY DICTIONARY AND CYCLOPEDIA (Whitney et al.)
(A) CRITICAL PRONOUNCING DICTIONARY ... (Walker)
(THE) STANDARD DICTIONARY ... (Funk)
WEBSTER'S THIRD NEW INTERNATIONAL ... (Gove)

Other literature:

Dilworth, Thomas (1740/58) New Guide to the English Tongue. London: H. Kent
Mencken, Henry L. (1919/63) The American Language (one-volume abridged edition by Raven I. McDavid). New York: A.A. Knopf & London: Routledge
Pickering, John (1816) A Vocabulary, or Collection of Words and Phrases Which Have Been Supposed to Be Peculiar to the United States of America. Boston: Cummings and Hilliard
Sledd, James and Ebbitt, Wilma R. eds. (1962) Dictionaries and THAT Dictionary. A Casebook on the Aims of Lexicographers and Targets of Reviewers. Chicago: Scott, Foresman

Sprague, William Buel (1874) The Life of Jedidiah Morse, D.D. New
    York: A.D.F. Randolph
Warfel, Harry R. ed. (1953) Letters of Noah Webster. New York:
    Library Publishers
Webster, Noah (1789) Dissertations on the English Language: with
    Notes, Historical and Critical. Boston: I. Thomas and Co.
Webster, Noah (1783) A Grammatical Institute of the English
    Language, Comprising, an Easy, Concise, and Systematic Method of
    Education. Hartford, Connecticut: Hudson and Goodwin

THE BILINGUAL DICTIONARY - VICTIM OF ITS OWN TRADITION?

Mary Snell-Hornby

é an-gin$_x$ uru$_4$ gar-ra	"A house with a foundation like heaven,
é dub-pisan-gin$_x$ gada mu-un-dul	A house which like a ... vessel has been covered with linen,
é uz-gin$_x$ ki-gal-la gubba	A house which like a goose stands on a (firm) base,
igi nu-bad ba-an-ku$_4$	One with eyes not opened has entered it,
igi-bad ba-an-ta-è	One with open eyes has come out of it.
ki-búr-bi édub-ba-a	Its solution: the school."

(Sumerian riddle, quoted Sjöberg 1976:159)

At the EURALEX Seminar "The Dictionary and the Language Learner", held in Leeds in April 1985, the author of the present paper ventured the following bold remarks:

> As there has always been a human need to communicate, even beyond language barriers, it is not surprising that foreign language learning, and with it translation and bilingual lexicography, have a very long history. Maybe that is the reason why this is an area of knowledge not only bound by tradition, but often even paralyzed by unquestioned fixed ideas and prejudices. One such fixed idea is epitomized in that naive question "What's x in English?", suggesting that a word "is" another word in the foreign language. This is the principle of elementary approximation underlying the vocabulary lists generations of schoolchildren are compelled to learn by heart, and it is unfortunately consolidated in the traditional small-size dictionaries such learners buy, use and stick to - perpetuating a practice that has in essence progressed no further than the ancient bilingual word lists on the clay tablets of Old Babylonia. (Snell-Hornby, forthcoming)

It is the purpose of this paper to substantiate those

claims and where necessary to modify them. A critical
look will be taken at the earliest beginnings of bilingual lexicography, whereby not so much the actual
linguistic material will be investigated as the cultural tradition and circumstances behind it. We shall
then see whether any cross-cultural links can be made
or parallels drawn with later developments of bilingual lexicography in Europe. Due to the vastness of
the field and the limited scope of this paper, only
a very broad and general view is possible and no final
conclusions can be reached - though it is hoped that
the following brief study will provide food for thought
and a basis for discussion. (1)

The bilingual word lists of Old Babylonia

Sumerian, the oldest written language in existence,
was used by the inhabitants of southern Mesopotamia
from the 4th to the 2nd millennium BC. The Sumerians
were characterized by what von Soden describes as "der
ganz ungewöhnlich stark ausgebildete Wille zur Ordnung"
(1974:23), which permeated their entire culture. No-
where is this inclination to impose order on a mass of
material better illustrated than in their rich legacy
of word lists, the earliest known beginnings of lexicography. The Sumerians believed that an object only
had real existence if it were given a name (von Soden
1974:33), and their lists were not in fact monolingual
dictionaries with headwords and definitions, but a complete documentation of the things around them.

During the 3rd millennium BC Sumer gradually fell
into the hands of the Akkadians, Semitic invaders from
northern Mesopotamia, who from about 2000 BC ruled the
whole region, and it is this period that is usually
referred to as 'Babylonian'. The Akkadians believed
they could best consolidate their political supremacy
by making the Sumerian cultural heritage their own
(von Soden 1974:25); among other things they adopted
the Sumerian cuneiform script (then in the form of
conventionalized linear drawings pressed into soft
clay tablets) for writing their own language (known
as Akkadian or Assyro-Babylonian). The impact of the
Sumerian culture on the Akkadians gave rise to the
oldest bilingual word lists known to us, in which the
Sumerian entries were provided with pronunciation
glosses and Akkadian translations. Some polyglot lists
also include Hittite, with rare examples of Hurrian
and Ugaritic (Civil 1976:124). The lists were used
mainly for the training of future scribes in the Old
Babylonian school, the eduba (a Sumerian word rendered in Akkadian as 'tablet house'). (Sjöberg 1976:159)

Though the script used by the Sumerians and Akkadians was identical, their languages were vastly different. As a member of the Semitic group, Akkadian was
an inflecting language like Hebrew and Arabic, while
Sumerian was an agglutinating language with no proven
relationship to any other tongue, though both morphological similarities and cultural contacts have been
established, inter alia with the Dravidian languages
of Southern India (cf. von Soden 1974:23). Equally
dissimilar were the Sumerians and Akkadians in world-
view and mentality: if the Sumerians tended to order
and organization, the Akkadians excelled in fine observation and explanation, which von Soden describes
as follows (1974:24):

> ... in der Kunst (...) vermochten sie dank ihrer
> Fähigkeit zu scharfer Beobachtung die Darstellung
> des Lebens, wie es ist, auf den Höhepunkten zu
> hoher Meisterschaft zu steigern.

It is against this linguistic and cultural background
that the first bilingual word lists have to be understood.

The Mesopotamian lexicographical legacy is imposing
not only in size (it runs into tens of thousands of
entries), but also because of the diversity in its compilation (cf. Civil 1976:124-5). For the present paper
we must limit ourselves to the most relevant aspects
only, above all the lexical content of the lists. Civil
notes nine groups, of which the Har-ra = hubullu group
(with more than 9,700 entries) is outstanding (1976:125):

> HAR-ra = hubullu. A thematic collection of twenty-
> four tablets, HAR-ra = hubullu includes legal and
> administrative terminology (tablets 1 and 2), trees
> and wooden artifacts (3-7), reeds and reed artifacts
> (8 and 9), pottery (10), hides and copper (11),
> other metals (12), domestic (13) and wild (14) ani-
> mals, parts of the body (15), stones (16), plants
> (17), birds and fish (18), textiles (19), geo-
> graphic terms (20-22), food and drinks (23 and 24).

The other groups include a continuation of the above,
with a thematic list of professions, kinship terms,
and various human activities, lists of compound words,
synonyms and antonyms, and a collection of simple signs
and compound logograms of the cuneiform script, along
with their pronunciation and Akkadian meanings. A later
genre consists of commentaries mainly oriented towards
the explanation of Akkadian words.

The lists of wild animals from the 14th tablet of the Har-ra = <u>hubullu</u> group, as presented by Landsberger (1934), provide some insight into the world-view of Ancient Mesopotamia. Below is an extract from the lists of rodents and related genera:

Text		Übersetzung	
		IV	V
péš.še.giš.ià.kú.e	[*kurusissu*]	Sesam fressende Maus	„
péš.ùr.ra	*ar-ra-bu*	Dachmaus	**Siebenschläfer**
péš.a.šà(g).ga	*ha-ri-ru*	**Feldmaus**	„Wühler", —
péš.igi.gùn.gùn.[na]	*bar-mu*	mehrfarbige Maus	—, (?)
péš.níg.gilim.ma	*aš-ti-ki-s*[*u*]	Maus der Vernichtung	**Ratte** (?)
péš.QA.gaz	*hu-lu-u*	.....-Gefäß-Maus	**Spitzmaus** (?)
péš.hul	„	böse Maus	„
péš.ki.bal	[*ak-ba-ru*]	den Ort verändernde Maus	**Springmaus**
péš.DU.DU.me	*as-*[*qu-du*]	(zusammen)tragende Maus	**Hamster** (?
DU.DU.me	„	(zusammen)tragendes (Tier)	„
dNin.kilim	*ši-ik-ku-u*	(Gott) Herrin der Mäuse (?)	**Mungo**
dNin.kilim.bar	*tar-pa-šu*	fremdartiger Mungo	**Fischotter** (?
dNin.kilim.íb.kur₄	*pu-ṣu-ud-du*	.... Mungo	**Iltis** (?)
dNin.kilim.tir.ra	*š/sak-ka-ru-u*	Waldmungo	**Marder** (?)
dNin.kilim.edin.na	*a-a-ṣu*	Steppenmungo	**Wiesel** (?

The column on the extreme left lists transcriptions of the Sumerian ideograms, Column IV their German translations, while the second column presents the Akkadian words with their translations in Column V. Words printed in bold type represent zoological species, and complete correspondence between the Sumerian ideogram and its Akkadian translation is indicated by —. This section shows clearly that the Sumerian categories in particular by no means correspond to the species familiar to us, while the Akkadian lists tend towards zoological interpretation. Thus the Sumerian 'roof-mouse' was interpreted as a kind of dormouse and the Sumerian 'mouse of destruction' as a rat. Sumerian categorization involved a good deal of evaluation, here illustrated by the 'nasty mouse', in the Akkadian list a shrew, while the physical categories were frequently interspersed with mythological elements. This is not illustrated above, but emerges clearly from the list of snakes, where Sumerian <u>muš.-ušumgal</u>, or 'giant caterpillar' was understood by the Akkadians to be a dragon.

As they stand, the lists - described above in their
final (canonical) form (cf. Civil 1976:125) - cannot be
viewed as complete or autonomous documents: they largely
went back to school exercises from the eduba, and are
hence fragments originally embedded in a rich oral teaching tradition, the essence of which is lost for ever (cf.
Civil 1976:130). However, on the basis of text-material,
a surprising amount has been reconstructed about life
in the eduba, and is described in a fascinating study by
Sjöberg (1976).

The medium of instruction, at least for more advanced
students, was most probably Sumerian. Evidence that this
was not the students' native tongue (and probably already
a dead language) is found in proverbs, such as "A scribe
who does not know Sumerian, what (kind of) a scribe is
he?" (Sjöberg 1976:161). Instruction aimed at active
proficiency in Sumerian, both oral and written, and there
is ample evidence that such proficiency was not easily
come by: firstly, many of the tablets excavated are
clearly the trainee scribes' own efforts, the clumsy
writing and inaccuracies reflecting the toil that went
into the copying of Sumerian 'vocab lists'; and secondly,
there are again texts available such as the following:

> If you have learned the scribal art, you had
>   recited all of it,
> the different lines, chosen from the scribal art,
> (the names of) the animals living in the steppe
>   to (the names of) artisans
> you have written, (but) after that you hate
>   (writing). (Sjöberg 1976:163)

In viewing the Sumerian-Akkadian word lists against
the background of their oral tradition, we must bear in
mind at least three points. Firstly, in the Old Babylonian schools the Sumerian culture was considered superior to the Akkadian; at the same time the Akkadians
had absorbed this superior culture and were themselves
developing it further. Secondly, the vast majority of
entries in the Sumerian word lists, and subsequently in
the bilingual word lists, denote concrete, static objects
or represent nomenclatures, although the genius of the
Akkadian language is seen by scholars to lie in the verb:
"Der Riesensphäre des Verbums steht ein kleiner, vollständig starrer Stock von Gegenstandsbegriffen gegenüber."
(Landsberger 1974:9). This linguistic clash might explain
the aversion the trainee scribes experienced in having
to cope with the strange vocabulary (cf. the proverb
quoted above). Thirdly, the nature of the bilingual word
lists at the same time owes much to the nature of the
Akkadians themselves: their empirical aptitude for fine

observation and skill in pragmatic explanation were
admirable in themselves, but they made the lists stop
short at a static inventory of items, whereby meta-
physical problems were not raised, the secret of inner
workings not pursued. It was only with the Greeks and
their dynamic spirit of critical inquiry that the foundations for Western philosophy and science could be laid.

Old Babylonia and the Western tradition

It is generally agreed that the Western tradition
of dictionary-making goes back to the Greeks, and it is
at that point too that Collison (1982) starts his history
of foreign-language dictionaries. At the same time it is
an indisputable fact that the Babylonians had their own
rich store of lexicographical lists at a much earlier
point in history. Is it possible that the Greeks -
through cultural ties or their imperialistic expansion
in the Near East - could have known of and drawn on the
cultural storehouse of Babylonia, that actually our
lexicographical tradition can be traced back to the
Sumerian word lists? The account of Babylonian lexicography given above might indeed tempt us to draw such
conclusions, but unfortunately there is no concrete
evidence on which to base them.

Two main observations are important here. Firstly,
it is certain that Greek lexicography developed auto-
nomously, beginning with the need to explain difficult
words from Homer. Secondly, although in everyday life
bilingualism must have been a common factor in Classical
Antiquity, the first known bilingual glossaries (Greek-
Latin) only date from the 2nd century AD (Goetz 1912).
Even in Mesopotamia itself, the ancient word lists were
not extended to include Aramaic or Persian; there are
clay tablets from the Seleucid Kingdom with Greek transcriptions of Akkadian words, but nothing that could be
described as a glossary or lexicon. The cuneiform script
fell into disuse around 70 AD with the decline of Seleucid
power, and from then on nothing was known of the Sumerian-
Akkadian word lists until their discovery in the 19th
century. In the early days of Bible translation no significant part seems to have been played by bilingual lexica:
St Jerome evidently had none at his disposal - he learnt
Hebrew himself, and for Aramaic he sought the counsel of
experts (Marti 1974:30-33). It is not impossible that
word lists were used in everyday life but have not been
preserved and are not mentioned in the works of literature, and it may be significant that the first evidence
of Greek-Latin glossaries was found in Syria (Goetz 1912),
but there is still no concrete link to the word lists of
Old Babylonia. Must we assume that the bilingual dictionary was invented twice?

After all that has been established, it would be reasonable to ask why a paper on the tradition of bilingual lexicography goes into the Babylonian word lists at all when they do not even form part of that tradition. The reason is that our discussion of Sumerian-Akkadian lexicography helps to throw light on a number of points significant for the development of the bilingual dictionary in Europe: it is in fact not an uncommon experience that an analysis of the unfamiliar and exotic helps one to recognize factors which sheer familiarity made one take for granted.

The first important point is that of cultural domination. At the time of the ancient bilingual word lists, Sumerian - probably already a dead language - was the accepted language of scholarship in Babylonian society, which at the same time was consciously absorbing and developing the older, superior culture. A similar constellation was to influence Western lexicography right up into modern times - and that was the situation caused by the overwhelming domination of Latin.

The history of lexicography from the early Middle Ages is already quite well-trodden ground (see Collison 1982), and only the most salient points need be mentioned here. Of major importance is the embryonic form of the future bilingual dictionary as interlinear glosses explaining difficult words. As in Old Babylonia and as with Ancient Greek, early lexicography was essentially a one-way track, making the distant and lofty world of scholarship and its strange, archaic terms accessible to an invariably passive recipient. Questions that concern us today, such as the type of user and his communicative needs, were totally irrelevant. Latin continued to dominate bilingual lexicography right into the 17th century, and also formed the source language for polyglot vocabularies such as the popular SEX LINGUARUM and Calepino's monumental DICTIONARIUM (see Stein 1985), even though these contained perfectly familiar and concrete everyday words. The change came with the growth of commerce and the rising importance of foreign travel in the 17th century, which both presupposed at least some communicative competence in foreign languages. Even with the decline of Latin however, cultural supremacy (conditioned by political power) continued to be a major factor in bilingual lexicography: this explains why dictionaries linking Romance language-pairs have a longer history than those linking the at one time 'weaker' Germanic languages English and German (Hausmann and Cop 1985).

The second main link between Old Babylonian word lists and the European dictionary is the vital connection with teaching in schools. The trainee scribe of the Baby-

lonian <u>eduba</u> was expected to reach active proficiency
in Sumerian, just as the pupil in the mediaeval monastery school gained active proficiency in Latin. As both
were however dead languages, performance could only be
assessed according to a system of abstract rules, without the intervention of a native speaker informant, and
vocabulary could only be interpreted in terms of what is
still known as 'translation equivalents' in the native
language. In the case of Latin (and Greek), as we all
know from school days, it was only a step to the elementary translation exercise involving the logical and consistent application of the rules learnt and the use of
the equivalents presented. The same kind of translation
exercise is today still mis-used in teaching living
languages. What is not yet understood is that the principles of active proficiency in a dead language are inadequate for communicative competence in the fuzzy, shifting
multi-dimensional world of a living foreign language.

In the case of the dictionary 'translation equivalent', both elements of the term are misleading: as
translation theorists are quick to point out, translation involves texts and not words, and equivalence is
for the most part an illusion. Moreover, the type of
relationship holding between lexemes of two different
languages can vary enormously. Elsewhere (Snell-Hornby,
forthcoming) I have differentiated between five main
groups of prototypes: the simplest relationship (i.e.
equivalence) exists at the level of terminology and
nomenclature; with concrete objects and basic human
activities, interlingual relationships are simpler than
with words involving perception and evaluation linked to
sociocultural norms. In the Sumerian-Akkadian lists of
the Har-ra = hubullu series, the entries are conspicu-
ously terms, names and concrete objects, a level where
equivalence is most easily reached (although von Soden
- 1974:117 - points out that even these terms hardly
ever corresponded exactly). It is equally striking that
even today the examples quoted both in contrastive semantics and in work on bilingual lexicography (cf. Kromann
et al. 1984) are for the most part likewise concrete
objects or basic activities, while the really complicated
problems of interlingual relationships go unnoticed.

The concept of 'Eigenbegrifflichkeit'

In his inaugural lecture "Die Eigenbegrifflichkeit
der babylonischen Welt", given at the University of
Leipzig in 1926, the great Sumerologist Benno Landsberger
emphasized that the best way to penetrate the culture of
the ancient Babylonians is to view it in its own terms
and not impose modern Western concepts on it (Landsberger
1974). Though his lecture may have been influenced by the

Humboldtian spirit then prevalent in Germany, his message
still remains a basic guiding factor in modern Sumero-
logy. Fifty years later M. Civil, while referring to the
methods of American linguistics and appealing to the la-
tent possibilities of language universals, still comes
to the conclusion: "Only by trying to look at the world
the way the ancient Mesopotamian did will the lexicographer properly understand his vocabulary." (1976:154)
During the course of his argumentation, Civil points out
the dangers of a 'faulty perspective', and names the
"ethnocentric approach" and the "Akkadocentric approach"
as the two main distorting factors (1976:142):

> By the ethnocentric approach I mean the unwarranted
> projection on Sumerian vocabulary of semantic cate-
> gories, presuppositions, and cultural classifications
> applicable only to the standard Western worldview, or
> perhaps to only part of it. (...) By the Akkadocentric
> approach I mean the procedure that stops the semantic
> investigation of a Sumerian word as soon as its Akka-
> dian equivalent is determined. (...) Whenever possi-
> ble, however, the meaning of a Sumerian word should
> be sought first in Sumerian contexts.

I have quoted Civil in such detail because the same principle basically applies - though usually to a lesser and
varying extent - to all bilingual lexicography and to
language learning in general: our understanding of a
foreign vocabulary is distorted if we force it into the
concepts of our own language and world view.

For a culture like the one of Ancient Babylonia in
the dim and distant past, there are of course special
difficulties, though Civil insists that we are dealing
with "messages from a past that is separated from us
perhaps more by linguistic and cross-cultural barriers
than by millennia" (1976:137). In other words, the problems are essentially the same for the bilingual lexicographer of today, though the strangeness of the Babylonian
world throws them into sharper relief. This comes out very
clearly in von Soden's study "Leistung und Grenze sumerischer und babylonischer Wissenschaft" (1974), which
discusses in detail whether the German concept of 'Wissenschaft' can be applied to the Babylonians at all: neither
in Sumerian nor in Akkadian can a word for it be found,
although both languages have a root form to express 'wissen' (meaning to know). Faithful to Landsberger's notion
of Eigenbegrifflichkeit, von Soden investigates the
Sumerian principle of the exhaustive ordering of names
(and hence things), and concludes by describing it as a
Listenwissenschaft (1974:35), unique in the history of man.
In contrast to that, the empirical and explanatory work
done by the Akkadians is described as "die ohne theore-

tische Nebenabsichten praktische Ziele verfolgende 'Wissenschaft' der Babylonier und Assyrer" (1974:74). (2)

Taking all that has been said so far into consideration, I should finally like to present some conclusions for general discussion. Firstly, to answer the question put in my title: it does indeed seem that bilingual lexicography has been manoeuvred into a stereotyped pattern of 'translation equivalents', a principle which, as Zgusta rightly points out (1984:147), lexicographers have followed since time immemorial, but which clashes with the notion that cultures and concepts must be viewed in their own terms, demanding a heuristic method of discovery procedures. I would also venture to suggest that the time is now ripe to break out of these stereotypes. A decisive factor in early lexicography was the already mentioned 'one-way track' conditioned by a prescriptive cultural domination: difficult words were explained to a passive recipient in the terms of his own vernacular. For everyday communication, on the other hand, bilingualism existed without the need for bilingual dictionaries. In modern lexicography the situation is quite different: in the place of an accepted cultural hierarchy we have a plurality of languages to be contrasted descriptively on an equal footing, and dictionaries are needed for active communication. (The present position of English as a lingua franca to facilitate such communication is not comparable to that of either Sumerian or Latin.) This means that the bilingual dictionary should help to clarify alien concepts against their own cultural background and not limit language to the status of a mere code consisting of varying labels. We are again required to see the dictionary in the context of school (or university) instruction, a place which (in the words of the Sumerian riddle quoted at the beginning of this paper) should open the pupil's eyes, instead of distorting his perspective with rough approximations presented as equivalents. Finally, an intriguing analogy can be drawn from the earliest lexicography: we may see the Sumerian principle of order as one pillar of dictionary-making and the Akkadian practice of observation and explanation as a second (i.e. the Listenwissenschaft followed by pragmatic analysis). There is however a third pillar needed if the dictionary is not to remain merely a static inventory of items, and it seems particularly necessary at the present stage of bilingual lexicography: a renewed spirit of critical inquiry to lay the foundations for new concepts and methods to cope with new and varied needs.

Notes

(1) I am most grateful to Professor Karl Oberhuber and Dr. Manfred Schretter (both of the Institute of Oriental Studies, University of Innsbruck) and to Professor Walter Burkert (Department of Classics, University of Zürich) for expert advice and information.

(2) The word Wissenschaft itself illustrates admirably the nature of Eigenbegrifflichkeit even among modern European languages. Rendered in German-English dictionaries as learning, scholarship or science, its full meaning can only be understood against the background of the specifically German conception of scholarship, as partially emerges from the definitions in BROCKHAUS-WAHRIG and the 6-volume GROSSE DUDEN. Its derivative wissenschaftlich is commonly used as an evaluative adjective extending beyond the range of learned, scholarly and scientific, the equivalents invariably offered in bilingual dictionaries. It is significant that in English monolingual dictionaries (as in the CONCISE OXFORD DICTIONARY and COLLINS ENGLISH DICTIONARY) scholarly is presented merely as a derivative of scholar, whereas in German dictionaries (see BROCKHAUS-WAHRIG and even the small 1-volume DUDEN BEDEUTUNGS-WÖRTERBUCH) wissenschaftlich is a fully-fledged headword.

References

Cited dictionaries (see Appendix):

BROCKHAUS-WAHRIG ... (Wahrig et al.)
COLLINS DICTIONARY OF THE ENGLISH LANGUAGE (Hanks et al.)
(THE) CONCISE OXFORD DICTIONARY (Fowler/Sykes)
DICTIONARIUM DECEM LINGUARUM ... (Calepinus)
DUDEN. BEDEUTUNGSWÖRTERBUCH ... (Grebe et al.)
DUDEN. (DAS) GROSSE WÖRTERBUCH DER DEUTSCHEN SPRACHE ... (Drosdowski et al.)
SEX LINGUARUM ...

Other literature:

Civil, Miguel (1976) "Lexicography" in Sumerological Studies in Honor of Thorkild Jacobsen ed. by S.J. Lieberman (Assyriological Studies 20). Chicago: U.P. 123-157
Collison, Robert L. (1982) A History of Foreign-Language Dictionaries (The Language Library). London: A. Deutsch

218   MARY SNELL-HORNBY

Goetz, Georg (1912) "Glossographie" in Realencyclopädie der Classi-
schen Alterthumswissenschaft ed. by G. Wissowa and W. Kroll.
Stuttgart: Metzler VII: 1435-1441
Hausmann, Franz J. and Cop, Margaret (1985) "Short history of
English-German lexicography" in Symposium on Lexicography II ed.
by Karl Hyldgaard-Jensen and Arne Zettersten (Lexicographica.
Series Maior 5). Tübingen: M. Niemeyer 183-197
Kromann, Hans-Peder et al. (1984) "Überlegungen zu Grundfragen der
zweisprachigen Lexikographie" Germanistische Linguistik 3-6//84:
159-238
Landsberger, Benno (1934) Die Fauna des alten Mesopotamien nach der
14. Tafel der Serie Har-Ra = Hubullu (Abhandlungen der philo-
logisch-historischen Klasse der Sächsischen Akademie der Wissen-
schaften 42, VI). Leipzig: Hirzel
Landsberger, Benno (1926/74) "Die Eigenbegrifflichkeit der babylo-
nischen Welt" (reprinted from Islamica II.1926). Darmstadt:
Wissenschaftliche Buchgesellschaft
Marti, Heinrich (1974) Übersetzer der Augustin-Zeit. Interpretation
von Selbstzeugnissen. München: Fink
Sjöberg, Åke W. (1976) "The Old Babylonian Eduba" in Sumerological
Studies in Honor of Thorkild Jacobsen ed. by S.J. Lieberman
(Assyriological Studies 20). Chicago: U.P. 159-179
Snell-Hornby, Mary (forthcoming) "Towards a learner's bilingual dic-
tionary" in The Dictionary and the Language Learner ed. by A.P.
Cowie (Lexicographica. Series Maior). Tübingen: M. Niemeyer
Soden, Wolfram von (1974) Leistung und Grenze sumerischer und baby-
lonischer Wissenschaft" (reprinted from Die Welt als Geschichte
2.1936). Darmstadt: Wissenschaftliche Buchgesellschaft
Stein, Gabriele (1985) "English-German/German-English lexicography:
Its early beginnings" Lexicographica 1: 134-164
Zgusta, Ladislav (1984) "Translational equivalence in the bilingual
dictionary" in LEXeter '83 Proceedings ed. by R.R.K. Hartmann
(Lexicographica. Series Maior 1). Tübingen: M. Niemeyer 147-154

SIXTEENTH-CENTURY ENGLISH-VERNACULAR DICTIONARIES

Gabriele Stein

To judge from the works that were printed and that have been brought
to scholarly notice, within the history of English lexicography the
sixteenth century was a period of intense lexicographical activity and
productivity. Under 'English lexicography' I subsume all those lexicographical works in which one of the languages dealt with is English.

The period begins in 1500 with the publication of the ORTUS VOCABU-
LORUM, the second Latin-English dictionary within the history of English
lexicography, and it ends with the publication of A DICTIONARIE IN
SPANISH AND ENGLISH in 1599. I have discussed the dictionaries compiled
during this period in detail in my book *The English Dictionary before
Cawdrey* (cf. Stein 1985). It may therefore suffice if I briefly focus on
certain facets of this intense lexicographical productivity:

1 As to the actual type and size of the word lists compiled we have to
  distinguish between vocabularies and dictionaries.

2 As to the number of languages covered in these works we may distinguish

  a) bilingual dictionaries, as for instance Sir Thomas Elyot's DIC-
     TIONARY of 1538 or Thomas Cooper's THESAURUS LINGUAE ROMANICAE &
     BRITANNICAE of 1565;

  b) tri- and quadrilingual dictionaries, as for instance Robert Estienne
     and John Veron's DICTIONARIOLUM PUERORUM TRIBUS LINGUIS, LATINA,
     ANGLICA & GALLICA CONSCRIPTUM of 1552 and John Baret's ALVEARIE,
     the first edition of which appeared in 1573 and dealt with English,
     Latin, and French. In the second edition of 1580 Greek had been
     added as a fourth language;

  c) polyglot dictionaries, as for instance Ambrosius Calepinus' DIC-
     TIONARIUM DECEM LINGUARUM ... of 1585, and

  d) polyglot vocabularies, as for instance the anonymously published
     work SEX LINGUARUM, LATINE, TEUTHONICE , GALLICE, HISPANICE,
     ITALICE, ANGLICE DILUCIDISSIMUS DICTIONARIUS of 1537.

3 With respect to the internal arrangement of the word lists we might
  distinguish between

  a) an alphabetical arrangement which holds for most works. One should
     however keep in mind that 'alphabetical order' in 16th-century
     lexicography is not yet fully and consistently alphabetical;

  b) a topical arrangement, as for instance in John Withals' SHORTE
     DICTIONARIE FOR YONGE BEGYNNERS of 1553 (the most popular English-

Latin dictionary in the 16th century) or in Adrianus Junius'
NOMENCLATOR of 1585;

c) a synonym arrangement as in Simon Pelegromius' SYNONYMORUM SYLVA
of 1580.

4 For the languages actually listed the following characterization
holds:

a) Bilingual dictionaries list besides English either Latin or French
or Spanish or Welsh or Italian;

b) All tri- and quadrilingual dictionaries typically include English
and Latin. The third language may either be French, Greek, or
Spanish, and in the case of the quadrilingual dictionary the two
additional languages are French and Greek. Noel van Barlement's
A boke intituled Italion, frynsche, englesshe and laten (?1567)
lists Italian instead of Greek - but as far as I know no copy of
this work has been traced so far.

c) Polyglot works all typically list Latin and English. They include
further languages, such as Hebrew, Dutch, German, Polish, Hungarian, etc.

As a generalization one might say that the works that list more than
two languages typically include Latin. The only works with no Latin component at all are bilingual word lists that deal with two vernaculars
spoken by native speakers at the time. It is on these that I would like
to concentrate in this article. The title therefore refers to 16th-
century lexicographical works in which English is contrasted with another spoken vernacular of the time. The title is not meant to restrict
the discussion to dictionaries in which English is the language of the
translation equivalents. It also covers those works in which English
figures as the headword language. But I thought that a title 'vernacular-
English/English-vernacular dictionaries' was too complicated.

I shall not characterize the works in question in any length or detail. Instead I would like to raise the following questions: Are there
any noteworthy differences in lexicographical approach and method between those 16th-century works that include Latin and those that concentrate on two spoken vernaculars? As to works including Latin I have
for instance shown elsewhere that those in which the word list is English are much more innovative in approach than those in which the head-
word language is Latin. If there are any differences are these substantial differences or differences of degree? I shall try to give an answer
to these questions on the basis of all the works that I have studied for
my book (Stein 1985).

The vernacular-English dictionaries under discussion are:

John Palsgrave's ESCLARCISSEMENT DE LA LANGUE FRANCOYSE, the first
     English-French dictionary, published in 1530;

William Salesbury's DICTIONARY IN ENGLYSHE AND WELSHE, in spite of
     its title the first Welsh-English dictionary, published in 1547;

Claudius Hollyband's DICTIONARIE FRENCH AND ENGLISH, published in 1593.

This is the most comprehensive French-English dictionary of the
sixteenth century. It was preceded by two other works: A dictionary of the same title published anonymously in 1570/71 and
Hollyband's TREASURIE OF THE FRENCH TONG of 1580. I have tried
to show elsewhere (cf Stein 1985) that all three works were
written by Hollyband.

John Florio's WORLDE OF WORDES, an Italian-English dictionary, published
in 1598; and

John Minsheu's DICTIONARIE IN SPANISH AND ENGLISH of 1599. This is the
second edition of Richard Percyvall's BIBLIOTHECA HISPANICA of
1591, a Spanish-English-Latin dictionary, in which the third
language, Latin, had been omitted.

Since the early beginnings of English-vernacular lexicography have been
studied by a number of scholars I do not have to discuss the very first
small word lists here and I shall concentrate on the five works mentioned. For French and English the best early historical accounts are
K. Lambley's excellent book on *The Teaching and Cultivation of the
French Language During Tudor and Stuart Times* (1920) and J.D. Anderson's
revised doctoral dissertation *The Development of the English-French,
French-English Dictionary* (1978), for Spanish and English there is R.J.
Steiner's monograph *Two Centuries of Spanish and English Bilingual
Lexicography (1590-1800)* (1970), and for Italian we have G. Tancke's
study *Die italienischen Wörterbücher von den Anfängen bis zum Erschei-
nen des 'Vocabolario degli Accademici della Crusca' (1612)* (1984).

Before discussing those differences which I regard as noteworthy I
have to put in a word of caution. In the sixteenth century we are still
at the beginning of English dictionary-making and the basis of comparison is therefore relatively small. This will have to be kept in mind for
all statements that aim at outlining tendencies of approach or development.

There are eight points which I would like to discuss. These are:

1) Matching dictionaries
2) Pronunciation and/or grammar
3) Standard vs non-standard
4) All-inclusiveness
5) Coverage
6) Order of entries
7) Literary references
8) Usage restrictions

1) Matching dictionaries

One of the striking, but not surprising differences is that dictionaries including Latin complemented each other. The decoding language
needs of the 16th-century Latin student could be met by the ORTUS
VOCABULORUM (1500, 1509, 1511, 1514, 1516, 1518, 1520, 1528, 1532),
THE DICTIONARY OF SYR THOMAS ELYOT (1538, 1542, 1545, 1548, 1552, 1559),
Thomas Cooper's THESAURUS LINGUAE ROMANICAE ...   (1565, 1573,
1578, 1584, 1587), and Thomas Thomas' DICTIONARIUM LINGUAE LATINAE ET
ANGLICANAE (1587, 1588, 1589, 1592, 1593, 1594, 1596). For the encoding
student of Latin there were a number of English Latin dictionaries

available, as for instance Richard Huloet's ABECEDARIUM ANGLICO-LATINUM
(1552, 1572), John Withals' SHORTE DICTIONARIE FOR YONGE BEGYNNERS
(1553, 1556, 1562, 1566, 1568, 1572, 1574, 1579, 1581, 1584, 1586, 1599),
Simon Pelegromius' SYNONYMORUM SYLVA (1580, 1585, 1594, 1598), and John
Rider's BIBLIOTHECA SCHOLASTICA (1589).

English-vernacular lexicography being younger than Latin-English/
English-Latin lexicography the first English-vernacular dictionaries
were not all matched by a dictionary in which the language order was
inverted. As to French, it is true that the dictionaries printed complemented each other for John Palsgrave's word lists are English-French
and those in Claudius Hollyband's works French-English. Yet there was
an interval of 40 to 50 years between the publications. Both works will
therefore not have been available to one and the same generation of
speakers. During the last three decades of the sixteenth century the
situation was considerably better because Huloet's and Baret's trilingual English-Latin-French dictionaries could meet the encoding
language needs of the English student learning French and they thus
complemented Hollyband's French-English dictionaries.

For William Salesbury's Welsh-English word list there was no corresponding English-Welsh dictionary.

According to our present-day knowledge there was no 16th-century
English-Italian dictionary to complement the first Italian-English
dictionaries, William Thomas' word list in his *Principal Rvles of the
Italian Grammar* (1550) and John Florio's WORLDE OF WORDES (1598).
Florio himself mentions in the list of books and authors which he con-
sulted when be compiled his dictionary *Dittionario Inghilese &
Italiano*. It is not clear whether there ever was any such English-
Italian dictionary or whether Florio had confused the order of the
two languages.

John Minsheu was the only 16th-century English lexicographer who
tried to provide the learner with a double dictionary. At the end of
his Spanish-English dictionary there is an English-Spanish index so
that the dictionary could also meet the encoding language needs of the
Englishman learning Spanish.

2) Pronunciation and/or grammar

In the English dictionaries that include Latin there is no introduction
to Latin pronunciation (nor to the pronunciation of the other language(s)
listed). An exception is Guillaume Morel's Latin-Greek-English dictionary of 1583 (VERBORUM LATINORUM CUM GRAECIS ANGLICISQUE CONIUNCTORUM
LOCUPLETISSIMI COMMENTARII). Nor is there a short grammar of Latin (or
the other language(s)). In the majority of the English-vernacular dictionaries there is such an introduction to pronunciation and/or grammar.
Palsgrave's ESCLARCISSEMENT DE LA LANGUE FRANCOYSE consists of three
books of which the first deals with French pronunciation, the second
and parts of the third with French grammar. The introductory matter of
William Salesbury's Welsh-English DICTIONARY includes a description of
English pronunciation for the Welsh dictionary-users. John Minsheu's
DICTIONARIE IN SPANISH AND ENGLISH has a grammar at the end (in Richard
Percyvall's trilingual Spanish-English-Latin dictionary of 1591 the
grammar preceded the dictionary). In the case of Claudius Hollyband the
three language components, pronunciation, grammar, and the lexicon were

dealt with and published separately. The list of his pedagogical and
linguistic works includes a book on French pronunciation, *De pronuntiatione linguae Gallicae* (1580) and on the verb system, *A Treatise
for Declining of Verbs* (1580).

It thus looks as if most of the compilers of dictionaries in which
English was contrasted with another 16th-century spoken vernacular
were scholars/teachers who supplied their students not only with a
dictionary but also with the basics on pronunciation and/or grammar
of the language of study.

3) Standard vs non-standard

Within the history of such languages as French, Italian, and English
the fifteenth and sixteenth centuries were the period during which the
question of the vernacular was debated publicly and during which one
particular regional and social variety of the language became established as the standard. 16th-century compilers of English dictionaries
that included Latin often claimed to have consulted 'good authors' for
their respective dictionaries but they did not discuss the question of
the standard and the dialects because the Latin standard model was
taken for granted. Compilers of vernacular dictionaries, however, had
to ask themselves which variety of the language they were recording
and thus teaching. Two of our lexicographers discuss the issue in
their dictionaries. John Palsgrave took the following position in his
ESCLARCISSEMENT:

> ... in all this worke I moost folowe the
> Parisyens / and the coûtreys that be conteygned
> bytwene the ryuer of Seyne and the ryuer
> of Loyre / which the Romayns called somtyme
> Gallya Celtica: for within that space is con-
> tayned the herte of Fraunce / where the tonge
> is at this day moost parfyte / and hath of
> moost auncyente so contynued / so that I
> thynke it but superfluous / and vnto the
> lernar but a nedelesse confusyon / to
> showe the dyuersite of pronuncyacion of
> the other frontier countreys ... There is no
> man of what parte of Fraunce so euer
> he be borne / if he desyre that his wri-
> tynges shulde be had in any estymacion /
> but he writeth in suche language as they
> speke within the boundes that I haue
> before rehersed ... (*The fyrst boke*, Fo. *xiii*[v]).

John Florio for his part discussed the question of the regional varieties of Italian in the *Epistle Dedicatorie* and expressed his concern
as follows:

> How shall we, naie how may we ayme at
> the Venetian, at the Romane, at the
> Lombard, at the Neopolitane, at so manie,
> and so much differing Dialects, and
> Idiomes, as be vsed and spoken in Italie,
> besides the Florentine?

4) <u>All-inclusiveness</u>

Another interesting aspect is the coverage of the dictionaries under
review. In dictionaries that include Latin we find two types of statements on the size of the word lists: either it is claimed that the dictionary includes more items than another rival dictionary published
earlier or the compiler explicitly says that his word list is selective
in order to keep the price down or because scholars do not agree about
the meaning of words. In the knowledge that Latin authors before them
had compiled full-size dictionaries our English compilers did not discuss the all-comprehensiveness of a dictionary. The situation was obviously very different for the pioneering English lexicographers who
compiled the first vernacular dictionaries. John Palsgrave was very
much aware of his great achievement of having put down the rules of
the French language and he claimed:

> After euery of whiche partes so cõpletely
> entreated of / shall folowe certayne tables /
> cõtayning all the wordes in our tong / after
> the order of a/b/c/ with the frenche wordes
> ioyned vnto them / To thentent that after
> the lernar can ... vnderstande any authour
> that writeth in the sayd tong by his owne
> study / without any other teacher. (*The thirde
> boke*, Fo. i.)

John Florio, nearly seventy years later, discussed the all-inclusiveness
of his dictionary in more realistic terms:

> If any man aske whether all Italian wordes
> be here? I answere him, it may be no: and
> yet I thinke heere be as many, as he is
> likely to finde (that askes the question)
> within the compasse of his reading; and
> yet he may haue read well too, I should
> thinke that very few wordes could escape
> those auctors I haue set downe, which I
> haue read of purpose to the absolute accom-
> plishing of this worke, being the most
> principall, choisest, and difficult in the
> toong; especially writing in such varietie
> not onely of matters, but of dialects: But
> what if I aske him againe how many hun-
> dred wordes he, and poßibly his teachers too
> were grauelled in? which he shall finde here
> explaned? If no other bookes can be so well
> perfected, but still some thing may be added,
> how much lesse a Word-booke? Since daily
> both new wordes are inuented; and bookes
> still found, that make a new supplie of olde.
> We see the experience in Latin, a limited
> toong, that is at his full growth: and yet
> if a man consider the reprinting of Latin
> Dictionaries, euer with additons of new store,
> he would thinke it were still increasing. And
> yet in these Dictionaries as in all other

that that is printed still is reputed
perfect. And so it is no doubt after the
customarie and poßible perfection of a
Dictionarie, which kinde of perfection if
I chalenge to mine (especially considering the yeerely increase, which is as
certainly in this, in French, in Spanish,
in Dutch, &c. as we finde by experience it is
in English; and I thinke I may well saie
more in this, then in the rest; yea in the rest
mostly from this) I hope no man that shall
expend the woorth of this worke in impartiall
examination, will thinke I challenge more
then is due to it.

5) Coverage

A difficult issue is the assessment of the vocabulary actually recorded
in the dictionaries under review. A computer analysis of the wordstock
contained in early English dictionaries would be most welcome for it
could provide us with

- a list of such items that occur in all or most dictionaries,
- lists of items that occur in one particular work only,
- lists of items that are literally the same or nearly the same in
  a number of dictionaries.

Such lists would help us to disentangle the intricate net of interrela-
tionships between the early dictionaries in Europe.

There is no doubt that there is more overlap in the wordstock listed
in 16th-century English dictionaries including Latin than in English
vernacular dictionaries. One particular vocabulary area which seems to
me to be conspicuous by its absence in the English-vernacular dictionaries is the field of rhetoric.

6) Order of entries

All English-vernacular dictionaries have an alphabetical arrangement,
to which in the case of Palsgrave is superimposed a word-class system.
There is no topical arrangement which we find in many of the polyglot
vocabularies and some of the Latin-English/English-Latin dictionaries.

7) Literary references

Some of the 16th-century English dictionaries that include Latin contain references to authors and works from which a particular item or a
sense of a word has been taken. These references characteristically
apply to Latin only. (Exceptions are Adrianus Junius' and Thomas
Thomas' dictionaries in which there is the same single reference to
Chaucer). In some of the English vernacular dictionaries we find
similar literary references which, however, are not restricted to
one of the language in the dictionary. In John Palsgrave's ESCLARCISSE-
MENT the dictionary part includes references to Geoffrey Chaucer and
John Lydgate as well as to the French writers Alain Chartier, Jean
Froissart, Jean Lemaire de Belges, and Jean de Meung.

John Florio refers to the English poet Chaucer, one particular
Italian work, the *Cento novelle antiche*, and the Italian poets and
scholars Ariosto, Boccaccio, Dante, and Petrach.

8) Usage restrictions

I do not think that there is any significant difference between our two
types of dictionaries in the occasional recording of old or dialectal
language use. Hollyband in his French-English dictionaries, however, is
the first compiler within the history of English lexicography who explicitly marks jocular and ironic language use. Cases in point are, for
instance:

> Vn *gentil fallot*, a trimme fellowe, a
> fine companion, this is spoken by
> mockerie.

> *Lu* [sic] *mu de cerf*, when the Hart cast-
> eth his hornes: also the muing of a
> Faulcon, it is taken also for the
> place where hee doth mue: so we
> say, *mettre en mue, mettre hors de*
> *mue:* also it is taken for a coupe or
> stie where Capons or other beasts
> are fatned: Finally, for a mockerie
> we say, *la mue d'vne fame*, when
> through Phisicke & drugs she hath
> changed her wrinkled skinne into a
> smooth and delicate hue.

I have tried to outline some lexicographical areas in which one
might perceive more independent and innovative thinking on the part
of those authors who compiled the first dictionaries in which English
and another 16th-century vernacular were described.

Monolingual English lexicography begins at the end of the period
under review. Further research is needed if we are going to find out
whether these beginnings

- are independent of the earlier development in English dictionary-
  making,
- whether there is an indebtedness to lexicographical works including Latin,
- or whether the compilers followed the bilingual English-vernacular
  dictionaries because, while treading on new ground, they had to
  provide a lexicographical description for a living language.

References

Cited dictionaries (see Appendix):

ABECEDARIUM ANGLICO-LATINUM ... (Huloet)
(AN) ALVEARIE OR TRIPLE DICTIONARIE ... (Baret)
BIBLIOTHECA HISPANICA ... (Percyvall)
BIBLIOTHECA SCHOLASTICA ... (Rider)
(A) DICTIONARIE, FRENCH AND ENGLISH (Hollyband)
DICTIONARIOLUM PUERORUM ... (Estienne/Veron)
DICTIONARIUM DECEM LINGUARUM ... (Calepinus)
DICTIONARIUM LINGUAE LATINAE ET ANGLICANAE (Thomas)
(A) DICTIONARY IN ENGLYSHE AND WELSHE ... (Salesbury)
(THE) DICTIONARY OF SYR THOMAS ELIOT KNIGHT (Elyot)
LESCLARCISSEMENT DE LA LANGUE FRANCOYSE (Palsgrave)
(THE) NOMENCLATOR, OR REMEMBRANCER ... (Junius/Higgins)
ORTUS VOCABULORUM
SEX LINGUARUM ...
(A) SHORTE DICTIONARIE FOR YONGE BEGYNNERS (Withals)
SYNONYMORUM SYLVA ... (Pelegromius)
THESAURUS LINGUAE ROMANICAE & BRITANNICAE ... (Cooper)
(THE) TREASURIE OF THE FRENCH TONG (Hollyband)
VERBORUM LATINORUM ... (Morel)
(A) WORLDE OF WORDES ... (Florio)

Other literature:

Anderson, James D. (1978) The Development of the English-French,
    French-English Bilingual Dictionary. A Study in Comparative
    Lexicography (Supplement to Word 28,3.1972 Monograph 6).
    London: W. Clowes
Desainliens, Claude (1580) De pronunciatione linguae Gallicae
    (reprint ed. by Robin C. Alston. Menston: Scolar Press 1970)
Hollyband, Claudius (1580) De pronuntiatione linguae Gallicae ...
    London: T. Vautrollerius
Hollyband, Claudius (1580) A Treatise for Declining of Verbs ...
    London: T. Vautrollerius
Lambley, Kathleen R. (1920) The Teaching and Cultivation of the
    French Language during Tudor and Stuart Times. With an Intro-
    ductory Chapter on the Preceding Period (Publications of the
    University of Manchester 129). Manchester: U.P.
Stein, Gabriele (1985) The English Dictionary before Cawdrey
    (Lexicographica. Series Maior 9). Tübingen: M. Niemeyer
Steiner, Roger J. (1970) Two Centuries of Spanish and English
    Bilingual Lexicography 1590-1800 (Janua Linguarum. Series
    Practica 108). The Hague: Mouton
Tancke, Gunnar (1984) Die italienischen Wörterbücher von den
    Anfängen bis zum Erscheinen des 'Vocabolario degli Accademici
    della Crusca' (1612). Tübingen: M. Niemeyer
Thomas, William (1550) Principal Rules of the Italian Grammar
    (reprint ed. by Robin C. Alston. Menston: Scolar Press)

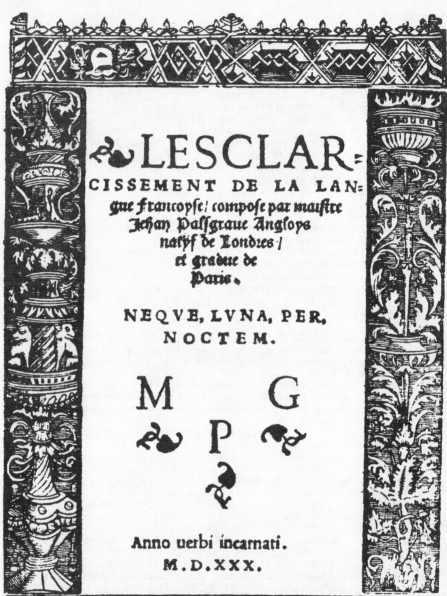

☙LESCLAR=
CISSEMENT DE LA LAN=
gue francoyse/ compose par maiſtre
Iehan Palſgraue Anglops
natyf de Londres/
et gradue de
Paris.

NEQVE, LVNA, PER.
NOCTEM.

M   G
☙   P   ☙
☙

Anno uerbi incarnati.
M.D.XXX.

THE THREE-CENTURY RECENSION IN SPANISH AND ENGLISH LEXICOGRAPHY

Roger J. Steiner

In showing the relationships among works of the first three
centuries of Spanish and English bilingual lexicogaphy, there are a
number of possible considerations, such as publishing practices,
political prejudices and commercial constraints, plagiarism, the
method of organizing the dictionary, the speaker(s) for whom a
dictionary is intended, the method of compiling the word list,
pronunciation, glossing, illustrative examples, and dozens of
others. Of. these considerations, publishers, politics, and
plagiarism will be the main threads which will tie this study of the
dictionaries together. Dictionaries were published for profit and
depended upon the business judgments of a publisher. Dictionaries
reflected the political situation in which they were written.
Dictionaries were often copies of their predecessors' works. What
we could call a 'recension' is a series of dictionaries each of
which contains plagiarized material of the predecessors.

Let us say something about the lexicographical works which
preceded the first dictionary of our study. The story of Spanish
bilingual lexicography precedes that of the monolingual, starting
with Alfonso Fernández de Palencia, whose UNIVERSAL VOCABULARIO
(Sevilla, 1490) used Latin as the headword and Spanish as the gloss.
Elio Antonio de Nebrija did the same kind of thing at Salamanca in
1492 with his DICTIONARIUM LATINO-HISPANICUM, and in 1495 he
reversed the entries to make the DICTIONARIUM HISPANO-LATINUM.
Pedro de Alcalá prepared a bilingual word list, Spanish and Arabic,
in 1505: VOCABULISTA ARAUIGO EN LETRA CASTELLANA. Polyglot
dictionaries included Spanish, starting at Antwerp in 1534 and
Venice in 1537. One of these polyglot dictionaries was the result
of the DICTIONARIUM LATINAE LINGUAE by Ambrosius Calepinus at Reggio
in 1502. It went through a century of frequent editions. A Spanish
and Italian bilingual dictionary by Cristóbal de las Casas
(VOCABVLARIO DE LAS DOS LENGVAS TOSCANA Y CASTELLANA) was printed in
1570 at Sevilla with a 1587 edition printed at Venice. Also in
1587, another Spanish-Latin dictionary saw the light of day at
Salamanca, completed by Alonso Sánchez de la Ballesta: DICTIONARIO
DE VOCABLOS CASTELLANOS, APLICADOS A LA PROPRIEDAD LATINA. Two
early essays at Spanish and English bilingual lexicography consisted
of small word lists from Spanish to English, the first by John
Thorius, appended to his The Spanish Grammar (1590) and the second
by William Stepney in a Spanish-English vocabulary appended to his
The Spanish Schoole-master (London 1591).

The first Spanish-English work worthy of the name of dictionary,
and therefore the first one in our study, was published in 1591 and

came out of the same intense political situation which had inspired
the two small word lists by Thorius and Stepney of about the same
time. It was compiled by none other than Richard Percyvall, who did
yeoman's service on Lord Burghley's staff in deciphering and
translating Spanish documents, including the sailing orders of the
Spanish Armada. He was ambitious, as shown by his meteoric rise to
fame, by his later membership in the House of Commons, and by his
position as one of the proprietors of the Virginia colony. It is
not surprising if he did indeed use his political influence to
secure the copyright which had been granted to John Wolfe in 1590
for a dictionary by Dr. Thomas D'Oylie, who had practiced medicine
in Belgium and Holland, 1581-1585, at a time when political reasons
favored the learning and use of the Spanish language in the Low
Countries. Percyvall adopts the Latin tag or meaning discrimination
which D'Oylie had used with each entry and seems to have borrowed a
good many medical terms from the good doctor's work. His publisher,
Richard Watkins, copyrighted the BIBLIOTHECA HISPANICA in 1591. It
contains two parts, the first a grammar, and the second a bilingual
DICTIONARIE... from Spanish to English.

    Percyvall had spent four years in Spain and had entrée into the
circles of antiquarians, lexicographers, and translators who were
interested in things Spanish. But he had to write most of his
dictionary without informants fresh from Spain because the very
conflict which made Spanish and English bilingual dictionaries a
necessity for the translation of documents, censorship, and
espionage, also reduced Percyvall's opportunity to fraternize with
those for whom a useful entry (supplied by Stepney, 1591) was "tiene
la cabeça enarbolada sobre la puente de Londres"/"he hath his head
upon London bridge". Percyvall knew very well how to keep his own
head from being impaled on London Bridge and he copied his
dictionary from standard sources, the works of Nebrija and of Las
Casas mentioned above. To this he put in some of his own work, as
he says in his preface, "casting in some small pittaunce of mine
owne, amounting well neere two 2000 wordes", or 15% of the
dictionary. Samplings bear out his veracity on this point, but half
of the new words are derived forms or expressions from other words
in the dictionary. The result turns out to be close to what might
be considered Standard Spanish, if one could conceive of a
'standard' at that time.

    Scholars now hold that a work by Sebastián de Covarrubias
(TESORO 1611) is an exemplary specimen of 16-century Peninsular
Spanish. Comparison of this monolingual work with Percyvall's
bilingual one indicates that Percyvall's spellings and meanings do
not deviate remarkably from those of Covarrubias. It must be said
that for a very short time Percyvall did have two native informants
straight from Spain, none other than two officers of the Spanish
Armada. Let Percyvall give us the account of it as he does in his
preface:

I ranne it ouer twise with <u>Don Pedro de Valdes</u>, and <u>Don Vasco de Sylua</u>; to whome I had accesse, by the fauour of my worshipfull friend Maister <u>Richard Drake</u>, (a Gentleman as vertuouslie minded as any, to further any good attempt); and hauing by their helpe made it readie for the presse with the English interpretation onely.

In 1599, Edmund Bollifant was allowed a copyright but had to give top billing on the title page to 'Ric. Perciuale <u>Gent</u>.', star each entry which was carried over from Percyvall's dictionary, and reduce the emphasis on the title page for his own lexicographer, John Minsheu, who, we have reason to belive, was at one time a colleague of Percyvall when they were both translators in the Foreign Office. Minsheu does not name Percyvall but writes in the preface about someone "puffed up with pride & swollen with fat of fortune". Percyvall had written a one-part, single-alphabet bilingual dictionary with Latin glosses added. It was mono-directional, that is, written for the speaker of only one of the languages, the Englishman. It had 184 pages and 12,500 entries.

Minsheu's DICTIONARIE of 391 pages had over four times as many entries. He adds them from one of Percyvall's own sources, the VOCABVLARIO of Las Casas. He looks into John Florio's Italian and English bilingual dictionary (A WORLDE OF WORDES 1598) to find the English for the Spanish glosses in Las Casas. He uses Latin dictionaries and bookish sources but removes Percyvall's Latin tags at the end of entries. What expands his dictionary the most is his addition of an English-Spanish part. He makes extensive use of John Rider (BIBLIOTHECA SCHOLASTICA: A DOUBLE DICTIONARIE 1589) and other sources already mentioned above to do this. Another main source of entries for the English-Spanish part is identified as the reversals from the Spanish-English part, but Minsheu does this in a thought-less, mechanical way. For example, the subentry <u>a place full of water</u>, s.v. **water**, is a perfectly useless source-language expression because it is so general in its application that it could include the River Thames. Yet Minsheu uses it as an entry expression and sets the equivalent <u>Regadízo</u> after it. Minsheu's revisions of Percyvall, for the most part, are not corrections but additions tacked on to verbatim borrowings from Percyvall.

Subsequent works of Minsheu add nothing to the progress of our recension, or series of revisions. In 1617, Minsheu published THE GUIDE INTO THE TONGUES, an encyclopedic polyglot work in eleven languages. The book contains a Spanish-English dictionary of 55,000 entries but it is only a glossary or vocabulary using words from the polylingual part of the work and from Minsheu's Spanish and English bilingual dictionary of 1599.

In 1623, John Haviland printed Minsheu's dictionary for a number of publishers: Edward Blount, William Aspley, Matthew Lownes, Thomas

Lownes, Humphrey Lownes, and George Latham. Usually only one of
these pubishers' names appears on the title page of the 1623
printing. At first sight the 1623 version looks like an identical
copy of the dictionary printed by Edmund Bollifant in 1599. Upon
close inspection one notes minor differences in typeface, orthography, and arrangement. It had to be a resetting, of course,
because in the early printing shops with movable type, the pages had
to be pied and the type reset for another page as the printing was
in progress. The fact that the 1623 is almost an exact copy of the
original 1599 is an indication that no original Spanish bilingual
lexicography was going on in the entire seventeenth century.

After the turn of the century, it became apparent to the London
publisher John Sawbridge that a dictionary purporting to be a new
work would sell. To this end he hired one Captain John Stevens.
The name lends a romantic naval air to the dictionary but in fact
the Stevens captaincy was in the Army and, aided by his bilingual
command of the two languages acquired from a childhood abroad, he
was a translator of Spanish literature. Indeed, the NEW SPANISH AND
ENGLISH DICTIONARY makes the pretense of using meanings and words
and citations from a whole pageful of titles of Spanish works. In
actual fact, Stevens followed Minsheu slavishly and one of the
Spanish and French dictionaries of César Oudin. His first volume
(1705) is an English-Spanish dictionary of 103 pages and 20,000
vocabulary entries. The second volume (1706) is a Spanish-English
dictionary of 415 pages and approximately 40,000 entries. An
'edition' of 1726 is printed for nine London publishers, none of
them George Sawbridge of the first edition. The body of the
dictionary is almost identical to the volumes printed by Sawbridge
in 1705 and 1706. The major change seems to be the elimination of
the grammar and dialogues which Stevens had stolen from Minsheu. In
a new preface, Stevens states that the only reason for his lexicographical work is a mundane, pecuniary one: "The only inducement ...
has been from the Booksellers". The most notable feature of the
Stevens dictionary is its bookish character. The work abounds in
proverbs and encyclopedic entries. Encyclopedic material intrudes
itself in entries in which it is out of place.

The first Spanish and English bilingual dictionary compiled by a
Spaniard was based on the dictionary of Captain John Stevens and
offered for sale as the work of Pedro Pineda, an émigré who had fled
from his native Andalusia for religious reasons. Pineda's NEW
DICTIONARY is not a mere copy of Stevens'. He added about 18,000
entries to the 60,000 entries taken from Stevens. What is extremely
important in the development of 18th-century lexicography is that
many of his new entries are valuable idiomatic words and expressions
like you hit the nail on the head. In order to pattern his
dictionary after living speech, Pineda went through Nathan Bailey's
monolingual English dictionary of 60,000 words and glossed as many
as he was able to with Spanish translations. Pineda is the first

lexicographer in the history of Spanish and English bilingual
lexicography to collect English words from a monolingual English
dictionary for use as entries in the English-Spanish part. He is
able to furnish translations for the English-Spanish part with
idiomatic accuracy because he was the first of these lexicographers
whose native tongue was Spanish. One might say that the English-
Spanish part is the first one to be not merely an appendage to the
Spanish-English part, which had occupied the greatest attention of
Minsheu and Stevens. The main contributions of Pineda to
lexicography were fourfold: (1) the introduction of living speech
into the entries; (2) the sound doctrine of short, concise glossing;
(3) the designation in a systematic manner of all the parts of
speech in an entry; (4) the indication of the pronunciation of
Spanish letters.

One drawback was that Pineda's lexicographical judgment and
practice were impaired by divagations into considerations that were
outside the concern of the lexicographer. He wrote abusive
definitions about the Spanish Academy and the Pope on the basis of
his own prejudices. The use of the dictionary as a political and
homiletical platform injured Pineda's standing as a lexicographer.

The subject of politics was kept alive in the preface of his
successor, Hippolyto San Joseph Giral Delpino, hired in 1763 by some
of the same publishers who had brought out the 1740 Pineda work.
Delpino severely criticized Pineda for letting prejudices alter
sound lexicographical practice. Delpino adapted entries from the
DICCIONARIO DE AUTORIDADES (The Dictionary of the Spanish Academy)
and from Johnson's DICTIONARY. The several thousand new entries
which Delpino contributed do not constitute a large number. The NEW
DICTIONARY was simply a new edition of Pineda, for Delpino retained
the bulk of Pineda's revolutionarily new and fruitful work, even as
he inveighed against him. Sofía Martín-Gamero has not understood
this in her study of Spanish and English dictionaries. She says
(Martín-Gamero 1961:143),

Pineda copia a Stevens sin el menor escrúpulo, y cuando
quiere introducir alguna novedad, es poco afortunado ...
sólo se encuentran innovaciones con respecto a Stevens
en las letras A, B y C del diccionario inglés-español.

She compounds the misunderstanding as she goes on, p. 187:

Delpino alarga las definiciones de las palabras inglesas
... el resultado es que de su pluma sale el primer diccionario inglés-español de alguna importancia que se
haya escrito.

The above should be said about Pineda and we can prove it simply by
comparing Pineda with Stevens, just as we prove Delpino's lack of

innovation by comparing his work to that of Pineda's. (See my history of Spanish and English bilingual dictionaries, Steiner 1970: 68-84). Delpino's book does include innovations such as explaining the pronunciation of certain English letters and sounds for the benefit of Spanish speakers. Another significant innovation was information provided concerning the level of speech, caste, or cultural status of headwords. He used a dagger to indicate slang or jocular words.

A name which was to resound in lexicography for over a century was that of Dr. Johnson's friend and the compiler of an Italian and English bilingual dictionary, Giuseppe Marcantonio Baretti. Yet Baretti spent half his life in Italy and very little of it in Spain. Some critics did not think that he understood either Spanish or English sufficiently to be involved with a dictionary of those languages. He was hired by one of the same publishers who published the Delpino dictionary. Baretti does not even pretend to call his DICTIONARY a new work; he calls it a 'second edition', Delpino's being the alleged 'first edition' in 1786, a word-for-word resetting of the 1778 work. Later the 'Successor to Mr. Nourse' (F. Wingrave, J. Johnson, J. Sewell, G.G. and J. Robinson, W. Richardson, R. Faulder, H. Murray, Vernor and Hood) brought out another identical printing in 1794. The work was pirated all over Europe with Baretti dictionaries continuing to come out during the early part of the next century. The greatest contribution of Baretti to Spanish and English bilingual lexicography was editorial: he attempted to make his dictionary more consistent, more correct, and neater than that of his predecessor by throwing out some of the accumulation of two centuries of lexicographical rubbish, underbrush, and overgrowth.

The honor of compiling the first Spanish and English bilingual dictionary to be printed in Spain belongs to the Irish Dominican friar, Father Thomas Connelly, confessor to the Royal family, and to his collaborator, the Carmelite friar described in the preface as 'companion and relation', Father Thomas Higgins, confessor at St. Ildephonsus. A vast DICCIONARIO NUEVO was printed at Royal expense. For fourteen years up to the age of seventy, Connelly worked at what became four quarto volumes: the Spanish-English dictionary of two volumes (1797) comprising 2053 pages and the English-Spanish dictionary of two volumes (1798) comprising 1395 pages. Connelly and Higgins welded together Dr. Johnson's DICTIONARY and the DICCIONARIO DE AUTORIDADES of the Spanish Academy by taking definitions verbatim from each one. This means that each headword not only has an equivalent in the target language but also a definition of the headword in the source language and a definition of the equivalent in the target language. In a way, the DICCIONARIO NUEVO can be considered three dictionaries in one: a monolingual English dictionary, a monolingual Spanish dictionary, and a bilingual Spanish and English dictionary. In actual practice the definitions make excellent discriminations and elaborations to clarify meaning. Of course, technical words such as nautical terms, terms of agriculture, etc., get a short standard treatment. Many entries use a variation of the complete treatment. But the majority of headwords receive the three-way treatment and, even with a word list not substantially larger than previous Spanish and English bilingual dictionaries, four large quarto-size volumes are needed.

Connelly and Higgins did not write disparaging definitions. It is interesting to compare their work with that of Delpino, who protested vociferously against Pineda's prejudices. Notice in the following confrontation the prejudicial entry **quaker** written by none other than Delpino:

Giral Delpino (1763)	Connelly/Higgins (1797)
A QUAKER, s. tembladór, especie singulár de Fanáticos en Inglaterra, adonde su secta se ha extendido mucho.	QUAKER, s. One of a certain religious sect. Quákaro, ó temblador, sectario cuyo principal instituto es temblar.

The dictionary compiled by Connelly and Higgins is the first Spanish and English bilingual dictionary to be:

(1) published and printed in Spain;
(2) authorized by other than a private business concern;
(3) free from the incubus of being modeled upon a predecessor;
(4) organized with an original and fundamentally new plan and method;
(5) divided into two approximately equal parts;
(6) equipped in almost every main entry and in many sub-entries with a bilingual set of particularizing words and definitions;
(7) fitted out with written accents on English vocabulary words;
(8) augmented by tables, one listing Christian names and one showing certain inflectional irregularities of English verbs.

The century ends with a glimpse of a name which is to dominate the nineteenth-century Spanish and English bilingual dictionaries when Henry Neuman is listed as the compiler of A MARINE POCKET DICTIONARY OF THE ITALIAN, SPANISH, PORTUGUESE, AND GERMAN LANGUAGES (London: Vernor and Hood, 1799). For all we know, Henry Neuman was simply a minor employee of Vernor and Hood, publishers who saw a market for a dictionary of nautical terms. His identity has not been established. As soon as his publishers received copies of the DICCIONARIO of Connelly and Higgins published in 1797 and 1798 in Spain, they took action with an expansion of their 1799 work into an all-purpose dictionary. They secured the cooperation of eleven other publishers in London to publish, in 1802, A NEW DICTIONARY OF THE SPANISH AND ENGLISH LANGUAGES ... BY HENRY NEUMAN.

In his preface, Henry Neuman says that he has had 'particular Recourse' to the Connelly and Higgins DICCIONARIO. Of course, he removed many definitions and condensed much of the material. He

depends upon Connelly and Higgins without actually copying them
verbatim, but he makes great use of their equivalents and translations. He provides a translation when they provide one and he
uses their definitions sometimes even when he also finds a translation. His one-page preface expresses his honor in presenting his
dictionary for the use of the 'first commercial and maritime Power
of Europe', viz., England. The preface in the 1817 Neuman has an
even more political slant. It is anti-French and pro-Spanish. The
English and Spanish are said to descend from the same race, and the
English language is said to show more similarity to Spanish than to
French - thus denying the obvious linguistic artifacts of the
centuries of French domination in England. One of the characteristics of the French, Neuman states, is bad breath because there is
a French word for such a person, Punais and Punaise. But "the
Spanish and English, being generally devoid of this quality, have no
corresponding term, and are without any such word". He goes on to
say:

> With every French thought and word something of colour and stage
> effect is associated; it is the spirit of the people and of
> their language, while that of Spain and England is metaphysical,
> or mere abstract truth and reason.

It was inevitable that sometimes the word list might resemble the
Baretti because the compilers of these dictionaries had each others'
works before them and would not want to be lacking in what the
competition had. Neuman does adopt Baretti's method of indicating
accent on the Spanish entry word. The accent is placed after the
vowel, as follows: **saborea'r**. But the translations and equivalents
of Neuman's dictionary definitely are not Baretti's. This is all
the more remarkable when one realizes that the chief publishers,
Vernor and Hood, also figured as two of the publishers of the 1794
Baretti.

What is even more remarkable is that the 'partnership' of NEUMAN
& BARETTI, a combination which will be announced on the title pages
of many editions throughout the century, started as late as 1823 in
a work called the 'fourth edition'. The partnership seems to have
been simply the application of the name of the long-gone Baretti to
the title page. This is proved by the fact that the Neuman and
Baretti of 1823 is identical, syllable for syllable and word for
word, to the so-called third edition of 1817, which has only
Neuman's name as a compiler. The publishers of the fourth edition
(1823) are different from those of the third edition (1817), but the
adding of the name Baretti to the title page is the only other
difference.

A Boston firm, Hilliard, Gray, Little, and Wilkins, used the
fourth edition (1823), published in London, to make an American
version which differs from the British only in the title page.

After the 'Second American, from the Fourth London Edition'
published in 1827, Hilliard, Gray, Little, and Wilkins published a
'Stereotype Edition' in 1832, that is, an edition printed on plates.
Inasmuch as the same plates were used in subsequent printings, the
so-called 'editions' are really 'printings'. Using the same plates,
Wilkins, Carter and Co. of Boston brought out a new printing in
1845/1847.

Meanwhile in England, the Neuman and Baretti received further
retouches from a Spanish émigré by the name of Mateo Seoane in an
1831 'fifth edition' of the NEW DICTIONARY printed for Longman,
Rees, and Co. by William Clowe. The Doctor don Mateo Seoane y
Sobral was born in Valladolid in 1791, was a student at the
university there, and received his medical degree at Salamanca.
When in England he showed successful determination in mastering
English and because of a long-standing reciprocity between the
universities of Oxford and Salamanca, he was allowed to build up a
large practice. He returned to Spain in 1834. Fellow political
refugees who helped him on the 1831 Neuman and Baretti were: Vicente
Salvá, Pablo de Mendibil, and Joaquín Villanueva. It was Seoane's
goal simply to add corrections and emendations. He and his collaborators produced a dictionary which found enormous success, and many
later editions were made. It was often pirated.

In America, twenty-one years after Seoane's work was published,
it found still another reviser. In New York, Appleton and Co.
hired a professor at Columbia and writer of pedagogical books to put
retouches on Seoane's Neuman and Baretti. The result in 1852 was:
"A PRONOUNCING DICTIONARY OF THE SPANISH AND ENGLISH LANGUAGES:
composed from the Spanish Dictionaries of the Spanish Academy,
Terreros, and Salvá, upon the basis of Seoane's Edition of Neuman
and Baretti, and from the English Dictionaries of Webster,
Worcester, and Walker: with the addition of more than eight thousand
words, idioms, and familiar phrases, the irregularities of all the
verbs, and a grammatical synopsis of both languages, by Mariano
Velázquez de la Cadena, professor of the Spanish Language and
Literature in Columbia College, New-York, and corresponding Member
of the National Institute, Washington". Subsequent printings were
made of this dictionary, e.g. in 1885. In 1900 Appleton and Co.
brought out a new edition: THE NEW PRONOUNCING DICTIONARY OF THE
SPANISH AND ENGLISH LANGUAGE, ed. J.S. Iribas and Edward Gray.

What did Iribas and Gray do to the Velázquez dictionary? Little
was retouched in the Spanish-English part, but revisions of the
larger entries on the English-Spanish side were frequent. The dusty
text contains entries like **aphthong, mug-house,** and tens of
thousands of other examples of old material which takes the space
which should be devoted to items and translations important in
contemporary life. Before Iribas and Gray started, most of the text
was a century old. Nevertheless, this 19th-century work, old even

in its time, underwent a scissors-and-paste job in 1959 and was
marketed as the NEW REVISED VELÁZQUEZ SPANISH AND ENGLISH DICTION-
ARY. A mere couple of thousand neologisms were substituted throughout the dictionary for older entries and over half of its material
was at least 142 years old. (There were other 19th-century dictionaries which do not find a place in our discussion, and some of these
are listed below in a Note.)

We have found in our study of three centuries of Spanish and
English bilingual lexicography that usually a lexicographer copies
from his predecessor - even our first lexicographer, Percyvall, who
copies from an unpublished manuscript. The lineal paternity of
Percyvall, Minsheu, Stevens, Pineda, and Delpino ends with Baretti.
Connelly and Higgins make a new start and are the source of a new
recension: Neuman, Seoane, Velázquez, Iribas and Gray, and even some
new revisers in the twentieth century, a period which does not lie
in the scope of our study. The main contribution from the old recension of 1591-1778 seems to be the name 'Baretti' on the new recension's title pages.

Note

Here are four other works published in the nineteenth century,
(1) a pocket dictionary by C.M. Gattel, NUEVO DICCIONARIO POR-
TÁTIL, ESPAÑOL E INGLES, I, 461 pp., II, 447 pp. 1803, pirated
in London by J. Johnson and Vernor, 1809; (2) the FIRST DIC-
TIONARY OF TWO LANGUAGES UNDER A SINGLE ALPHABET by the Reverend
don Felipe Fernández, printed in 1811. (Spanish-English entries
and English-Spanish entries follow one another on the same page
thus eliminating the necessity to decide which side of the dictionary to use.); (3) the DICCIONARIO INGLES-ESPAÑOL Y ESPAÑOL-
INGLES by Francisco Corona Bustamente, 1878; and (4) the NUEVO
DICCIONARIO INGLES-ESPAÑOL attributed to J.M. López and E.R.
Bensley in a Paris publication of 1888. The debt to the Velázquez dictionary is admitted on the title page, but the dictionary is fundamentally the same as the one compiled by F.
Corona Bustamente above.

References

Cited dictionaries (see Appendix):

BIBLIOTHECA HISPANICA ... (Percyvall)
BIBLIOTHECA SCHOLASTICA ... (Rider)
DICCIONARIO DE AUTORIDADES (Spanish Academy)
DICCIONARIO INGLES-ESPAÑOL ... (Corona Bustamente)
DICCIONARIO NUEVO DE LAS DOS LENGUAS ESPAÑOLA E INGLESA (Con-
    nelly/Higgins)

(A) DICTIONARIE IN SPANISH AND ENGLISH (Minsheu)
DICTIONARIO DE VOCABLOS CASTELLANOS ... (Sánchez de la Ballesta)
DICTIONARIUM HISPANO-LATINUM (Nebrija)
DICTIONARIUM LATINAE LINGUAE (Calepinus)
DICTIONARIUM LATINO-HISPANICUM (Nebrija)
(A) DICTIONARY OF THE ENGLISH LANGUAGE (Johnson)
(A) DICTIONARY, SPANISH AND ENGLISH, AND ENGLISH AND SPANISH
    (Baretti)
(THE) FIRST DICTIONARY OF TWO LANGUAGES ... (Fernández)
(THE) GUIDE INTO THE TONGUES (Minsheu)
(A) MARINE POCKET DICTIONARY OF THE ITALIAN, SPANISH, PORTUGUESE AND
    GERMAN LANGUAGES (Neuman)
NEUMAN AND BARETTI DICTIONARY see (A) NEW DICTIONARY OF THE SPANISH
    AND ENGLISH LANGUAGES and (A) PRONOUNCING DICTIONARY ...
(A) NEW DICTIONARY OF THE SPANISH AND ENGLISH LANGUAGES ... (Neuman
    et al.)
(A) NEW DICTIONARY OF THE SPANISH AND ENGLISH LANGUAGES ... (Seoane
    et al.)
(A) NEW DICTIONARY, SPANISH AND ENGLISH AND ENGLISH AND SPANISH
    (Pineda)
(THE) NEW PRONOUNCING DICTIONARY OF THE SPANISH AND ENGLISH LANG-
    UAGES (Iribas/Gray)
(THE) NEW REVISED VELÁZQUEZ SPANISH AND ENGLISH DICTIONARY (Navarro
    Hinojosa)
(A) NEW SPANISH AND ENGLISH DICTIONARY ... (Stevens)
NUEVO DICCIONARIO INGLÉS-ESPAÑOL (López/Bensley)
NUEVO DICCIONARIO PORTÁTIL, ESPAÑOL E INGLES (Gattel)
(A) PRONOUNCING DICTIONARY ... (Velázquez de la Cadena)
TESORO DE LA LENGUA CASTELLANA, O ESPAÑOLA (Covarrubias y Horozco)
UNIVERSAL VOCABULARIO ... (Fernández de Palencia)
VOCABULISTA ARAUIGO EN LETRA CASTELLANA (in Alcalá)
VOCABVLARIO DE LAS DOS LENGVAS TOSCANA Y CASTELLANA (Las Casas)
(A) WORLDE OF WORDES ... (Florio)

Other literature:

Alcalá, Pedro de (1505) Arte para ligeramete saber la legua arauigo.
    Granada: J. Varela
Martín-Gamero, Sofía (1961) La Enseñanza del inglés en España desde
    la edad media hasta el siglo XIX (Biblioteca Románica Hispánica
    2). Madrid: Editorial Gredos
Steiner, Roger J. (1970) Two Centuries of Spanish and English
    Bilingual Lexicography, 1590-1800 (Janua Linguarum. Series
    Practica 108). The Hague: Mouton
Stepney, William (1591) The Spanish Schoole-master. London: R. Field
    for J. Harison
Thorius, John (1590) The Spanish Grammar. London: J. Wolfe

APPENDIX A: BIBLIOGRAPHY OF CITED DICTIONARIES

(This list unites all the references to dictionaries in this
volume. It gives the information in the following order: (1) title,
(2) common abbreviation, (3) name(s) of compiler(s)/editor(s), (4)
place(s) of publication, (5) name(s) of publisher(s), (6) date(s) of
earliest and/or important later publication, (7) information on re-
print(s) if available. - Ed.)

ABECEDARIUM ANGLICO-LATINUM, PRO TYRUNCULIS
    Richard Huloet. London: G. Riddel 1552 (Reprint ed. Robin C.
    Alston. Menston: Scolar Press 1970)
(AN) ADVANCED LEARNER'S ARABIC-ENGLISH DICTIONARY
    Habib A. Salmoné. London: Trübner 2 volumes 1890
(THE) ADVANCED LEARNER'S DICTIONARY OF CURRENT ENGLISH (ALD)
    A.S. Hornby et al. Oxford: U.P. 1948/74/80
(AL-) 'AIN see KITĀB AL-'AIN
(AN) ALPHABETICAL DICTIONARY ...
    in Wilkins, John (1668) Essay towards a Real Character and a
    Philosophical Language. London: J.M. for Gellibrand and Martin
    (Reprint ed. Robin C. Alston. Menston: Scolar Press 1968)
(AN) ALVEARIE OR TRIPLE DICTIONARIE, IN ENGLYSHE, LATIN AND
    FRENCH ...
    John Baret. London: H. Denham 1573
AMERICAN COLLEGE DICTIONARY (ACD)
    Clarence L. Barnhart et al. New York: Random House 1947/60
(AN) AMERICAN DICTIONARY OF THE ENGLISH LANGUAGE
    Noah Webster. New York: S. Converse 2 volumes 1828 (Reprint New
    York: Johnson Reprint 1977)
(THE) AMERICAN HERITAGE DICTIONARY ... (AHD)
    William Morris/M. Berube. Boston: Houghton Mifflin 1969/82
(THE) AMERICAN PHONETIC DICTIONARY OF THE ENGLISH LANGUAGE
    Daniel S. Smalley. Cincinnati OH: Longley Bros. 1855
(THE) AMERICAN STANDARD OF ORTHOGRAPHY AND PRONUNCIATION AND IM-
    PROVED DICTIONARY OF THE ENGLISH LANGUAGE
    Burgiss Allison. Burlington NJ: J.S. Meehan 1815
ARABIC-ENGLISH DICTIONARY FOR THE USE OF STUDENTS
    Joseph G. Hava, S.J. Beirut: Catholic Press 1899
(AN) ARABIC-ENGLISH LEXICON
    Edward W. Lane. London: Williams and Northgate 8 volumes 1863-93
    (Reprint Beirut: Librairie de Liban 1968)
(AN) ARABIC-ENGLISH VOCABULARY OF THE COLLOQUIAL ARABIC OF EGYPT
    Socrates Spiro-Bey. Cairo: Al-Mokattam & London: B. Quaritch
    1895
AUSFÜHRLICHES ... LATEINISCH-DEUTSCHES LEXICON ...
    Immanuel J.G. Scheller. Leipzig: K. Fritsch 3 volumes 1788/1804

BBC PRONOUNCING DICTIONARY OF BRITISH NAMES ...
     Graham E. Pointon. Oxford: U.P. 1971/83
BIBLIOTHECA HISPANICA. A DICTIONARIE IN SPANISH, ENGLISH AND LATINE
     Richard Percyvall. London: J. Jackson for R. Watkins 1591
BIBLIOTHECA SCHOLASTICA: A DOVBLE DICTIONARIE
     John Rider. Oxford: I. Barnes 1589 (Reprint ed. Robin C. Alston.
     Menston: Scolar Press 1970)
BIOGRAPHICAL DICTIONARY OF THE PHONETIC SCIENCES
     Arthur J. Bronstein et al. New York: Lehman College Press 1977
BOL'ŠOJ AKADEMIČESKIJ SLOVAR' see SLOVAR' SOVREMENNOGO RUSSKOGO
     LITERATURNOGO JAZYKA
(THE) BOOK OF JARGON
     Don Ethan Miller. New York: Macmillan 1981
BROCKHAUS-WAHRIG. DEUTSCHES WÖRTERBUCH IN SECHS BÄNDEN
     Gerhard Wahrig et al. Wiesbaden: F.A. Brockhaus & Stuttgart:
     Deutsche Verlags-Anstalt 1980-84
CAMBRIDGE ENCYCLOPEDIA OF ARCHAEOLOGY
     Andrew Sherratt. Cambridge: U.P. 1980
CATHOLICON
     Johannes F. Balbus (Balbi). Anon. 1286 (Printed version Mainz:
     J. Gutenberg 1460)
(THE) CENTURY DICTIONARY AND CYCLOPEDIA (CDC)
     William D. Whitney et al. New York: Century 10 volumes 1889-1897
CHAMBERS TWENTIETH CENTURY DICTIONARY (TCD)
     Thomas Davidson/Elizabeth M. Kirkpatrick. Edinburgh: W. and R.
     Chambers 1901/83
CHAMBERS UNIVERSAL LEARNERS' DICTIONARY (CULD)
     Elizabeth M. Kirkpatrick. Edinburgh: W. and R. Chambers 1980
(A) CHINESE AND ENGLISH VOCABULARY IN THE PEKINESE DIALECT
     George C. Stent. Shanghai: Imp. Maritime Customs Press 1871
(A) CHINESE-ENGLISH DICTIONARY
     Herbert A. Giles. London: B. Quaritch & Shanghai etc.: Kelly and
     Walsh Ltd. 2 volumes 1892/1912
(A) CHINESE-ENGLISH DICTIONARY
     Robert H. Mathews. Shanghai: China Inland Mission/Presbyterian
     Mission Press 1931 (Revision Cambridge MA: Harvard U.P. 1943)
CHINESE-ENGLISH DICTIONARY OF CONTEMPORARY USAGE
     Chi Wen-shun. Berkeley etc.: U. of California P. 1977
CHINESE-FRENCH VOCABULARY
     in Michael Boym. China Illustrata. Amsterdam 1670
CHINESE-LATIN VOCABULARY
     in Michael Boym. China Illustrata. Amsterdam 1667
CIYUAN (Chinese Etymological Dictionary)
     Lu Erkui et al. Shanghai 1915 (Reprint Beijing: Commercial Press
     4 volumes 1979)
(A) CLASSICAL DICTIONARY OF THE VULGAR TONGUE
     Francis Grose. London: S. Hooper 1785
COLLINS DICTIONARY OF THE ENGLISH LANGUAGE (CED)
     Patrick Hanks et al. London & Glasgow: Collins 1979
COLLINS ENGLISH DICTIONARY see COLLINS DICTIONARY OF THE ENGLISH

LANGUAGE
COMPENDIOUS DICTIONARY OF THE ENGLISH LANGUAGE
    Noah Webster. New Haven CT: Increase Cooke 1806
(A) COMPENDIOUS DICTIONARY OF THE LATIN TONGUE
    Robert Ainsworth. London: Longman 1752/96
(A) COMPLETE DICTIONARY OF THE ENGLISH LANGUAGE ...
    Thomas Sheridan. London: C. Dilly 1780/89
COMPREHENSIVE PRONOUNCING AND EXPLANATORY DICTIONARY OF THE ENGLISH
    LANGUAGE ...
    Joseph Worcester. New York: Collins and Hannay 1830
(A) CONCISE DICTIONARY OF THE ENGLISH AND HUNGARIAN LANGUAGES
    László Országh. Budapest: Franklin 1948
(THE) CONCISE OXFORD DICTIONARY (COD)
    Henry W. Fowler and Francis G. Fowler/John B. Sykes. Oxford:
    Clarendon P. & Oxford U.P. 1911/1982
(THE) CONCISE PRONOUNCING DICTIONARY OF BRITISH AND AMERICAN ENGLISH
    (CPDBAE)
    John Windsor Lewis. Oxford: U.P. 1972
(LA) CONCORDE DES DEUX LANGAGES
    Jean Lemaire de Belges. Anon. 1510 (Reprint ed. Jean Frappier.
    Paris: Droz 1947)
(DE LA) CONFORMITE DU LANGAGE FRANÇOIS AVEC LE GREC
    Henri Estienne. Anon. 1565 (Reprint ed. Leon Feugère. Paris: J.
    Delalain)
(A) CRITICAL PRONOUNCING DICTIONARY AND EXPOSITOR OF THE ENGLISH
    LANGUAGE
    John Walker. London: G. and J. Robinson 1791 (Revision see NEW
    CRITICAL PRONOUNCING DICTIONARY OF THE ENGLISH LANGUAGE)
DA QING QUAN SHU (A Comprehensive Dictionary of the Great Qing
    Dynasty)
    Shen Qiliang. Beijing: Wan Yu Zhai 12 volumes 1683
DEUTSCHES WORTERBUCH
    Jacob Grimm and Wilhelm Grimm et al. Leipzig: Hirzel 16 volumes
    in 32 1854-1961
DEUTSCHES WORTERBUCH
    Gerhard Wahrig. Gütersloh: Bertelsmann 1966/80
DICCIONARIO DE AUTORIDADES
    Madrid: Real Academia Española 6 volumes 1726-1737
DICCIONARIO INGLÉS-ESPAÑOL Y ESPAÑOL-INGLÉS
    Francisco Corona Bustamente. Paris: Garnier 1878
DICCIONARIO NUEVO DE LAS DOS LENGUAS ESPAÑOLA E INGLESA
    Thomas Connelly/Thomas Higgins. Madrid: P.J. Pereyra 4 volumes
    1797-98
DICTIONAIRE COMIQUE, SATYRIQUE, CRITIQUE ...
    Philibert J. le Roux. Amsterdam: M. Ch. le Cene 1718/35
DICTIONAIRE FRANCOISLATIN
    Robert Estienne. Paris: R. Estienne 1539/1549
DICTIONAIRE FRANÇOIS-LATIN
    Jean Nicot. Paris: J. Dupuys 1573
DICTIONAIRE UNIVERSEL ...

Antoine Furetière. The Hague: A. and R. Leers 1690 (Reprint
Genève: Slatkine Reprints 3 volumes 1970)
(A) DICTIONARIE, FRENCH AND ENGLISH
Claudius Hollyband. London: T.O. for T. Woodcock 1593
(A) DICTIONARIE IN SPANISH AND ENGLISH
John Minsheu. London: E. Bollifant 1599 (Reset London: J.
Haviland for E. Blount et al. 1623)
(A) DICTIONARIE IN SPANISH, ENGLISH, AND LATINE in BIBLIOTHECA
HISPANICA
DICTIONARIO DE VOCABLOS CASTELLANOS, APLICADOS A LA PROPRIEDAD
LATINA
Alonso Sánchez de la Ballesta. Salamanca: J. and A. Renaut 1587
DICTIONARIOLUM PUERORUM, TRIBUS LINGUIS LATINA, ANGLICA & GALLICA
CONSCRIPTUM
Robert Estienne/John Veron. London: R. Wolfius 1552 (Reprint New
York: Da Capo Press 1971)
DICTIONARIUM ANGLO-BRITANNICUM ...
John Kersey. London: J. Wilde for J. Phillips 1708 (Reprint ed.
Robin C. Alston. Menton: Scolar Press 1969)
DICTIONARIUM BRITANNICUM see (A) MORE COMPLEAT UNIVERSAL ETYMO-
LOGICAL ENGLISH DICTIONARY
DICTIONARIUM DECEM LINGUARUM ...
Ambrosius Calepinus (Calepino). Lyon: E. Michel 1585
DICTIONARIUM ... FRANTZÖSISCH-TEUTSCH
Matthias Kramer. Nürnberg: M. Endter 1712
DICTIONARIUM HERLOVIANUM ...
Povl J. Colding. København: Imp. S. Sartorii 1626
DICTIONARIUM HISPANO-LATINUM
Elio Antonio de Nebrija. Salamanca: Anon. 1495
DICTIONARIUM LATINAE LINGUAE
Ambrosius Calepinus (Calepino). Reggio: Imp. D. Berthochi 1502
DICTIONARIUM LATINO-HISPANICUM
Elio Antonio de Nebrija. Salamanca: Anon. 1492
DICTIONARIUM LINGUAE LATINAE ET ANGLICANAE
Thomas Thomas. London: R. Boyle 1587 (Reprint ed. Robin C.
Alston. Menston: Scolar Press 1972)
DICTIONARIUM QUADRILINGUE SUEDICUM GERMANICUM LATINUM GRAECUM
Ericus J. Schroderus (unpublished) 1640 (Printed version ed. B.
Hesselman. Uppsala: Almqvist & Wiksell 1929)
DICTIONARIUM QUINQUE NOBILISSIMARUM EUROPAE LINGUARUM LATINAE,
ITALICAE, GERMANICAE, DALMATICAE ET UNGARICAE
Fausto Vrančič. Venezia: N. Morettus 1595 (Reprint Zagreb: Liber
U.P.)
DICTIONARIUM SEPTEM DIVERSARUM LINGUARUM, VIDELICET LATINE, ITALICE,
DALMATICE, BOHEMICE, POLONICE, GERMANICE ET UNGARICE
Petrus Loderecker. Praha: E typ. Ottmariano 1605
DICTIONARIUM, SEU LATINAE LINGUAE THESAURUS
Robert Estienne. Paris: R. Estienne 1531
DICTIONARIUM UNGARO-LATINUM
Albert Szenczi Molnár. Nürnberg: Anon. 1604

(A) DICTIONARY IN ENGLYSHE AND WELSHE ...
    William Salesbury. London: J. Waley 1547 (Reprint ed. Robin C.
    Alston. Menston: Scolar Press 1969)
DICTIONARY OF AMERICAN REGIONAL ENGLISH (DARE)
    Frederic G. Cassidy. Cambridge MA: The Belknap Press Vol. I 1985
(THE) DICTIONARY OF CANADIAN ENGLISH (BEGINNING/INTERMEDIATE/SENIOR
    DICTIONARY)
    Clarence L. Barnhart/Walter S. Avis et al. Toronto: Gage 1962/73
(A) DICTIONARY OF ENGLISH PRONUNCIATION WITH AMERICAN VARIANTS
    Harold E. Palmer et al. Cambridge: W. Heffer 1926
(A) DICTIONARY OF MODERN ENGLISH USAGE
    Henry W. Fowler. Oxford: Clarendon P. 1926/65
(A) DICTIONARY OF MODERN WRITTEN ARABIC
    Hans Wehr. Ithaca NY: Cornell U.P. 1961/1976
(THE) DICTIONARY OF SYR THOMAS ELIOT KNIGHT
    Thomas Elyot. London: T. Berthelet 1538 (Reprint ed. Robin C.
    Alston. Menston: Scolar Press 1970)
DICTIONARY OF THE CHINESE LANGUAGE
    Robert Morrison. Macao: Honorable East India Press 6 volumes
    1815-1823
(A) DICTIONARY OF THE ENGLISH LANGUAGE
    Samuel Johnson. London: W. Strahan for J. and P. Knapton, T. and
    T. Longman et al. 2 volumes 1755 (Reprint ed. Robert W. Burch-
    field. London: The Times & Salem NH: The Ayer Co. 1979)
(A) DICTIONARY OF THE ENGLISH LANGUAGE
    Joseph Worcester. Boston: Hickling, Swan and Brewer 1860
(A) DICTIONARY OF THE HO-KEEN (FUJIAN) DIALECT OF THE CHINESE LANG-
    UAGE
    William H. Medhurst. Macao: Honorable East India Press 1832
DICTIONARY OF THE OLDER SCOTTISH TONGUE ... (DOST)
    William Craigie/Adam Jack Aitken. Aberdeen: U.P. 33 parts from
    1933
(A) DICTIONARY OF THE SPANISH AND ENGLISH LANGUAGES
    Mariano Velázquez de la Cadena. New York: Appleton 1852 (Re-
    vision see NEW REVISED VELÁZQUEZ SPANISH AND ENGLISH DICTIONARY)
(A) DICTIONARY, SPANISH AND ENGLISH, AND ENGLISH AND SPANISH
    Hippolyto S.J. Giral Delpino. London: A. Millar, J. Nourse, P.
    Vaillant 1763
(A) DICTIONARY, SPANISH AND ENGLISH, AND ENGLISH AND SPANISH
    Giuseppe M. Baretti. London: J. Nourse 1778/1786
DICTIONNAIRE ALPHABÉTIQUE ET ANALOGIQUE DE LA LANGUE FRANÇAISE
    Paul Robert et al. Paris: Société du Nouveau Littré Le Robert
    (GRAND ROBERT 6 volumes & supplement 1964/74, LE PETIT ROBERT 1
    volume & supplement 1967/72)
DICTIONNAIRE BURLESQUE
    César-Pierre Richelet (unpublished) 1689
DICTIONNAIRE CHINOIS, FRANÇAIS ET LATIN
    M. deGuignes. Paris: Anon. 1813/1815
DICTIONNAIRE COMIQUE ... see DICTIONAIRE COMIQUE, SATYRIQUE,
    CRITIQUE ...

(LE) DICTIONNAIRE DE L'ACADEMIE FRANÇAISE
      Paris: J.B. Coignard 4 volumes & 2 supplements 1694 (Reprints
      Tokyo: France Tosho Reprints 1967 & Genève: Slatkine Reprints
      1968)
DICTIONNAIRE DE LA LANGUE FRANÇAISE
      Emile Littré. Paris: Hachette 1863-77 (Abridged reprint ed. A.
      Beaujean. Paris: Gallimard 1959)
DICTIONNAIRE DES ARTS ET DES SCIENCES
      Thomas Corneille. Paris: J.B. Coignard 1694
DICTIONNAIRE DES MOTS OBSCURES see (LA) PORTE DES SIENCES ...
DICTIONNAIRE DU FRANÇAIS CONTEMPORAIN ... (DFC)
      Jean Dubois et al. Paris: Librairie Larousse 1966/80
DICTIONNAIRE FRANÇOIS ...
      César-Pierre Richelet. Genève: J.H. Widerhold 1680 (Reprint
      Tokyo: France Tosho Reprints 1969) (Revised as DICTIONNAIRE
      PORTATIF DE LA LANGUE FRANÇOISE ... by Noël F. de Wailly. Lyon:
      A. Leroy 1770/1811)
DICTIONNAIRE FRANÇOIS-LATIN see DICTIONAIRE FRANCOISLATIN
DICTIONNAIRE LE PETIT ROBERT see DICTIONNAIRE ALPHABETIQUE ET
      ANALOGIQUE ...
DICTIONNAIRE UNIVERSEL DES NOMS PROPRES
      Paul Robert et al. Paris: Société du Nouveau Littré 4 volumes
      1974
DIZIONARIO PORTOGHESE-CINESE
      Matteo Ricci/Michele Ruggieri. Anon. c. 1600
DOKŁADNY SŁOWNIK POLSKO-ANGIELSKI
      Erazm Rykaczewski. Berlin: B. Behr 1849
DUCTOR IN LINGUAS see EGEMON EIS TAS GLOSSAS
DUDEN. BEDEUTUNSWORTERBUCH ...
      Paul Grebe et al. (Vol. 10, Der Duden in 10 Bänden). Mannheim:
      Bibliographisches Institut 1970
DUDEN. BILDWORTERBUCH DER DEUTSCHEN SPRACHE
      Kurt D. Solf et al. (Vol. 3, Der Duden in 10 Bänden). Mannheim:
      Bibliographisches Institut 1935/77
DUDEN. DEUTSCHES UNIVERSALWORTERBUCH
      Günther Drosdowski et al. Mannheim: Bibliographisches Institut
      1983
DUDEN. (DAS) GROSSE WÖRTERBUCH DER DEUTSCHEN SPRACHE IN SECHS BÄNDEN
      Günther Drosdowski et al. Mannheim: Bibliographisches Institut
      1976-81
DUDEN. RECHTSCHREIBUNG (DR)
      Horst Klien et al. (Der grosse Duden, Wörterbuch und Leitfaden
      der deutschen Rechtschreibung). Leipzig: VEB Bibliographisches
      Institut 1957/85
DUDEN. RECHTSCHREIBUNG DER DEUTSCHEN SPRACHE UND DER FREMDWORTER
      (DR)
      Dudenredaktion (Vol. 1, Der Duden in 10 Bänden). Mannheim: Bib-
      liographisches Institut 1929/86
DUDEN. (VOLLSTÄNDIGES) ORTHOGRAPHISCHES WÖRTERBUCH DER DEUTSCHEN
      SPRACHE

Konrad Duden. Leipzig: Bibliographisches Institut 1880/1914
EGEMON EIS TAS GLOSSAS/DUCTOR IN LINGUAS/THE GUIDE INTO THE
    TONGUES ...
    John Minsheu. London: I. Browne 1617
ELIĀS' MODERN DICTIONARY ARABIC-ENGLISH
    Eliās A. Eliās. Cairo: Eliās' Modern Press 1922
ELIĀS' MODERN DICTIONARY ENGLISH-ARABIC
    Eliās A. Eliās. Cairo: Eliās' Modern Press 1913/1954
(THE NEW) ENCYCLOPAEDIA BRITANNICA
    Chicago etc.: Encyclopaedia Britannica 15th edition 30 volumes
    1976
(THE) ENCYCLOPAEDIA METROPOLITANA ...
    Samuel T. Coleridge et al. London: B. Fellowes and J.J. Griffin
    59 parts 1817-1845/1849
ENCYCLOPEDIC WORLD DICTIONARY
    Patrick Hanks. London & New York: Hamlyn 1971
ENGLESKO-HRVATSKE KNJIŽEVNE VEZE
    Rudolf Filipović. Zagreb: Liber U.P. 1972
ENGLISH-ARABIC DICTIONARY ...
    Francis Steingass. London: W.N. Allen 1882 (Revision see
    LEARNER'S ENGLISH ARABIC DICTIONARY)
(AN) ENGLISH-ARABIC LEXICON
    George P. Badger. London: C. Kegan Paul 1881 (Reprint Beirut:
    Librairie de Liban 1967)
(AN) ENGLISH-ARABIC VOCABULARY OF THE MODERN AND COLLOQUIAL ARABIC
    OF EGYPT
    Socrates Spiro-Bey. Cairo: Al-Mokaṭṭam & London: B. Quaritch
    1895 (Revision Cairo: Eliās' Modern Press 1929)
(THE) ENGLISH DICTIONARIE ...
    Henry Cockeram. London: E. Weaver/N. Butter 1623 (Reprint ed.
    Robin C. Alston. Menston: Scolar Press 1968)
(AN) ENGLISH DICTIONARY ...
    Elisha Coles. London: S. Crouch 1676 (Reprint ed. Robin C.
    Alston. Menston: Scolar Press 1969)
(AN) ENGLISH EXPOSITOR ...
    John Bullokar. London: J. Legatt 1616 (Reprint ed. Robin C.
    Alston. Menston: Scolar Press 1967)
ENGLISH-HUNGARIAN DICTIONARY
    László Országh. Budapest: Akadémiai Kiadó 1960
ENGLISH PRONOUNCING DICTIONARY see EVERYMAN'S ENGLISH PRONOUNCING
    DICTIONARY
(AN) ENGLISH PRONOUNCING DICTIONARY FOR JAPANESE STUDENTS
    Sanki Ichikawa. Tokyo: Kenkyusha 1923
(AN) ETYMOLOGICAL DICTIONARY OF THE SCOTTISH LANGUAGE ...
    John Jamieson. Edinburgh: U.P. for W. Creech et al. 2 volumes
    1808, supplement 2 volumes 1825
EUROPÄISCHER SPRACHSCHATZ
    Johann Rädlein. Leipzig: J.F. Braun 1711
EVERYMAN'S ENGLISH PRONOUNCING DICTIONARY (EPD)
    Daniel Jones/A.C. Gimson. London: Dent 1917/1977

EVERYMAN'S FRENCH-ENGLISH, ENGLISH-FRENCH DICTIONARY, WITH SPECIAL
    REFERENCE TU CANADA
    Jean-Paul Vinay et al. London: Dent 1962
FAN ER YA (Foreign, i.e. Tangut, Er Ya)
    Yuan Hao/Yeli Renrong. Shaanxi: Anon. c. 1030
FAN HAN HE SHI ZHANG ZHONG ZHU (Foreign-, i.e. Tangut-, Chinese
    Glossary 'as Timely as a Pearl in a Palm')
    Gule Maocai. Anon. 1190 (Reprint Tianjin: Yi'an Tang Jing Pu
    1924)
FAN YU QIAN ZI WEN (Sanskrit One-Thousand Character Text)
    Yi Jing. Chang'an: Anon. 6th century (Printed version 1727)
(THE) FIRST DICTIONARY OF TWO LANGUAGES (English and Spanish) UNDER
    A SINGLE ALPHABET
    Don Felipe Fernández. London: J. McCreery for the author 1811
(THE) GAGE CANADIAN DICTIONARY
    Clarence L. Barnhart/Walter S. Avis. Toronto: Gage 1973/83
GAMBLA SWEA OCH GOTHA MÅLES FATEBUR
    Georg Stiernhielm. Stockholm: P. von Selow 1642
GLOSSOGRAPHIA, OR A DICTIONARY OF HARD WORDS ...
    Thomas Blount. London: H. Moseley and T. Newcomb 1656 (Reprint
    ed. Robin C. Alston. Menston: Scolar Press 1971)
GRAMMATISCH-KRITISCHES WÖRTERBUCH DER HOCHDEUTSCHEN MUNDART ...
    Johann Christoph Adelung. Leipzig: B.C. Breitkopf 5 volumes
    1774-86
GRAND ET NOUVEAU DICTIONNAIRE FRANÇOIS ET FLAMAND
    'L.V.I.V.I.F.' Bruxelles: J. de Grieck 1707
(A) GREEK-ENGLISH LEXICON
    Henry G. Liddell/Robert Scott. Oxford: Clarendon P. & Oxford
    U.P. 1843/1925/40
(THE) GUIDE INTO THE TONGUES see EGEMON EIS TAS GLOSSAS
HANDWOORDEBOEK VAN DIE AFRIKAANSE TAAL ... see VERKLARENDE HAND-
    WOORDEBOEK VAN DIE AFRIKAANSE TAAL
HARRAP'S SHORTER FRENCH AND ENGLISH DICTIONARY
    Jean E. Mansion. London: Harrap 1967
HARRAP'S STANDARD FRENCH AND ENGLISH DICTIONARY
    Jean E. Mansion. London: Harrap 1939
HUA YI YI YU (Chinese-Foreign Glossary)
    Huoyuanjie/Mayichihei. Anon. 1382 (Revised as ZENG DING HUA YI
    YI YU ...)
HUNGARIAN AND ENGLISH DICTIONARY
    Arthur B. Yolland. Budapest: Franklin (Part I English-Hungarian)
    1908
HUNGARIAN-ENGLISH DICTIONARY
    László Országh. Budapest: Akadémiai Kiadó 1953
IANUA LINGUARUM ...
    William Bathe. London: R.F. for M. Lownes 1615
IANUA LINGUARUM RESERATA ...
    John A. Comenius (Komenský). Amsterdam: L. Elzevier 1631
INSTAURATIO MAGNA
    Francis Bacon. London: J. Billium 1620

(AL-) JAMHARA FĪ-L-LUGHA
    Abū Bakr M. ibn Duraid. Anon. 9th century (Printed version Hyderabad 1344 A.H. & Maṭba'at Majlis Dā'irat al-Ma'ārif 4 volumes 1924-1932)
JANUA LINGUARUM RESERATA see IANUA LINGUARUM RESERATA
JI LIN LEI SHI (Hen Grove Analogies)
    Sun Mu. Anon. c. 1100
(AL-) KĀMOOS ...
    Majd ul-Dīn M.I.Y. al-Firūzābādī. Anon. 14th century (Printed version see QĀMŪS AL-MUHĪṬ)
KANG XI ZI DIAN (Kangxi Dictionary)
    Zhang Yushu et al. 1716 (Reprint Beijing: Zhonghua Shuju 1981)
KITĀB AL-'AIN
    Al-Khalil ibn Aḥmad. Anon. 8th century (Printed version Baghdad: Maṭba'at al-Ṣafi 6 volumes from 1967)
KITĀB AL-AMTHĀL see MAJMA AL-AMTHĀL
KITĀB AL-MU'ARRAB
    Abū Manṣūr M. al-Jawālīqī. Anon. c. 1100 (Printed version ed. Aḥmad M. Shākir. Cairo: Dār al-Kutub al-Miṣriyah 1969)
(A) LEARNER'S ENGLISH-ARABIC DICTIONARY
    Francis Steingass. Beirut: Librairie de Liban 1966
LESCLARCISSEMENT DE LA LANGUE FRANCOYSE
    John Palsgrave. London: R. Pynson 1530 (Reprint ed. Robin C. Alston. Menston: Scolar Press 1969)
LEXICI RUNICI ...
    Olaus Wormius (Worm)/Magnus Olafsson. København: M. Martz 1650
LEXICON ARABICO-LATINUM
    Georg W. Freytag. Halle: C.A. Schwetschke 4 volumes 1830-37
LEXICON LATINO-POLONICUM
    J... Maczyński. Regiomonti Borussiae: J. Daubmannus 1564
LEXICON LATINO-SCONDICUM ...
    Ericus J. Schroderus. Uppsala: H. Käyser 1637
LEXICON OF CONTEMPORARY ENGLISH see LONGMAN LEXICON ...
LEXIS. DICTIONNAIRE DE LA LANGUE FRANÇAISE
    Jean Dubois. Paris: Librairie Larousse 1975
LIAO GUO YU JIE (Explanations of the Liao Language)
    Tuoketuo. Anon. 13th-14th century
LIBER DE SIMPLICIBUS
    Niccolò Roccabonella. Zadar: Anon. c. 1445
LINGUAE LATINAE LIBER DICTIONARIUS QUADRIPARTITUS
    Adam Littleton. London: T. Bassett et al. 2 volumes 1678
LISĀN AL-'ARAB
    Abū al-Faḍl J. M. ibn Manẓūr. Anon. 13th century (Printed version Beirut: Dār Ṣadir 15 volumes 1955-56)
(THE) LITTLE OXFORD DICTIONARY
    George Ostler/Julia Swannell. Oxford: Clarendon P. & Oxford U.P. 1930/1980
LONGMAN ACTIVE STUDY DICTIONARY OF ENGLISH (LASDE)
    Della Summers. Harlow & London: Longman 1983
LONGMAN DICTIONARY OF AMERICAN ENGLISH (LDAE)

Arley Gray et al. Harlow & New York: Longman 1983
LONGMAN DICTIONARY OF CONTEMPORARY ENGLISH (LDOCE)
    Paul Procter et al. Harlow & London: Longman 1978
LONGMAN LEXICON OF CONTEMPORARY ENGLISH
    Tom McArthur. Harlow & London: Longman 1981
(THE) MACQUARIE DICTIONARY
    Arthur Delbridge et al. St. Leonards NSW: Macquarie Library 1981
(A) MAGYAR NYELV ERTELMEZŐ SZOTÁRA
    Géza Bárczi/László Országh. Budapest: Akadémiai Kiadó 7 volumes
    1959-62
(A) MAGYAR NYELV SZOTÁRA
    Gergely Czuczor/János Fogarasi. Pest: G. Emich 6 volumes
    1862-1874
MAJMA' AL-AMTHĀL (Book of Proverbs)
    A. M. al-Maidānī. Anon. c. 1100 (Printed version ed. M.M.D.
    'Abd al-Hamīd. Cairo: Al-Maktaba al-Tijāriya al-Kubra 2 volumes
    1959)
(AL-) MANĀR (AN) ENGLISH-ARABIC DICTIONARY
    Hasan S. Karmi. London: Longman & Beirut: Librairie de Liban
    1970
(A) MARINE POCKET DICTIONARY OF THE ITALIAN, SPANISH, PORTUGUESE AND
    GERMAN LANGUAGES
    Henry Neuman. London: Vernor and Hood 1799
(AL-) MAWRID (A) MODERN ENGLISH-ARABIC DICTIONARY
    Munīr Ba'albaki. Beirut: Dār al-Ilm lil-Malāyēn 1967
MEMORIALE DELLA LINGUA ...
    Giacomo Pergamini. Venezia: G.B. Ciotti 1602
MENG GU YI YU (Explanations of the Mongolian Language)
    Anon. 13th-14th century
MERRIAM-WEBSTER'S (FIFTH) COLLEGIATE DICTIONARY (W5)
    Editorial Staff. Springfield MA: Merriam 1941
(A) MORE COMPLEAT UNIVERSAL ETYMOLOGICAL ENGLISH DICTIONARY
    (also called DICTIONARIUM BRITANNICUM)
    Nathan Bailey. London: T. Cox 1730
MUHĪT AL-MUHĪT
    Butrus al-Bustāni. Beirut: Anon. 2 volumes 1867-1870 (Reprint
    Beirut: Maktabat Lubnan 1966)
(AL-) MUHĪT FĪ-L-LUGHA
    Al-Sāhib ibn 'Abbād. Anon. 10th century (Printed version ed.
    M.H. al-Yāsīn. Baghdād: Matba'at al-Ma'ārif from 1975)
(AL-) MUHKAM WA L-MUHĪT AL-A'ZAM
    Abū al-Hassan A.I. ibn Sīda. Anon. 11th century (Printed version
    ed. M. al-Saqqa et al. Cairo: Al-Halabi 6 volumes 1958-72)
NASIONALE WOORDEBOEK (NW)
    Meyer de Villiers et al. Cape Town: Nasou 1977/85
NBC HANDBOOK OF PRONUNCIATION
    James F. Bender. New York: T. Crowell 1943/64
NEDERDUITSCH TAALKUNDIG WOORDENBOEK
    Petrus Weiland. Amsterdam: J. Allart 11 volumes 1799-1811
NEUMAN AND BARETTI DICTIONARY see A NEW DICTIONARY OF THE SPANISH

AND ENGLISH LANGUAGES and (A) PRONOUNCING DICTIONARY OF THE
SPANISH AND ENGLISH LANGUAGES
(THE) NEW CENTURY CYCLOPEDIA OF NAMES
     Clarence L. Barnhart et al. New York: Appleton-Century-Crofts
     1954
(THE) NEW COLLINS COMPACT ENGLISH DICTIONARY
     William T. McLeod. London & Glasgow: Collins 1984
(THE) NEW COLLINS CONCISE DICTIONARY OF THE ENGLISH LANGUAGE (NCCD)
     William T. McLeod. London & Glasgow: Collins 1982
(A) NEW CRITICAL PRONOUNCING DICTIONARY OF THE ENGLISH LANGUAGE ...
     R.S. Coxe. Burlington NJ: D. Allinson 1813
(A) NEW DICTIONARY OF THE SPANISH AND ENGLISH LANGUAGES ...
     Henry Neuman et al. London: Vernor and Hood et al. 1802/1817
     (Reprint Paris: S.H. Blanc 1848)
(A) NEW DICTIONARY OF THE SPANISH AND ENGLISH LANGUAGES
     Mateo Seoane y Sobral et al. London: W. Clowe for Longman, Rees
     and Co. 1831
(A) NEW DICTIONARY, SPANISH AND ENGLISH AND ENGLISH AND SPANISH
     Pedro Pineda. London: F. Giles et al. 1740
(A) NEW ENGLISH DICTIONARY ...
     'J.K.' London: H. Bonwicke 1702 (Reprint ed. Robin C. Alston.
     Menston: Scolar Press 1969)
(A) NEW ENGLISH DICTIONARY ON HISTORICAL PRINCIPLES see OXFORD
     ENGLISH DICTIONARY
(A) NEW GENERAL ENGLISH DICTIONARY ...
     Thomas Dyche/William Pardon. London: R. Ware 1735
(THE) NEW OXFORD ENGLISH DICTIONARY (NOED) see OXFORD ENGLISH
     DICTIONARY
(THE) NEW PRONOUNCING DICTIONARY OF THE SPANISH AND ENGLISH LANG-
     UAGES
     Juan L. Iribas/Edward Gray. New York: Appleton 1900
(THE) NEW REVISED VELÁZQUEZ SPANISH AND ENGLISH DICTIONARY
     Ida Navarro Hinojosa. Chicago: Follett 1959
(A) NEW SPANISH AND ENGLISH DICTIONARY ...
     John Stevens. London: G. Sawbridge 2 volumes 1705-1706
(THE) NEW WORLD OF ENGLISH WORDS ...
     Edward Phillips. London: E. Tyler for N. Brooke 1658 (Reprint
     ed. Robin C. Alston. Menston: Scolar Press 1969)
9,000 WORDS: A SUPPLEMENT TO WEBSTER'S THIRD NEW INTERNATIONAL
     DICTIONARY
     Merriam-Webster Editorial Staff. Springfield MA: Merriam-Webster
     1983
NOMENCLATOR, OMNIUM RERUM PROPRIA NOMINA ...
     Adrianus Junius. Antwerpen: C. Plantinus 1577
(THE) NOMENCLATOR, OR REMEMBRANCER ... AND NOW IN ENGLISH
     Adrianus Junius/Iohn Higgins. London: R. Newberie and H. Denham
     1585
(DEN) NORSKE DICTIONARIUM ELLER GLOSEBOG ...
     Christen Jenssøn. København: Anderssøn 1646 (Reprint ed. Torleiv
     Hannaas. Kristiania: Aeldre norske sprogminder 3 1915)

NORSK-ENGELSK ORDBOK/NORWEGIAN-ENGLISH DICTIONARY
    Einar Haugen et al. Oslo: Universitetsforlaget & Madison: U. of
    Wisconsin P. 1965/84
NOUVEAU DICTIONNAIRE PROVERBIAL, SATIRIQUE ET BURLESQUE
    Antoine Caillot. Paris: Douvain 1826/1829
NUEVO DICCIONARIO INGLES-ESPAÑOL
    Jose M. López/Edward R. Bensley. Paris: Garnier 1888
NUEVO DICCIONARIO PORTÁTIL, ESPAÑOL E INGLES
    Claude M. Gattel. Paris: Bossange, Masson et Besson 2 volumes
    1803 & London: J. Johnson and Vernor 1809
OPERA NVOVA CHE INSEGNA A PARLARE LA LINGVA SCHIAVONESCA ALLI
    GRANDI, ALLI PICOLI ET ALLE DONNE ...
    Pietro L. Valentiano. Ancona: Anon. 1527
ORBIS SENSUALIUM PICTUS QUADRILINGUIS
    John A. Comenius (Komenský). Nürnberg: M. Endter & London: C.
    Mearne 1658/1685
ORIGEN Y ETYMOLOGIA DE TODOS LOS VOCABLOS ORIGINALES DE LA LENGUA
    CASTELLANA
    Fernando del Rosal (unpublished - Madrid: National Library Ms.)
    1601
ORTUS VOCABULORUM
    Anon. 1500 (Reprint ed. Robin C. Alston. Menston: Scolar Press
    1968)
OXFORD ADVANCED LEARNER'S DICTIONARY OF CURRENT ENGLISH see ADVANCED
    LEARNER'S DICTIONARY OF CURRENT ENGLISH
OXFORD AMERICAN DICTIONARY (OAD)
    Eugene Ehrlich et al. New York: Oxford U.P. 1980
(THE) OXFORD ENGLISH-ARABIC DICTIONARY OF CURRENT USAGE
    Nakdimon S. Doniach. Oxford: U.P. 1972
(THE) OXFORD ENGLISH DICTIONARY (OED) title before 1897: NEW ENGLISH
    DICTIONARY ON HISTORICAL PRINCIPLES (NED)
    James Murray et al. Oxford: Clarendon P. & Oxford U.P. 12 vol-
    umes and supplement 1884-1933 (see also SUPPLEMENT TO THE OED),
    computerised version (THE) NEW OXFORD ENGLISH DICTIONARY (NOED)
    from 1986
PATRIOT WOORDEBOEK AFRIKAANS-ENGELS/DICTIONARY CAPE DUTCH-ENGLISH
    D.F. du Toit. Paarl: D.F. du Toit 1902
PETIT LAROUSSE ILLUSTRE
    Pierre Larousse. Paris: Larousse 1949/60
(A) PHONETIC DICTIONARY OF THE ENGLISH LANGUAGE
    Daniel Jones/Hermann Michaelis. Hannover: C. Meyer & New York:
    G.E. Stechert 1913
(A) PHONOGRAPHIC PRONOUNCING DICTIONARY OF THE ENGLISH LANGUAGE
    William Bolles. New London: Bolles and Williams 1846
(THE) POCKET OXFORD DICTIONARY OF CURRENT ENGLISH (POD)
    Henry W. Fowler/Robert E. Allen. Oxford: U.P. 1927/1984
(LA) PORTE DES SIENCES OU RECEUIL DES TERMES ET DES MOTS LES PLUS
    DIFICILES A ENTENDRE ... AVEC UN DICTIONNAIRE DE PLUSIEURS
    AUTRES MOTS & TERMES AUSSI OBSCURS
    'D.C.S.D.S.S.' (= François Cassandre). Paris: J.B. Coignard 1682

PROEVE VAN KAAPSCH TAALEIGEN
   in: Changuion, Anthoni N.E. (1848) De Nederduitsche taal in
   Zuid-Afrika hersteld. Rotterdam: J. van der Vliet
PROMPTORIUM PARVULORUM ...
   Anon. London: R. Pynson 1440/1499 (Reprints ed. A.L. Mayhew.
   London: Kegan Paul 1908; ed. Robin C. Alston. Menston: Scolar
   Press 1968)
(A) PRONOUNCING DICTIONARY OF AMERICAN ENGLISH (PDAE)
   John S. Kenyon/Thomas A. Knott. Springfield MA: G. and C.
   Merriam 1944/53
(A) PRONOUNCING DICTIONARY OF THE SPANISH AND ENGLISH LANGUAGES ...
   Mariano Velázquez de la Cadena. New York: Appleton and Co. 1852
(AL-) QĀMŪS AL-MUHĪT
   Majd ul-Dīn M.I.Y. al-Firūzābādī. Anon. 14th century (Printed
   version Cairo: Maṭba'at al-Ḥalabi 4 volumes 1952)
QING WEN ZONG HUI (Comprehensive Collection of the Manchu Languages)
   Zhikuan/Zhipei. Beijing: Wan Yu Zhai 12 volumes 1897
RANDOM HOUSE DICTIONARY OF THE ENGLISH LANGUAGE (RHD)
   Laurence Urdang/Jess Stein. New York: Random House 1966/73
READER'S DIGEST GREAT ILLUSTRATED DICTIONARY IN TWO VOLUMES
   Robert F. Ilson et al. London etc.: Reader's Digest 1984
RJEČNIK HRVATSKOGA ILI SRPSKOGA JEZIKA (ARJ)
   Zagreb: Yugoslav Academy of Sciences and Arts 23 volumes
   1882-1975
ROGET'S THESAURUS see THESAURUS OF ENGLISH WORDS AND PHRASES
SA'ĀDEH'S ENGLISH-ARABIC DICTIONARY ...
   Khalīl Sa'ādeh. Cairo: Al-Garīdah Press 1911 (Reprint Beirut:
   Librairie du Liban 2 volumes 1974)
(TĀJ AL-LUGHA WA-AL-) ṢAḤĀḤ (AL-'ARABIYYA)
   Abū Naṣr I.I.H. al-Jauharī. Anon. 10th century (Printed version
   Cairo: Dār al-Kitāb al-'Arabi 6 volumes 1956-58)
SCOTT, FORESMAN BEGINNING DICTIONARY
   Clarence L. Barnhart. Garden City NY: Doubleday 1952/76
SEX LINGUARUM, LATINAE, GALLICAE, HISPANICAE, ITALICAE, ANGLICAE, &
   TEUTONICAE, DILUCIDISSIMUS DICTIONARIUS ...
   Anon. Augustae Vindelicorum: P. Ulhardus c. 1530/37
SEX LINGUARUM LATINE, TEUTHONICE, GALLICE, HISPANICE, ITALICE,
   ANGLICE, DILUCIDISSIMUS DICTIONARIUS ...
   Anon. Southwarke: J. Nicolson for J. Renys 1537
(A) SHORTE DICTIONARIE FOR YONGE BEGYNNERS
   John Withals. London: T. Berthelet 1553
(THE) SHORTER OXFORD ENGLISH DICTIONARY (SOED)
   William Little et al./Charles T. Onions et al. Oxford: Clarendon
   Press 1933/73
6,000 WORDS: A SUPPLEMENT TO WEBSTER'S THIRD NEW INTERNATIONAL
   DICTIONARY
   Merriam-Webster Editorial Staff. Springfield MA: G. and C.
   Merriam 1976
SLANG AND ITS ANALOGUES ...
   John S. Farmer/William E. Henley. London: Printed for sub-

scribers only 1890-1904
SLOVAR' RUSSKOGO JAZYKA ... (RAD)
Jakov Karlovič Grot et al. Moskva: Akademija Nauk 6 volumes
1891-1937
SLOVAR' SOVREMENNOGO RUSSKOGO LITERATURNOGO JAZYKA (BAD)
Fedot Petrovič Filin et al. Moskva: Akademija Nauk 17 volumes
1950-65
SLOVNIK ČESKO-NĚMECKÝ
Josef J. Jungmann. Praha: R.W. Spinsky 5 volumes 1835-39
SŁOWNIK GWAR POLSKICH
Jan Karłowicz. Kraków: Akademia Umiejętności 6 volumes 1900-1911
SŁOWNIK JĘZYKA POLSKIEGO (SJPDor)
Witold Doroszewski. Warszawa: PAN 11 volumes 1958-1969
SŁOWNIK JĘZYKA POLSKIEGO (SW)
Jan Karłowicz et al. Warszawa: Nakładem prenumeratorów 8 volumes
1900-1927 (Reprint Warszawa: PIW 1952)
SŁOWNIK JĘZYKA POLSKIEGO ...
Tadeusz Lehr-Spławiński. Warszawa: Trzaska, Evert i Michalski
1938-39
SŁOWNIK JĘZYKA POLSKIEGO (SL)
Samuel B. Linde. Warszawa: XX. Piiarów 6 volumes 1807-14
(Reprint Warszawa: PIW 1951)
SŁOWNIK JĘZYKA POLSKIEGO
Mieczysław Szymczak et al. Warszawa: PWN 1978-81
SPECIMEN LEXICI RUNICI ... see LEXICI RUNICI ...
(A) STANDARD DICTIONARY OF THE ENGLISH LANGUAGE ...
Isaac K. Funk. New York: Funk and Wagnalls 1893
(THE) STUDENT'S ARABIC-ENGLISH DICTIONARY
Francis Steingass. London: Crosby Lockwood 1884 (Reprint Ann
Arbor: U. of Michigan P. 1974)
(A) SUPPLEMENT TO THE OXFORD ENGLISH DICTIONARY
Robert W. Burchfield. Oxford: U.P. 4 volumes 1972-1986
SVENSK-ENGELSK FACKORDBOK ...
Ingvar E. Gullberg. Stockholm: Norstedt 1964
SYNONYMORUM SYLVA ...
Simon Pelegromius. London: T. Vautrollerius 1580
(A) TABLE ALPHABETICALL ...
Robert Cawdrey. London: I.R. for E. Weaver 1604
TAHDHĪB AL-LUGHA
Abū Manṣūr M.I.A. al-Azharī. Anon. 10th century (Printed
version Cairo: Al-Dār al-Miṣriyya lil-Talīf wal-Tarjama 15
volumes 1964-67)
TĀJ AL-'ARŪS ...
Muḥib ul-Din A.F.M.M. al-Zabīdī. Anon. 1767 (Reprint Cairo:
Al-Matba'ah al-Khayriah 10 volumes 1870-90)
TESORO DE LA LENGUA CASTELLANA, O ESPAÑOLA
Sebastián de Covarrubias y (H)Orozco. Madrid: L. Sánchez 1611
THESAURUS LINGUAE LATINAE see DICTIONARIUM, SEU LATINAE LINGUAE
THESAURUS
THESAURUS LINGUAE ROMANICAE & BRITANNICAE ...

Thomas Cooper. London: H. Wykes 1565
THESAURUS OF ENGLISH WORDS AND PHRASES ...
    Peter M. Roget. London: Longman, Brown, Green and Longmans 1852
    (Revision ed. Susan M. Lloyd. Harlow & London: Longman 1982)
THESAURUS POLONO-LATINO-GRAECUS ...
    Gregorius Cnapius (Knapski). Cracoviae: Typis F. Caesario 1621
THORNDIKE-BARNHART BEGINNING DICTIONARY
    Edward L. Thorndike/Clarence L. Barnhart. Chicago: Scott, Fores-
    man 1952
THORNDIKE-BARNHART COMPREHENSIVE DESK DICTIONARY
    Clarence L. Barnhart. Garden City NY: Doubleday & Chicago:
    Scott, Foresman 1951/67
THORNDIKE-BARNHART HIGH SCHOOL DICTIONARY
    Edward L. Thorndike/Clarence L. Barnhart. Chicago: Scott, Fores-
    man 1952/65
THRESOR DE LA LANGUE FRANÇOYSE
    Jean Nicot. Paris: Douceur 1606
TOLKOVYJ SLOVAR' ŽIVOGO VELIKORUSSKOGO JAZYKA
    Vladimir Ivanovich Dal'. St. Petersburg & Moskva: Izd. M.O.
    Vol'fa 1863-66
(A) TONIC DICTIONARY OF THE CHINESE LANGUAGE IN THE CANTON DIALECT
    S. Wells Williams. Canton: Office of the Chinese Repository 1856
(THE) TREASURIE OF THE FRENCH TONG
    Claudius Hollyband. London: H. Bynneman 1580
TWEETALIGE WOORDEBOEK/BILINGUAL DICTIONARY (Afrikaans-English/
    English-Afrikaans) (BD)
    Daniel B. Bosman et al. Cape Town: Tafelberg 1967/84
UNIVERSAL AND CRITICAL DICTIONARY OF THE ENGLISH LANGUAGE ...
    Joseph Worcester. Boston & Philadelphia: Wilkins, Carter and Co.
    1846
(AN) UNIVERSAL ETYMOLOGICAL ENGLISH DICTIONARY ...
    Nathan Bailey. London: E. Bell et al. 1721/1724
UNIVERSAL VOCABULARIO EN LATIN Y EN ROMANCE
    Alfonso Fernández de Palencia. Sevilla: P. de Colonia 1490
VARIARUM RERUM VOCABULA CUM SUECA INTERPRETATIONE
    Olavus Petri. Stockholm: Anon. 1538 (Reprint ed. Aksel Ander-
    sson. Uppsala: Almqvist 1890)
VELÁZQUEZ SPANISH AND ENGLISH DICTIONARY see DICTIONARY OF THE
    SPANISH AND ENGLISH LANGUAGES and NEW REVISED VELÁZQUEZ SPANISH
    AND ENGLISH DICTIONARY
VERBORUM LATINORUM CUM GRAECIS ANGLICISQUE CONIUNCTORUM ...
    Guillaume Morel. London: H. Bynneman for R. Hutton 1583
VERKLARENDE HANDWOORDEBOEK VAN DIE AFRIKAANSE TAAL ... (HAT)
    Pieter C. Schoonees et al./Francois F. Odendal et al. Johannes-
    burg: Voortrekkerpers & Doornfontein: Perskor
VERSUCH EINER ALLGEMEINEN DEUTSCHEN SYNONYMIK IN EINEM KRITISCH-
    PHILOSOPHISCHEN WOERTERBUCHE DER SINNVERWANDTEN WOERTER DER
    HOCHDEUTSCHEN MUNDART
    Johann August Eberhard. Halle & Leipzig: J.G. Ruff 6 parts
    1795-1802

VERSUCH EINES VOLLSTÄNDIGEN ... WÖRTERBUCHES see GRAMMATISCH-
  KRITISCHES WÖRTERBUCH DER HOCHDEUTSCHEN MUNDART
VOCABOLARIO DEGLI ACCADEMICI DELLA CRUSCA ...
  Accademia della Crusca. Venezia: G. Alberti 1612
VOCABULA DALMATICA QUE UNGARI SIBI USURPARUNT
  in DICTIONARIUM QUINQUE ... LINGUARUM ...
VOCABULA SCLAVONICA
  in Georgievič (Djurdjevič), Bartholomaeus (1544) De afflictione
  tam captivorum quam etiam sub Turcae tributo viventium Christi-
  anorum ... Antwerpen: Typis Copenij
VOCABULARIUM AD USUM DACORUM ...
  Christiern Pedersen. Paris: Anon. 1510 (Reprint ed. I. Bom/N.
  Haastrup. København: Akademisk Forlag 1973)
(A) VOCABULARY OF THE CANTON DIALECT
  Robert Morrison. Macao: Honorable East India Press 3 volumes
  1828
(A) VOCABULARY OF THE SHANGHAI DIALECT
  Joseph Edkins. Shanghai: Presbyterian Mission Press 1869
VOCABULISTA ARAUIGO EN LETRA CASTELLANA
  in Pedro de Alcalá (1505) Arte para ligeramete saber la legua
  arauigo. Granada: J. Varela
VOCABVLARIO DE LAS DOS LENGVAS TOSCANA Y CASTELLANA
  Cristobál de las Casas. Sevilla: F. de Aguilar 1570 & Venezia:
  D. Zenaro 1572/87
VOLLSTÄNDIGE ANWEISUNG ZUR DEUTSCHEN ORTHOGRAPHIE NEBST EINEM
  KLEINEN WÖRTERBUCH FUR DIE AUSSPRACHE, ORTHOGRAPHIE, BIEGUNG UND
  ABLEITUNG
  Johann Christoph Adelung. Leipzig: Weygand 1788/90
VOLLSTÄNDIGES ORTHOGRAPHISCHES WÖRTERBUCH DER DEUTSCHEN SPRACHE see
  DUDEN. (VOLLSTÄNDIGES) ORTHOGRAPHISCHES WÖRTERBUCH
WAR WORDS see WORLD WORDS
WEBSTER'S (EIGHTH) NEW COLLEGIATE DICTIONARY (W8)
  Editorial Staff. Springfield MA: Merriam 1973
WEBSTER'S NEW STUDENT'S DICTIONARY (WNSD)
  Editorial Staff. Springfield MA: Merriam 1974
WEBSTER'S NEW WORLD DICTIONARY OF THE AMERICAN LANGUAGE (WNW)
  David B. Guralnik. New York: Collins & Cleveland OH: Simon and
  Schuster 1953/76/83
WEBSTER'S NINTH NEW COLLEGIATE DICTIONARY (W9)
  F.C. Mish et al. Springfield MA: Merriam 1983
WEBSTER'S (SECOND) NEW INTERNATIONAL DICTIONARY
  William A. Neilson. Springfield MA: Merriam 1934
WEBSTER'S (SEVENTH) NEW COLLEGIATE DICTIONARY (W7)
  Editorial Staff. Springfield MA: Merriam 1963
WEBSTER'S THIRD NEW INTERNATIONAL DICTIONARY ... (WIII)
  Philip B. Gove. Springfield MA: Merriam 1961, supplements see
  6000 WORDS, 9000 WORDS
WHAT'S WHAT: A VISUAL GLOSSARY OF THE PHYSICAL WORLD
  David Fisher/Reg Bragonier. Maplewood NJ: Hammond 1981
WOORDEBOEK VAN DIE AFRIKAANSE TAAL (WAT)

Pieter C. Schoonees (Vol. 1–4)/F.J. Snijman (Vol. 5–6)/Daniel C.
    Hauptfleisch (from Vol.7). Pretoria: Die Staatsdrukker 1951–84
WOORDENBOEK DER NEDERLANDSCHE TAAL
    Matthias de Vries et al. The Hague: M. Nijhoff 25 volumes from
    1882
(THE) WORLD BOOK DICTIONARY
    Clarence L. Barnhart and Robert K. Barnhart. Chicago: World Book
    & Childcraft International 2 volumes 1963/79
(A) WORLDE OF WORDES, OR MOST COPIOUS AND EXACT DICTIONARIE IN
    ITALIAN AND ENGLISH
    John Florio. London: A. Hatfield for E. Blount 1598 (Reprint
    Hildesheim & New York: Olms 1972)
WORLD WORDS (formerly called WAR WORDS)
    W. Cabell Greet. New York: Columbia U.P. 1944/48
WU JU YUN FU (Chinese Rhyme Dictionary)
    Chen/Y.I. Hu. Anon. Qing Dynasty
XI FAN YI YU (Translation of the Tibetan Language)
    Anon. 11th century
XI RU ER MU ZI (An Audio and Visual Guide for Foreign Scholars)
    Nicolas Trigault. Hangzhou: Anon. 3 volumes 1626
YI QIE JING YIN YI (The Sound and Meaning of the Tripitaka)
    Xuan Ying. Chang'an: Anon. 7th century
YU PIAN (Jade Chapters)
    Gu Yewang. Anon. 6th century
YU ZHI ZENG DING QING WEN JIAN (The Enlarged Imperial Manchu
    Language Survey)
    Fu Heng et al. Anon. 41 volumes 1771, 5 supplements
ZENG DING HUA YI YI YU see HUA YI YI YU
ZI ER JI (Handbook for the Beijing Dialect)
    Thomas Wade. Shanghai: Inspectorate General of Customs (Reprint
    London: W.H. Allen 3 volumes 1886)

APPENDIX B: SEMINAR PROGRAMME

SESSION	THEME, SPEAKERS	CHAIRMEN
Saturday 22 March		
9.00-10.30	Three classical traditions 1 Chien/Creamer 2 Snell-Hornby 3 Haywood	Hartmann
11.00-12.30	Early European cross-currents 4 (Filipović) 5 Kibbee 6 Steiner Discussion on Resource Centres	Kirkness
2.00-3.30	The English dictionary I 7 Dolezal 8 Osselton 9 Stein	Mugdan
4.00-6.00	The English dictionary II 10 Hüllen 11 McArthur 12 Bronstein 13 Read	Hanks
Sunday 23 March		
9.00-10.30	National developments I 14 Haugen 15 Magay 16 Piotrowski	Jackson
11.00-12.30	National developments II 17 El-Badry 18 Gouws 19 Hatherall	Cowie
2.00-3.30	Pioneers of three genres 20 Bray 21 Merkin 22 Wolfart	Aitken
4.00-5.30	The English dictionary III 23 Ilson 24 Allen 25 Cassidy	Gates

APPENDIX C: LIST OF PARTICIPANTS

AITKEN, Prof. A. Jack
   University of Edinburgh/Dictionary of the Older Scottish
   Tongue

ALLEN, Dr. Robert E.   (Sp.)
   Oxford University Press/Oxford Dictionaries

BOTHOF, Mr. G.J.
   Bothof Vertaalbureau (Nijmegen)

BRAY, Dr. Laurent   (Sp.)
   Universität Erlangen-Nürnberg/Angewandte Sprachwissenschaft

BRONSTEIN, Prof. Arthur J.   (Sp.)
   City University of New York/Graduate School

CASSIDY, Prof. Frederic G.   (Sp.)
   University of Wisconsin (Madison)/Dictionary of American
   Regional English

CHIEN, Mr. David   (Sp.)
   University of Exeter/Dictionary Research Centre &
   China University of Science and Technology (Hefei, Anhui)/
   Department of English

COOPER, Dr. Margaret A.
   University of Edinburgh/Centre for Speech Technology
   Research

COP, Ms. Margaret
   Universität Erlangen-Nürnberg/Erlanger Zentrum für
   Wörterbuchforschung

COWIE, Mr. Anthony P.
   University of Leeds/School of English

CREAMER, Mr. Thomas   (Sp.)
   Takoma Park, Maryland

DE BHALDRAITHE, Prof. Tomás
   Ollamh le Canúineolaíocht na Gaeilge (Dublin)

DOLEZAL, Dr. Fredric   (Sp.)
   University of Southern Mississippi (Hattiesburg)/
   Department of English

EL-BADRY, Mrs. Nawal H.   (Sp.)
   University of Exeter/Dictionary Research Centre &
   University of Cairo/Department of English

EMERY, Mr. Peter G.
   University of Bath/School of Modern Languages

FILIPOVIĆ, Prof. Rudolf   (Paper not read
   Yugoslav Academy of Science (Zagreb)   due to illness)

GATES, Prof. Edward
   Indiana State University (Terre Haute)/
   Department of English

GEMMINGEN, Dr. Barbara von
   Universität Düsseldorf/Romanisches Seminar

GOUWS, Dr. Rufus H.   (Sp.)
   University of Exeter/Dictionary Research Centre &
   Universiteit van Stellenbosch/Department of Afrikaans
   and Dutch

HANKS, Mr. Patrick W.
   University of Birmingham/COBUILD

HARTMANN, Dr. Reinhard R.K.
   University of Exeter/Dictionary Research Centre

HATHERALL, Mr. Glyn   (Sp.)
   Ealing College of Higher Education/School of Language
   Studies

HAUGEN, Prof. Einar   (Sp.)
   Harvard University (Cambridge, Massachusetts)

HAUGEN, Dr. Eva L.
   Belmont, Massachusetts

HAYWOOD, Mr. John A.   (Sp.)
   Lewes, East Sussex

HULLEN, Prof. Werner   (Sp.)
   Universität-GHS Essen/Literatur- und Sprachwissenschaften

ILSON, Dr. Robert F.   (Sp.)
   University of London/Survey of English Usage

JACKSON, Dr. Howard T.
   City of Birmingham Polytechnic/English and Communication
   Studies

KIBBEE, Prof. Douglas A.   (Sp.)
   University of Illinois (Urbana)/Department of French

KIRKNESS, Dr. Alan
    Institut für deutsche Sprache (Mannheim)

KNOWLES, Prof. Francis E.
    University of Aston (Birmingham)/Modern Languages

LI, Mr. Xiang-Ying
    St. Mary's College (University of London)/English Department
    & Nanjing Institute of Forestry/Department of English

MAGAY, Dr. Tamás   (Sp.)
    Akadémiai Kiadó (Budapest)

McARTHUR, Dr. Tom   (Sp.)
    Cambridge University Press/'English Today'

MERKIN, Prof. Reuven   (Sp.)
    Bar-Ilan University (Ramat-Gan) &
    Hebrew Language Academy (Jerusalem)

MOON, Ms. Rosamund
    University of Birmingham/COBUILD

MUGDAN, Dr. Joachim
    Universität Münster/Linguistik

NIC PHÁIDIN, Dr. Caoilfhionn
    Royal Irish Academy (Dublin)

OSSELTON, Prof. Noel E.   (Sp.)
    University of Newcastle/School of English

PIOTROWSKI, Mr. Tadeusz   (Sp.)
    Uniwersytet Wrocławski/Muzeum Przyrodnicze

READ, Prof. Allen W.   (Sp.)
    Columbia University (New York, N.Y.)

SCHWARZ, Ms. Catherine
    W. & R. Chambers (Edinburgh)

SEATON, Ms. M. Anne
    W. & R. Chambers (Edinburgh)

SNELL-HORNBY, Dr. Mary   (Sp.)
    Universität Zürich/Englisches Seminar

STEIN, Prof. Gabriele   (Sp.)
    Universität Hamburg/Seminar für Englische Sprache
    und Kultur

APPENDIX

STEINER, Prof. Roger J.   (Sp.)
    University of Delaware/Linguistics

STELLINGSMA, Mr. Hans
    Fryske Akademy (Ljouwert/Leeuwarden)

SWANEPOEL, Prof. Piet H.
    Universiteit van Suid-Afrika (Pretoria)/Afrikaans
    and Dutch

THOMPSON, Dr. Della J.
    Oxford University Press/Oxford Dictionaries

WARBURTON, Ms. Yvonne
    Oxford University Press/New Oxford English Dictionary

WOLFART, Prof. H.C.   (Sp.)
    University of Manitoba (Winnipeg)/Linguistics

LIST OF CONTRIBUTORS

ALLEN, Dr. Robert E.
  (Oxford U.P./Oxford Dictionaries)
  37a St. Giles
  Oxford OX1 3LD
BRAY, Dr. Laurent
  (U. Erlangen-Nürnberg/
  Angewandte Sprachwissenschaft)
  Glückstraße 5
  D-8520 Erlangen
BRONSTEIN, Prof. Arthur J.
  (City U. of N.Y./Graduate School)
  33 West 42nd Street
  New York, NY 10036, USA
CHIEN, Mr. David
  (China U. of Science and
  Technology, Hefei, Anhui, P.R.C.)
CREAMER, Mr. Thomas
  6619 Westmoreland Avenue
  Takoma Park, MD 20912, USA
DOLEZAL, Dr. Frederic
  (U. of Southern Mississippi)
  721 Milan Street
  New Orleans, LA 70115, USA
EL-BADRY, Mrs. Nawal H.
  (U. of Exeter/Language Centre)
  2 Stoke Valley Road, Penn-
  sylvania, Exeter EX4 5DA
FILIPOVIĆ, Prof. Rudolf
  (Yugoslav Academy of Sciences)
  42 Moše Pijade
  YU-41000 Zagreb

GOUWS, Dr. Rufus H.
    Department of Afrikaans and Dutch
    University of Stellenbosch
    Stellenbosch 7600
    R. South Africa
HATHERALL, Mr. Glyn
    (Ealing College of Higher
    Education/School of Lang. Studies)
    11 Lindfield Road
    London W5 1QS
HAUGEN, Prof. Einar
    (Harvard U.)
    45 Larch Circle
    Belmont, MA 02178, USA
HAYWOOD, Mr. John A.
    4 The Rowans
    Prince Edwards Road
    Lewes, East Sussex BN7 1BD
HÜLLEN, Prof. Werner
    (U.GHS Essen/Literatur- und
    Sprachwissenschaften)
    Universitätsstraße 12
    D-4300 Essen 1
ILSON, Dr. Robert F.
    (U. of London/Survey of
    English Usage)
    58 Antrim Mansions
    Antrim Road
    London NW3·4XU
KIBBEE, Prof. Douglas A.
    (U. of Illinois/Dept. of French)
    2090 Foreign Languages Building
    University of Illinois
    Urbana, IL 61801, USA
MAGAY, Dr. Tamás
    (Akadémiai Kiadó)
    Alkotmány Utca 21, P.O. Box 24
    H-1363 Budapest

McARTHUR, Dr. Tom
  (Cambridge U.P./English Today)
  22-23 Ventress Farm Court
  Cherry Hinton Road
  Cambridge CB1 4HD
MERKIN, Prof. Reuven
  (Bar-Ilan U. & Hebrew Language
  Academy)
  35 Tchernikhovsky Street
  Jerusalem 92587, Israel
OSSELTON, Prof. Noel E.
  (U. of Newcastle/School of
  English)
  The University
  Newcastle upon Tyne NE1 7RU
PIOTROWSKI, Mr. Tadeusz
  (U. Wroclawski/Muzeum
  Przyrodnicze)
  Sienkiewicza 21
  PL-50335 Wroclaw
READ, Prof. Allen Walker
  39 Clarenmont Avenue
  New York, NY 10027, USA
SNELL-HORNBY, Dr. Mary
  (U. Zürich)
  In der Au 38
  CH-8706 Meilen
STEIN, Prof. Gabriele
  (U. Hamburg)
  Seminar für Englische Sprache
  und Kultur
  Von-Melle-Park 6
  D-2000 Hamburg 13
STEINER, Prof. Roger J.
  (U. of Delaware/Linguistics)
  University of Delaware
  Newark, DE 19716, USA

In the STUDIES IN THE HISTORY OF THE LANGUAGE SCIENCES (SiHoLS) series the following volumes have been published thus far, and will be published during 1986:

1. KOERNER, E.F. Konrad: *The Importance of Techmer's "Internationale Zeitschrift für Allgemeine Sprachwissenschaft" in the Development of General Linguistics.* Amsterdam, 1973.

2. TAYLOR, Daniel J.: *Declinatio: A Study of the Linguistic Theory of Marcus Terentius Varro.* Amsterdam, 1974. 2nd pr. 1986.

3. BENWARE, Wilbur A.: *The Study of Indo-European Vocalism; from the beginnings to Whitney and Scherer: A critical-historical account.* Amsterdam, 1974. t.o.p. 2nd pr. 1986.

4. BACHER, Wilhelm: *Die Anfänge der hebräischen Grammatik* (1895), together with *Die hebräische Sprachwissenschaft vom 10. bis zum 16. Jahrhundert* (1892). Amsterdam, 1974.

5. HUNT, R.W. (1908-1979): *The History of Grammar in the Middle Ages. Collected Papers.* Edited with an introduction, a select bibliography, and indices by G.L. Bursill-Hall. Amsterdam, 1980.

6. MILLER, Roy Andrew: *Studies in the Grammatical Tradition in Tibet.* Amsterdam, 1976.

7. PEDERSEN, Holger (1867-1953): *A Glance at the History of Linguistics, with particular regard to the historical study of phonology.* Amsterdam, 1983.

8. STENGEL, Edmund (1845-1935), (ed.): *Chronologisches Verzeichnis französischer Grammatiken vom Ende des 14. bis zum Ausgange des 18. Jahrhunderts, nebst Angabe der bisher ermittelten Fundorte derselben.* Amsterdam, 1976.

9. NIEDEREHE, Hans-Josef & Harald HAARMANN (with the assistance of Liliane Rouday), (eds.): *IN MEMORIAM FRIEDRICH DIEZ: Akten des Kolloquiums zur Wissenschaftsgeschichte der Romanistik/Actes du Colloque sur l'Histoire des Etudes Romanes/Proceedings of the Colloquium for the History of Romance Studies, Trier, 2.-4. Okt. 1975).* Amsterdam, 1976.

10. KILBURY, James: *The Development of Morphophonemic Theory.* Amsterdam, 1976.

11. KOERNER, E.F. Konrad: *Western Histories of Linguistic Thought. An annotated chronological bibliography, 1822-1976.* Amsterdam, 1978.

12. PAULINUS a S. BARTHOLOMAEO (1749-1806): *Dissertation on the Sanskrit Language.* Transl., edited and introduced by Ludo Rocher. Amsterdam, 1977.

13. DRAKE, Glendon F.: *The Role of Prescriptivism in American Linguistics 1820-1970.* Amsterdam, 1977.

14. SIGERUS DE CORTRACO: *Summa modorum significandi; Sophismata.* New edition, on the basis of G. Wallerand's *editio prima*, with additions, critical notes, an index of terms, and an introd. by Jan Pinborg. Amsterdam, 1977.

15. PSEUDO-ALBERTUS MAGNUS: *Quaestiones Alberti de Modis significandi.* A critical edition, translation and commentary of the British Museum Inc. C.21.C.52 and the Cambridge Inc.5.J.3.7, by L.G. Kelly. Amsterdam, 1977.

16. PANCONCELLI-CALZIA, Giulio (1878-1966): *Geschichtszahlen der Phonetik* (1941), together with *Quellenatlas der Phonetik* (1940). New ed., with an introd. article and a bio-bibliographical account of Panconcelli-Calzia by Jens-Peter Köster. Amsterdam, 1986. n.y.p.

17. SALMON, Vivian: *The Study of Language in 17th-Century England.* Amsterdam, 1979.

18. HAYASHI, Tetsuro: *The Theory of English Lexicography 1530-1791.* Amsterdam, 1978.

19. KOERNER, E.F. Konrad: *Toward a Historiography of Linguistics. Selected Essays.* Foreword by R.H. Robins. Amsterdam, 1978.
20. KOERNER, E.F. Konrad (ed.): *PROGRESS IN LINGUISTIC HISTORIOGRA-PHY: Papers from the International Conference on the History of the Language Sciences, Ottawa, 28-31 August 1978.* Amsterdam, 1980.
21. DAVIS, Boyd H. & Raymond K. O'CAIN (eds.): *FIRST PERSON SINGULAR. Papers from the Conference on an Oral Archive for the History of American Linguistics. (Charlotte, N.C., 9-10 March 1979).* Amsterdam, 1980.
22. McDERMOTT, A. Charlene Senape: *Godfrey of Fontaine's Abridgement of Boethius the Dane's MODI SIGNIFICANDI SIVE QUAESTIONES SUPER PRISCIANUM MAIOREM.* A text edition with English transl. and introd. Amsterdam, 1980.
23. APOLLONIUS DYSCOLUS: *The Syntax of Apollonius Dyscolus.* Translated, and with commentary by Fred W. Householder. Amsterdam, 1981.
24. CARTER, M.. (ed.): *ARAB LINGUISTICS, an introductory classical text with translation and notes.* Amsterdam, 1981.
25. HYMES, Dell H.: *Essays in the History of Linguistic Anthropology.* Amsterdam, 1983.
26. KOERNER, Konrad, Hans-J. NIEDEREHE & R.H. ROBINS (eds.): *STUDIES IN MEDIEVAL LINGUISTIC THOUGHT,* dedicated to Geoffrey L. Bursill-Hall on the occassion of his 60th birthday on 15 May 1980. Amsterdam, 1980.
27. BREVA-CLARAMONTE, Manuel: *Sanctius' Theory of Language: A contribution to the history of Renaissance linguistics.* Amsterdam, 1983.
28. VERSTEEGH, Kees, Konrad KOERNER & Hans-J. NIEDEREHE (eds.): *THE HISTORY OF LINGUISTICS IN THE NEAR EAST.* Amsterdam, 1983.
29. ARENS, Hans: *Aristotle's Theory of Language and its Tradition.* Amsterdam, 1984.
30. GORDON, W. Terrence: *A History of Semantics.* Amsterdam, 1982.
31. CHRISTY, Craig: *Uniformitarianism in Linguistics.* Amsterdam 1983.
32. MANCHESTER, M.L.: *The Philosophical Foundations of Humboldt's Linguistic Doctrines.* Amsterdam 1985. n.y.p.
33. RAMAT, Paolo, Hans-Josef NIEDEREHE & E.F. Konrad KOERNER (eds.): *THE HISTORY OF LINGUISTICS IN ITALY.* Amsterdam, 1986. n.y.p.
34. QUILIS, Antonio & Hans J. NIEDEREHE (eds.): *THE HISTORY OF LINGUISTICS IN SPAIN.* Amsterdam, 1986. n.y.p.
35. SALMON, Vivian (ed.): *A READER ON THE LANGUAGE OF SHAKESPEARE.* Amsterdam, 1986.
36. SAPIR, Edward: *Appraisals of his Life and Work.* Edited by Konrad Koerner. Amsterdam, 1984.
37. Ó MATHÚNA, Seán P.: *William Bathe, S.J., 1564-1614: a pioneer in linguistics.* Amsterdam, 1986.
38. AARSLEF, Hans, Louis G. KELLY & Hans-Josef NIEDEREHE: *PAPERS IN THE HISTORY OF LINGUISTICS. Proceedings of ICHoLS III, Princeton 1984.* Amsterdam, 1986.
39. PETRUS HISPANUS: *Summulae Logicales.* Translated and with an introduction by Francis P. Dinneen, S.J. Amsterdam, 1986.
40. HARTMANN, R.R.K. (ed.): *THE HISTORY OF LEXICOGRAPHY. Papers from the Dictionary Research Centre Seminar at Exeter, March 1986.* Amsterdam, 1986.
41. COWAN, William, Michael K. FOSTER & Konrad KOERNER (eds.): *NEW PERSPECTIVES IN LANGUAGE, CULTURE, AND PERSONALITY. Proceedings of the Edward Sapir Centenary Conference (Ottawa, 1-3 October 1984).* Amsterdam, 1986.